HISTORY OF AMERICAN THOUGHT AND CULTURE

Paul S. Boyer, *General Editor*

Darwinism
and the
Divine in America

Protestant Intellectuals and Organic Evolution,
1859–1900

JON H. ROBERTS

The Frank S. and Elizabeth D. Brewer Prize Essay
of the American Society of Church History

The University of Wisconsin Press

Published 1988

The University of Wisconsin Press
114 North Murray Street
Madison, Wisconsin 53715

The University of Wisconsin Press, Ltd.
1 Gower Street
London WC1E 6HA, England

First printing

Printed in the United States of America

For LC CIP information see the colophon

ISBN 0-299-11590-9

For Sharon
ILYS

Contents

Preface

DESPITE the existence of an already thriving "Darwin industry," the impact of the theory of organic evolution on nineteenth-century American Protestant theology remains surprisingly obscure. Some issues that played a prominent role in determining the course of discussion regarding this problem have been virtually ignored. The debate within the American Protestant community over the ethical implications of the transmutation hypothesis, for example, has received lamentably little attention. Still other issues, such as the role of evolutionary thought in fostering more immanentist conceptions of God's relationship to the world and broader visions of divine revelation, though not entirely neglected, merit more detailed analysis than they have thus far received. Most important, we lack a comprehensive analytical overview of the public dialogue that occurred among nineteenth-century American Protestant intellectuals who grappled with the theory of organic evolution.

I have attempted to provide such an overview. A brief rehearsal of the argument I advance in the text is perhaps in order. In Part 1, I submit that before the publication of Charles Darwin's *Origin of Species* in 1859, most American Protestant intellectuals valued science, and especially natural history, for supplying data that appeared to be invaluable for defending many of the major tenets of the Christian world view. These individuals conceded that the conclusions of science sometimes seemed to clash with the Scriptures, but they managed to devise a number of formulas that accommodated the meaning and truth of the Bible to the results of scientific investigation. Charles Darwin's work, however, could not be so easily assimilated; it appeared to challenge the basic tenets of both natural and revealed theology. From 1859 to 1875, however, American Protestant thinkers devoted little effort to analyzing the theological implications of the transmutation hypothesis. Because they were convinced that the study of God's works would confirm the teachings of His Word, they simply assumed that any theory as patently subversive of Christian theology as that of Charles Darwin must perforce be a spurious interpretation of natural history. Accordingly, most Protestants who analyzed the theory of organic evolution prior to 1875 focused their efforts on showing that it was bereft of scientific merit. Toward this end, they availed themselves of the arsenal of anti-evolutionary arguments advanced by scientists since the eighteenth century.

Convinced that the transmutation hypothesis was patently absurd, many American Protestant thinkers found it necessary to ponder the questions of why the *Origin of Species* had been published and why it received at least some support. The answers they returned to these questions were strongly informed by their conviction that the partisans of unbelief were currently engaged in an all-out effort to invest a naturalistic world view with the name and prestige of science. Both the promulgation of and the support for the theory of organic evolution appeared to be among the numerous manifestations of this effort.

As long as the bulk of support for the transmutation hypothesis came from outspoken critics of the Christian world view, this diagnosis remained quite plausible. In the decade after 1865, however, an ever-increasing number of scientists endorsed the theory of organic evolution. By 1875, a large number of the clergy and theologians in the United States recognized that the scientific community had defected to the evolutionists' camp. This recognition changed the focus of the Protestant intellectual community's analysis of the transmutation hypothesis. Arguments concerning the scientific merits of that hypothesis increasingly gave way to discussion of its theological implications.

In Part 2, I attempt to reconstruct the course of that discussion from 1875 to 1900. Many Protestants in this period concluded that the theory of organic evolution was inconsistent with traditional apologetic strategies and conventional interpretations of God's relationship to nature, the narrative of the creation and early history of the world recorded in Genesis, and the ethical philosophy embodied in the gospel. Notwithstanding this assessment, scientists' conversion to the theory of evolution convinced most commentators within the American Protestant community during the last quarter of the nineteenth century that it was necessary to accept the theory and to accommodate Christian theology to its dictates. Significant differences characterized the way in which they approached this task. Some Protestant evolutionists were determined to demonstrate that the theory of evolution required only minimal adjustments in the traditional understanding of God, epistemology, and the nature of the divine-human encounter. Others, though no less committed to most of the established categories of Christian theology, favored more radical alterations in the way those categories were expressed and defended. Many of these thinkers valued evolutionary rhetoric in lending credibility to their theological revisions. Many also came to believe that the concept of evolution was not simply a description of natural history but a paradigm for the way in which God operated throughout His creation.

A minority of American Protestant thinkers continued to reject the theory of organic evolution in favor of the doctrine of special creation. Of the numerous factors prompting them to adopt this position, biblical considerations were paramount. Most special creationists within the Protestant intellectual community in the United States were convinced that it was simply impossible to subscribe to the transmutation hypothesis without abandoning the claim that the Scriptures were a reliable source of religious truth. In defending this position, most of these Protestants committed themselves to a view of the Bible that precluded them from interpreting efforts to accommodate the Christian world view to the theory of organic evolution as anything more than an implicit capitulation to the forces of secularism.

I am aware that my issue-oriented approach runs the risk of imposing more coherence than actually existed on the welter of opinions that emerged during the course of the nineteenth-century American Protestant community's consideration of the transmutation hypothesis. This risk is all the greater because few religious thinkers addressed themselves to every issue in the discussion. It is therefore simply impossible to ascertain with any certainty the position that most of them held concerning each of the issues that are treated in the text. These considerations notwithstanding, I am convinced that it is possible to discern in the mosaic of ideas and attitudes manifested in the public dialogue a series of coherent underlying patterns. I have attempted to reconstruct those patterns.

Another danger of a thematic analysis of the history of thought is that of reducing the rich texture of human experience to a cluster of colorless abstractions. I have sought to combat this problem by periodically interjecting brief biographical sketches of some of the most prominent figures in the evolutionary controversy. These sketches, I should emphasize, do not securely ground the ideas held by the subjects of my study in their social context. I am not in principle opposed to the "social history of ideas." Nor do I doubt that ideas concerning science and religion have often been used to promote or defend particular views about society. Neither, however, am I convinced that views concerning nature and nature's God are *always* or *necessarily* rooted in social and political concerns, and I must confess that much of the secondary literature I have read that attempts to ground theological and scientific beliefs in such concerns seems to me to assume precisely what it should be setting out to prove: that such a relationship actually exists. This is obviously not the place to engage in a sustained discussion of this issue. Suffice it to say that during the course of my research I was unable to find in the backgrounds, social standing, or class status of the participants in the Darwinian controversy clues that helped me to predict the stance they adopted toward the theory of evolution or better understand the particular ideas they espoused. Perhaps I am not as troubled as I should be about this. At any rate, I have found the theological issues that arose in the wake of the theory of organic evolution to be sufficiently complex, significant, and compelling in their own right to justify systematic investigation and explication.

My reluctance to focus my analysis on the views of a small group of "representative" participants in the public dialogue on the evolutionary hypothesis stems largely from doubts about just how much such studies really reveal about the larger group they allegedly exemplify. When, for whom, and to what extent, for example, was Charles Hodge's attack on Darwinism representative? How resonant was Asa Gray's mode of reconciling Darwinism with belief in the existence of God? Is the fact that several Calvinists found it possible to embrace Darwinism sufficient to establish an affinity between those two modes of interpreting reality? I am persuaded that it is simply impossible to answer such questions or to chart the changing patterns of thought within the American Protestant intellectual community in its attempts to come to grips with the theory of evolution without examining the positions of a large group of controversialists.

Toward that end, I have endeavored to assay much of the literature relating to the transmutation hypothesis published by American Protestant thinkers between 1859 and 1900. I have not limited my investigation to works devoted exclusively to an analysis of that hypothesis, for I discovered during the course of my research that the response of many Protestants to the theory of evolution could be gleaned only by examining works that were not primarily devoted to that topic. Nor is my work limited to a consideration of the views of Protestant clergymen and theologians. The dramatis personae of my study also includes a number of scientists and other lay men and women who expressed opinions concerning the theological implications of the transmutation hypothesis. I am aware that some of my more methodologically inclined readers may find my working definition of the term "Protestant intellectual community" disconcertingly broad and imprecise. This concern, I believe, is unjustified. Sharp boundary lines between science and theology simply did not exist during the nineteenth century. Not only did ministers and theologians frequently address themselves to scientific issues, but many scientists were avid participants in theological discussions. Nor have I discerned meaningful ideological differences between divinity school professors, clergymen, and lay thinkers who published works dealing with the religious aspects of the theory of evolution. My desire to treat the evolutionary controversy comprehensively prompted me to cast my net widely and to deal with the issue of the effect of occupational commitments on theological perspectives only when it seemed relevant.

I have found it necessary to impose certain limits on the scope of my investigation. Although I have made selective use of the private correspondence of some of the participants in the discussion, I have largely ignored manuscript sources. Such sources would doubtless yield a number of illuminating insights, but the focus of my investigation is the public posture of Protestants who assessed the theological implications of the theory of organic evolution rather than their private ruminations. Second, with the exception of a few forays into the *Independent*, I have restricted my investigation of the periodical literature to the quarterly journals of opinion. I am convinced that an examination of the weekly denominational magazines would yield a fertile harvest, and I hope that someone will undertake such an examination. But at an early stage in my research, it became abundantly clear that the quarterlies provided such a rich and voluminous source of data that a comprehensive search of the weeklies would involve a commitment of time that would simply be prohibitive. Finally, I have concentrated on the views of members of the more "main-line" Protestant denominations (Congregationalists, Presbyterians, Methodists, Baptists, Disciples, Lutherans, Episcopalians, Reformed, Unitarians, and Universalists). Several terminological issues require comment. First, I am aware that my use of the term "intellectual" in referring to the subjects of my study has a rather odd ring. Some of my more heretical friends and colleagues have even suggested—facetiously, I think—that the phrase "Protestant intellectual" is self-contradictory. My decision to employ this term is primarily motivated by a desire to call attention to the fact that the subjects discussed in the text treated Christian theology as a set of ideas and employed reasoned discourse in discussing the relationship between those ideas and the theory of organic evolution. I should also note that in formulating generalizations about the views of these "people of ideas," I have sought to mitigate rhetorical monotony by using a number of collective terms—"Protestant intellectuals," "Protestant thinkers," "church people," "religious thinkers," and the like—interchangeably.[1]

Finally, I recognize that the title of this book suggests that I regard the terms "Darwinism" and "theory of organic evolution" as synonymous. I hope that the text of my work indicates that I am aware that scientists actually differentiated the general theory of organic evolution from Darwin's more specific hypothesis regarding the mechanisms by which evolution had occurred. Religious thinkers, too, drew that distinction when they found it relevant to their concerns. Nevertheless, one of the spoils of Darwin's triumph in forcing scientists to reconsider their verdict on transmutation was that in common parlance Darwinism became synonymous with the theory of organic evolution. I therefore think there is some warrant for juxtaposing the terms.

Though my work deals primarily with the Protestant intellectual community, my fascination with the relationship between science and religion grows out of a longstanding interest in the changing significance of theological discourse within American culture. A casual glance at the contemporary cultural landscape is sufficient to engender skepticism about claims that the intensity of piety in the United States has measurably declined. This skepticism finds reinforcement in a large body of scholarly literature that challenges the usefulness of the concept of secularization. Still, I think it is undeniable that for well over a century Christian theology has played a rather inconsequential role in shaping the direction, dynamics, and pattern of American intellectual life. As late as 1850, few American artists and writers interpreted experience without paying at least lip service to theological concerns. By 1900, however, numerous realms of human inquiry were proceeding with little or no reference to the tenets of Christian thought. For many Americans piety became almost exclusively a private affair, divorced from discussions of nature and society.

In my judgment, science has been instrumental in accounting for this change. Not too many years ago, the history of the relationship between science and Christian theology was generally depicted as the story of the steady triumph of the forces of enlightenment over the stubborn resistance of the forces of obscurantism. In recent years, historians have succeeded in exposing this story for the caricature that it is. They have quite properly noted that the metaphor of "warfare" is inappropriate in describing the relationship that generally obtained between the work of scientists and that of Protestant clergymen and theologians. Indeed, for much of modern history, proponents of the Christian world view regarded the scientific enterprise as an ally in defending their faith. To suggest, however, that this implies that tension between science and theology was nonexistent is to substitute one fiction for another. It is unnecessary to applaud the crude positivism that has animated celebrations of this tension to recognize that the increasing success of science in describing the phenomena disclosed in nature and society has been attended by a growing inclination to ignore the categories of Christian theology in discussing those phenomena. The theory of organic evolution played a crucial role in this process by significantly widening the boundaries within which scientific analysis appears to be possible.[2]

My study, which deals with a group of thinkers for whom theological concerns remained paramount even in the face of an increasingly comprehensive scientific picture of the cosmos, is an admittedly oblique approach to the problem of secularization. Nevertheless, I am convinced that an examination of the role that Protestant apologists played in the glorification of the scientific investigation of the natural world and the responses they made when confronted by one of the major results of that investigation sheds a good deal of light on the process by which the currency of Christian theology became devalued in the intellectual life of the West. At an early stage in their confrontation with science, Protestant thinkers opted to eschew ontological reflection concerning the relationship between God as Being Itself and the beings that inhabit the universe in favor of an analysis of the relationship between Creator and creation grounded on the discoveries disclosed by science concerning the structure and behavior of phenomena. It seems to me that this decision greatly contributed to the transfer of cultural authority and prestige from theology to science, the impoverishment of the religious vision of the world, and the desacralization of nature. The problem with adopting an apologetic position that relied so heavily on collusion with science was not, as many twentieth-century commentators have suggested, that it precluded Protestants from endorsing a division of labor that would accord science the right to interpret "facts" and religion the responsibility for determining values. Christianity is concerned with more than values; a view of God's relationship to nature is also deeply embedded within the faith. But there are other ways of interpreting the natural world than that of science, other conceptions of God in His relationship to the world than that of a supernatural Mechanic. In the late nineteenth century, a number of American Protestant intellectuals enthusiastically explored these alternatives. By that time, however, the historical moment in which a sacramental view of nature could vie with science on anything like an equal basis had already passed. Many intellectuals had come to share the mind-set that alternatives to the scientific mode of apprehending the world could be ignored as unnecessary and uninteresting. In turn, the absence of a theological interpretation of the cosmos in the discourse of intellectuals has rendered religious belief less compelling for many Americans who have looked to these thinkers as the arbiters of truth.

Acknowledgments

WHILE working on this book I have incurred numerous intellectual and personal debts, and it is a pleasure to be able to acknowledge the most significant of these. Donald Fleming has followed my project since its inception and has been a source of consistent encouragement. I have found his enthusiasm for "large" topics liberating and his rigorous standards challenging. His comments on numerous drafts of this manuscript have improved both its style and its substance considerably. Bernard Bailyn, Stephan Thernstrom, and Harold Woodman have interests that are considerably different from my own, but they have nevertheless consistently given me good counsel. I have also come to rely upon Ronald Numbers for shrewd and friendly advice. My colleagues at the University of Wisconsin-Stevens Point have provided me with a congenial intellectual environment in which to work.

This book owes a great deal to the insights, the critical judgment, and the warm support of numerous friends and colleagues. Christopher Jedrey and Fred Anderson have not only given several drafts a close reading, but they have also listened to my speculations about the relationship between science and religion with far more patience and responsiveness than one can reasonably expect from even the best of friends. My work has also enormously profited from the criticisms and suggestions of other friends and colleagues who have read all, or significant parts, of this book at various stages. These individuals include Jeffrey Adler, Donald Bellomy, Laura Bando, John C. Greene, Oscar Handlin, William R. Hutchison, James H. Kettner, Kenneth M. Ludmerer, Ronald Numbers, Robert Silverman, Stephan Thernstrom, Frank Miller Turner, and members of the New World Colloquium in Church History at Harvard Divinity School. Needless to say, these individuals should not be implicated in whatever errors remain in this book.

The year I embarked upon this study, Michael McGiffert generously offered me a large number of books relating to the Darwinian controversy from his own personal library. Frank Schwartz served as my research assistant in the final stages of this project, and I greatly appreciate both his diligence in tracking down fugitive sources and his critical acumen. Patricia Denault devoted painstaking care and exhibited extraordinary patience in typing several drafts of the manuscript. Paul Boyer has been most supportive and enthusiastic in his role as general editor of the series, and no author could ask for a more genial, sensitive, and encouraging editor than Barbara Hanrahan of the University of Wisconsin Press. Thanks are also due to Susan Tarcov, whose careful attention to detail and sharp eye for awkward sentence constructions have made this book better than it would have been without her efforts.

Several groups and institutions have contributed to the completion of this book. Financial support for the first phase of this project came from a Ford Foundation Graduate Prize Fellowship at Harvard University. At the postdoctoral stage, the Charles Warren Center for the Study of American History at Harvard University gave me a generous grant to supplement a sabbatical that helped enable me to expand my research and to elaborate my ideas. I would also like to express my appreciation to the American Society of Church History, which awarded my manuscript the Brewer Prize for 1985.

Without the enormous support of my family, this book would never have been written. I suspect that my parents, Anna Belle and Robert E. Roberts, did not always understand why I chose to enter academe; I am therefore all the more grateful to them for refusing to try to dictate the direction of my life and for encouraging me to follow my own visions. On some occasions my son Jeff was forced to tolerate my rejections of his gracious invitations to cavort with him. On other occasions, though, I gave in, and while this meant a delay in the publication of this book, I would like to thank Jeff for helping me to maintain a proper sense of priorities. My greatest debt is to my wife, Sharon. She has supported my fascination with this project, endured my periods of preoccupation, served as a friendly critic, and in more ways than I can recount contributed to the meaningfulness of the venture. Words fail to express my gratitude to her for allowing me to love my work and her at the same time.

Part One

1859–1875

1

"The Firmament Sheweth His Handywork": Darwin's Theory in Its Theological Context

THE response of literate Americans to the *Origin of Species* was a compound of fascination and consternation. Less than two years after its publication in 1859, a Methodist reviewer observed that "perhaps no scientific work has ever been at once so extensively read, not only by the scientific few, but by the reading masses generally; and certainly no one has ever produced such commotion."[1]

The individual responsible for this commotion was Charles Darwin. The son of a prosperous physician and the grandson of a notorious champion of the concept of transmutation, Darwin was born in Shrewsbury, England, in 1809. After abandoning a career in medicine, he attended Cambridge University with the intention of taking holy orders. The intellectual life of the school did little to engage Darwin's interest, but it did foster some important and lasting friendships for the young student, most notably with the botanist John Henslow. It was Henslow who later secured for him a position on board HMS *Beagle*, a surveying ship bound for South America. Darwin would never have been able to take advantage of this opportunity, however, if his uncle had not succeeded in persuading his father that training in natural history was quite "suitable" for aspiring clergymen.[2]

In looking back on the development of his thought, Darwin reflected that this voyage, which lasted from December 1831 until October 1836, was the most important event of his life. Not only did it prompt him to devote his career to the study of natural history, but it exposed him to the wealth of biological and geological phenomena that impelled him

3

to question his assumptions regarding the immutability of species. For example, his investigations in South America convinced him that existing plants and animals resembled extinct ones in important respects. In addition, he discovered that contiguous species on the South American continent were, though "closely allied," nevertheless distinct and that the species on the various islands of the Galapagos archipelago were somewhat different, even while bearing a distinctly "South American character." The long hours aboard ship also gave Darwin the opportunity to read and ponder the first two volumes of a work that was to have a profound impact on the course of his thought, Charles Lyell's *Principles of Geology*. Darwin concluded that Lyell's approach, which attempted to account for the history of the earth in terms of the gradual operation of natural agencies, was exemplary, and he began to consider seriously the possibility that the history of life might be susceptible to similar analysis.[3]

In July 1837 Darwin, no longer convinced of the fixity of species, began his first notebook addressing that "mystery of mysteries," the origin of species. Drawing on his reading of a wide variety of works on science and philosophy, he developed a theory of speciation predicated on the gradual and naturalistic principles he had found so appealing in Lyell's work. By 1844 most of the essential features of his theory of descent with modification by natural selection had taken form.[4]

Darwin proceeded from the assumption that adaptation was central to any discussion of natural history. This assumption, which he shared with most natural historians, had received classic expression in the work of William Paley, one of the few authors whom Darwin had found worthwhile during his studies at Cambridge. Paley had maintained in his *Natural Theology* (1802) that the cosmos was replete with phenomena bearing the same marks of "contrivance" as mechanisms designed by human beings. To illustrate this point, he had focused primarily on organisms. The eye itself, he asserted, constituted sufficient grounds for inferring the existence of an intelligent and benevolent Creator. But this structure was just one of a plethora of contrivances that abounded in the organic world. Muscles, bones, vessels, joints, organs—all provided cumulative evidence of the existence of a divine Designer who displayed "no signs of diminution of care by multiplicity of objects, or of distraction of thought by variety."[5]

If Paley's work provided Darwin with a storehouse of data attesting to the prevalence of adaptation in the organic world, it was Darwin's own observation that there were numerous, slight, hereditable differences among individuals in a species that gave him a clue as to how adaptation might be explained by means of "secondary" agencies. He reasoned that in an environment characterized by constant change, some variants would be better adapted than the original forms of species. In order to disprove the doctrine of the fixity of species and to demonstrate that transmutation had occurred, he needed to find a natural mechanism that would give these beneficial variations a directionality great enough to produce a population of individuals sufficiently different from their ancestors to be considered new species.[6]

In the work of breeders who selected characteristics they deemed desirable in domesticated plants and animals Darwin found the needed "principle of change." Persuaded that the barrier between varieties and species was not insurmountable, he began casting about for an explanation of how nature could achieve results superior even to those of artificial selection. In 1838, his reading of Thomas Malthus' *Essay on the Principle of Population* gave Darwin the clue he had been looking for. Malthus had maintained that human populations tended to multiply geometrically, pressing constantly on limited resources. Darwin now saw that such population pressure among organisms generally, by generating a competitive struggle among the individuals within a species, was also responsible for maintaining the relatively stable populations of plants and animals.[7]

Darwin was not the first naturalist to point to the existence of a competitive struggle for survival, but his predecessors had generally emphasized struggle among different species rather than competition among individuals within the same species. Moreover, though some had used the notion of struggle to explain the extinction of inferior varieties and species, they had overlooked the *creative* possibilities of competition. Darwin, on the other hand, reasoned that in a struggle for limited resources, those individuals best adapted to their circumstances would survive to leave the greatest number of progeny. In turn, the best adapted of these progeny would themselves leave a greater number of descendants. After many generations, Darwin argued, the remaining population of individuals would have diverged from the ancestral population sufficiently to merit designation as a new species.[8]

In 1842 Darwin set down some of his views in a short abstract, which he enlarged to a 230-page "Essay" in 1844. He was aware, however, that scientists had given a hostile reception to other works espousing the transmutation of species, and he refused to publish any account of his theory before he had collected data sufficient to compel a skeptical scientific community to take it seriously. Impatience, he feared, was the shortest road to obscurity.[9]

In 1846, following the publication of his *Geology of South America*, Darwin embarked on an eight-year study of barnacles. This time was not

wasted. Not only did his research secure for him the biological credentials that gave his later work added credibility, but he also gained
greater knowledge of and experience in dealing with variations within
a species and differences among species.[10]

In 1856 Charles Lyell, one of the first people to become privy to Darwin's heterodox speculations, persuaded Darwin to begin drafting his
theory for publication. Lyell feared that the cautious Darwin might not
get proper credit for his ideas. On May 14, 1856, Darwin began work on
a long statement of his theory. It was only about half finished when
Lyell's worst fears were realized. On June 18, 1858, Darwin received a
paper, "On the Tendency of Varieties to depart indefinitely from the
Original Type," that captured the essence of his own views.[11]

The author of this paper was Alfred Russel Wallace, a surveyor
turned natural historian. Wallace had long believed that the independent creation of each species by divine fiat was inconsistent with the
way the rest of the world had been shown to operate, and by 1845 he
had become convinced that species originated by means of transmutation. It was not until 1858, however, that he hit upon a mechanism
capable of accounting for such transmutation: natural selection.[12]

Thanks to a suggestion from Lyell and the botanist Joseph Hooker,
another of Darwin's confidants, an abstract of Darwin's 1844 "Essay"
and an 1857 letter outlining his theory were read along with Wallace's
paper before the Linnaean Society of London on July 1, 1858, and the
papers were published in the Linnaean Society's *Journal of Proceedings*.
These papers had little immediate impact on the scientific community,
but the episode did impel Darwin to write a short "abstract" of his
views. This abstract quickly became a large book, which was published
on November 24, 1859, under the title *On the Origin of Species by Means
of Natural Selection, or the Preservation of Favoured Races in the Struggle for
Life*.[13]

The *Origin of Species* was in many respects simply a larger version of
his "Essay" of 1844. The natural selection of variations that had
"chanced to arise" remained central to his discussion of transmutation.
But Darwin modified his organizational scheme and added conclusions
he had since reached. The most important of these was the "principle
of divergence." Recognizing that the great diversity of organisms
within a single location could not be explained solely by factors such as
climate, Darwin had concluded by the 1850s that different varieties of a
species sometimes found unoccupied "niches" within the "economy of
nature" that enabled them to escape competition and hence survive.
This principle, which explained how new species could coexist with

original ones, played an important role in enabling Darwin to account for diversity as well as adaptation.[14]

Darwin realized that both his claims to originality and his prospects for convincing the scientific community to accept his theory depended on his mechanism explaining how transmutation occurred. Accordingly, he placed the analogy between artificial selection and natural selection at the heart of his work. He also emphasized that his theory provided a scientific explanation for phenomena that special creationists had necessarily regarded as brute facts. For example, "rudimentary" organs, which served no purpose, could be explained as the result of inheritance from earlier individuals for whom the organs had played adaptive roles. Similarly, if the transmutation hypothesis were correct, embryological and morphological similarities among different organisms could be attributed to common ancestry, and the geographical distribution of species could be ascribed to migration and divergent variation from the center of their origin.[15]

Darwin devoted a good portion of his book to answering anticipated objections to his theory. He conceded that observational evidence for transmutation was lacking, but he argued that demands for such evidence were unreasonable, for the process worked far too slowly for anyone to witness it. The closest one could come to providing empirical evidence for descent by modification was the fact of artificial selection. More troublesome was the lack of paleontological evidence for transmutation. Because Darwin emphasized that change was quite gradual, the absence of intermediate fossil forms in the geological strata was particularly problematic. He was therefore compelled to stress the fragmentary nature of the geological record.[16]

Darwin clearly hoped to avoid inflaming the passions of pious reviewers. He refrained from any discussion of spontaneous generation. He did not dwell on the origin of humanity. He also explicitly credited God with having "impressed on matter" the laws governing the universe. Nevertheless, in rejecting the doctrine of special creation, Darwin was challenging a vision of natural history that had become fundamental to the way most religious thinkers conceived of the relationship between the organic world and its Creator. For this reason, in the period from 1859 to 1875 they characteristically assumed that the Darwinian hypothesis was an assault on "the fundamental principles both of natural and revealed religion."[17]

The conviction of American Protestants that Darwin's theory undermined natural theology becomes comprehensible only when that theory is placed within the context of mid-nineteenth-century Christian apologetics in the United States. Throughout the nineteenth century American religious thinkers, haunted by the specter of unbelief, devoted a great deal of attention to defending their belief in a supernatural Deity. By 1859, most of these thinkers assumed that the most important repository of evidence attesting to God's existence was the natural world. Actually, nature had few rivals. Though Protestants themselves embraced the Bible as a source of religious truth, they were aware that scriptural testimony carried little weight with those who were wavering on the more fundamental issues of God's existence and attributes. Recognizing this, the Congregational clergyman Joseph Haven, Jr. declared that "until natural theology has done its work, all other theology is impossible." Nor did formal metaphysics seem to offer much promise in constructing a credible natural theology. The commitment of most American Protestant thinkers in the first six decades of the nineteenth century to "common sense realism" both manifested and justified their contempt for the "airy region of metaphysics," an enterprise they associated with the sophistry of medieval scholasticism and the acid of philosophical skepticism. The reverent study of nature, on the other hand, had yielded a much richer harvest, a body of data witnessing to the existence of a providential Creator.[18]

In the two centuries prior to publication of the *Origin of Species*, the venerable argument from design constituted the bulwark of Anglo-American apologetics. William Paley's *Natural Theology* was only one of the most celebrated of a profusion of works seeking to show that the order, structure, and function of natural phenomena could be reasonably explained only if they were seen as the work of a benevolent, supernatural Designer. So compelling was the argument, many Protestants believed, that "none but a mind wilfully obtuse, or one that had been perverted by logical subtilties and metaphysical abstactions ever failed to receive it with perfect trust at the first view."[19]

Not everyone agreed with this assessment. In the eighteenth century, two of Europe's most incisive intellects, David Hume and Immanuel Kant, subjected the argument from design to severe scrutiny. These thinkers did not deny that the universe might have been fashioned by an intelligent, supernatural Deity, but they insisted that the argument from design failed to prove that this was the case. The order disclosed in the universe, they contended, was insufficiently analogous to contrivances designed by finite minds to justify the inference that it was the product of a divine mind. Other thinkers emphasized that the presence of so much evil and suffering should be sufficient to deter human

beings from appealing to the order of nature for proof of the perfect benevolence of God. Voltaire, for example, found in the Lisbon earthquake of 1759 a persuasive indication that "man's the victim of
unceasing woe." Such a world, he held, was incapable of establishing
the existence of a benevolent Governor.[20]

Such criticisms left apologists unmoved. For the most part, they eschewed systematic and detailed refutations of the objections advanced
against the argument from design in favor of compiling an ever larger
number of instances of divine handiwork. In carrying out this agenda,
most defenders of the faith found the scientific study of nature quite
useful. To be sure, from the very outset of the Reformation some Protestant thinkers warned that scientific investigation would divert attention from spiritual affairs. Such apprehension, however, did not
represent the dominant view. Samuel Harris, a Congregational clergyman who eventually went on to a distinguished career as a professor of
theology at Yale, gave expression to the position characteristically held
by nineteenth-century American Protestant intellectuals when he declared in 1852 that "if God is the Creator of the universe, how is it possible but that the study of the creation be interlinked at every point with
the study of the Creator, and thus become, to the devout mind, the
study of theology." Most Protestants were inclined to blame philosophical speculation for whatever inroads unbelief was making. In contrast,
"the calm investigation of science, stamped with the seal of Christian
charity, is found to be the best of all swords and all shields."[21]

For their part, scientists helped to cement the alliance between science and religion by justifying scientific inquiry in theological terms.
This mode of defense clearly helped to legitimate and even hallow their
pursuits, but it would be a mistake to assume that this was the only
consideration motivating scientists to align their work with the theological enterprise. Both institutionally and intellectually, the boundary between science and theology in the United States was quite obscure
throughout much of the nineteenth century. Many scientists were also
clergymen, and many others were pious Christians who valued the
study of nature as a means of kindling awareness of the existence of a
wise and gracious Creator. These thinkers found it reasonable to suppose that "the religious applications of science are its most important
use," and they were among the most enthusiastic partisans of natural
theology.[22]

The effect of basing apologetics on the systematic study of nature
was profound. The conviction that science furnished "statements,
specifications, facts, details, that will illustrate the wonderful perfec-

tions of the infinite Creator" prompted many Protestant clergymen and theologians to champion the cause of science. This support was of crucial importance in determining the status and popularity of science within American culture. At the same time, however, the fact that scientific investigation was ongoing and the fact that the theoretical framework within which that investigation took place underwent periodic change encouraged—even forced—defenders of the faith to follow scientific discussions with a watchful, and sometimes wary, eye. Finally, and perhaps most important, the scientific mode of analyzing phenomena became decisive in shaping the way in which Protestants thought about nature and nature's God. Their use of the insights gleaned from investigations of the natural world tended to foster arguments evoking admiration for the skill of its Creator rather than awe in the face of the mystery of existence. Concomitantly, God was envisioned less as the source and power of Being than as an ingenious cosmic Architect Whose existence was "to be proved like any other fact in natural science, by arguments of the same kind, though superior in number and force." Order rather than Being became the major category in Protestants' understanding of reality.[23]

These consequences seemed far less obvious to most religionists than the value of scientific knowledge in confounding the forces of skepticism. At no time did science appear more conducive to the apologetic enterprise than during the first half of the nineteenth century. Of special importance in this regard was the work of paleontologists, which gave defenders of the Christian world view access to a wealth of data that enabled them to go well beyond Paley in showing that natural history was a variorum of divine wisdom and benevolence. Like Paley, most nineteenth-century apologists believed that the organic world was the source of the most vivid illustrations of divine design. The fossil record provided additional evidence of the ubiquity of design by showing that species that had long since perished were, like those currently in existence, well adapted to the environments in which they had lived.[24]

Many, probably most, American natural theologians joined Paley in arguing that the usefulness of organic structures in enabling plants and animals to adapt to their environment was to be ascribed to neither chance nor necessity but to the work of a divine Creator. Many students of the organic world continued to use the concept of purpose—adaptation—in their morphological investigations long after the idea of final cause had become irrelevant in the physical sciences. Other natural historians, though convinced that plants and animals were generally well adapted to their environments, recognized not only that it was impossible to discern purpose in every structure, but also that the same structures performed different functions and that the same functions could be performed by different structures. For these thinkers, the utilitarian formulation of the argument from design seemed less compelling. Most of them continued to believe, however, that the structure of organisms implied the existence of an intelligent Designer. Contending that the fact that all organisms were modifications of a few basic structural types was too remarkable to be the result of chance, they inferred that "unity of type" was indicative of a rational divine plan. This claim proved to be most popular among scientists, but some nonscientists also found the idea of "unity of plan" an attractive way of formulating the argument from design. Still other apologists employed both versions of the argument. However they chose to construct and defend the argument from design, they could agree that the phenomena of the organic world were "all so many individual protests against the Atheist's creed; that all is the work of chance, or of a blind unintelligent necessity."[25]

This view was reinforced by the apparent directional pattern of the fossil record. Most paleontologists believed that the fossils in more recent geological strata were generally of a more highly developed character than those in older strata. This "progressive" interpretation of the fossil record led Christian apologists to infer that in the prehistory of the planet, as in human history, the divine plan had been enacted gradually.[26]

If the history of life suggested God's unwillingness to countenance "a stagnant and unprogressive creation," it also appeared to bear witness to the conviction that He "has always exercised over the globe a superintending Providence." Belief in God's providential concern for His creatures was central to the Christian faith. In defending this belief, most Protestants relied on phenomena that could not be described by reference to the laws of nature. The fossil record seemed ideally suited to this purpose, for it appeared to disclose "a group of organic statuary too remarkable to be slid in and out by the simple operations of material law." The disparities among fossils in different strata, apologists argued, provided strong evidence of the "direct interposition, often repeated and distinctly visible, of the same almighty power, which originated the whole design at first, and still presides over every movement of the complicated machinery." And because each of these acts appeared to be inexplicable in terms of natural law, many Protestants believed that the fossil record supplied evidence capable of refuting the standard argument against miracles. Since the eighteenth century, individuals who denied the reality of miracles had typically joined David Hume in arguing that the testimony of human witnesses regarding alleged miraculous occurrences was less credible than the lesson of common experience that the universe operates in a uniform manner. The appearance of successive groups of new species during the course of natural history seemed to give the lie to the notion that the world was a scene of unvaried activity. From the "MYRIAD MIRACLES recorded indelibly upon the 'everlasting rocks,'" apologists inferred that it was unreasonable to assume that the miracles recorded in the Bible were incredible.[27]

If the interpretation of the history of life as a succession of independent creations of ever more highly developed species served to broaden the scope of supernatural activity and attest to God's providential concern for the world, the fact that myriads of species had become extinct in a "grim, gloomy, and deadly" preadamite world could hardly fail to perplex thinkers who believed in an omnipotent and benevolent God. Many religious intellectuals, committed to the view that "seeming evil must have a beneficent design and tendency," thus searched diligently for clues that would help justify God's mode of creation. Much of their speculation on this problem proceeded from the assumption that the human species had been created in the image of God and thus enjoyed a special status in the world. From this perspective, they reasoned that "all the arrangements of this world" had been created "with ultimate reference to man." In this vein, some thinkers, persuaded that humanity lived in a world irrevocably blemished by Adam's sin, held that the death disclosed in the fossil record prefigured the Fall and the Cross. Other Protestants favored a different approach and linked the creation of the successive races of plants and animals to the establishment of a "habitable abode" for human beings. The eminent Yale geologist James Dwight Dana, for example, submitted that vegetation had preceded animal life in order to remove carbonic acid from the air and to provide oxygen necessary for the existence of animal life. Other commentators noted that the remains of plants and animals had fertilized the soil and produced coal deposits instrumental to human welfare. Still others suggested that fossils served humanity's spiritual needs "by becoming grounds for praise in the estimation of the living, unfolding to them the impress of the wisdom of God."[28]

It was impossible to account for all preadamite phenomena in this manner, however, and the contention that "evil appears in the world only as incidental to the good" remained an article of faith rather than an established fact. Some Protestants made their peace with this state of affairs by contending that in order to demonstrate the goodness of God, it was enough to show that the preponderance of phenomena were manifestly beneficent. Others contended that the perception of "blemishes in the works of God" was due to the "partial and imperfect" view of finite creatures attempting to apprehend the purposes of an infinite Creator. Although this contention was not unreasonable, it did place religious thinkers in the position of arguing for God's existence on the basis of what human beings had discerned about the nature of the divine plan and for His benevolence at least partly on the basis of what they had not. To mitigate this tension, some Protestants urged that "time and the progress of knowledge" would show more clearly the goodness of God. Others held that a proper apprehension of God's benevolence required the supplementary testimony of the Bible.[29]

The existence of God, the reality of His providential concern for His creation, the veracity of miracles, the importance of humanity as the focus of divine plan—all these doctrines appeared to be legitimate inferences from the clearest disclosures of scientific investigation. If, as some historians have contended, natural theology had become a feckless, desultory, and even insignificant concern long before the publication of the *Origin of Species*, this was not recognized by most American Protestant intellectuals. Admittedly, a few thinkers cautioned that "it is a poor Divinity which rests its claim to godhead on the instincts of the beaver or the sagacity of the ant." Most of them, however, continued to regard the inference from nature to God as an unassailable basis for defending the validity of the Christian world view. In this spirit, Josiah Parsons Cooke, a professor of chemistry at Harvard, submitted that "the existence of an intelligent Author of nature, infinite in wisdom and absolute in power, may be proved from the phenomena of the material world with as much certainty as can be any theory of science."[30]

In view of the widespread conviction that "the manner in which living beings originate . . . touches upon beliefs which are the very foundation of all religion," it is not surprising that defenders of the faith within the American Protestant community tended to view any challenge to the idea that each species had been independently created by means of a "special" divine creative act as a threat to their faith. Edward Hitchcock, a Congregational clergyman and well-known geologist, clearly enunciated this view when he observed in 1835 that "the production of new forms of animal and vegetable life must be regarded, as it ever has been, as the highest and most astonishing exercise of creative power; and if that power can be supposed to reside in the laws of nature, it seems to us that there is no phenomenon in the universe that will require a higher power: and we are reduced at once to materialism and atheism."[31]

It was in this spirit that religious thinkers confronted the transmutation hypothesis. By the middle of the nineteenth century, the concept of gradual development had become quite important in analyzing both human history and a wide range of natural phenomena. Biology was not exempt from this concept's influence, and historians have succeeded in compiling a long list of "evolutionists" who preceded Charles Darwin. Most of these precursors lived on the European continent, long assailed by English and American religious thinkers alike as the dwelling place of infidelity. Like the proverbial bad penny, however, the transmutation hypothesis continued to turn up. In 1844 a popular exposition of the hypothesis appeared in the English-speaking world: *Vestiges of the Natural History of Creation*.[32]

The author of this work, which was published anonymously, was the Scottish publisher Robert Chambers. A respectable self-taught geologist, Chambers loved science but disdained the narrow-mindedness and "intellectual timidity" he saw in most of its practitioners. For him, scientists not only were guilty of "doing little for the establishment of comprehensive views of nature," but also seemed intent on sabotaging the work of anyone who suggested such views. Chambers staked whatever hopes he had for acceptance of his speculations on informed laymen like himself.[33]

Chambers, who was a deist, disavowed any intention of undermining belief in a divine Creator. At issue, he insisted, was not whether but how God governed phenomena. For his own part, Chambers was convinced that natural law was a more intellectually plausible and emotionally satisfying explanation of natural history than arbitrary divine fiat. This conviction informed his discussion of the history of life.[34]

Noting that scientific investigation had shown that gradual, lawful change characterized the history of both the heavens and the earth, Chambers held that it was reasonable to infer that the development of life also proceeded from "one law or decree of the Almighty," the law of development. The notion that each species required God's "immediate exertion," he maintained, was "a very mean view of the Creative Power." Although he ascribed the origin of life itself to the animation of inorganic elements by means of electricity, he did not believe that spontaneous generation could account for the appearance of the new species—the "vestiges of creation"—contained in the fossil record. In accounting for the adaptation of plants and animals, which "was as perfect in those early ages as it is still," he invoked a "generative law" that was as fuzzy as it was fanciful. Chambers contended that new species arose by means of small sudden leaps caused by the "protracted gestation" of existing species under the "peculiar conditions" provided by an environment increasingly favorable to the existence of more complex forms. These leaps, he emphasized, were no more remarkable or miraculous than "the silent advance of an ordinary mother from one week to another of her pregnancy."[35]

The problem with this theory was that it failed to explain precisely why the adaptation of organisms to their environment occurred. In grappling with this problem, Chambers offered the rather vague suggestion that "organic life presses in wherever there is room and encouragement for it," but in the end he was reduced to acknowledging that it was God Who ensured the parallel advances of new species with their environment. To him, this was additional evidence that "*design* presided in the creation of the whole—design again implying a designer, another word for a CREATOR." Given this view, it is little wonder that Chambers felt entitled to believe that he had achieved his goal of presenting his theory "with as little disturbance as possible to existing beliefs."[36]

Still, the view of natural history embodied in *Vestiges* did challenge established views. Chambers believed that the cosmos was the work of a "transcendently kind" divine Utilitarian Who worked by means of dependable law operating for the greatest good for the greatest number. He acknowledged the possibility of "a system of Mercy and Grace behind the screen of nature," but he inferred that "the individual, as far as the present sphere of being is concerned, is to the Author of Nature a consideration of inferior moment." For him it was enough that the natural world "has the fairness of a lottery, in which every one has the like chance of drawing the prize."[37]

Most reviewers of *Vestiges* within the American Protestant intellectual community indignantly rejected Chambers' work as a disingenuous attempt to undermine belief in a providential moral Governor. "Of what avail is it to give us the idea of a Creator," a reviewer for the Presbyterians' *Biblical Repertory* asked, "if He who created does not govern us?" Tayler Lewis, a professor at the University of the City of New York and an avid participant in discussions of the relationship between science and religion, offered a representative statement of a widely shared concern. Lewis held that in spite of the fact that the author of *Vestiges* "does not deny the existence of a God in express terms," it was nevertheless true that "the doctrine of the book is atheism,—blank atheism, cold, cheerless, heartless, atheism." In justification of this indictment, Lewis observed that the God recognized by the author of *Vestiges* "is the hearer of no prayer, he is the administrator of no particular providence; he has no love for right, and no burning indignation against wrong. . . . This deity never wrought a miracle, never created a world in time by any special act aside from necessarily eternal influences, never was the author of any new state of things, or ever brought to a special end any old dispensation."[38]

The assessment Protestants made of the implications of *Vestiges* anticipated their interpretation of the *Origin of Species*. Darwin's account of speciation was more aggressively naturalistic than anything Chambers had envisioned and could hardly fail to seem inimical to Christian supernaturalism. In contrast to the "orthodox theory in science," which appeared to "write the name of God on every organic structure so plainly that even the fool can scarcely fail to read it," the Darwinian hypothesis accounted for the characteristics of organisms most commonly cited as evidence of design by a continuous process of random variation and *natural* selection, and it attributed unity of type to descent from a common ancestor rather than to a master plan actualized by a supernatural Designer. Adaptive structures were less clearly the effect of Mind than the cause of survival. Moreover, if Darwin were correct, adaptation was not as ubiquitous as Protestants who ascribed each species to independent special creation had assumed; in the competitive struggle that pervaded nature, plants and animals that were relatively less adapted simply did not survive. Nor did Darwin's theory imply that adaptation was perfect; it presupposed only that "new and improved varieties will inevitably supplant and exterminate the older, less improved and intermediate varieties." In fact, Darwin held that evolution occurred precisely because organisms were not perfectly adapted to the conditions of their existence. Moreover, as those conditions changed, plants and animals that were relatively adapted frequently became less so. Little wonder, then, that many American Protestant intellectuals concluded that the Darwinian hypothesis undermined the conviction that the history of life was the realization of a creative plan initiated and governed by a Christian Deity. Some of them accused Darwin of attributing the origin of species to "the inevitable and unforeseen results of the blind working of nature's laws." Others, possibly because they equated natural law with the uniform regularities of Newtonian physics, charged that Darwin's account of speciation "openly dispenses with law itself . . . and throws itself without reserve upon the illimitable ocean of accident." However they interpreted the Darwinian mechanism, they could agree that the *Origin of Species* suggested "views on the modes of action of the Creator, and on the ways of Providence, that are repugnant to the most cherished feelings and hopes of man." Unlike the doctrine of special creation, which clearly attested to God's interest in His creation and His willingness to "interfere in other respects should the universe demand such an interposition," Darwin's theory tended "to efface every impression of an acting Deity."[39]

One of the most influential statements of this position was presented by Charles Hodge, Princeton Seminary's Professor of Exegetical, Didactic, and Polemic Theology. During the course of his long and productive career, Hodge trained some three thousand clergymen, more than any other American theologian in the nineteenth century. These students and the readers of his several books and the 142 articles he published in the prestigious *Princeton Review*, a journal he edited until 1871, found Hodge to be an able defender of Old School Calvinism. The pugnacious Hodge was already a veteran of numerous theological conflicts when he joined battle with Darwinism. In his *Systematic Theology* (1872–73), a massive three-volume work elaborating the doctrinal tenets of the Reformed orthodoxy he had espoused throughout his career, Hodge contended that Darwin's theory was nothing more than an unproved "hypothesis," inconsistent with both the Bible and natural theology. Noting that Darwinism was antithetical to the notion that the world had been supernaturally designed, he warned that "there is no more effectual way of getting rid of a truth than by rejecting the proofs on which it rests." In an impromptu speech at a session of the General Conference of the Evangelical Alliance in 1873, he charged Darwin and his followers with believing that the organic world was a product of "unintelligent, undesignating forces." The next year Hodge published his most complete indictment of the transmutation hypothesis in his book *What Is Darwinism?*[40]

Hodge repeated his allegation that Darwin held that all organisms "may be accounted for by the blind operation of natural causes, without any intention, purpose or cooperation of God." This explained, he thought, why opponents of Christianity had eagerly embraced Darwin's theory of organic evolution after rejecting earlier ones. Though he acknowledged that Darwin had retained an "infinitesimal spark of supernaturalism" by professing belief in a divine Creator, Hodge insisted that "the denial of design in nature is virtually the denial of

God." He thus found the answer to his title question all too clear: "What is Darwinism? It is Atheism."[41]

A few intellectuals sought to defend Darwin's theory against charges of heresy. One of the most enthusiastic of these defenders was America's preeminent botanist, Asa Gray. In 1842, after rejecting the study of medicine for natural history, Gray became Fisher Professor of Natural History at Harvard. In the course of his career he not only distinguished himself as a scholar but did much to popularize the study of botany in the United States. And, like numerous other American scientists, he combined a rigorous devotion to science with a commitment to a liberal variant of evangelical Christianity.[42]

In 1846 Gray published a biting review of *Vestiges* and the *Sequel* Chambers had published in its defense. He not only indicted the author of these works for substituting unsupported, confused speculation for solid research, but contended that Chambers' view of natural history "gives birth to conclusions as incongruous with any common theistic scheme as they are revolting alike to our religious and our common sense." Nevertheless, though Gray was convinced that the evidence of natural history indicated that God had created each organism "specifically after its kind" in accordance with "a foreordained, harmonious plan," he also insisted on trying the transmutation hypothesis before the court of science, acknowledging that "we must receive it, if proven, and build up our religious belief by its side as well as we may."[43]

Gray found Darwin's exposition of the development hypothesis far more convincing than Chambers' speculations. This assessment, which will be discussed at some length in the next chapter, prompted him to revise his views concerning the theological implications of the theory of organic evolution, for he was convinced that no valid scientific theory could truly be irreligious. Gray addressed himself to the religious implications of the Darwinian hypothesis in a review of the *Origin of Species* that appeared in the March 1860 issue of the *American Journal of Science*. He acknowledged that Darwin's theory was compatible with atheism but insisted that this was equally true of all "physical theories." Darwin thus created no new problems for believers. But if scientific hypotheses were themselves ipso facto neither theistic nor atheistic, this did not mean that there was no evidence in nature for the existence of God. On the contrary, he urged, the order pervading the universe provided the "philosophical theist" with strong grounds for affirming the existence of a divine Mind, Will, and Personality overseeing "the bringing to pass of new and fitting events at fitting times."[44]

Aware that the readership of scientific journals was limited, Gray also published three articles on the *Origin of Species* anonymously in the *Atlantic Monthly*. One of the purposes of these articles was to allay fears regarding the theological implications of the Darwinian hypothesis. Gray reiterated his view that scientific theories were, as explanations of events employing secondary causes, inherently neither theistic nor atheistic. He insisted, however, that "a theistic view of Nature is implied in his [Darwin's] book." In defending this claim, he reminded his readers that Darwin had acknowledged that God had created life itself; if the issue of divine intervention in the natural world was at issue, "one interposition admits the principle as well as more."[45]

Like most American Protestant intellectuals, however, Gray was not enamored of the idea that God's role in nature had ceased after the initial creation. He therefore turned to the question of the relationship between Darwinism and design. Gray reiterated his position that acceptance of the Darwinian hypothesis "would leave the doctrine of final causes, utility, and special design just where they were before." The idea that species originated by natural causes, he contended, was no more threatening to the claim that plants and animals were the product of design than the idea that individuals had entered the world by the natural process of birth. Gray held, in fact, that a careful analysis of the Darwinian hypothesis would reveal that the inference from the "orderly arrangements and admirable adaptations pervading the organic world" to "an ordaining and directing intelligence" remained as persuasive as it had ever been. He emphasized that "though natural selection is scientifically explicable, variation is not." Persuaded that the history of life suggested that "variation has been led along certain beneficial lines," he reasoned that this implied the existence of a divine Designer and exonerated this Designer from charges of incompetence or malevolence. If Darwin's view of natural selection implied that the history of life resembled a game of dice, these dice had been loaded by a merciful and intelligent Deity.[46]

Gray was not the only thinker who sought to "baptize" the *Origin of Species* in the period from 1859 to 1875. Shortly after arriving from Scotland in 1868 to assume the presidency of the College of New Jersey (later Princeton), James McCosh, a prolific author and influential philosopher, began telling his students that when the transmutation hypothesis was "properly limited and explained," it was perfectly in accord with theism. In his influential *Christianity and Positivism*, a series of lectures delivered in 1871 at Union Theological Seminary and published the same year, he insisted that "we are not precluded from seeking and discovering a final cause, because we have found an efficient cause." Christians could thus subscribe simultaneously to the theory of organic evolution and to the doctrine that God was the Creator and Designer of organisms.[47]

Prior to 1875, most American Protestant intellectuals were not as conciliatory in their approach to the transmutation hypothesis as Asa Gray and James McCosh. Gray's effort to recast the argument from design in a Darwinian mold by conferring upon God the role of directing the course of variation was largely ignored. Protestant thinkers quite correctly interpreted Darwinian variation as a "random" phenomenon, unrelated to the requirements of adaptation. Francis Bowen, the editor of the *North American Review* from 1843 to 1854 and Harvard's Alvord Professor of Natural Religion, Moral Philosophy, and Civil Polity from 1853 to 1889, thus noted that the principle of natural selection "would have nothing to do,—it would not be *selection*,—if the Individual Variations were not multiplied at random, and were not purposeless in character."[48]

Bowen and most of the other American thinkers who assessed the religious implications of Darwin's hypothesis in the fifteen years after publication of the *Origin of Species* assumed that the apologetic value of natural history remained inextricably bound up with the inability of science to account for the origin of species by physical agencies. If they could accept Gray's contention that the Darwinian hypothesis did not alter the *fact* of adaptation, they could also recognize that the role of natural selection in the hypothesis served to obscure, if it did not altogether sever, the link between adaptation and a divine Designer. Gray's acknowledgment that the Darwinian hypothesis was compatible with either theism or atheism gave them small comfort. Daniel R. Goodwin, an Episcopal clergyman who in 1860 became provost of the University of Pennsylvania, voiced the concern of many Protestant intellectuals when he observed that "natural theology is not simply the *belief* in God, but the *evidence* for that belief from nature and reason. If the theory of 'natural selection' is consistent with the belief in God, yet does it not overthrow the evidence for that belief?"[49]

The consensus among apologists that the doctrine of special creation was central to the defense of the Christian world view ensured that the Darwinian hypothesis would be widely perceived as a challenge to the structure of natural theology. The attitude that American Protestants would adopt in the face of the theory's inconsistency with prevailing interpretations of the Bible was similarly predictable, but the underlying basis for that attitude was considerably more complex. From the outset of the development of modern science, Protestants had been forced again and again to grapple with the problem of "reconciling" science and the Bible. Though they had typically complained bitterly when scientists advanced ideas that conflicted with their interpretation of the Bible, they had accepted these ideas once it became clear that they had become part of the corpus of accepted science. This pattern of accommodation, however, resulted more from the ability of Protestant exegetes to convince themselves that little was at stake in the compromises they made than from a systematic position concerning the scope of biblical authority. Actually, by the middle of the nineteenth century the voluminous literature dealing with the relationship between science and the Bible had yielded only an amalgam of not altogether consistent formulas that had been hammered out in response to the imperatives of the moment. Carefully articulated, widely accepted prescriptions for responding to ideas set forth in the name of science that conflicted with the biblical narrative were rarely presented and even more rarely heeded.[50]

Protestant intellectuals could agree that however valuable the natural world might be in promoting belief in an omnipotent God, it was necessary to look to the Scriptures for a disclosure of many of the truths enabling humanity to elude the snares of Satan. In defending the claim that the Bible was a vehicle of divine revelation, they invoked a variety of "evidences," most notably the "organic unity" of the Scriptures and the confirmation of biblical teachings furnished by miracles and the fulfillment of prophecies. Such evidence, even if taken at face value, did not actually demonstrate that every passage of the Bible had been divinely inspired. Nevertheless, most American Protestant intellectuals during the first three quarters of the nineteenth century believed that once they had justified the claim that God had revealed Himself to the authors of Scripture, it was reasonable to assume that all the words of these individuals "are to be received not as the words of men, but as they are in truth, as the words of God." This conviction was embodied in a doctrine of "plenary" inspiration that attributed inerrancy to the contents of the Scriptures. The New School Presbyterian scholar Albert Barnes, whose *Commentaries* sold more than a million copies, described the "old and established doctrine of the church" regarding biblical inspiration as the belief

that truths are recorded there which in fact have their origin *directly* in the mind of God, and have been imparted by him to the minds of the writers by a direct communication; that those truths are above any natural power of the writers to originate them, to discover them, or to express them; and that in recording them, however much they may have been left to their own peculiarities of modes of expression or language, they have been so guided by the Holy Spirit as to be preserved from error; that this principle applies to every part of the sacred volume; that the Bible is in fact, and to all intents and purposes, *one book*, whose real author is the Spirit of God.[51]

To many Protestants, the veracity of the Bible justified the notion that biblical theology was no less a "science" than astronomy or biology. As Charles Hodge put it, "the Bible is to the theologian what nature is to the man of science. It is his storehouse of facts." Just as the task of the scientist was to interpret natural phenomena, so that of the theologian was to infer the proper order of "data" contained in the Scriptures and to deduce Christian doctrine from them.[52]

The idea that nature and the Bible were partners in revealing divine truth to humanity appealed to Protestants of widely different theological perspectives. Proponents of this position, convinced that "there can be no contradiction between what God does and what he says," affirmed that truths gleaned from the study of nature would necessarily accord with the testimony of the Bible. In fact, however, ideas posited in the name of science sometimes conflicted with prevailing interpretations of biblical passages. During the nineteenth century, much of this conflict centered on work emanating from the study of geology. Geologists, in focusing on changes that had occurred during the history of the planet, entered a preserve long inhabited by biblical theology. By 1840, the interpretation of the earth's past embraced by most geologists differed significantly from that embodied in conventional interpretations of the Scriptures. Geologists agreed, for example, that the earth was much older than the six thousand years commonly allowed by biblical expositors. They also recognized that the testimony of the fossil record ran counter to the belief that the world had been created in six twenty-four hour days. Finally, most had abandoned the notion that geological evidence lent support to the traditional interpretation of the biblical flood as a deluge that covered the entire globe.[53]

These developments engendered an enormous literature dedicated to establishing the proper relationship between science and the Bible. Proceeding from the assumption that God's works would be found consistent with His Word, many Protestants assumed that the closer science came to an accurate interpretation of the natural world, the closer it would conform to the testimony of the Bible. To some religionists, this suggested that biblical testimony was relevant to discussions of natural history. Noting that science "depends upon the investigations of imperfect and fallible men," James Read Eckard, a professor of history and rhetoric at Lafayette College and a part-time pastor to a Presbyterian church in Asbury, New Jersey, concluded that "there is no real wisdom except such as exists in subordination to the Bible, and in sympathy with that holy church which God himself has constituted the 'Pillar and Ground of the Truth.' " If Protestants believed that the facts obtained by scientific investigation were unassailable, even sacred, they were also convinced that the interpretation of these facts was often problematic. In dealing with data relating to events that lay outside the realm of human observation, interpretation was especially tenuous. This prompted some thinkers to suggest that "lest we should err in our inferences from the works of God, we have a clearer revelation of all that nature reveals, in his word." From this perspective, a number of Protestant intellectuals insisted that it was entirely appropriate to regard biblical testimony as "data" that could help resolve questions relating to natural history. Daniel R. Goodwin thus declared that "to enunciate doctrines in palpable contradiction to the testimony of the Scriptures—passing over their testimony in silence—is neither consistent with respect for the Christian religion, nor with the rules of scientific procedure."[54]

In itself, however, this idea provided little assistance in resolving apparent conflict between science and the Bible, for most Protestant thinkers simply could not bring themselves to join Eckard in assuming that "revealed religion, as understood by the church of Christ," was always "entitled to a high pre-eminence over the theories of science." Instead they took the position that while the Bible itself was infallible, interpretations of it were not. This view made it theoretically possible for Christians to countenance the idea of abandoning interpretations of the Bible that were inconsistent with scientific conclusions, but it also rendered the problem of establishing the proper relationship between science and the Bible immeasurably more complex. The shibboleth that apparent conflict between God's two "books" was due to an erroneous interpretation of either nature or the Bible provided no basis for determining whether the interpretive blunder in any given case of discord was to be ascribed to the scientist or to the biblical expositor. It was clearly incumbent on religious thinkers to reconcile divergent views of the natural world. But how?[55]

Much of the discussion of this question within the American Protestant community focused on the problem of arriving at reliable principles for interpreting the Scriptures. To this end, many Protestants urged that biblical passages were generally to be interpreted literally.

For thinkers who applied this principle to passages relating to natural history, the task of resolving inconsistencies between the scriptural narrative and the conclusions of scientists presented little difficulty; they simply denounced the latter. Most nineteenth-century American religious intellectuals, however, did not feel compelled to interpret the biblical account of creation in a literal manner. It was with little exaggeration that the outspoken Francis Bowen could declare in 1849 that "the literal interpretation of the first chapter of the book of Genesis has come to be regarded by nearly all educated Christians in the same light with the Papal opposition to the doctrine that the earth revolves round the sun."[56]

Natural science played an important role in undermining biblical literalism. During the course of the nineteenth century, the faith of educated Americans in science became sufficiently great that a number of Protestants warned that individuals would "sooner question the truth of Revelation, with all its overpowering evidence, than cast away demonstrated principles of science." One thinker noted that because "all parties" agreed that God was the author of nature, the appearance of contradiction between science and the Bible might lead some individuals to conclude that God was not the author of the latter. From this vantage point, the biblical literalist seemed to be engaged in a dangerous form of folly.[57]

Most Protestants agreed that the biblical authors had employed "popular" rather than scientific language in conveying truths relating to natural history. A representative statement of this position appeared in the work of Moses Stuart of Andover Seminary, an eminent theologian and one of the early practitioners of biblical criticism in the United States. Stuart submitted that God had "accommodated" the words of the Mosaic narrative "to the feelings, views, and methods of expression, existing in the time of Moses." But if Moses "knew nothing and therefore could teach nothing" of science, this was of no consequence: "the Bible was not designed to teach the Hebrews astronomy or geology."[58]

Stuart employed this position as a springboard for asserting that biblical expositors should endeavor to interpret the meaning of the Scriptures without taking into account the conclusions of modern science. "The question, what Moses meant," he insisted, "is one of *philology*." Tayler Lewis concurred, insisting in 1856 that "the *Bible* is to be *interpreted*, not reconciled with anything but itself." Most Protestant intellectuals, however, were reluctant to disjoin biblical theology from the disclosures of science. Paradoxically, for numerous thinkers this reluctance stemmed at least in part from belief in the infallibility of the Bible.

Many Protestants who joined Stuart in denying that the purpose of the biblical authors was to teach scientific truth nevertheless insisted that the Scriptures did not "teach falsehoods whether in physics or metaphysics." The fact that the Bible described the natural world in non-scientific language did not mean that its description was untrue; it simply meant that its description was not based on the categories of analysis employed by scientists. From this vantage point, many proponents of the doctrine of plenary inspiration reasoned that science could aid expositors in understanding the meaning of biblical passages. The Presbyterian clergyman James A. Lyon of Columbus, Mississippi, thus extolled science as "an indispensable concomitant of the Bible, in order to unfold and illustrate its great and ever-expanding truths." Similarly, Charles Hodge credited scientists with having "in many things taught the church how to understand the Scriptures."[59]

During the first three quarters of the nineteenth century Protestants expended a good deal of energy in attempting to show that just as belief in the veracity of the Bible had been accommodated to the astronomical innovations of the sixteenth and seventeenth centuries, so the "apparent" discord between geology and the Scriptures could be eliminated through reinterpretation of the latter without detriment to belief in the plenary inspiration of the Bible. Numerous commentators reinterpreted passages relating to the Flood to make it resemble the kind of limited, local affair that geological investigation seemed to require. The age of the earth elicited considerably more controversy, but it centered on the proper mode of reinterpreting the Scriptures rather than on the desirability of reinterpretation. During the second quarter of the nineteenth century, the majority of Protestant intellectuals came to believe that since any attempt to bring earth history within the bounds of traditional chronology was in vain, "the only alternative is, to find a longer period in Genesis." Two approaches to this problem proved particularly popular. One of these was predicated on the notion that between the initial creation described in the first verse of Genesis and the world inhabited by man, there had been a long interval during which the events described by geologists had occurred. Then, in six literal days God had "renovated" the world to correspond to its present configuration. The other mode of reconciliation rendered the word "day" an indefinitely long geological period.[60]

Both views provoked objections. Critics of the "interval" theory pointed out that passages in Exodus explicitly stated that God made all things in six days. In addition, the suggestion that organisms preserved as fossils had been created in a long interval between the "beginning" and the "renovation" appeared to be irreconcilable with the biblical statement that prior to the first day, the earth was "without form and void." Nor did the theory seem to allow enough time for what the Mosaic account asserted had been created since the first day. Finally, the return to chaos presupposed by the "renovation" appeared to be incompatible with the progressive nature of the fossil record. There were also problems with the figurative interpretation of the word "day." If, for example, a day were actually an epoch, what meaning could be attached to the words "morning and evening"? Moreover, philologists like Moses Stuart insisted that the grammatical and historical meaning of the term "day" in Genesis accorded with a twenty-four-hour period.[61]

The force of these criticisms succeeded in driving a few Protestants to abandon efforts to reconcile the words of the narrative of creation with the discoveries of geology and to content themselves with asserting that the author of Genesis had simply intended to affirm that the world had been created by a providential Deity. Others enjoined their readers to "wait, in a believing and patient spirit, for more light." Most, however, embraced one of the prevailing views and sought to explain away the difficulties as well as they could. More significant than the particular approach they advocated was the assumption they shared that biblical interpretation could profit from the insights of modern science and that scriptural "language is elastic enough to warrant a change without violence or unfairness" when the results of scientific investigation necessitated such a change. The widespread acceptance of this view was instrumental in enabling Protestants to accommodate their faith to the conclusions of geologists.[62]

The alacrity with which most Protestants accepted geological conclusions that contradicted the conventional understanding of the Mosaic narrative was doubtless fostered by their ability to convince themselves that neither the idea of a universal Noachian deluge nor traditional conceptions of the age of the earth were central to the structure of Christian theology. Many of them also believed, however, that some passages relating to the natural world could "never be set aside by the ultimate results of any true science." The "plain sense" of these passages was so integral to the Christian scheme of redemption that one could not take positions that contravened it without undermining Christianity itself. As with so many other issues relating to biblical authority, there was no consensus among the Protestants who adopted this position as to just which passages enjoyed this privileged status. There was general agreement, however, that at least two hypotheses that received a good deal of attention in mid-nineteenth-century America were indicative of a presumptuous reliance on "the wisdom of men" rather than on the teachings of God: "polygenism" and the transmutation hypothesis.[63]

Prior to the second quarter of the nineteenth century, most speculation on human diversity proceeded from the assumption that all human beings had descended from a common progenitor. After 1840, however, an increasing number of ethnologists came to believe that neither variation nor the impact of the environment could account for the differences among the races. Noting that these differences had remained constant throughout recorded human history, they rejected the idea that all races had descended from a common source in favor of the notion that they had been created separately.[64]

Strong support for polygenism appeared in the work of Louis Agassiz, a Swiss natural historian who emigrated to the United States in 1846. A prolific writer, Agassiz's contributions in the fields of paleontology and historical geology gave him a distinguished position in the Continental scientific community, and when he assumed a position as professor of geology and zoology at Harvard's Lawrence Scientific School in 1848, he quickly gained renown as America's most eminent natural historian. But Agassiz was not only a scholar. He also used his considerable talents to make science intelligible and interesting to the general public. His popular lectures served as an important conduit of scientific information to the American Protestant community.[65]

It was only after arriving in America that Agassiz reached the conclusion that the human species, like other forms of life, was confined to distinct and clearly defined regions. Though he maintained that all human beings were members of the same species, he denied that the Negro and Malay races had descended from the descendants of Noah.[66]

In 1850 Agassiz espoused this belief in the plural origin of the races in two articles published in the Unitarian *Christian Examiner*. Noting that the locations where races of man resided corresponded to the provinces of the animal kingdom, he asserted that this correspondence constituted grounds for believing that differences among the human races were as "primitive" as those separating animals in one province from those of another. Agassiz found additional support for this view in the absence of evidence suggesting that any race had migrated far from its birthplace. Moreover, he argued, the Eqyptian tombs showed that Negroes were no less different from Caucasians five thousand years ago than they were in his own time; hence, "to assume them to be of the same order, and to assert their common origin, is to assume and to assert what has no historical or physiological or physical foundation." Finally, he suggested, a consistent God would not have given all human beings a common center of origin while giving other organisms plural origins. On the basis of these considerations, Agassiz concluded that the human races had originated not from a single pair but from separate communities created by God in their present zones of habitation.[67]

Agassiz denied that his position militated against belief in the unity of humanity. The moral and intellectual similarities among human beings proved that they had all been created in the image of God, not that they had a single origin. The real basis for asserting the oneness of humanity was the awareness that all human beings showed of higher moral obligations rather than actual genetic connections.[68]

Although Agassiz was anxious to separate what he regarded as scientific questions from religious dogma, he had no wish to inflame religious passions. Accordingly, he submitted that there was not a single passage in the Bible that affirmed either the existence of a "common centre" from which humanity had originated or the differentiation of the descendants of Adam and Eve. References in the Bible relating to the origin and nature of humanity, he contended, either attested to the general view of human unity that Agassiz himself embraced or applied to the white race whose genealogy Genesis recorded.[69]

Agassiz next entered the polygenist discussion in 1854, when he published a short introductory essay to *Types of Mankind*, a large, tendentious compendium of material in support of the diversity of mankind. The inflammatory, irreverent style of this work's authors, the Egyptologist and popular lecturer George R. Gliddon, and Josiah C. Nott, a physician from Mobile, Alabama, could hardly have presented a starker contrast to Agassiz's restrained defense of polygenism. Both Gliddon and Nott were apparently theists, but they spurned the notion that the Scriptures were an appropriate guide to ethnology. Accordingly, they coupled their discussion of the physical types and geographical distribution of man with a stinging rebuke of the "Biblical dunces" who insisted on invoking Scripture in opposition to polygenism.[70]

A few Protestant commentators received the claims of polygenists with relative equanimity. The Boston Unitarian N. L. Frothingham, for example, submitted that "we are no less men, on the supposition of several original heads, than on that of two such individuals only." Frothingham recognized that Agassiz's conclusions were irreconcilable with a literal interpretation of the scriptural account of humanity's Fall, but this did not trouble him, for he regarded that story as "a didactic invention intended to account for the introduction of evil into the world which God had made 'very good,'" rather than as a description of actual historical events. Although Frothingham was himself "inclined" toward the idea that all human beings descended from a single pair, he insisted that scientific investigation should be allowed to proceed untrammeled by scriptural dogma.[71]

Most American Protestant intellectuals viewed polygenism less charitably. To these thinkers, the plural origin of the human species constituted an assault on one of the fundamental teachings of the Bible: the creation of humanity. A representative statement of this position was presented by Thomas Smyth, the pastor of Charleston's Second Presbyterian Church and a member of the American Association for the Advancement of Science. Smyth regarded efforts to exclude the Mosaic narrative from the discussion of humanity's origin as "unscientific" arrogance. Though he believed that scientists were entitled to discuss whether the races of man were variations of a single species or different species altogether, he insisted that the origin of humanity was an issue to be decided not by consulting scientists but by examining the Scriptures. From this perspective, Smyth dismissed Agassiz's suggestion that God had used the same plan in creating humanity that He had employed in creating other species; nothing was more clearly affirmed in the Bible than the uniqueness of human beings. By undermining belief in the "common relation of all men to the first man Adam, and to the second Adam who is Christ," Smyth declared, polygenism represented a threat to a doctrine on which "the whole scheme of divine mercy is founded, and an interest in its unspeakable blessings offered to 'EVERY CREATURE IN ALL THE WORLD.' "[72]

Smyth's hostile assessment of polygenism was widely shared. Even in the South, where views of black inferiority were most dramatically institutionalized, most Protestants continued to believe that the drama of salvation embodied in the Scriptures was predicated on the unity of humanity. Albert Barnes considered individuals who urged that polygenism could be reconciled with the Scriptures to be guilty of the sheerest sophistry: "By no fair rules of exegesis; by no possible torture of language, can the teachings of the Bible be made consistent with the belief that the different 'races' of men upon the earth have each had a separate origin." Others focused less attention on efforts to compromise than on the "antibiblical spirit" that motivated the work of many of polygenism's most outspoken proponents. In this vein, a reviewer of *Types of Mankind* in the Episcopalian *Church Review* charged that Nott and Gliddon were engaged in "a crusade . . . against all reverence and respect for the Bible as the Word of God." For critics who shared this view, the fate of the doctrine of plenary inspiration, even Christianity itself, was at stake in the debate over human origins.[73]

Similar reasoning drove many American Protestants to assail *Vestiges of the Natural History of Creation.* These thinkers were convinced that the view of human beings implicit in that work was inimical to that which was revealed in the Scriptures. Not only was Chambers' scheme inconsistent with a biblical view of providential activity, but it obliterated the notion that humanity enjoyed a unique status in its relationship to God. The notion that human beings had developed from lower organisms, one clergyman complained, implied either that "immortality is an essential and inherent attribute of the Infusoria" or that humanity was "destitute of immortality." The development hypothesis also undermined the scriptural exposition of the origin of sin and its remedy. If that hypothesis were correct, it would be necessary to "look for the virus of depravity far back of Adam." By the same logic, Christ's atonement would necessarily include "all those generations of animalculae from which man has descended."[74]

Significantly, Protestant thinkers did not regard their criticism of either polygenism or *Vestiges* as a challenge to established scientific doctrine. The comprehensive evolutionism espoused in *Vestiges* never received the approbation of the scientific community. Polygenism was considerably more successful in attracting support from natural historians, but the controversy was too confused by extraneous polemics to yield a clear consensus among them. By 1860, although some discussion of that issue continued to be heard, the focus of debate among individuals concerned with the problem of human origin had shifted to the transmutation hypothesis. Religious thinkers were thus able to maintain their view of the validity of biblical precepts without feeling that they were opposing a view of the natural world that had been given the imprimatur of science.

By 1859, the efforts of American Protestant intellectuals to come to grips with the problem of relating the testimony of the Scriptures to the pronouncements of modern science had resulted in a welter of slogans but no clear-cut, widely acknowledged principles that could determine which of these slogans to invoke in future confrontations with hypotheses concerning natural history. The ambiguity characterizing their views of the relationship between science and the Bible was epitomized in the Presbyterian clergyman Richard Gladney's declaration that science and the Bible were "the mutual interpreters of each other." This irenic position may well have succeeded in defusing tension, but it hardly constituted a formula for systematically delineating the realms of authority appropriate to science and biblical testimony.[75]

The absence of such a formula occasioned little concern among American Protestant thinkers in their confrontation with the Darwinian hypothesis. They were quick to recognize that this hypothesis was inconsistent with the biblical exposition of the creation of every plant and animal "after its kind." A few religionists took the position that a modified interpretation of the meaning of the phrase could effect a reconciliation of the Scriptures with the Darwinian theory if that theory were ever established. Many others were convinced that the problem of reconciliation went deeper than abandoning the literal interpretation of a biblical passage. The scenario of creation envisioned in Darwin's theory was so fundamentally at odds with the scriptural view, these thinkers maintained, that if it were ever shown to be true, the Bible would become nothing more than "an unbearable fiction."[76]

Most Protestants, however, saw no reason to present detailed analyses of the theological implications of an unproved speculation. In the 1860s commentators who were concerned with relating biblical testimony to modern thought focused more of their attention on the problems raised by *Essays and Reviews* (1860)—a volume composed of seven essays written by a group of English Protestants committed to the proposition that the principles of historical criticism should be used in interpreting the biblical text—than on those presented by Darwinism. This is not surprising. Compared with an assault on the doctrine of plenary inspiration emanating from within the ranks of Christendom itself, a speculative work seemingly akin to the discredited *Vestiges* appeared to merit little expenditure of intellectual energy.[77]

For most American Protestant intellectuals who addressed themselves to the Darwinian hypothesis in the period from 1859 to 1875, the focus of attention lay elsewhere. These thinkers reasoned that a hypothesis that appeared to threaten the Christian world view was most effectively countered through "a thorough investigation, which may determine whether the obnoxious opinion rest[s] on positive and sufficient proof, or merely on vague and precarious inference." In the fifteen years after publication of the *Origin of Species*, American Protestant intellectuals directed their efforts at convincing their readers that Darwin's "theory and all its possibilities are no better proof than the dream of an inebriate or the visions of a madman."[78]

2

"Science, Falsely So Called": The Assault on the Scientific Merits of the Theory of Organic Evolution

ALTHOUGH the attention that American religious intellectuals gave to the *Origin of Species* was motivated by their concern for its theological implications, most of these thinkers sought to discredit the theory in the period prior to 1875 by demonstrating that it was scientifically untenable. This strategy reflected their awareness that science had come to enjoy enormous prestige among large numbers of educated Americans as an arbiter of truth. By showing that the transmutation hypothesis was inconsistent with the disclosures of scientific investigation, they could effectively destroy its credibility.[1]

Most American Protestant thinkers were confident that it would not be difficult to impeach Darwin's theory. Several considerations contributed to this confidence. The assumption that God was the Author of nature as well as of the gospel led Protestants to reason that a theory as inconsistent with the Christian world view as that of Charles Darwin would also conflict with the facts of natural history.

This supposition was reinforced by the hostile reception scientists had given the transmutation hypothesis prior to the *Origin of Species*. Most natural historians believed that both observation of living organisms and examination of the fossil record, which revealed radical discontinuities between the species of different strata and gaps between the major branches of organisms, proved that species were discrete units within nature. Most also assumed that the requirements of adaptation imposed fixed limits to the degree of variability in each species. Indeed, many scientists regarded the fixity of species as a necessary condition of fruitful biological investigation. Natural historians who could agree on little else thus joined forces in denying that different species had arisen from a common progenitor. The eminent French paleontologist Georges Cuvier opposed Jean de Lamarck's transmutation hypothesis in the early years of the nineteenth century. Charles Lyell, convinced that "species have a real existence in nature and that each was endowed, at the time of its creation, with the attributes and organization by which it is now distinguished," devoted much of the second volume of his *Principles of Geology* to refuting (and inadvertently publicizing) Lamarckianism. Scientists were also virtually unanimous in repudiating the transmutation hypothesis espoused in *Vestiges of the Natural History of Creation*. Charles Darwin was but one of many natural historians who found Chambers' geology "bad, and his zoology far worse."[2]

Satisfied that scientists' verdict against the development hypothesis was unequivocal, American Protestant thinkers who initially joined battle with the *Origin of Species* did so in a spirit of weary confidence. To be sure, they recognized that Darwin was one of England's most respected naturalists. Many were aware, too, that Darwin's work was the ablest treatment of the transmutation hypothesis yet advanced. William North Rice, a professor of geology at Wesleyan University whose thesis, "The Darwinian Theory of the Origin of Species," earned the first Ph.D. in geology granted by Yale, declared that "it would be difficult to conceive of a theory of development which should combine more elements of strength." Nonetheless, Protestants judged the Darwinian hypothesis as only the most recent version of an "old exploded theory." Just as their own response to Darwin's precursors foreshadowed, even conditioned, their reception of his work, so they assumed that the scientific community would offer the *Origin of Species* no more support than it had shown previous works espousing transmutation.[3]

The initial response of scientists seemed to justify this assumption. Of particular importance in this regard were the writings of Louis Agassiz. Agassiz's world view, shaped by his European education and essentially fixed by the time he reached America, was based less on research than on a set of a priori postulates derived from his commitment to metaphysical idealism. If he acknowledged that scientific generalizations depended on careful investigation of natural phenomena, he also believed that the data obtained by such investigation "will teach us little or nothing till we place them in their true relations, and recognize the thought that binds them together as a consistent whole." He also believed that it was impossible to place the facts of natural history in their true context without recognizing that the units of classification that scientists used were categories of thought in the mind of the Creator. Likening natural history "to a drama, the plan of which was complete in the mind of its author before the first scene was written out," he concluded that in studying nature, minds were meeting Mind. The ultimate end of natural history resided in "the analysis of the thoughts of the Creator of the Universe, as manifested in the animal and vegetable kingdoms." For Agassiz, metaphysics and science were inseparable.[4]

Unlike most natural historians, who believed that individuals within a species were bound together by descent from a common ancestry, Agassiz regarded morphological similarities among the individuals composing a species as embodiments of the same idea in the mind of God. As a result, he maintained that "the unity of a species does not involve a unity of origin and that a diversity of origin does not involve a plurality of species." This position enabled him to assert that all human beings were members of the same species while affirming that the different races had been separately created.[5]

Agassiz's belief that species were immutable categories of thought precluded him from viewing the evolutionists' suggestion of a genetic connection among species as anything more than unintelligible nonsense. Adding to his animus against the transmutation hypothesis was the conviction that "there will be no scientific *evidence* of God's working in nature until naturalists have shown that the whole creation is the *expression of thought* and not the *product of physical agents*." Not surprisingly, Agassiz criticized *Vestiges* as nothing more than a tired rehash of arguments that the "French school" had been making for over half a century. Such arguments, unconfirmed by valid scientific evidence, were "not worthy [of] a critical examination by a serious scientific man." His endorsement of polygenism was also prompted by his concern that transmutation constituted the only plausible alternative to that view. In 1854 he noted that if the diversity and geographical distribution of human beings and animals were not primordial aspects of a divine "general plan" ordained by God, they were due to the activity of physical agents. Because he believed that human beings and animals were "modified by the same laws," he inferred that adoption of the latter alternative would entail the acceptance of some version of the development hypothesis. This was unacceptable.[6]

For his part, Agassiz believed that "the intervention of a Creator is displayed in the most striking manner, in every stage of the history of the world," and he advanced a number of arguments in defense of this belief. In the first place, he found in the fossil record unequivocal evidence of the existence of a "successive, gradual, progressive creation, planned by the Almighty in the beginning, and maintained in its present state by his providential action." Both the teachings of his mentor, Georges Cuvier, and his own investigation of glacial action convinced him that a series of "catastrophes" had periodically rent the earth's surface. Unlike Cuvier, however, Agassiz believed that each of these catastrophes had destroyed all life and that there was "a complete break between the present creation and those which precede it." This precluded a genetic connection between the species of one era and those of the next; life was periodically created anew by a providential Deity.[7]

Agassiz found even more compelling evidence for "the direct intervention of a Supreme Intelligence in the plan of the Creation" in the geographical distribution of species. Each species, he contended, inhabited a sharply circumscribed geographical region. Such discontinuity was indicative not of migrational dispersion but of a "premeditated plan," a plan that had been "marked out on the first day of creation," and "maintained unchanged through ages."[8]

Agassiz continued his assault on the idea of the efficacy of physical agencies in his *Contributions to the Natural History of the United States*, the first two volumes of which were published two years before Darwin's work appeared. Although much of this multivolume work was addressed primarily to specialists, he prefaced the first volume with a less technical "Essay on Classification" (later issued separately) that clearly revealed the philosophical assumptions informing his scholarship. As in his other works, Agassiz affirmed that in tracing the structure of organisms and the order in which they appeared, "the human mind is only translating into human language the Divine thought expressed in nature in living realities." Convinced that physical agents, operating alone, produced only chaos, he insisted that the structure, distribution, and order of succession of plants and animals "proclaim aloud the One God, whom man may know, adore, and love."[9]

The perspective from which Agassiz analyzed natural history ensured that he would judge the *Origin of Species* quite harshly. In November 1859 he received a copy of this work from Darwin, who appended a note expressing the hope that Agassiz would credit him with having "earnestly endeavoured to arrive at the truth." Agassiz was not appeased. Darwin had repeatedly referred to Agassiz by name in turning the results of Agassiz's research into arguments on behalf of evolution, and Agassiz undoubtedly found the work infuriating, even acutely embarrassing. The work, he told Asa Gray, was *"poor—very poor!!"*[10]

In 1860, Agassiz conducted a campaign against the Darwinian hypothesis in a variety of forums, including the Boston Society of Natural History and the American Academy of Arts and Sciences. In July his criticism of Darwinism appeared in the pages of the *American Journal of Science*, where readers learned that Darwin's arguments "have not made the slightest impression on my mind, nor modified in any way the views I have already propounded." Because he believed that the connection among individuals composing a species was ideal rather than material and that only the characteristics corresponding to the immutable ideas in the mind of God were inherited, he contended that new species "cannot be the result of a gradual material differentiation of the objects themselves." On the other hand, his conviction that species were fundamental "categories of thought, embodied in individual living forms," prompted him to criticize what he took to be Darwin's position that the divisions in the animal kingdom were "altogether artificial." In Agassiz's judgment, Darwinians were hopelessly inconsistent: "If species do not exist at all, as the supporters of the transmutation theory maintain, how can they vary? and if individuals alone exist, how can the differences which may be observed among them prove the variability of species?"[11]

Agassiz held that transmutationists were no less committed than proponents of the doctrine of special creation to the idea that the characteristics of organisms had arisen "spontaneously"; they differed from their opponents only in ascribing these new characteristics to "physical agents." This ascription was untenable. It was necessary to "look to the original power that imparted life to the first being for the origin of all other beings, however mysterious and inaccessible the modes by which all this diversity has been produced must remain for us."[12]

In assailing Darwin's theory, Agassiz drew on his vast store of knowledge of natural history. There were as many simple types now as ever. Each geological stratum teemed with fossil forms radically distinct from those that preceded them. Darwin overestimated the delicacy of organisms and thus the imperfection of the geological record. Migration could not explain the geographical distribution of species. Relentlessly, Agassiz hammered at Darwin's "illogical deductions and misrepresentations of the modern results of Geology and Paleontology." If the transmutation hypothesis were true, Agassiz reasoned, the geological record would exhibit an uninterrupted succession of types that gradually blend into one another; it revealed instead that each geological period was characterized by "definite specific types . . . built upon definite plans." In promulgating his "fanciful theory," Darwin, like earlier proponents of transmutation, had wrongly assumed "that the most complicated system of combined thoughts can be the result of accidental causes." Until the facts of nature were themselves disproved, Agassiz informed his readers, he would continue to regard the development hypothesis "as a scientific mistake, untrue in its facts, unscientific in its method, and mischievous in its tendency."[13]

In large measure Agassiz was merely rehashing views he had held since his arrival in America. This is not surprising, for his conviction that each species was an embodiment of a separate divine idea rather than a collection of genetically linked populations precluded him from giving serious consideration to theories advocating transmutation. Unable to see anything in the concept of natural selection that would require rethinking his position, he regarded Darwin as a confederate of Lamarck and the author of *Vestiges of the Natural History of Creation*.

Agassiz's assessment of the transmutation hypothesis was enormously influential. His reputation for solid scientific scholarship and his academic clout gave him a powerful voice in the international scientific community. American Protestant intellectuals had little difficulty convincing themselves that his position represented the view of most scientists, and they regarded his vigorous defense of the doctrine of special creations as, quite literally, a godsend. Although Agassiz's idealism clashed with the "common-sense" realism embraced by most Protestants in the United States in 1859, his theistic interpretation of nature earned for him the respect and praise of religious intellectuals. Ironically, Agassiz's heretical stand during the polygenesis controversy may well have given even greater force to his rejection of the transmutation hypothesis. Protestants proved quite willing to forgive his earlier doctrinal deviations and to embrace him as a fellow traveler. In 1863 J. M. Manning, who was serving as the chaplain of the Forty-third Regiment of the Massachusetts Volunteers, praised Agassiz for demonstrating that Darwin's theory "rests on a purely fictitious basis." Lyman Atwater, a pugnacious Presbyterian divine not inclined toward flattery, crowned Agassiz the "prince of naturalists" and commended him for "earnestly and eloquently protesting against this whole development or evolution theory." And Heman Lincoln, a professor at the Baptists' Newton Theological Institution, credited Agassiz "with the penetration of a seer." Again and again between 1859 and 1875, Protestant intellectuals alluded to Agassiz's defense of theism and his condemnation of Darwinism.[14]

For his part, Agassiz did a great deal to foster the immense respect the American public had for him by devoting his time to producing lectures and publications designed to educate the public. This made his views more accessible to nonscientists. At the same time, he became less interested in discussing his views with other members of his profession. His refutation of Darwin's theory in the *American Journal of Science* was the last occasion in which he discussed the transmutation hypothesis in a professional scientific forum. Agassiz's curtailment of his professional life disappointed, even irritated, many scientists.[15]

Not all natural historians judged the Darwinian hypothesis as harshly as Agassiz. Agassiz's colleague at Harvard, Asa Gray, found a good deal of merit in Darwin's position. Although in 1847 Gray had lauded Agassiz's refutation of "Lamarckian or 'Vestiges' views" as "the most original and fundamental confutation of materialism" he had ever heard, he thereafter steadily moved away from Agassiz's conception of natural history. In part, the rift can be attributed to Gray's resentment at having been eclipsed by a distinguished emigré. But their growing disagreement went further. At bottom, Gray and Agassiz entertained fundamentally different conceptions of biological classification and of the possibility of accounting for the origin of species in scientific terms. Unlike Agassiz, who considered a species to be an ideal category embracing individuals who embodied a similar divine thought, Gray emphasized the crucial role of genetic connection in understanding natural history. Agassiz believed that problems involving the origin, historical succession, and distribution of species were inescapably metaphysical and that the task of science was complete once it had shown that "the organization of living beings in their connection with the physical world prove[s], in general, the existence of a Supreme Being." Gray, on the other hand, was prepared to countenance the idea that the succession of organisms that had appeared during the history of life were linked together in a nexus open to scientific investigation and describable by means of "physical" theory.[16]

Gray's relationship with Darwin began in 1855, when Gray's favorable review of the English botanist Joseph Hooker's book arguing that species of plants were more widely distributed than commonly believed prompted Darwin to initiate a correspondence. The next year Darwin told Gray that he found the willingness of scientists to stop short of a scientific explanation of speciation profoundly unsatisfying, and he confided that he had "come to the heterodox conclusion, that there are no such things as independently created species—that species are only strongly defined varieties." In 1857 Gray became a member of the elite group who saw a written outline of Darwin's theory prior to publication.[17]

In view of his hostility to previous theories of transmutation, it is hardly surprising that Gray did not immediately become an uncritical devotee of Darwin's hypothesis. Still, his receptivity to the possibility of accounting for the origin of species by means of "secondary" agencies prevented him from rejecting out of hand the idea of transmutation. Darwin's inquiries led Gray to reexamine the striking similarities he had found between the florae of East Asia and eastern North America. This examination convinced Gray that the plants in the two regions had descended from a common ancestor. It also convinced him that "variation in species is wider than is generally supposed" and that such variation was heritable. These conclusions were instrumental to Gray's later conversion to Darwinism.[18]

Gray considered Darwin's exposition of his theory "masterly" and promised him "fair play" in America. Toward this end, he praised the *Origin of Species* in a review in the *American Journal of Science* as "a legitimate attempt to extend the domain of natural or physical science." The supernatural, he insisted, should be invoked only upon the "failure of every attempt to refer the phenomenon in question to causal laws." Though he acknowledged that unresolved difficulties remained and denied that Darwin's theory had been proved, he emphasized that because the theory "chimes in with the established doctrines of physical science," it "is not unlikely to be largely accepted long before it can be proved."[19]

Gray elaborated upon this position in the *Atlantic Monthly*. Speculation about the origin of species, he noted, was the inevitable result of scientific discussion of the historical succession and geographical distribution of species. In an age in which the recognized domain of secondary causes was steadily expanding, the traditional doctrine of special creation had become increasingly doubtful. Gray did not believe it necessary or appropriate to repudiate the idea of supernatural creation. The question, he asserted, was not whether such creation had taken place, but when and how many times. In his judgment, it was necessary to appeal to science to answer these questions.[20]

Gray noted that the conventional view of the origin of species and Darwin's theory were equally hypothetical. Though he endorsed the idea that more than one species had evolved from a formerly homogenous one, he suggested that the hypothesis of more extensive evolution be held "in cool suspense or in grave suspicion." Gray acknowledged that individuals "who regard the derivative hypothesis as satisfactorily proved, must have loose notions as to what proof is," but he added that "those who imagine it can be easily refuted and cast aside, must . . .

have imperfect or very prejudiced conceptions of the facts concerned and of the questions at issue."[21]

Though Gray was not the only scientist who took a sober look at Darwin's theory, few scientists rushed to embrace it. In Europe, no consensus emerged immediately after publication of the *Origin of Species*, but it is clear that few scientists were willing to give the Darwinian hypothesis an enthusiastic endorsement. Although the response of American scientists to the hypothesis was retarded somewhat by the Civil War, which destroyed numerous channels of scientific communication, Darwin's work attracted some attention. In 1863 Jeffries Wyman, Hersey Professor of Anatomy at Harvard and president of the Boston Society for Natural History termed the origin of species "the great question of the day." Wyman, who abhorred controversy, did not openly endorse Darwin's theory. He did note, however, that the idea that chemical elements had somehow come together and instantaneously combined into various species was "entirely opposed by the observed analogies of nature." Nevertheless, few American scientists endorsed the theory of organic evolution. Frederick A. P. Barnard, who had served as a professor of mathematics and natural history before becoming president of Columbia University, asserted in 1864 that it was only the "ingenuity displayed by its advocates" that had secured for the transmutation hypothesis "more than a momentary attention." Like other speculative theories, it would be "trodden out of life" by the scientific community, for "nothing can claim a permanent place in science which fails to attain the certainty of truth." Scientific error, Barnard declared, "has only to be let alone, and it will inevitably die of itself."[22]

Most Protestant clergymen and theologians shared Barnard's faith in the ability of the scientific community to detect error, and they assumed that scientists would, after brief consideration, repudiate Darwin's work. This assumption largely accounts for the decline in the volume of attention accorded it by religious thinkers after the initial flurry of reviews appeared. It was not until the 1870s that Darwinism again became the subject of sustained consideration within the American Protestant intellectual community. This pattern was not, as some historians have suggested, due primarily to a preoccupation with the Civil War and Reconstruction; even a cursory examination of books, journals, and popular magazines published during the War and its aftermath is sufficient to indicate that American Protestant intellectuals continued to discuss a host of timely and important theological issues. The relative paucity of works on the Darwinian hypothesis in this period was rather a measure of their confidence that scientists would "soon consign it to its appropriate place in the museum of curious and fanciful speculations."[23]

Not all religious thinkers were willing to rely entirely on natural historians to discredit the Darwinian hypothesis. Just as scientists frequently considered the religious implication of scientific theories, so nonscientists made determined efforts to show their readers that the Darwinian hypothesis was inconsistent with the facts of natural history. In justifying these efforts, some thinkers concurred with Daniel R. Goodwin, who declared that "when such a theory is inconsistent with the principles of Christianity or Theism, no matter though it may be disguised in a scientific form, and may bristle all over with scientific terminology, we feel authorized, without any special scientific training, to attempt an exposure of its fallacious and groundless character." Others saw their role primarily as one of communicating the arguments scientists were advancing against Darwinism to nonscientists in religious journals and other organs of opinion. Whatever their rationale, many clergymen and theologians avidly participated in efforts to discredit Darwin's theory. Occasionally, their criticisms were garbled and preposterous. More often, they echoed objections that were leveled against the theory by their friends within the scientific community.[24]

Five days after publication of the first edition of the *Origin of Species*, Charles Darwin wrote Asa Gray that his work was "grievously hypothetical, and large parts by no means worthy of being called induction." Three months later, however, in a letter to Joseph Hooker, he offered a criterion for evaluating his theory that rendered complaints about the "hypothetical" character of his work largely irrelevant: "I have always looked at Natural Selection as an hypothesis which, if it explains several large classes of facts would deserve to be ranked as a theory deserving acceptance."[25]

This claim, which was one that Darwin and his followers were to make over and over again in defense of the plausibility of the transmutation hypothesis, was guaranteed to evoke suspicion in thinkers living in a culture that venerated "Baconianism" as the basis of scientific methodology. To be sure, by 1859 the meaning of Baconianism had become quite elastic, and many scientific practitioners and theorists alike were convinced that speculation and deduction played a legitimate role in fostering the development of useful theoretical constructs. Still, most of them continued to assume that scientific theories were acceptable only if they were confirmed by inductions from facts gleaned by observation and/or experiment. Nonscientists were also enamored of the Baconian method, for they believed that it was the surest route to the certainty they associated with science. Asa Mahan, a prominent philosopher who served as the first president of Oberlin College, presented in 1872 a typical statement of the prevailing view within the American Protestant intellectual community: "*Science is knowledge systematized*. Into a scientific process, nothing but what is *absolutely known* can enter." The Methodist clergyman Randolph Sinks Foster, the president of Drew University, concurred, noting that "science wastes no time in stammering and muttering of conjectures and possibilities; that is the method of doubt, not of knowledge."[26]

Thinkers who shared this view assumed that "the question of transmutation is one of *fact* and can only be determined by positive evidence." To these thinkers, Darwin's acknowledgment of "difficulties" in his theory and his emphasis on the analogy of natural selection with human selection rather than on more "direct evidence" of transmutation amounted to a tacit confession of his inability to do justice to the data of natural history. These thinkers made an extended effort to show that Darwin's work was nothing more than "hypothesis," a term that Anglo-American intellectuals characteristically employed pejoratively as a synonym for unbridled speculation.[27]

Toward this end, American religious intellectuals—scientists and nonscientists alike—commonly noted that throughout recorded history species had remained unchanged. Moreover, they emphasized, by Darwin's own admission, it was impossible to observe one species evolving into another. And if observation yielded no support for Darwin's hypotheses, investigation of the fossil record appeared positively to disprove it. Whereas Darwin's theory required a host of intermediate, "transitional" varieties, paleontologists had found clearly marked species suddenly appearing and disappearing. Critics also maintained that the order of fossils contradicted Darwin's theory. The fossil record did not always display progression from simple to more advanced organic forms; higher species within a biological order sometimes preceded simpler ones. Nor had progenitors been found for the rather advanced forms of life that were present in even the lowest geological strata. Such considerations were sufficient to prompt Luther Tracy Townsend, a Methodist clergyman teaching at Boston Theological Seminary (later Boston University School of Theology), to relegate his consideration of Darwin's hypothesis to a footnote. "The leading facts of geology are so utterly at variance with the theory of 'transmutation of species,' " he declared in 1869, "that no additional refutation is necessary."[28]

Darwin attempted to neutralize the force of paleontological objections by appealing to the imperfections in the fossil record. His critics took this to be a particularly flagrant example of his "genius for special pleading." Francis Bowen, for example, complained that the strategy of "speculatists" such as Darwin was "to admit any evidence from paleontology *in favor* of any theory or speculation, but to deny the competency of the same science to bear testimony *against* it." These thinkers recognized that the fossil record was incomplete, but they also recognized that paleontological research had been steadily filling in gaps throughout the nineteenth century. Convinced that "all that is *known* of the past geological periods, contradicts the theory," they upbraided Darwin for relying on "a vast *unknown* which *may* furnish abundant proof of the theory."[29]

Aware that neither contemporary observation nor the geological record could provide positive evidence for his hypothesis, Darwin sought to establish its plausibility by asserting that nature's selection of those specimens best adapted to their environment was analogous to the efforts of human beings to breed desirable varieties of domesticated plants and animals. To American religious intellectuals, this was tantamount to employing natural selection as a "magician's wand" endowed with intelligence, omnipotence, omniscience, and benevolence—in short, with "all the attributes of the Divine Creator." The proper analogue of conscious human activity, they insisted, was certainly not "an unintelligent natural selection." Emphasizing that no "mere jugglery of words" could decipher the riddles of natural history, Protestant thinkers reminded their readers that natural selection was simply a term to describe the preservation of varieties, not a creative power. Even if it were granted that natural selection could occasionally produce stable new varieties, it was quite another thing to produce new species, genera, orders, and kingdoms. Actually, in nature varieties generally either did not transmit their differences to their offspring or else lost their distinctiveness after several generations. Even human beings could not transcend the "appointed line of life" God had given each species. Although domestic breeders could consciously select valued individuals and scrupulously guard against the dilution of desired traits, they had been limited to establishing and preserving mere varieties, which, unless "kept near a certain line," either reverted to the specific norm or become diseased. Moreover, once they were returned to nature they tended to revert, thus suggesting that domestication was an "unnatural" condition.[30]

Observation, paleontological evidence, and experience with domesticated species all appeared to suggest the immutability of species. Members of the American Protestant intellectual community thus repudiated Darwin's claim that species were not fixed entities but merely "well-marked and permanent varieties" and that well-marked varieties were "incipient species." Darwin, they maintained, had violated "the first principles of inductive logic" in founding his theory on varieties rather than stable species. Leonard Withington, a Congregational clergyman in Newburyport, Massachusetts, maintained that to deny the stability of species was to "throw all creation into one heap of confusion." The eminent liberal theologian Horace Bushnell similarly concluded that the science of biology depended on the fixity of species: "If there is no stability or fixity in species, then, for aught that appears, even science itself may be transmuted into successions of music, and moonshine, and auroral fires. If a single kind is all kinds, then all are one, and since that is the same as none, there is knowledge no longer."[31]

Religious thinkers were convinced that nature was more charitable to the scientific enterprise than Darwin had implied. The fixity of species appeared to be guaranteed by organisms' "natural repugnance" to interbreeding. Fertility was frequently viewed as a criterion of common descent. On those rare occasions when the union of individuals of two different species actually produced offspring, their progeny were infertile, thereby ensuring that the aberration would not be perpetuated. William North Rice submitted that the sterility of hybrids was sufficient to show the absurdity of claiming that "varieties and species differ only in degree," and he suggested that "there is between them a radical difference in nature and in origin." To put it another way, Darwin's theory raised the seemingly insurmountable problem of accounting for intersterility among species that had allegedly descended from a common ancestor and the infertility of hybrids. Noting that even outspoken champions of the Darwinian hypothesis were stymied by this problem, many Protestant critics regarded the problem of the intersterility as the most formidable objection to the Darwinian hypothesis.[32]

Anticipating this objection, Darwin devoted a chapter of the *Origin of Species* to defending the proposition that "neither sterility nor fertility affords any clear distinction between species and varieties." It was his belief that sterility, far from being an inherent, "endowed" quality ordained "to prevent the confusion of all organic forms," was actually the "simply incidental" effect of such causes as close interbreeding and the removal of organisms from their "natural conditions." Opponents of the development hypothesis responded by contending that the isolated cases Darwin had found to disprove the universality of hybrid sterility were "perversions of nature or monstrosities, and therefore entitled to but little weight." Even Darwin could not deny that there was a "general tendency towards a sterility more or less nearly complete." Several critics noted that Darwin himself had conceded a crucial point: no perfectly fertile animal hybrid had ever been discovered. Until such a hybrid was produced, the line dividing varieties from species remained intact. And "no *believed* or *guessed* specimens [would] serve."[33]

Many American religious thinkers coupled their frontal assault on the Darwinian hypothesis with the claim that Darwin's work failed to account for many of the most fundamental features of the organic world. One of the most obvious of these was the origin of life itself. Unable to explain this event by means of natural causes, Darwin had acknowledged that God had "breathed" life into at least one primordial organism. A number of religious thinkers responded by suggesting that it was more reasonable to believe that God had created all species than that He had created merely the primordial forms. The radical Unitarian clergyman Francis Ellingwood Abbot argued that the development hypothesis was "philosophically worthless" if it could not "altogether dispense" with special creations. The notion that the history of life was the result of periodic special creations at least had the merit of legitimizing miracles. By contrast, a single creation was an "absolute anomaly." Abbot therefore concluded that "it is a severer tax on 'faith' to accept Mr. Darwin's solitary creation than to accept the innumerable creations of his opponents." William North Rice advanced a similar criticism. Noting the lack of evidence for intermediate links between groups possessing radically different "plans of structure," he held that insofar as Darwin could circumvent that problem by claiming that more than one primordial form had been created, he destroyed "that universal analogy on which, more than on any matters of fact, the Darwinian theory depends."[34]

Like Asa Gray, some Protestants observed that Darwin had not accounted for the origin of variations. This hardly surprised them, for they believed that "the smallest infinitesimal advance from one species to another is as impossible to conceive of, except as proceeding from a direct Creative Power, as the whole distance from vesicle to man." They were equally convinced of Darwin's inability to explain either the "ten thousand exquisite diversities and marvelous adaptations of organic nature" or the unity of plan disclosed in the organic world. If even the "smallest or meanest specimens" of life displayed adaptation superior to that of humanity's most artful creations, they reasoned, it was preposterous to suggest that "perfect" organs such as the eye had resulted from "the blind workings of nature's laws." How much more reasonable it was, wrote Joseph P. Thompson, the influential pastor of the Congregationalists' Broadway Tabernacle, to regard the universe as "the 'patent office' of the Creator."[35]

Among the most impressive of God's "patents" was instinct. It is not surprising, therefore, that some Protestant intellectuals inveighed against Darwin's contention that instincts had arisen from the "slow and gradual accumulation of numerous, slight, yet profitable, variations." Although there was some disagreement about whether instinct was absolutely invariable, these Protestants agreed that one instinct could not evolve from another, and they found it significant that Darwin had been unable to adduce a single instance of such a development.[36]

Some Protestants paid particular attention to the problem of the correlation of instinct and physical structure. Francis Bowen and John Amory Lowell, a cotton manufacturer and financier, who as president of the Boston Athenaeum, member of the Harvard Corporation, and trustee of the Lowell Institute played a prominent role in the promotion of science in America, held that Darwin's theory required "an almost infinite series" of coincidental parallels between variations in instinct and variations in structure. If, as Darwin proposed, variations were "aimless and accidental," there was "no ground to expect that the *variations* of structure and instinct should be even simultaneous, much less nicely correlated to each other." For Darwin, whose theory presupposed that changes in both structure and instinct took place by "insensible steps," it seemed reasonable to assume that at any given time the potential disparity would be rather small. Lowell and Bowen demurred. If the correlation were not precise, they believed, variations in either instinct or structure would confer no advantage and hence not be selected; they might even be fatal to the organism. To illustrate this, John Amory Lowell chose an example that was plausible only if one ignored Darwin's emphasis on the nature of the evolutionary process: if an animal evolved lungs from gills without a simultaneous change in its instinct for swimming under water, it would drown. It was far more reasonable to attribute the harmonious development to the wisdom of a divine Designer.[37]

In the first few years after publication of the *Origin of Species*, much of the criticism of Darwin's hypothesis centered on the idea of transmutation *per se*. In the late 1860s, however, Darwin's explanation of how it had occurred increasingly became the focus of critical attention. One of the most important critiques of natural selection, appearing in the *North British Review* in 1867, was a long article written by the Scottish engineer Henry Charles Fleeming Jenkin. Jenkin was convinced that there were definite limits to the extent of variation and did not enthusiastically embrace any theory of organic evolution. His most telling objections, however, concerned the "efficiency of Natural Selection." These objections were not new, but it was Jenkin who most effectively brought them to the attention of Darwin and other interested members of the intellectual community.[38]

Although Jenkin conceded that natural selection could conceivably improve "organs already useful to great numbers of a species," he insisted that it was wholly unable to "create or develop new organs, and so originate species." Like most nineteenth-century naturalists, Jenkin believed that an organism's attributes were characteristically intermediate between those of its two parents. This fact, he argued, was fatal to the Darwinian hypothesis, for favorable variations, which in Darwin's view were "apparently fortuitous in their character," would be "utterly outbalanced by numerical inferiority." Over several generations favorable variations would be progressively diluted as a result of the free intermingling of advantaged and average individuals. Such "swamping" would frustrate selection; after a number of generations, there would be no improved individuals to select.[39]

Even if the problem of swamping were somehow overcome, Jenkin maintained that recent computations by physicists proved that "the age of the inhabited world" was "limited to periods utterly inadequate for the production of species according to Darwin's views." In 1863, Jenkin's friend William Thomson (later Lord Kelvin), employing the second law of thermodynamics, computed the earth's age to be only about 98 million years. Thomson concluded that even allowing for error, the earth was only from 20 to 400 million years old. This was "preposterously inadequate," Jenkin asserted, for "the action of the Darwinian theory."[40]

In 1871, the English zoologist St. George Jackson Mivart, a pious Roman Catholic and convinced evolutionist, subjected the efficacy of natural selection to a sophisticated critique in his influential *On the Genesis of Species*. Mivart argued that

evolution has not taken place by the action of "Natural Selection" *alone*, but through it (amongst other influences) aided by the concurrent action of some other natural law or laws, at present undiscovered; and probably that the genesis of species takes place partly, perhaps mainly, through laws which may be most conveniently spoken of as special powers and tendencies existing in each organism; and partly through influences exerted on each by surrounding conditions and agencies organic and inorganic, terrestrial and cosmical, among which the "survival of the fittest" plays a certain but subordinate part.[41]

To support this contention, Mivart employed a "cumulative argument" intended to show the inadequacy of Darwin's view that evolution resulted from the gradual accumulation of "individually slight, minute, and insensible" variations by means of natural selection. In the first place, a utilitarian principle like natural selection might explain the preservation of variations "sufficiently considerable to be useful from the first to the individual possessing them," but it could not "account for the conservation and development of the minute and rudimentary beginnings, the slight and infinitesimal commencements, however useful those structures may afterwards become." It was even less credible that natural selection had preserved structures that appeared to be "positively hurtful" to individuals, such as a rattlesnake's rattle or a cobra's hood, structures that, according to Mivart, warned potential victims.[42]

Because minutely graduated transitional forms had not been found in the fossil record and there were abundant examples of heritable variations that seemed to have originated suddenly, Mivart joined other scientists in asserting that variation was more saltatory than Darwin had believed. Like Jenkin, Mivart noted that Darwin's explanation of the evolutionary process was irreconcilable with Thomson's estimates of the age of the earth. Mivart's solution to these difficulties was to "admit that new forms of animal life of all degrees of complexity appear from time to time with comparative suddenness."[43]

Finally, Mivart rejected Darwin's notion that variations were undirected, or "fortuitous," in favor of the view that "there are positive tendencies to development along certain special lines." It was highly unlikely that the selection of fortuitous variations was sufficient to account for the marvelous symmetries—the "serial, bilateral, and vertical homologies"—that were present in the organic world. These phenomena were rather the result of "the action of some special innate power or tendency . . . possessed by the organism itself" and "controlled and subordinated by the action of external conditions." This power, Mivart believed, served the very function that Asa Gray more than a decade before had argued was necessary: it directed variations along lines beneficial to organisms.[44]

Prior to 1875, few nonscientists within the American Protestant community were prepared to follow Mivart in accepting the transmutation hypothesis. To them, the assault on the efficacy of natural selection served as additional evidence that the theory of organic evolution was untenable.[45]

In the judgment of many Protestants, the most telling argument against the transmutation hypothesis concerned an issue Darwin had been reluctant to address: the origin of the human race. Long before 1859, Darwin had concluded that the human species, like other species, had evolved by means of natural selection. Because he believed that this issue was "surrounded with prejudices," however, he decided to avoid it altogether in the *Origin of Species*. He confined himself to observing that when his views of natural history were accepted, "light will be thrown on the origin of man and his history."[46]

The issue, however, was not so easily avoided. Unlike Asa Gray, who interpreted Darwin's silence as a mandate for affirming "the separate and special creation of man," most American religious thinkers regarded Darwin's sidestepping of the issue of human genealogy as an effort to avoid making manifest the fact that his theory implied that "the monkey is his [man's] brother, and the horse his cousin, and the oyster his remote ancestor."[47]

A special relationship obtains between God and His human children in the Christian world view. This not only made it easy for Protestant apologists to assume that the human species was "the crowning work of the infinite Creator," but it ensured that they would give ideas relating to the origin of humanity their strictest scrutiny. Both the polygenesis controversy and the discussion generated by *Vestiges of the Natural History of Creation* convinced these thinkers of the need for vigilance in the face of challenges to the biblical view of human creation. Their awareness of the heretical implications of the Darwinian hypothesis was vividly reinforced in the decade after publication of the *Origin of Species* by the appearance of a number of works by avowed transmutationists espousing the view that the human species had evolved from other animals.[48]

One of the most important of these was Charles Lyell's *The Geological Evidences of the Antiquity of Man* (1863). This long, rambling exposition was written to expose the public to the growing body of data indicating that humanity was much older than the conventional view suggested. Lyell's earlier work had been instrumental in changing people's conception of the age of the earth; he now forced thinkers to reconsider seriously the age of the human species.[49]

The reaction of American religious thinkers to Lyell's defense of human antiquity was mixed. A few simply denied the validity of his conclusions. Others disputed the inferences he drew from his evidence. One critic, for example, asserted in the *Methodist Quarterly Review* that the contemporaneous existence of humanity and extinct animals indicated not that the human species was older than previously suspected, but that the other animals were younger than scientists had previously believed. For the most part, however, American Protestant intellectuals greeted Lyell's discussion of human antiquity with relative equanimity. Few of them held that Christians were obliged to believe that the Scriptures fixed the age of humanity. Most believed that the notion that human beings had existed before "the present epoch of human history" was no more inconsistent with the message of the Scriptures than the idea that different flora and fauna had preceded contemporary species of plants and animals.[50]

The willingness of many American Protestants to reconsider the antiquity of humanity may have been conditioned by the debate over polygenism. Advocates of the separate origin of the different races had marshaled evidence that racial differences had persisted for thousands of years, and they maintained that there had not been sufficient time for the races to have diverged from a single type. If the human race were only six thousand years old, this was a formidable argument, but as Lyell observed, "the difficulty becomes less and less, exactly in proportion as we enlarge our ideas of the lapse of time."[51]

Lyell also believed, however, that if, "in the course of time," the different races of humanity had descended from a common stock, there was good reason to believe that "closely allied species of animals and plants" had also sprung from a common progenitor. Virtually all religious thinkers rejected this position. Although convinced that the races of man were merely varieties of a single species, Protestant intellectuals denied that the common origin of these varieties buttressed the notion that different species had developed from a common ancestor. Additional time, they insisted, may have been a necessary condition for the occurrence of transmutation, but it was not a sufficient one.[52]

Protestant thinkers were aware that the issue of human antiquity could be divorced from the development hypothesis. Many also recognized, however, that many individuals who advocated extending the age of humanity also favored the idea of transmutation. They were thus probably not surprised that Lyell concluded the *Geological Evidences* with five chapters on the development hypothesis. Most of the animosity Lyell encountered from the American religious community focused on his relatively brief discussion of organic evolution.

Actually, Lyell's discussion hardly constituted a ringing endorsement of the Darwinian hypothesis; Darwin himself was bitterly disappointed by Lyell's "excessive caution." Lyell observed that transmutation was the only scientific explanation of the history of life; the doctrine of separate creation constituted "an avowal that we deem the question to lie beyond the domain of science." But although he maintained that Darwin's theory had unquestionably rendered transmutation a more probable hypothesis for the populating of the world than ever before, he accorded it only a provisional status. Lyell had no trouble believing that it had "pleased the Author of Nature that the origin of new species should be governed by some secondary causes analogous to those which we see preside over the appearance of new varieties." But like Asa Gray, whose work he greatly admired, Lyell believed that a "Variety-making Power" provided the raw material on which natural selection operated. He thus joined many American Protestant intellectuals in denying that the transmutation hypothesis actually explained the *creation* of species and warned proponents of the hypothesis not to "deify secondary causes or immeasurably exaggerate their influence." Darwin's theory was a description of, not a substitute for, divine creativity.[53]

Lyell acknowledged that if many of the most compelling arguments for the Darwinian hypothesis were not to be scrapped, it would have to be applied to humanity, but he denied that the gap between the brutes and the human species was "absolutely insensible." Among the "new and powerful" variations created by God were "the moral and intellectual faculties of the human race." Because Lyell was convinced that variations were supernaturally directed, he saw no reason to concur with Darwin's assumption that life had always advanced by means of minute changes. On the contrary, he asserted that "the space which separated the highest stage of the unprogressive intelligence of the inferior animals from the first and lowest form of improvable reason manifested by Man" had been "cleared at one bound."[54]

When Darwin criticized this position, Lyell was unmoved. The leap he had postulated, he informed Darwin, was no more "un-Darwinian" than the birth of a genius to ordinary parents. As late as 1869, he was still trying to convince Darwin that the origin of humanity's moral and intellectual nature "was a real innovation, interrupting the uniform course of the causation previously at work on the earth." Lyell was similarly unrepentant in responding to Darwin's complaint about the treatment his theory had received at Lyell's hands. He felt obliged to "plead guilty" to the charge that he had less than wholeheartedly endorsed Darwin's theory, but he expressed confidence that he had converted to transmutation many individuals who would have rejected a more dog-matic presentation. Moreover, he predicted, "hundreds who have bought my book in the hope that I should demolish heresy, will be aw-fully confounded and disappointed."[55]

He was right. His discussion of transmutation served notice to Dar-win's critics that Lyell, "infected with the same credulous skepticism" as Darwin, had gone over to the camp of the enemy. Lyell's reservations about transmutation, so dismaying and distressing to Darwin, were lost on many thinkers. C. H. Hitchcock, Edward Hitchcock's son and a geologist who had also pursued theological studies, noticed only that Lyell had shown "more care to argue in favor of the development views than against them." Although Hitchcock acknowledged that Lyell had not endorsed the "hideous doctrines" generally attending the applica-tion of the transmutation hypothesis to man, he reproached Lyell for affirming that the human species had acquired all of its faculties "by purely natural processes." Another reviewer criticized Lyell for em-bracing "the visionary notions" of Darwin and his followers and sug-gested that one of his motives for writing the *Geological Evidences* had been to provide Darwinians with "all the time demanded by their speculations."[56]

The outrage attending Lyell's rather reserved discussion of trans-mutation paled before that generated by the work of Thomas Henry Huxley. Although a much younger man than Darwin and Lyell, Huxley was already a highly respected biologist when the *Origin of Species* ap-peared. He had met Darwin in 1851, and by 1854 they had become close friends. Having scratched his way up from lowly circumstances into a professional niche in English science, Huxley was well fitted by both temperament and experience to assume the role of Darwin's "bulldog."[57]

Huxley had long believed that the doctrine of special creations was unsupported by the evidence, but he had found expositions of the transmutation hypothesis prior to the *Origin of Species* wholly unper-suasive. He was thus "inclined to say to both Mosaists and Evolution-ists, 'a plague on both your houses!' " Darwin's theory was the "flash of light" that brought him into the circle of convinced transmutation-ists. Although Huxley recognized that the Darwinian hypothesis had its difficulties, he was confident that Darwin had "demonstrated a true cause for the production of species." Huxley predicted that Darwin would encounter "curs which will bark and yelp." But Darwin was not to worry; Huxley would be prepared: "I am sharpening up my claws and beak in readiness."[58]

In the years following publication of the *Origin of Species*, Darwin's opponents frequently feel prey to Huxley's pugnacity. Like Agassiz, though with different purposes in mind, Huxley was committed to bringing the results of scientific investigation to nonscientists. In a long, enthusiastic review of the *Origin of Species* for the April 1860 edition of the *Westminster Review*, Huxley praised the work as "the most compendious statement of well-sifted facts bearing on the doctrine of species that has ever appeared." By contrast, he charged, the hypothesis of special creations was nothing more than "verbal hocus-pocus" that had too long served as "a mere specious mask for our ignorance." Darwin's work, Huxley averred, "does not so much prove that natural selection does occur, as that it must occur."[59]

In 1863 Huxley, who had for some time been fascinated with the problem of the relationship between human beings and other primates, disregarded the advice of several of his friends and published *Evidence as to Man's Place in Nature*. The three essays in this short work broke little new ground. They soberly examined what Huxley regarded as the "question of questions for mankind[,] . . . the place which Man occupies in nature and . . . his relations to the universe of things." Answers to this question, he maintained, had heretofore been inadequate, and it was the duty of "every good citizen" to derive more satisfactory answers. This duty provided his avowed "excuse" for publishing his essays.[60]

Huxley's first essay reviewed previous discussions of the "man-like apes" and delineated the principal physical and behavioral characteristics of these creatures. His concluding essay dealt with the antiquity of humanity. Like Lyell, he acknowledged that no known fossil skull could serve as a link between man and the apes, but he insisted that the "very high antiquity" of the Engis and Neanderthal skulls confirmed the assumptions of the development hypothesis. The polemical thrust of Huxley's book was most prominent in his second essay, entitled "On the Relations of Man to the Lower Animals." Huxley, who was able to draw on a good deal of nineteenth-century research in comparative anatomy and physiology attesting to biological connections between human beings and other animals, contended that embryological development alone was "sufficient to place beyond all doubt the structural unity of man with the rest of the animal world, and more particularly and closely with the apes." But other evidence also supported this conclusion. After systematically reviewing the structural characteristics of human beings and the higher apes, Huxley concluded that "whatever system of organs be studied, the comparison of their modifications in the ape series leads to one and the same result—that the structural similarities which separate Man from the Gorilla and the Chimpanzee are not so great as those which separate the Gorilla from the lower apes." Huxley also addressed himself to the issue of humanity's allegedly unique brain. As with other anatomical characteristics, he argued, the real cerebral "hiatus" lay not "between Man and the man-like apes, but between the lower and the lowest Simians." Even the "very striking difference in absolute mass and weight between the lowest human brain and that of the highest ape" was of negligible import, for even greater differences existed among human brains.[61]

Huxley acknowledged that the differences between human beings and their "blurred copies," the apes, were significant enough to rule out the possibility of direct descent. He also conceded that "in the present creation" no link between humanity and the apes could be found. Nevertheless, he submitted, the differences between human beings and the apes, though sufficient to place humanity in a classificatory family separate from the apes, did not justify making the human species a separate order.[62]

Huxley concluded this essay with the assertion that "if any process of physical causation can be discovered by which the genera and families of ordinary animals have been produced, that process of causation is amply sufficient to account for the origin of Man." Only one such process had any scientific credibility: "that propounded by Mr. Darwin." Thus, "the question of the relation of man to the lower animals resolves itself, in the end, into the larger question of the tenability or untenability of Mr. Darwin's views." As usual, Huxley did not mince words. Though he granted that Darwin's theory would remain "provisional" as long as the progeny "produced by selective breeding from a common stock . . . are fertile with one another," he maintained that it was "as near an approximation to the truth as, for example, the Copernican hypothesis was to the true theory of the planetary motions."[63]

By linking Darwin's theory to the problem of humanity's origin, Huxley confirmed the suspicion of religious thinkers that Darwin's disciples would be satisfied only after they had persuaded others that "Bacon, Newton, Plato, the orang-outang and the ape . . . are derived from the same origin." The theory that humanity had developed from lower animals, the eminent Episcopalian clergyman Phillips Brooks warned, would result in "the depreciation of the individuality of man, the loss of his special type of being, and inevitably the confusion of his human responsibility in the intricate series of the apes." "If such speculations be science or its legitimate deductions," a reviewer of Huxley's work for the *New Englander* suggested, "then, indeed, 'tis folly to be wise."[64]

Religious thinkers insisted, however, that such speculations were *not* science. In support of this position, Protestants noted that a vast gulf separated the human species from apes. Neither Huxley nor anyone else had discovered transitional links capable of bridging that gulf. The absence of such links, they held, was sufficient to create "a strong presumption in favor of the common view" of the separate creation of humanity. This presumption was reinforced by the available evidence, which seemed to indicate that humanity had always differed structurally from other primates. Religionists brushed aside Huxley's argument that the gap between the most inferior human being and the highest ape exceeded that separating different human beings as an attempt to evade the real issue. Daniel R. Goodwin, for example, observed that even if the gap between the human species and apes was comparable to that which divided other species, this proved nothing; transmutationists had not found the links necessary to bridge those gaps either. Huxley had thus assumed what he should have been attempting to prove: that the origin of *other* species could be explained by transmutation.[65]

While Huxley and other transmutationists concentrated on the similarities between man and other primates, religious thinkers emphasized the differences. For some this amounted to little more than anthropocentric chest-thumping. The Universalist I. C. Knowlton, for example, asserted that "man's large brain renders him the intellectual king, and women's sweet features constitute her the beauteous queen of all the earth." More frequently, however, the discussion centered on substantive issues. Protestant critics asserted that the size and structure of man's brain, his capacity for speech, his hand, and a number of other structural features were sufficiently different from those of other primates to justify placing man in a separate zoological category.[66]

Neither Huxley nor other transmutationists denied the presence of structural differences between human beings and the apes, and as long as the issue was the extent of those differences, there was ample room for argument over whether the differences were sufficient to set the human species apart from all other animals. Religious intellectuals could clinch their case for humanity's structural uniqueness only if they could point to a peculiarity that clearly constituted a difference of kind. In 1863, shortly after the publication of Huxley's book, the American naturalist James Dwight Dana attempted to do just that. Dana maintained that although man shared a number of attributes with other mammals, he also possessed "structural characteristics that leave no question of man's independent position in the class of Mammals." The human species alone stood erect and thus possessed forelimbs that

could be used in service of the brain. Dana considered this subordination of "a very large anterior portion of the body" to the brain—what
he called "cephalization"—to be "a structural expression of the domi-
nance of mind" unique to humanity. Dana was convinced that cephalization was not merely a slight variation but "profoundly a criterion of
grade."[67]

Darwin dismissed Dana's argument as "utterly wild." American religious thinkers did not. Those who sought to establish the zoological
uniqueness of humanity frequently employed Dana's argument in the
1860s. A critic of Huxley's work for the Episcopalian *American Quarterly
Church Review* was so favorably impressed with Dana's views that he
cribbed virtually all of an article Dana had published on cephalization
as part of his own. Similarly, C. H. Hitchcock insisted that Dana's argument was so conclusive that other arguments against transmutation
were unnecessary.[68]

For all their concern with anatomy, American Protestant intellectuals
believed that the essence of human uniqueness resided elsewhere. For
them, as for Dana, the "outer being" was significant primarily as it was
"made to show forth the divine feature of the inner being." This feature—the image of God in humanity and the most obvious and important evidence of "the immense chasm betwixt us and the other
creatures that inhabit this globe"—was to be found "preeminently in
our personality, and the qualities which perfect and adorn it."[69]

Three elements of personality appeared to Protestant intellectuals to
be especially decisive in setting the human species apart from other animals. One of these was intelligence. The ability of human beings to
reason and to communicate their ideas by means of language enabled
them to apprehend general principles, establish culture, and initiate
new ideas and institutions. By contrast, the Creator had given other animals instinct. The difference between animal instinct and human intelligence, religious thinkers believed, was one of kind rather than of
degree.[70]

In the judgment of many American Protestant intellectuals, the possession of a conscience was as significant as reason in setting human
beings apart from other organisms. Though there was some difference
of opinion among these thinkers as to whether or not the dictates of
conscience were the same in all times and cultures, they could agree
that the capacity for judging between right and wrong and the feeling
of obligation to act in accordance with perceptions of virtue were universal attributes of humanity and that "not the least trace" of these attributes could be found in other species. The Reverend James A. Lyon

articulated a view that was not uncommon among these thinkers when he cited the "moral sense" as "the grand distinction between man, made in the image of God, and the brute creation."[71]

Finally, religious thinkers maintained that the human species alone possessed a "spiritual element" enabling it to recognize and worship its Creator. A representative statement of this position was offered by I. C. Knowlton in 1863. "There is not the least evidence," he observed, "that any animal is devotional, nor that there ever lived a tribe of men, however degraded, that was not devotional."[72]

By the third quarter of the nineteenth century, some thinkers were prepared to abandon the claim that the "moral and intellectual preeminence" of human beings set them radically apart from other animals. These critics argued that many mental traits ascribed to humanity alone were also present in nascent forms in other animals. As early as 1855, the English philosopher Herbert Spencer, whose views will be discussed at greater length in later chapters, had contended in his *Principles of Psychology* that mental attributes, from the simple reflex action of the polyp to the complex operations of human reason and emotion, could be viewed as a continuum of "insensible steps." Persuaded that "all mental phenomena are incidents of the correspondence between the organism and its environment," Spencer believed that the development of complex mental capacities was a gradual process in which organisms became increasingly successful at adjusting to their environment. Spencer's ideas were not immediately influential, but his affirmation of the biological basis of psychology and his insistence on links between the mental capacities of human beings and other animals were omens of theories to come.[73]

By 1859 Darwin was convinced that human mental attributes were not radically different from those of other animals. He devoted little attention in the *Origin of Species*, however, to the relationship between the human mind and the mental capacities of other animals. He simply suggested that "a little dose . . . of judgment or reason, often comes into play, even in animals very low in the scale of nature" and predicted that when the natural world was interpreted from an evolutionary perspective, psychology would "be based on a new foundation, that of the necessary acquirement of each mental power and capacity by gradation." Most important, the thrust of his theory impelled many of his followers to take the issue of change within the organic world more seriously than ever before and to apply that concept to psychology.[74]

During the 1860s a number of other thinkers, most of whom were proponents of the transmutation hypothesis, provided additional support for the claim that the human mind was not utterly different from that of other animals. T. H. Huxley, for example, maintained in 1861 that household pets manifested intellectual and emotional characteristics commonly associated with human beings. This implied, he argued, that "there is a unity in psychical as in physical plan among animated beings." Even Charles Lyell insisted that "no impartial judge can doubt that the roots, as it were, of those great faculties which confer on Man his immeasurable superiority above all other animate things are traceable far down in the animate world."[75]

American Protestant intellectuals responded to such claims by reiterating that humanity possessed "powers entirely distinct and diverse in kind from every thing yet discovered in the mere animal." These thinkers, convinced that only "infinite Intelligence and Goodness" could account for human personality, denounced the transmutation hypothesis as "revolting to common sense and experience." Some Protestants reminded their readers that evolutionists had failed to produce evidence of the kind of "innumerable slight variations" capable of bridging the gap between the mental capacities of brutes and those of human beings. Others sought to undercut the transmutation hypothesis by denying that the mind was the kind of entity to which the mechanism of transmutation applied. Protestant intellectuals were rarely very systematic in delineating their view of the relationship of mind to brain. Although scientific advances in anatomy and physiology made it progressively more difficult for these thinkers to sustain the view that the mind was wholly independent of the structure and activity of the brain, many of them coupled an acknowledgment that the mind was "conditioned" by the brain with a vehement denial that "thought is merely a function of the bodily organization." In their view, mind and matter were related but ultimately distinct, and the laws governing the physical world were inoperative in analyzing mental phenomena. Some critics thus argued that in view of the significant differences between the intellectual and moral capacities of the human species and those of the most highly developed apes, if Huxley was correct in claiming that the brains of the two orders were quite similar, this would only reinforce their position that mind was not dependent on cerebral structure. Or to put the argument another way, even if Darwinians could demonstrate that the human physical structure had evolved, this would prove nothing concerning the origin of those features that most significantly set human beings apart from other animals.[76]

By 1869, Protestants who assailed the notion that the theory of evolution by natural selection was capable of explaining the origin of the human species could claim the co-founder of that theory as an ally. Alfred Russel Wallace was not immediately inclined to doubt that humanity was the product of natural processes. On the contrary, in 1864 he published a paper suggesting that natural selection was sufficient to account for human evolution. By 1869, however, he no longer believed this to be a tenable position. In an article published in the *Quarterly Review*, Wallace maintained that both prehistoric peoples and "the lowest savages" in the contemporary world possessed a number of physical characteristics—"the brain, the organs of speech, the hand, and the external form"—that "developed in advance of the needs of its possessor." Natural selection, he argued, could not account for these characteristics, for it preserved only those features of immediate value to an individual's survival. A year later he amplified this position in an article entitled "The Limits of Natural Selection as Applied to Man." Wallace submitted that members of primitive tribes apparently possessed latent capacities for a number of complex mental operations that exceeded their needs. They also possessed a sense of right and wrong that was too powerful, too widespread, and too invested with "sanctity" to be explicable in terms of purely utilitarian considerations. The presence of such characteristics convinced Wallace that an "Overruling Intelligence" had overseen organic evolution, "directing variations and so determining their accumulation, as finally to produce an organization sufficiently perfect to admit of, and even to aid in, the indefinite advancement of our mental and moral nature."[77]

Darwin and most of his followers were predictably dismayed by Wallace's position. American religious intellectuals, on the other hand, regarded the admission by "one of the most extreme of the Darwinians" that the human species possessed "original characteristics for which Natural Selection cannot account, and which bear the marks of Overruling Design," as an important concession to the position they had held all along. But in sharp contrast to Wallace, who remained committed to the idea that evolution by natural selection was sufficient to account for the origin of other species, they viewed the inability of that process to explain the appearance of human species as "a providential testimony to the absurdity" of the entire transmutation hypothesis.[78]

In 1871 Darwin finally broke his self-imposed silence on the origin of the human species with the publication of his two-volume *The Descent of Man, and Selection in Relation to Sex*. The longest section of the work elaborated Darwin's views concerning sexual selection, a subject to which he had only briefly alluded in the *Origin of Species*. Darwin held that in the higher animals a number of characteristics survived, not because they directly aided the individual in adapting to his environment, but because they gave the animal a competitive advantage in the contest for mates and consequently the production of offspring. Because adaptive advantages were meaningless if they were not inherited, sexual selection constituted a vitally important corollary to natural selection.[79]

Darwin's view of sexual selection received little attention from religious intellectuals in the United States. This was not true of the other major subject of his work, the origin of the human species. Darwin praised that species as "the wonder and glory of the Universe" but insisted that it was a product of the evolutionary process outlined in the *Origin of Species*. Humanity, he asserted, had evolved from animals "covered with hair, both sexes having beards; their ears were pointed and capable of movement; and their bodies were provided with a tail, having the proper muscles." Even earlier, the progenitors of human beings "apparently consisted of a group of marine animals, resembling the larvae of existing Ascidians." Only people's "natural prejudice" and "arrogance" prevented them from acknowledging their ancestry.[80]

Darwin admitted that he could not offer a detailed account of the prehistoric development of humanity, and he conceded that transitional forms linking human beings to their animal kin had yet to be discovered. The method he employed to establish the credibility of his position was the by now familiar one of impeaching the fossil record and attempting to show that the human species was separated from other animals by differences of degree rather than of kind. While conceding that sizable gaps differentiated humankind from its nearest living relatives, the apes, Darwin emphasized that the general bodily structure, the embryological development, and the rudimentary organs of human beings resembled those of other animals. If the human species was the product of a "separate act of creation," he argued, such similarities would be "mere empty deceptions."[81]

Nor were the intellectual, spiritual, and moral attributes of the human species sufficiently distinctive to set it outside the evolutionary process. Other animals, Darwin insisted, possessed mental characteristics, such as the potential for improvement and the ability to use tools, that had traditionally been ascribed to humanity alone. Even the religious impulse was not uniquely human: "we see some distant approach to this state of mind, in the deep love of a dog for his master, associated with complete submission, some fear, and perhaps other feelings."[82]

Like many other thinkers in the nineteenth century, Darwin believed that the strongest warrant for claiming that the human species was unique resided in humanity's possession of a "moral sense," which he defined as the capacity for "comparing his past and future actions or motives, and of approving or disapproving of them." Unlike other thinkers, however, Darwin chose to analyze the moral sense "exclusively from the side of natural history." Toward this end, he presented a schematic view of the evolution of conscience.[83]

Darwin contended that from the very outset of their appearance on earth, human beings had possessed the "social instincts" of "love and sympathy" for others. These instincts, which bound individuals together in discrete social groups and impelled them to act in accordance with "what is best in the long run for all the members," had been inherited from other animals by natural selection and continued to confer advantages in the struggle for existence on human tribes that had a large number of individuals possessing them. These social instincts constituted "the prime principle of man's moral constitution."[84]

If, however, the roots of conscience were to be found in the social instincts, the birth of conscience itself was contingent on humanity's acquisition of sufficient intelligence to permit it to reflect upon its actions. Darwin did not deny that human beings were unique in feeling that they ought to obey certain impulses and in regretting their failures to do so, but he insisted that "any animal whatever, endowed with well-marked social instincts, would inevitably acquire a moral sense or conscience, as soon as its intellectual powers had become as well, or nearly as well developed, as in man." Human life as Darwin envisioned it was a drama in which each individual chose between conflicting instincts. Because humanity had only recently emerged from "a state of barbarism," its more primitive instincts—for self-preservation, lust, vengeance, and the like—sometimes proved stronger than its social instinct. Darwin insisted, however, that human beings judged their conduct by the more enduring social instinct, and when they concluded that they had failed to act in accordance with the social good, they incurred the misery attending "any unsatisfied instinct." This misery was manifested in shame, in pangs of "conscience."[85]

The next stage in the development of conscience, Darwin believed, was marked by the acquisition of language, which enabled groups to reinforce the natural instinct of individuals to behave in ways conducive to community welfare by providing them with clear prescriptions for acting in ways that would most effectively meet community needs. Because human beings were social animals, they were sensitive to the approbation and disapprobation of others. Finally, the dictates of conscience were "strengthened by habit" and passed down by inheritance to later generations. Eventually, "desires and passions" became subordinate to the "social sympathies," and the struggle between them abated. Moreover, although Darwin assumed that natural selection played an important role in fostering the advance of human moral and intellectual faculties, he also believed that with the advance of civilization, the role of education, religion, and other such influences became more important than that agency. The golden rule emerged as the basis of moral conduct. In time, too, the scope of human sympathies gradually expanded from the immediate group to the nation and even "to the men of all nations and races."[86]

Though Darwin's reputation ensured that his work would receive attention, his contribution did not alter the terms of the debate over the origin of humanity. To be sure, a number of outraged reviewers denounced Darwin's position as one that "degrades mankind in his origin to a level with the worms of the dust." The animosity Darwin incurred, however, was of a piece with the opprobrium that religious thinkers had heaped upon evolutionary interpretations of the origin of humanity during the 1860s. Moreover, the primary way in which Protestants sought to counter Darwin's theory in the first few years after publication of the *Descent of Man* was not markedly different from their earlier strategy. Most reviewers eschewed detailed consideration of the religious implications of human evolution and concentrated instead on invoking the litany of arguments based on the data of natural history that had already become quite familiar to readers of literature relating to the origin of humanity. To a number of reviewers, Darwin's discussion of the origin of the human species served only to confirm how absurd his general theory really was.[87]

In contrast to Darwin, who emphasized the similarities between human beings and other animals, American Protestant thinkers continued to point to the "immense interval between even savage man and the highest brute" and the absence of intermediate forms bridging that interval. Because most of them rejected the general idea of organic evolution, they were understandably unmoved by Darwin's argument that the gap between the human species and other primates was no greater than that which existed among other species. They also emphasized that the existence of anatomical similarities did not prove that humanity was descended from lower animals; it indicated only that the Creator had employed a uniform plan in creating organisms.[88]

Over and over again, religious thinkers insisted that a wide array of intellectual, spiritual, and moral characteristics distinguished human beings from other animals. They flatly denied that humanity's intelligence had gradually evolved from instinct. Though a number of them conceded that some other animals were not totally bereft of reason, they emphasized that only human beings could think conceptually, reflect on their experience, and act voluntarily in accordance with the dictates of reason. Other animals were primarily motivated by instinct, and whatever reasoning powers they possessed were limited to associations of habitual impressions.[89]

American religious thinkers also denied that the evolutionary hypothesis could account for either humanity's belief in spiritual agencies or its desire for immortality. They did not deny that animals were capable of devotion, but they regarded Darwin's equation of a dog's instinctual loyalty to his master and humanity's rational worship of God as ludicrous.[90]

Finally, American Protestant intellectuals rejected Darwin's view of the development of the human moral sense from the social instincts. To them, the notion that moral conduct could be ascribed to the promptings of instincts that human beings held in common with other animals seemed to be less an explanation of morality than an implicit denial of it. The sense of duty prompting love of one's fellow man, they contended, could be reduced to neither community pressure nor the "love of applause."[91]

Recognizing that Darwin was a highly respected scientist, a number of members of the American Protestant intellectual community pondered the question of what had prompted him to promulgate a theory that violated "every principle of reason and logic" and contradicted "all the facts of natural history." Most of these thinkers ascribed Darwin's theory not simply to a mistake in scientific judgment but to adherence to a world view antithetical to Christianity. From their vantage point, not only the effect but the very intent of the Darwinian hypothesis was to undermine belief in Christian theology. Darwinism, they believed, was embedded within a larger movement that was assuming an increasingly prominent role in philosophical discussions: scientific naturalism.[92]

3

"In the Twinkling of an Eye": From Naturalist Ploy to Scientific Theory

THROUGHOUT the nineteenth century, the image of the Christian as warrior in the struggle against irreligion played a prominent role in the rhetoric of American Protestant intellectuals. Again and again, their spokesmen boasted, the forces of unbelief had been defeated on the field of battle. But infidelity was protean and tenacious: "Driven from one stronghold, it plants itself in another; driven from them all, it swings the circle and begins anew."[1]

In the third quarter of the century, a number of combatants on the American front warned that the enemies of Christendom were mounting a new offensive. "Never since the crucifixion," Amherst's president, W. A. Stearns, lamented in 1870, had Christianity "been assailed with such variety and persistency of argument." The primary target of this offensive, most American Protestant intellectuals believed, was to undermine the credibility of supernaturalism. By promoting unfounded speculations suggesting that the universe was a network of "inflexible and virtually omnipotent laws," the partisans of unbelief were engaged in an all-out effort to undermine the faith of educated men and women in the presence of an active Deity.[2]

Religious thinkers believed that science would become, as Andrew Preston Peabody, Harvard's Plummer Professor of Christian Morals, put it in 1864, "the Armageddon—the final battlefield— in the conflict with infidelity." Because they were convinced that scientific inquiry, properly pursued, was "God's interpreter to man of his universal Scripture," they were confident that it would disclose the presence of a providential Deity acting in the natural world. On the other hand, they also recognized that science, "if perverted, may become a dangerous antagonist to religion." Accordingly, they coupled their praise of "true science" with determined efforts to show that it was incapable of ascertaining all of reality.[3]

Toward this end, defenders of the faith denounced the idea that every feature of the natural world was comprehensible in terms of natural laws. These thinkers were not opposed in principle to the idea that such laws existed. By regarding them simply as descriptions of the way in which God had ordained matter to act, and by interpreting them teleologically as the means by which the Deity had provided the intelligibility and stability that enabled human beings to make their way in the world, Protestant apologists made a plausible case for the contention that these laws were an integral part of the divine plan. They emphasized, however, that there was no reason to assume that the "secondary" causes embodied in natural laws enjoyed "a presumptive advantage over primary, personal power." Francis Bowen thus assailed Darwin's theory on the grounds that it seemed to be predicated on the assumption "'that a horse should create a horse is conceivable; but that God should create a horse is inconceivable.'" The Presbyterian theologian Robert Lewis Dabney of Union Theological Seminary (Virginia) submitted that if, as Christians believed, God had originally created the universe, it was no less reasonable to believe that He had subsequently intervened immediately in the world. The assumption that natural events were always due to natural causes was therefore unwarranted. Dabney and other American religious thinkers insisted that the question of whether God employed direct power or natural agencies to accomplish His purposes could be resolved only by appealing to the facts. To substitute secondary agencies for the supernatural as an explanation of events on any other grounds was to substitute philosophical dogmatism for science.[4]

There was not, and by the very nature of the case could not be, any empirical evidence of immediate supernatural activity. Still, wherever there was no compelling evidence to the contrary, most Protestant intellectuals were inclined to ascribe natural events to direct supernatural intervention. This is hardly surprising. The doctrine that human history had been punctuated by the immediate intervention of a providential Deity in the natural order was the central tenet of their faith. Any instances of supernatural activity in nature would buttress their claim that the Deity actively supervised His creation. Conversely, if the natural world were nothing more than a complex of secondary causes and effects operating with machinelike regularity, the Christian's belief in a "superintending Providence" became much less plausible. Efforts to redraw the boundary between science and theology thus evoked little enthusiasm, while theories that seemed to suggest that God had "surrendered the universe to the government of mere natural laws" encountered heavy criticism from Protestant apologists.[5]

Defenders of the faith also inveighed against the proposition that ascertainable knowledge was limited to information obtainable by empirical observation of the natural world. There remained, they believed, "a sphere of knowledge beyond that over which science in kingly dignity presides." Samson Talbot, president of the Baptists' Denison University, gave voice to the prevailing view among American Protestant intellectuals when he declared in 1872 that "mere physical science, which begins and ends with nature, which seeks only mechanical causes, never can construct a philosophy of all being and knowing."[6]

The idea that science was limited in its ability to decipher reality was precisely what an increasing number of Anglo-American polemicists appeared to be bent on denying. The vantage point from which American Protestant thinkers analyzed Darwinism was strongly informed by their concern that they were living in an era characterized by an aggressive form of unbelief seeking to undermine the credibility of Christian supernaturalism in the name of science. In the first section of this chapter the work of some of the most prominent opponents of the Christian world view will be briefly surveyed in an effort to show that this concern was far from groundless.

No one proved more brazen in his willingness to confront the armies of the Lord than T. H. Huxley. Huxley's favorable review of Darwin's theory in the April 1860 issue of England's *Westminster Review* gave him a publicist's role analogous to that of Asa Gray. There was, however, a crucial difference. Unlike Gray, who was anxious to conciliate religionists, Huxley chose to taunt them. He thus observed in 1860 that "extinguished theologians lie about the cradle of every science as the strangled snakes beside that of Hercules." This was only one of many barbs that Huxley directed against orthodox Christianity. During the course of his career he avoided few opportunities to rebuke the pious for what he believed to be their ignorant and obdurate hostility to new ideas. In 1871, for example, he asserted that no one should "imagine he is, or can be, both a true son of the Church and a loyal soldier of science." Though Huxley tended to equate orthodoxy with biblical literalism and the church with Roman Catholicism, the strident language he often employed in his discussion of Christian theology antagonized even Protestants who had little sympathy for the literal interpretation of the Scriptures or Catholicism.[7]

Huxley's assault on Christianity had a substantive as well as rhetorical component. His reading of history convinced him that the advance of science was attended by the "elimination of the notion of creative, or other interferences, with the natural order of the phaenomena which are the subject-matter of that science." This process was epitomized by the development of the concept of cosmic evolution, which affirmed that "the whole world, living and non-living, is the result of the mutual interaction according to definite laws, of the forces possessed by the molecules of which the primitive nebulosity of the universe was composed." In 1864, a year after he had jarred the sensibility of Christians by espousing the evolution of the human species in *Man's Place in Nature*, he announced that "Teleology, as commonly understood, had received its deathblow at Mr. Darwin's hands." In his 1868 reflections entitled "On the Physical Basis of Life," Huxley declared that thought was simply an "expression" of changes in the molecular structure of protoplasm. Because he believed that the ultimate nature of reality was unknowable, he contended that it made little difference from a philosophical perspective whether matter was conceived of in terms of spirit or spirit in terms of matter. He insisted, however, that the progress of science had been accompanied by "the extension of the province of what we call matter and causation, and the concomitant gradual banishment from all regions of human thought of what we call spirit and spontaneity." Nor did Huxley have any desire to arrest this trend: "with a view to the progress of science the materialistic terminology is in every way to be preferred." Two years later he denied that the gap between the inorganic and the organic was unbridgeable by natural causes. Life had originated, he suggested, by "the evolution of living protoplasm from not living matter." It is little wonder that one Presbyterian divine, upon hearing that Huxley had been invited to speak at the newly founded Johns Hopkins University in 1876, observed sardonically that "it was bad enough to invited Huxley. It were better to have asked God to be present. It would have been absurd to ask them both."[8]

Joining Huxley in the assault on the Christian world view was Herbert Spencer, a polymath who devoted much of his career to exploring the ramifications of the view "that the Universe and all things in it have reached their present forms through successive stages physically necessitated." Spencer derived "great satisfaction" from Darwin's theory and was even instrumental in making popular two terms that were increasingly employed in discussions of it, "evolution" and "the survival of the fittest." Accordingly, throughout his life he sought to lay to rest the popular misconception that he was Darwin's disciple.[9]

As early as 1852 Spencer had publicly announced his "profession of faith" in the transmutation hypothesis. The special creation of species, he argued, explained nothing, was totally unsupported by factual evidence, and could not even be conceptualized. Although he suggested no mechanism by which transmutation might have occurred, he was confident that "if a single cell may, when subjected to certain influences, become a man in the space of twenty years; there is nothing absurd in the hypothesis that under certain other influences, a cell may, in the course of millions of years, give origin to the human race."[10]

In Spencer's judgment, transmutation was merely one aspect of a process of development that characterized the entire universe. In 1851 he had read an account of the embryologist Karl Ernst von Baer's idea that "the development of every organism is a change from homogeneity to heterogeneity." He was so taken with this idea that he made it the basis of a theory of progressive change that encompassed all phenomena. By 1857 Spencer was on record as holding that "from the earliest traceable cosmical changes down to the latest results of civilization," it was possible to discern the "same evolution of the simple into the complex, through successive differentiations."[11]

Spencer devoted much of the rest of his life to the creation of a multivolume "Synthetic Philosophy" that he believed would demonstrate the universal applicability of evolution. The initial volume of this project, *First Principles,* appeared in 1862. Spencer's primary concern in this work was to show that the law of evolution, which he defined as "*a change from an indefinite, incoherent homogeneity, to a definite, coherent heterogeneity; through continuous differentiations and integrations,*" was capable of accounting for all natural phenomena. He prefaced this discussion, however, with a section on "the Unknowable" in which he attempted to show that a "fundamental harmony" existed between science and religion. The basis for this harmony, he contended, was that both enterprises pointed to the "most certain of all facts—that the Power which the Universe manifests to us is utterly inscrutable." The abiding element of all religions was a belief in some Power that could account for the unfathomable mystery of existence. Similarly, "ultimate Scientific Ideas"—space, time, matter, motion, and so on—were "all representative of realities that cannot be comprehended."[12]

Spencer submitted that the tension that often characterized the relationship between science and religion was the product of "the imperfect separation of their spheres and functions." By disclosing "the established order of the Universe," science had purged religion of a host of superstitious elements. But scientists sometimes forgot that their data were merely manifestations of a persistent Force, "an incomprehensible, Omnipresent Power." Religion reminded humanity of the existence of "that unascertained something which phenomena and their relations imply." Too often, however, religionists, afflicted with "the impiety of the pious," had insisted on endowing the "Unknown Cause" with anthropomorphic attributes. In reality, he proposed, the Unknowable possessed not personality but an unspecified "something" that was "higher" than personality. "A permanent peace will be reached," Spencer concluded, "when Science becomes fully convinced that its explanations are proximate and relative; while Religion becomes fully convinced that the mystery it contemplates is ultimate and absolute."[13]

The Spencerian world view reached an audience in the United States not only through Spencer's own works but also through publicity given his views by American disciples. One of the most active of these was Edward Livingston Youmans, an energetic advocate of the view that science held the key to the destruction of "the baneful superstitions by which, for ages, men's lives were darkened." Though suffering from periodic attacks of blindness, Youmans was a busy and popular lecturer on the lyceum circuit and the scientific editor for D. Appleton and Company, which published American editions of the works of Darwin and others whom religious thinkers regarded as suspect. Youmans edited Appleton's "International Scientific Series," a library of volumes written for the public by many of the world's leading scientists. In 1872, backed by Appleton's, be became the founding editor of *Popular Science Monthly,* through which he continued his efforts to bring the latest results of scientific investigation to the attention of the reading public.[14]

In the first edition of the *Monthly* Youmans observed that "the ascertainable order of things proves to be much more extensive than was at first suspected; and the inquiry into it has led to sphere after sphere of new investigation, until science is now regarded as not applying to this or that class of objects, but to the whole of nature." Convinced that the history and operation of the cosmos could be comprehended by means of natural laws, he greeted with unmitigated hostility every attempt to account for natural events by invoking a supernatural Deity. Tension between science and religion, he asserted, was the "natural and inevitable" result of religionists' obdurate refusal to grant scientists a truly free rein in the investigation of nature.[15]

An early and devoted convert to the Spencerian conception of reality, Youmans extolled the idea of cosmic evolution as "a great and established fact" that "accounts for the origin, continuance, and disappearance of the changing objects around us." Because he viewed it as "a definite verifiable principle educed from a more comprehensive range of facts than any other generalization ever attempted," he regarded evolution as the cornerstone of any valid philosophical interpretation of the universe. Though the *Monthly* published numerous articles unrelated to evolution, there was some justice in the observation of one critic that the magazine might more appropriately be called "Evolution Monthly."[16]

Like Youmans, whose efforts he would later eulogize in a biography, the free-lance writer and lecturer John Fiske was a zealous publicist for science and a self-proclaimed disciple of Herbert Spencer. In 1874, Fiske published his voluminous *Outlines of Cosmic Philosophy*, an expanded version of a series of lectures on the "positive philosophy" he had earlier presented as a visiting instructor at Harvard. Taking a cue from Spencer, he held that such problems as "the origin of the universe, the nature of its First Cause, and the ultimate constitution of the matter which it contains" were irresolvable, for the nature of ultimate reality was inscrutable. Knowledge was limited to the classification of experiences "produced in us by unknown external agencies." Science simply systematized this knowledge and constructed verifiable hypotheses concerning the connections between experiences. Fiske held that modern science, by showing that the universe was cosmos rather than chaos, laid the foundation for a truly "Cosmic Philosophy." The "proper business" of philosophers was not ontological speculation but the coordination of "those seemingly separate groups of scientific truths which scientific specialists have not the leisure, and often neither the desire nor the ability, to coördinate."[17]

Fiske embraced the Spencerian notion that the orderly "progress toward higher complexity and higher organization" disclosed by the investigation of nature could be formulated in a general "Law of Evolution." In the three chapters he devoted to the origin of species, he contrasted the special creation hypothesis, "originating in the crude mythological conceptions of the ancient Hebrews," with Darwin's theory, which accorded with other scientific efforts to describe the cosmos by means of "agencies such as are daily seen in operation about us." The doctrine of special creation, he urged, should be consigned "to that limbo where hover the ghosts of the slaughtered theories that were born of man's untutored intelligence in early times."[18]

In some respects Fiske's *Outlines* was little more than a restatement of the Spencerian philosophy. But whereas Spencer regarded his discussion of the Unknowable primarily as a vehicle for deflecting the hostility of religious thinkers, Fiske was genuinely interested in religious questions. Unlike Spencer, whose hostility to prevailing expressions of theism led to avoidance of the use of the term "God," Fiske's conviction that "no theory of phenomena, external or internal, can be framed without postulating an Absolute Existence of which phenomena are the manifestations" led him to claim that "the affirmation of God's existence" was the very basis of his Cosmic Philosophy.[19]

Like many other religious thinkers, Fiske believed that no system of theology that set itself against the conclusions of science would long endure. He took a more extreme view than most of his contemporaries, though, in asserting that theists could harmonize science and religion only if they based their assertions concerning the divine on "science alone." In six chapters he outlined his conception of the only version of theism he believed to be compatible with the scientific view of the natural world.[20]

Fiske contended that it was possible to infer the existence of "an unconditioned Power existing independently of consciousness, to which no limit is conceivable in time or space, and of which all phenomena, as known to us, are the manifestations." Beyond this, however, real insight into the nature of that First Cause was impossible: whereas knowledge depended on classifiable relationships among experimental phenomena, the Absolute First Cause existed "out of all relation." In Fiske's judgment, the assumption that "the highest form of Being as yet suggested to one petty race of creatures by its ephemeral experience of what is going on in one tiny corner of the universe is necessarily to be taken as the equivalent of that absolutely highest form of Being in which all the possibilities of existence are alike comprehended" was preposterous. Those who insisted on ascribing anthropomorphic attributes to the Deity were guilty of finitizing the Absolute. "*Personality* and *Infinity*," he argued, were "terms expressive of ideas which are mutually incompatible." Persuaded that intelligence, will, and other personal attributes were simply mechanisms by which organisms adjusted more adequately to their environment, Fiske inferred that those who would assign those attributes to God were in effect suggesting that He was "a product of evolution."[21]

Rejecting this "gross and painful conception" of God as irreconcilable with the deepest insights of both religion and science, Fiske interpreted the history of philosophy "as a continuous process of *deanthropomorphization*." He believed that the anthropomorphic symbol "Spirit" was superior to the materialistic symbol "Force" in characterizing the First Cause and that it would never be possible wholly to eliminate anthropomorphism from religious discourse. He predicted, however, that humanity's acceptance of the concept of cosmic evolution would promote the elimination of the crude forms of anthropomorphism that still characterized contemporary theological discussion and the substitution of the concept of a Power "utterly and forever unknowable." Far from viewing this as cause for despair, he insisted that the inscrutability of the Absolute was precisely what made It an object of worship.[22]

Of fundamental importance to the Christian concept of God was the notion that He was responsive to the needs of His children. In the early seventies, a spirited challenge to this notion appeared in the work of John Tyndall, a noted British physicist who devoted a good deal of his career to spreading the gospel of naturalism to the educated public. In 1872 Tyndall, who had long questioned the notion that prayer could affect natural phenomena, used one of England's leading journals, the *Contemporary Review*, to present and endorse a proposal submitted to him by a friend (Sir Henry Thompson) for an "exhaustive and complete" experiment by which the extent of "the action of 'Providence' in physical affairs" could be ascertained. For a period of three to five years, believers were to make special petitions on behalf of people in a designated hospital ward. The mortality rate in this ward would then be compared with that in wards that had not enjoyed the benefit of special prayers.[23]

In a subsequent article on this subject Tyndall asserted that, because believers had assigned *"physical value"* to prayer, students of science were justified in investigating it by the same methods they would use for other kinds of "physical energy." If experimental results indicated that God did not in fact alter physical states of affairs, believers might profitably redirect their petitions to more "practicable objects." To add insult to injury, Tyndall highlighted the stakes in this controversy by emphasizing that if, as Christians believed, God were analogous to an "earthly father," it was reasonable to suppose that He would grant the requests of His children by intervening on their behalf.[24]

The "prayer test" inevitably raised the hackles of American religious thinkers. They found it so patently absurd that they were tempted to regard it as nothing more than an irreverent jest at their expense. But the sober tone and analysis that characterized Tyndall's presentation forced them to proceed on the assumption that he had been completely serious in setting forth his challenge.[25]

Protestant intellectuals advanced several arguments designed to show that Tyndall's proposal was an invalid test of the efficacy of prayer. They reminded their readers that because God required faith as a condition for answering prayer, individuals who assumed that He would submit to a neutral "test" would be disappointed. They also charged that Tyndall had fundamentally misconstrued the claims believers made with regard to prayer. Christians did not discount the possibility that God might interfere with natural laws in responding to a believer's petition, but because these laws were themselves expressions of God's will, it was unreasonable to assume that He would frequently contravene them. Some noted, too, that God often employed those very laws in answering prayers. It would thus be presumptuous to deny that His hand was involved in cases where individuals were healed "by an original strength of constitution, or by the well-timed application of a remedy." Finally, Protestant thinkers denied that God's response to prayer could be evaluated by means of a criterion arbitrarily laid down by the experimentalist. The nature of His response was conditioned by a multitude of circumstances beyond the ken of human beings. Because healing might conflict with an even higher purpose, it could not be employed as the basis for deciding whether God had responded to petitions. Prayers made in the proper spirit, religious intellectuals reminded their readers, were always informed by the conviction that God's will was paramount.[26]

From the vantage point of American Protestant thinkers, Tyndall offered living testimony to the fact that "those who have excelled in physical experiments are not, *therefore,* fitted to discuss philosophical or religious questions." Lacking both the faith to offer prayer in the proper spirit and the understanding to recognize an answer to it, Tyndall appeared to be in spiritual jeopardy. Religionists acted accordingly; when Tyndall arrived in America in 1872 to deliver a series of scientific lectures, he found many American believers fervently praying for his salvation.[27]

Contrition and repentance, however, were preconditions for salvation, and Tyndall was impenitent. In his 1874 presidential address before the British Association at Belfast he depicted the history of efforts to account for "the sources of natural phenomena" as an epic struggle in which the oft-martyred forces of science had gradually triumphed over the forces of pious superstition. Acknowledging his debt to F. A. Lange's *History of Materialism*, Tyndall commended those who throughout the history of Western civilization had attempted to account for natural phenomena by means of physical agencies.[28]

Tyndall submitted that the nineteenth century was an age of "great generalizations," most notably the doctrine of the conservation of energy and the theory of evolution. Spurning special creation as tanta-

mount to no explanation at all, Tyndall heartily praised that "most
terrible of antagonists," Charles Darwin, whom he characterized as an
opponent of teleology, and Huxley, whom he credited with populariz-
ing Darwin's doctrine. There was one issue, however, on which Tyndall chided Darwin for timidity: he had not endeavored to explain how
life itself had originated. In 1870 Tyndall had interpreted the evolutionary hypothesis as a theory implying that all phenomena, including
the human mind, "were once latent in a fiery cloud." He reaffirmed
this view in his Belfast address, contending that "anthropomorphism,
which it seemed the object of Mr. Darwin to set aside, is as firmly associated with the creation of a few forms as with the creation of a multitude." In the interest of consistency, Tyndall asserted that "two
courses, and two only, are possible. Either let us open our doors freely
to the conception of creative acts, or, abandoning them, let us radically
change our notions of matter." In words that could hardly fail to reso-
nate ominously within the American Protestant community, Tyndall
made his own choice clear: "Abandoning all disguise, the confession
that I feel bound to make before you is that I prolong the vision [of physical forces] backward across the boundary of the experimental evidence, and discern in that matter, which we in our ignorance, and
notwithstanding our professed reverence for its Creator, have hither-
to covered with opprobrium, the promise and potency of every form
and quality of life." Though he acknowledged that this confession
amounted to an endorsement of materialism, he affirmed that "the
whole process of evolution is the manifestation of a Power absolutely inscrutable to the intellect of man." Hence, he concluded, "there is . . .
no very rank materialism here."[29]

For their part, American religious thinkers failed to see "how mystery mitigates the rankness of the materialism." The Belfast Address
served only to reinforce the conviction of these thinkers that Tyndall
was seeking to undermine belief in the supernatural. Indeed, a number
of them concurred with Professor John W. Mears of Hamilton College,
who called Tyndall's address "the boldest challenge which English-
speaking theologians and philosophers had ever received from the materialist and atheist side."[30]

Tyndall, Huxley, Spencer, Youmans, and Fiske were only some of the
most celebrated names in a sizable roster of individuals whose views
tended to reduce, even eliminate, the role of supernatural activity in
the world. The confluence of such views in the third quarter of the
nineteenth century convinced American Protestant intellectuals that
the forces of unbelief, led by a talented cadre of militant heretics, were

engaged in an all-out effort to invest materialism with the name and prestige of science. The healthy American sale of many of the books written by well-known partisans of scientific naturalism, as well as the enthusiastic reception accorded Spencer and Huxley during their visits to the United States, suggested the prevalence of "an uneasy feeling in regard to the foundations of belief." The appropriate response to this challenge seemed to be clear enough: "Those set for the defence of the gospel must therefore gird on their armor. They must watch, detect, expose, confront and overpower their foe. Valiant for the truth, speaking it in love, strengthened by Him who is the Truth, they shall conquer." By 1870, no problem was attracting more attention in the mainstream Protestant theological quarterlies and in the multitude of other theological works published in the United States than the threat of unbelief posed by the work of scientific naturalists.[31]

None of the ruling assumptions of scientific naturalism was the object of more sustained criticism from Protestant apologists in the United States than the idea that matter and the laws describing its operation were sufficient to account for natural phenomena. It was this idea, they believed, that accounted for the enthusiastic support that the concept of evolution received at the hands of scientific naturalists. Not all American Protestant intellectuals would have gone as far as the Methodist critic who asserted that "the only form of infidelity from which Christianity has anything to fear is the *Theory of Development*." Most of them could agree, however, that the view of the universe as "a self-evolving system of laws" was the most comprehensive "device for banning God" from the natural world yet contrived by opponents of supernaturalism. Some, in fact, believed that cosmic evolution was "not merely the only actual, but also the only *possible* competitor of Theism as an explanation of Nature."[32]

A representative statement of the conviction that evolution and naturalism were intimately related was offered by Enoch Fitch Burr, the pastor of the Congregational Church in Hamburg, Connecticut, and Lecturer on the Scientific Evidences of Religion at Amherst from 1868 to 1874. Burr's study of mathematics and astronomy at Yale culminated in 1848 in the publication of the creditable *Results of Analytical Researches in the Neptunian Theory of Uranus*. After becoming a village pastor, he manifested his continuing interest in science by publishing several volumes dealing with the relationship between science and religion. In one of these works, published in 1873, Burr addressed himself to the metaphysical implications of the evolutionary philosophy: "Founded by

[margin annotation: materialism]

atheism, claimed by atheism, supported by atheism, used exclusively in the interest of atheism, suppressing without mercy every jot of evidence for the Divine existence, and so making a positive rational faith in God wholly impossible, the Doctrine of Evolution may well be set down as not only a foe to Theism, but a foe of the most thorough-going sort."[33]

Religious intellectuals were aware, of course, that many proponents of scientific naturalism had allowed that the phenomena disclosed by the investigation of nature were manifestations of an underlying Reality that was, as Huxley put it, "Unknown and Unknowable." The concept of an Unknowable Deity, treated most extensively in the work of Herbert Spencer and John Fiske, provoked an enormous volume of discussion within the American Protestant intellectual community. Emerging from this discussion was widespread agreement that the Unknowable was "a barren abstraction" wholly unacceptable as an object of worship. Christians did not want their spiritual quest to culminate in mystery; they wanted to find the personal God of the Bible. Unworthy of being worshiped, an Unknowable Absolute was really no God at all. "The result of Mr. Spencer's religious theory," wrote the Congregational clergyman J. E. Barnes of Darien, Connecticut, in 1863, "is to leave us, like slaves, before the throne of an utterly incognizable Power." Barnes allowed that Spencer's conception of God would commend itself to individuals who were "ready to welcome whatever promises to release them from the unpleasant sense of standing related to a Personal Deity," but he insisted that it was "miserably inadequate" to meet the spiritual needs of most individuals, who felt impelled to worship "a Being, who, though infinitely transcending human conception, is not wholly 'unknowable' and unapproachable, but stands related to man, as, in the highest sense, a Father and a Friend."[34]

Similar reasoning was applied to the conception of God embodied in the work of the "American Spencer," John Fiske. Most Protestants repudiated Fiske's claim to have envisioned a "higher and purer" view of Christian theism. The impersonal Absolute might well be an "object of awe," but it was not an object of worship, love, or devotion.[35]

Reinforcing this view was the widespread conviction among American Protestant thinkers that acknowledgment of an Unknowable Deity represented not a pious confession of faith in a God transcending human thought but a tactical ploy, a "condescension to old-fashioned notions," aimed at easing believers into the camp of materialism. In this spirit, a critic writing anonymously in the Episcopalian *American Church Review* submitted that when proponents of naturalism disclaimed belief in the idea that "there is *no* God, there is only nature," what they really meant was that "there is no God *but* nature: or Nature is God." And "materialistic pantheism," Protestants assured their readers, was no less pantheism, no less materialism, no less antagonistic to belief in the God of Christianity.[36]

Though most religious thinkers considered the invocation of an Unknowable little more than a covert endorsement of materialism, they also recognized that the choice of that term spoke volumes about the epistemological assumptions of its adherents. The "skepticism" embraced by mid-nineteenth-century infidels was most clearly discernible in its repudiation of any knowledge other than that obtained by "observation, analysis, and induction." The same unbelievers who exalted nature as their true god regarded the scientific method as the sole means by which that god revealed itself to humanity.[37]

In defending the position that the Bible was a legitimate source of knowledge, Protestant thinkers advanced several arguments. Some contended that the assumption that all discoverable truth resulted from the scientific investigation of nature was wholly arbitrary. "What folly would it be," S. A. Ort, a Lutheran clergyman who served as a professor at Wittenberg College, asked rhetorically, "for the naked eye to say to the telescope, 'There are no worlds beyond the limits of my vision.' . . . Would it be sensible for the ear to tell the nose, 'There are no odors,' or for the nose to say to the ear, 'There is no sound.' And how much more authority has science to declare the whole field of knowledge is circumscribed by its limits?"[38]

Even more fundamentally, many Protestants insisted that, all protestations to the contrary notwithstanding, the principles underlying naturalism were not truly based on the "scientific method" at all. Such conceptions as the uniformity of nature and the "veracity of the senses" called for eyes of faith akin to those required for believing the testimony of Scripture. And some of the speculations of the partisans of unbelief required a leap of faith much greater than anything required by the Bible. One Lutheran clergyman thus observed that individuals who denied the credibility of the miracles of the Bible were often the very individuals who "invent and spin out from their fancy such fables, which are a thousand times more incredible than the juvenile stories of Grimm, Hauf, Bechstein, Anderson, and the Thousand and One Nights put together."[39]

Because science served as the source of many of the slogans and furnished many of the most prominent supporters of supernaturalism, it is not surprising that some members of the American Protestant intellectual community expressed growing concern about the tenor of modern scientific investigation during the third quarter of the nineteenth century. By 1875, the increasing tendency of scientists to "deify matter" and to heap opprobrium upon Christian theology appeared to be one of the most obvious features of the age. In accounting for the indifference, even hostility, of scientists to supernaturalism, some Protestants cited a one-sidedness stemming from the "too exclusive study of the phenomena of matter." Others imputed the unwillingness of some scientists to set "bounds to their idea of nature" to an arrogance bred by the recent accomplishments of science in pushing back "the domain of the unknown" and nurtured by the sinful proclivities of humankind.[40]

Most Protestants refused to consign science to unbelief. Indeed, the prestige of the scientific enterprise within educated circles was sufficiently great to convince many of them that the clergy needed even greater acquaintance with natural science. The real source of opposition to supernaturalism, Protestant thinkers emphasized, was not science but a philosophical system that sought to capitalize on its prestige. Although they were aware that such a system would naturally be especially appealing to some scientists, they derived a great deal of solace and hope from the fact that a host of natural historians remained faithful to Christianity. They insisted that when practitioners of science reduced reality to nature and knowledge to the experience of natural phenomena, they were abandoning the arena in which they were authorities and were speaking as philosophers. Not all religious thinkers shared the perspective of the critic writing in the Methodists' *Southern Review* who enjoined individuals "who have studied matter, and matter alone," to "stand aloof from the domain of philosophy." Most assumed, however, that scientists possessed neither special authority in philosophy nor unique insight into ultimate reality.[41]

For this reason, Protestant thinkers were infuriated when scientists hostile to Christian supernaturalism insinuated that anyone who disagreed with them was guilty of obscurantism. In fact, they insisted, statements made by Huxley, Tyndall, and others manifested "a dogmatism as bold and arrogant as ever fell from the lips of the most bigoted and narrow-minded theologian of the dark ages." In the judgment of religious thinkers, it was perverse and unfair that they should be branded as opponents of science merely because they refused to make the same philosophical leaps as their skeptical antagonists.[42]

Given their impatience with charges of obscurantism, it is not surprising that American Protestant intellectuals looked askance at the notion that the history of thought could be seen as the steady triumph of science over the forces of obdurate theology. This interpretation, which was frequently espoused by scientific naturalists, received its most full-blown expression in the 1870s in the work of John William Draper, an Anglo-American chemist and historian who in 1860 had been the main speaker at the famous meeting of the British Association in which Huxley had clashed with Wilberforce over evolution. In 1874, Draper's *History of the Conflict between Religion and Science* appeared as one of the volumes in the "International Scientific Series." If the title did not betray Draper's position, the preface left no doubt about the author's perspective. "The history of science," he declared, "is not a mere record of isolated discoveries; it is a narrative of the conflict of two contending powers, the expansive force of the human intellect on one side, and the compression arising from traditionary faith and human interests on the other."[43]

Though Draper concentrated his attack on the Roman Catholic church, Protestant thinkers were not appeased. Many conceded that Christians had sometimes objected to scientific theories later proven correct. They reminded their critics, however, that theologians had made and would continue to make adjustments in theology whenever advances in science necessitated them. Draper's work had thus unfairly depicted religion. In the guise of objectivity, he had sought "to sow the seeds of discord" by placing contemporary controversies within a historical context that would cast Christians as Cardinal Bellarmine to Huxley's Galileo.[44]

It was in this fiercely polemical intellectual environment that American Protestant thinkers confronted the Darwinian hypothesis. From the very outset of their consideration of Darwin's work, American Protestant intellectuals had emphasized that the theory of organic evolution played a central role in the philosophical outlook of individuals who were hostile to Christian theology. Most of the avid support for the Darwinian hypothesis, they charged, proceeded from "those who are glad to seize any plausible method of excluding Deity from his creation." More than one critic observed that it was a telling comment on the philosophical tenor of the transmutation hypothesis that most individuals who favored the heretical idea that the human race comprised more than one independently created species had embraced the equally subversive view that all species sprang from a common ancestor. As time went on, many defenders of the faith, disturbed by the bellicosity with which the proponents of naturalism were prosecuting their case, came to assume that not only the support but the very promulgation of the Darwinian hypothesis was inspired by a philosophical animus against the Christian world view. For these thinkers, Darwin was not simply the disinterested advocate of a fallacious scientific hypothesis; he was one of those partisans of unbelief who, recognizing that "this is a scientific age," sought "to give their speculations the similitude of science."[45]

Darwin himself fostered this opinion. In spite of the fact that he had gravitated toward a materialistic (though not atheistic) view of the world long before 1859, he largely eschewed discussion of philosophical issues in the *Origin of Species*. In subsequent years, however, Darwin became both increasingly unwilling to credit God with playing a meaningful role in the world and more candid about his assessment of the philosophical implications of his views. These tendencies can be rather dimly glimpsed in his *On the Various Contrivances by Which British and Foreign Orchids are Fertilized by Insects* (1862), where Darwin maintained that structures that had originally served one function could gradually adapt to serve another. This position implied that biological roles were the result not of intention or design but of the gradual change in organisms and constituted what Darwin termed in a letter to Asa Gray a " 'flank movement' on the enemy." But this implication proved to be so subtle that it eluded most Protestant reviewers.[46]

Darwin was anything but subtle in his "Concluding Remarks" to his two-volume *The Variation of Plants and Animals under Domestication* (1868). Gray's position that a providential Creator had directed the course of variation, he asserted, was inimical to the spirit of his theory. Darwin observed that "if we assume that each particular variation was from the beginning of all time preordained, the plasticity of organisation, which leads to many injurious deviations of structure, as well as that redundant power of reproduction which inevitably leads to a struggle for existence, and as a consequence, to the natural selection or survival of the fittest, must appear to us superfluous laws of nature." This passage confirmed Protestant thinkers' suspicions that the Darwinian God was "a cold and lifeless abstraction which could kindle no devotion in the soul" and clearly unmasked Darwin as yet another proponent of the naturalistic world view. Accordingly, by the late sixties the charge that Darwin's "incredible philosophical romance" had been written to lend credibility to a conception of nature bereft of the presence of an active Deity assumed a more prominent role in Protestants' analysis of the theory.[47]

This charge was the final link in a chain of reasoning about Darwinism that most American Protestants found enormously convincing. These thinkers began from the conviction that because the God of grace was also the God of nature, a valid interpretation of natural history would confirm the essential tenets of Christianity. This connection, coupled with their conviction that the effect of the Darwinian theory was to undermine the Christian world view, led Protestants to reason that Darwin's hypothesis was irreconcilable with the facts of natural history. In turn, their belief that the transmutation hypothesis was unfounded speculation, combined with a heightened awareness of the menace represented by scientific naturalism, convinced them that the real animus behind the promulgation of the hypothesis was hostility to Christian supernaturalism.

Nevertheless, although American Protestant intellectuals gave Darwin's theory a good deal of attention in the period from 1859 to 1875, few of them regarded it as peculiarly noteworthy. Besieged by what they considered to be quite literally one damned idea after another, religious thinkers rarely clearly differentiated serious challenges to prevailing formulations of Christian theology from more ephemeral and flippant proposals. The early seventies thus found them devoting almost as much attention to Tyndall's prayer test as to the theory of organic evolution. The siege mentality of Protestant thinkers also helped to blur their vision of the changing status of the latter theory among scientists. For even while they were confidently proclaiming that the transmutation hypothesis would share the fate of other pseudoscientific conceits, the community to whom they had traditionally turned for guidance in such matters was radically reevaluating its position regarding the theory of organic evolution.[48]

By the middle of the 1860s it was apparent that the scientific community had no intention of rejecting the Darwinian hypothesis out of hand. Darwin was not a crackpot but a highly respected scientist, and few of his colleagues were inclined to dismiss his work with the same contempt they had shown *Vestiges of the Natural History of Creation.*

Protestant clergymen and theologians tended to assume that when scientists paid homage to the doctrine of special creation, they were embracing the biblical sense of the term "creation." In fact, however, by the middle of the nineteenth century the term had taken on a variety of meanings within the scientific community. For some natural historians, such as Louis Agassiz, it continued to denote a series of miraculous events. For others, however, the term "creation" referred to a process describable by a yet unknown natural law. Many scientists adopting this position believed that this law had been initiated and governed by God. These individuals, when combined with those who endorsed the view that species had been miraculously created, were sufficiently numerous to lead Asa Gray to conclude in 1863 that "most naturalists believe that the origin of species is supernatural." But a minority of scientists avoided references to the divine and viewed "creation" simply as the work of an unknown natural agency responsible for the appearance of new species.[49]

Prior to the publication of the *Origin of Species*, natural historians readily acknowledged that science was unable to account for the origin of species. The intractability of that problem led many of them to refrain altogether from discussing the issue. Few, however, shared James Dwight Dana's belief that "hypotheses as to the precise mode of creating a species are presumptuous." Though most scientists countenanced the idea of supernatural intervention in the natural world when they could not account for phenomena by reference to secondary causes, by the middle of the nineteenth century even the most pious members of the scientific community assumed that it was "clearly the duty of science to seek for some other explanation" of the origin of species than "half a million distinct miracles." If they were willing to allow that the issue of ultimate origins was beyond the purview of science, they were also adamant in their insistence that science had the right to determine just when origins became ultimate and the responsibility, as Huxley put it, "to reduce the fundamental incomprehensibilities to the smallest possible number."[50]

In his campaign to secure scientific support for his hypothesis, Darwin did his best to exploit scientists' growing discontent with the idea of miraculous creation and to minister to the desire to account for speciation in terms of natural agencies. His argument that the idea that the origin of species was the product of "secondary" causes more clearly accorded with the thrust of scientific thought than the notion that species had originated by periodic divine fiat was shrewdly designed to give his theory credibility within a scientific community that was seeking to assert its autonomy within the culture. In contrast to special creation, which presupposed that the agency responsible for the appearance of new species lay beyond the reach of human apprehension, the Darwinian hypothesis described speciation in terms of phenomena and processes that were familiar to natural historians. Equally effective was the invidious distinction Darwin drew between the explanatory power of his theory and that of the doctrine of special creation. Actually, it was not, as he and his followers suggested, that evolution could account for phenomena that were otherwise inexplicable. After all, an omnipotent Creator could account for *any* phenomenon. The fundamental difference lay rather in the role that the two explanations conferred on scientists. The doctrine of special creation presupposed that the reason for the structural affinities among extinct and extant species lay beyond the realm of science. The natural historian's task was thus limited to investigative forays into a past connected to the present only by a "plan" in the mind of the Creator. To many scientists this seemed to be a "pernicious" limitation on scientific explanation. By contrast, Darwin's theory offered a way of discussing speciation in terms of natural agencies, the only kind of agencies amenable to scientific discourse. In so doing, it opened the relationships of organisms through time to scientific investigation.[51]

These considerations were sufficient to ensure that natural historians would give the Darwinian hypothesis the fair hearing that Asa Gray had demanded, but they were not enough in themselves to convert scientists to the hypothesis. It was also necessary to convince them that the theory of organic evolution accorded more closely with the data of natural history than had previously been believed. The actual transmutation of species was not susceptible to observation. Accordingly, supporters of the theory were forced to emphasize more indirect kinds of evidence.

In this vein, a number of natural historians in the 1860s called attention to the salience of variation among organisms and pointed to the existence of gradations in the structures and the instincts of individuals within a species. In themselves, however, such data did not go very far in establishing the validity of the transmutation hypothesis. What was needed was evidence that variation was both heritable and cumulative. It was therefore enormously significant that in the two decades after publication of the *Origin of Species*, scientists unearthed fossil sequences that included the kinds of "intermediate forms" that critics of evolution had demanded. In the early 1860s specimens of the reptilelike birds (*Archaeopteryx*) and birdlike reptiles (*Compsognathus*) were found. These findings were supplemented in the seventies by the even more celebrated discovery of a series of horses from the vast American fossil beds. In 1874 the American paleontologist O. C. Marsh announced that this series "suppl[ied] every important intermediate form" from the Eocene *Orohippus* to the living horse and that "the line of descent appears to have been direct." On the basis of such findings, Huxley maintained that if the theory of evolution "had not existed, the palaeontologist would have had to invent it."[52]

Important gaps in the fossil record still remained. A fossil sequence exhibiting minute gradations in form from one species to another was not discovered until 1875, and even then it received little attention from the scientific community. Nor did the fossil record disclose unimpeachable evidence that phyla were linked together by a common ancestor. Nevertheless, the data that did exist suggested that further research would confirm the hypothetical links that evolutionists had postulated on the basis of data from embryology and anatomy. By 1875 the evidence was sufficiently convincing to encourage most scientists to adopt the theory of organic evolution as their "working hypothesis." When the English clergyman Charles Kingsley reported in 1863 that "Darwin is conquering everywhere," he was guilty of some hyperbole. But in the decade from 1865 to 1875, most influential members of the scientific community did become converts to the theory. In the United States, for example, the geologist William North Rice acknowledged only a few years after he had rejected the theory in his doctoral thesis that evolution was the most probable explanation for the history of life. Similarly, Joseph Le Conte, Alexander Winchell, and numerous other scientists who had once rejected the theory became enthusiastic proponents of the idea of organic evolution.[53]

The most celebrated of these converts was James Dwight Dana. By 1874 Dana no longer believed that the fossil record unequivocally opposed evolution. Instead, he reasoned that "since the physical progress of the globe was under the action of natural law, so the same may naturally have been true of its organic progress." Though he continued for some time to insist that the creation of man had required a special act of God, he now concluded that "the evolution of the system of life went forward through the derivation of species from species, . . . and with few occasions for supernatural intervention."[54]

Many younger naturalists did not need to be converted at all. For them evolution was not a cause célèbre but the fundamental assumption informing their investigations. By the mid-seventies even virtually all of Louis Agassiz's students, thanks in large measure to an intellectual independence that Agassiz himself had fostered in them, embraced the evolutionary hypothesis.[55]

Not all scientists were converted. As late as 1867 Agassiz privately predicted that he would "outlive this mania," and he went to his grave unconvinced by the arguments of the evolutionists. In an *Atlantic Monthly* article that appeared in January 1874, a month after his death, he finally acknowledged that Darwin had "placed the subject on a different basis from that of all his predecessors, and . . . brought to the discussion a vast amount of well-arranged information, a convincing cogency of argument, and a captivating charm of presentation." Nevertheless, Agassiz continued to insist that the Darwinian hyhpothesis was "merely conjectural" and, in view of the actual sequence of the fossil record, not even "the best conjecture possible in the present state of our knowledge." Agassiz remained convinced that the history of life was the result of "repeated acts of creation."[56]

John William Dawson, a well-known paleontologist and the principal of McGill University, was another scientist who viewed the theory of evolution as an egregious error. An early and vigorous opponent of Darwin's theory, Dawson continued to emphasize that it was supported by neither observation nor the fossil record. Like Agassiz, he preached this view outside scientific forums. In the 1870s he wrote several works for the lay public that condemned the transmutation hypothesis as "a system destitute of any shadow of proof, and supported merely by vague analogies and figures of speech, and by the arbitrary and artificial coherence of its own parts."[57]

Although Agassiz and Dawson were the most prolific scientific opponents of the theory of organic evolution, a number of other scientists in the early seventies either actively rejected or withheld their assent from the theory. J. Lawrence Smith, professor of chemistry at the University of Louisville, Kentucky, used the occasion of his presidential address to the American Association for the Advancement of Science to caution his colleagues against following the example of people like Darwin, whom he regarded "more as a metaphysician with a highly-wrought imagination than as a scientist." Smith also emphasized, however, that the transmutation hypothesis should be examined rather than execrated, and he refused to dismiss the possibility that it was "grounded on truth."[58]

By 1875 the ranks of outspoken opponents of the theory of organic evolution within the scientific community had grown quite thin. Asa Gray, who became the first president of the AAAS to endorse Darwin's theory, observed in 1872 that evolutionary ideas had "so possessed the minds of the naturalists of the present day that hardly a discourse can be pronounced or an investigation prosecuted without reference to them." By 1877 O. C. Marsh was prepared to argue that "to doubt evolution is to doubt science."[59]

In the fifteen years following publication of the *Origin of Species*, a revolution in the field of natural history had occurred. It was a quiet revolution, a change of perspective rather than a storming of the heights. The striking rapidity with which the scientific community cast its verdict in favor of a theory that shattered the traditional understanding of the history of life attested to the lack of commitment many natural historians felt toward the doctrine of special creation. To be sure, not all converts found change to be painless. Whatever sources of appeal the transmutation hypothesis may have had for natural historians, many doubtless shared the experience of David Starr Jordan, who recalled going "over to the evolutionists with the grace of a cat the boy 'leads' by its tail across the carpet!" Still, if, as Huxley maintained, a theory's "right to exist is coextensive with its power of resisting extinction by its rivals," most members of the scientific community were prepared to affirm by 1875 that the theory of organic evolution was a most hardy variety.[60]

In the last quarter of the nineteenth century natural historians bestowed upon Darwin the honor generally accorded the leader of a successful revolution. Indeed, by the mid-seventies comparisons of his achievement with that of Isaac Newton were not uncommon. Ironically, though, in spite of the fact that they generally acknowledged that Darwin's work had succeeded in convincing scientists to endorse the theory of evolution and tended to equate "Darwinism" and "organic evolution" in common parlance, most natural historians ultimately could not bring themselves to believe that Darwin's explanation of how that process occurred was entirely adequate.[61]

By the early seventies, the criticism of Fleeming Jenkin, Lord Kelvin, St. George Jackson Mivart, and others had succeeded in convincing most natural historians that natural selection was simply incapable of performing the task that Darwin had originally assigned to it. Increasingly speculation centered on the origin and nature of variation. Though evolutionists generally conceded that natural selection weeded out unfit individuals and preserved useful variations, many came to regard variation as the central mechanism of evolutionary theory.[62]

Prominent among the critics were American scientists. The paleontologist A. S. Packard, Jr., expressed the position of most evolutionists in the United States when he submitted in 1877 that "Darwinism is but one of a number of factors of a true evolution theory." Noting that natural selection accounted "for the *preservation* of forms [rather] than for their origination," Packard emphasized that it "comes in play only as the last term of a series of evolutionary agencies or causes." American evolutionists commonly adopted a view of transmutation that they characterized as "neo-Lamarckian." This "American school," led by the eminent paleontologists Edward Drinker Cope, Alpheus Hyatt, and Packard, urged that variation was more saltatory, more rapid, and more adaptive than Darwin had suggested. Variations, they maintained, were induced by environmental conditions, fostered by the use and disuse of structures that organisms already possessed, and inherited by subsequent generations.[63]

American neo-Lamarckianism was only one of many manifestations of a pervasive dissatisfaction with Darwin's account of the dynamics of transmutation. In fact, until well into the twentieth century, only a small minority of evolutionists credited natural selection with being the primary agent of transmutation. Most natural historians, convinced that variation was more systematically related to the adaptive needs of organisms than Darwin had suggested, consigned natural selection to a rather subordinate place in the evolutionary process. This move was to have a significant impact on the subsequent history of both scientific and religious thought.[64]

In the short period between 1875 and 1880, most religious intellectuals came to recognize that scientists had rendered a clear verdict in favor of the theory of organic evolution. This recognition marked the beginning of a new phase in the "interminable Darwinian discussion" within the American Protestant intellectual community. Prior to 1875 few religious thinkers had seen much reason to engage in a systematic investigation of the theological implications of a theory lacking the endorsement of science. During the last quarter of the nineteenth century, however, Protestants engaged in a sustained dialogue about what terms of relationship should be established between evolution and Christian theology. In the course of this dialogue the consensus that had heretofore existed within the American Protestant intellectual community in its approach to the theory of evolution was shattered, and there emerged within that community a new division, a division cutting across traditional theological, denominational, and geographical lines. Most American Protestant intellectuals could agree that the evolutionary hypothesis was irreconcilable with the prevailing formulations of numerous Christian doctrines. They differed radically among themselves, however, in the inferences they drew from this conclusion. Some insisted that it constituted sufficient grounds for rejecting the hypothesis. Others just as adamantly maintained that it made theological restatement imperative. The last quarter of the nineteenth century witnessed the development and elaboration of each of these positions.[65]

Part Two

1875–1900

4

"Put on the Whole Armor of God":
The Theological Critique

DURING the last quarter of the nineteenth century, a sizable number of Protestant intellectuals in the United States continued to advance arguments against the theory of organic evolution. The nature of their criticism, however, shifted significantly. Prior to 1875, members of the American religious community devoted little sustained attention to the theological implications of the transmutation hypothesis. Most chose instead to concentrate on what they viewed as its scientific deficiencies. The wholesale conversion of scientists to the theory of organic evolution vitiated the effectiveness of this mode of analysis. Accordingly, after 1875 most critics of Darwinism within the American Protestant community altered their emphasis. They now sought to prove the theory of organic evolution invalid by showing its inconsistency with central elements of the Christian message.

This does not mean that the older mode of analysis was entirely abandoned. Some American Protestants continued to insist that the transmutation hypothesis was grounded on nothing more than a series of dubious speculative suppositions. This conviction prompted the Baptist clergyman Ebenezer Nisbet to recount a story he had heard about an insane individual who claimed that the only thing preventing him from creating a young pig from " 'black puddings, pigs' bones, and bristles' " was a lack of " 'vital warmth.' " "Darwinism," Nisbet suggested, "is forever like the lunatic, looking for his pig to appear; is all right if it only had something it has not got,—something wanting there, something wanting almost everywhere." To Nisbet, as to many other Protestants, it was clear that "Darwinism requires so many unproven hypotheses for its support, and so completely fails to explain what we find in nature, that it is not worthy even of provisional acceptance as the key for the solution of the mystery of the *modus operandi* of the rise of terrestrial organisms."[1]

Protestants who indicted the theory of organic evolution on scientific grounds after 1875 repeated many of the same arguments that had been leveled against the theory throughout the nineteenth century. They continued to emphasize, for example, that not a single instance of the transmutation of one species into another had been observed in all human history. Nor, they argued, did the fossil record lend support to the theory of organic evolution. In spite of diligent efforts to uncover transitional, "intermediate" forms capable of bridging the gap between species, few had been found. The fossil record disclosed neither the "insensible gradations" integral to Darwin's theory of change nor the common ancestors joining the more major groups of animals. Moreover, the discovery of fossil series of closely aligned species did not in itself constitute support for the transmutation hypothesis, for many organisms that resembled each other were clearly not related by descent. Recognition of this fact led one religious thinker to submit that the series of horses pieced together by paleontologists no more warranted the inference that some had evolved from others than would the future discovery of bones of contemporary white men in areas once inhabited by Indians imply that the former group of individuals had descended from the latter.[2]

These writers acknowledged that a complete record of organic history did not exist and that it was therefore necessary to draw inferences from the fossils that remained. In their judgment, this did nothing to resolve the problems attending the transmutation hypothesis. If evolution were really an accurate account of the origin of species, some commentators submitted, some of "Nature's failures" would surely have been preserved in geological strata; yet none had been discovered. On the contrary, wrote one Methodist critic, "the whole drift of geological evidence, as pictured on the ancient strata, declares that species have ever sprung, by divine law, power, and act, into sudden and complete existence." Though varieties might well be "far more numerous than we expected," there was every reason to assume that "the complete record, perfectly understood," would indicate that "true species have nevertheless suddenly originated."[3]

Many American Protestant intellectuals continued to regard human evolution as a particularly egregious instance of the scientific insufficiency of the Darwinian hypothesis, and they often went to great lengths to ridicule the notion that the human species was simply "a developed Rhizopod." Robert Lewis Dabney, for example, suggested that "no one has taken a young ape and educated it into a man. When that is done, there will be a beginning in the demonstration of this hypothesis, and not until then." Dabney, who had participated in more intellectually weighty controversies with evolutionists, doubtless knew better, but his rhetoric illustrates the emotionally charged attitude that most Protestants brought to the issue of human origins.[4]

Even critics who, like Dabney, found the issue an occasion for venting their spleen rarely depended on emotional appeals alone to carry their case. Rather, most proponents of the doctrine of special creation sought to undermine the credibility of the transmutation hypothesis by focusing on what they regarded as the enormous gulf between human beings and other animals. Not only did they point to current differences between humans and other primates, but they also invoked the fossil evidence, which suggested that the gap had never been bridged. As in the period prior to 1875, however, these thinkers were especially impressed not by anatomical differences but by what they took to be humanity's radical superiority in the realms of intellect and morality. Reason, many contended, was a "*royal* endowment" rendering humanity "immeasurably exalted above the brute." A few were prepared to acknowledge that "the brutes can infer and reason, after a fashion, from instance to instance," but they typically coupled this admission with the insistence that "compendious thought, and thus . . . symbolical knowledge, is entirely beyond and cannot be conceived as developed out of the lower intelligence of the brutes." Human beings, on the other hand, could engage in abstract thought and translate such thought into language. Other Protestants noted that only human beings enjoyed intellectual and cultural progress. The Reverend Samuel Z. Beam, who published an article in the *Reformed Quarterly Review* in 1888 pronouncing "Evolution a Failure," defended his claim that humanity had no intellectual "affinity" with other animals by noting that "the [human] mind goes on advancing, every new generation taking up the truth where the last one left it, and going on to higher knowledge, and adding new discoveries for the benefit of subsequent generations."[5]

Many critics were equally convinced that humanity's possession of a moral sense constituted a refutation of the theory of organic evolution. "No ape," the Reverend John Moore insisted, "ever shows any measure of this faculty large enough to be discerned by the most powerful moral microscope." J. H. McIlvaine, pastor of Newark's High Street Presbyterian Church, alleged that evolutionists' account of the origin of

conscience left man's "consciousness of moral obligation" totally unex-
plained. He emphasized that "the admiration we feel for an act of noble
self-sacrifice, the promptings of great and heroic souls, our indignation
at injustice and iniquity—all these and other similar facts are inexplicable on the hypothesis of our derivation from ape-like creatures, in
which no such susceptibility has ever appeared." Far from explaining
the salient features of man's moral sense, McIlvaine concluded, proponents of evolutionary ethics were forced "to deny, or at least to ignore
them."[6]

Critics of Darwinism cited the objections against Darwin's emphasis
on natural selection that had been advanced by Fleeming Jenkin, Lord
Kelvin, Mivart, and others. The work of these critics led some Protestants to conclude that the "inability [of evolution by natural selection]
to perform the task assigned it is daily growing clearer and clearer." In
contrast to scientists, who characteristically regarded these arguments
merely as qualifications and refinements of the general theory of organic evolution, many of the theory's opponents within the American
Protestant community chose to believe that they demonstrated the untenability of the more general hypothesis.[7]

Protestant critics were convinced that the evidence of natural history
attested to the existence of limits on the extent to which species could
vary. Persuaded that the fixity of species was a divinely dictated "ne
plus ultra built squarely across the path which neither art nor force can
remove," Enoch Fitch Burr averred that "it has never been passed, save
in hypothesis." Proponents of this position were thus not surprised
that Darwin was unable to account for how descendants could have become infertile with the species from which they had diverged.[8]

The commitment of some Protestant intellectuals to the fixity of species was rooted in philosophical considerations as well as in an assessment of the data of natural history. The transmutation hypothesis,
these thinkers argued, was actually a "theory of the annihilation of species." Thomas Hill, a Unitarian clergyman who served as the president
of Harvard from 1862 to 1868, maintained that the "lawlessness" implicit in the idea that species had originated from the interplay of "random" variation with the concatenation of environmental forces was
"discordant with all of the analogies of science" and repugnant to common sense. It was also antithetical to the divine rationale informing creation. Hill reasoned that the organic world could serve as "a school-
house for minds" only if species remained basically constant. Accordingly, God had made the infertility of hybrids a law of nature and had
confined variations among individuals in a species "within strict lim-

its." A similar view on the fixity of species led a Hartford, Connecticut, clergyman to assert that the notion that one major organic group had evolved from another by means of genetic descent was as inconceivable as "changing a triangle into a square, by some evolutionary process."[9]

Attacks on the scientific validity of the transmutation hypothesis became more problematic in the face of the mass exodus of scientists to the evolutionists' camp. Although a few diehards maintained that the theory of organic evolution had failed "to obtain general currency" among scientists, most recognized that it was the "favorite scientific creed of the day" and redirected their efforts to discounting the significance of this fact. D. S. Gregory, an individual who served both as president and as professor of Christian philosophy and mental sciences at Lake Forest University (Illinois) while becoming prominent within conservative Protestant circles, emphasized that the status of a scientific theory could not be ascertained simply by "counting noses." The "unanimous vote" of lesser scientists against the verdict of Louis Agassiz, John William Dawson, Armand de Quatrefages, and other eminent savants who "agree in pronouncing the doctrine of evolution unscientific and false" counted for little. The Lutheran clergyman John A. Earnest of Rhinebeck, New York, agreed, expressing the hope that the opposition of distinguished scientists to the theory of organic evolution would fortify believers "when charlatans in science and timid brethren in the pulpit tell us we are in conflict with science . . . if perchance we have the courage to say that we prefer the cosmogony of Moses to that of Evolution."[10]

Nevertheless, during the last quarter of the nineteenth century, the roster of scientists opposed to the transmutation hypothesis steadily dwindled in both number and stature. Critics employed several tactics to counter this trend. One was to point to the division over evolution within the scientific community that remained and to insist that the persistence of disagreement about a hypothesis as old as transmutation was itself sufficient to cast doubt on its merits. Another was to compensate for the dearth of scientific opposition by citing, with little regard for chronology or alterations in position, that opposition which had been expressed earlier in the century. Still another tactic was to emphasize that although Darwinism "must stand or fall by the test of the facts of science," the ability to decide that question was not limited to scientists. Critics could hardly deny that scientists commanded special knowledge, but many rejected the idea that scientists were specially qualified to assess the merits of the generalizations and interpretations they based upon that knowledge. In this vein, J. H. McIlvaine insisted that nonscientists were "often quite as good judges of the nature, validity and force of their [scientists'] proofs, and of the soundness of their reasonings, as they themselves can possibly be. For logic is one and the same thing in all the departments of human thought and life."[11]

One of the clearest affirmations of this populist conception of validation as it applied to the transmutation hypothesis was presented by the eminent attorney George Ticknor Curtis. In *Creation or Evolution?* (1887), Curtis put his extensive experience in constructing courtroom briefs and his proven flair for writing appealing prose in the service of opposition to the evolutionary hypothesis. Curtis held that the proper judges of the validity of that hypothesis were not simply scientists but "the whole intelligent part of mankind." It was "not by the numbers of those who propound or accept it, or by any amount of mere authority," that the theory was to be evaluated, "but by the soundness of the reasoning by which its professors support it." Employing this standard, he concluded that "the whole doctrine of the development of distinct species out of other species makes demands upon our credulity which are irreconcilable with the principles of belief by which we regulate, or ought to regulate, our acceptance of any new matter of belief."[12]

Many critics, convinced that the conversion of scientists to the hypothesis had been precipitate, were unsympathetic to many of the considerations that prompted scientists to embrace the theory of organic evolution. McIlvaine, for example, cautioned his readers that the fact that the theory could account for a wealth of ostensibly disparate data was insufficient to establish its validity. During the course of history many erroneous hypotheses had satisfied that criterion. It was unreasonable, he urged, to endorse the transmutation hypothesis, with its "unsolved difficulties," when "another and totally different hypothesis, namely that of the distinct and independent creation of species," better accounted for the phenomena of natural history.[13]

Nor were critics of the theory of organic evolution inclined to assume, like most scientists and many nonscientists, that it was necessary to invoke natural, or "secondary," agencies in order to lay claim to a valid explanation of natural phenomena. On the contrary, they deplored what they regarded as "the excessive tendency of modern science to resolve everything into the operation of general laws, or into what we call secondary causes." That God occasionally intervened in the natural world no more restricted the scope of scientific endeavor than did the use of human intelligence and will. Even Darwin had presupposed an initial "special" creation; to embrace transmutation as a "working hypothesis" simply because it enabled scientists to describe a wider range of phenomena in naturalistic terms suggested only that "anything is more credible to the Darwinist, than that God, after one act of immediate creation, will ever repeat it." Such "parsimony" was a baseless metaphysical presumption, not a legitimate scientific principle. In reality, critics asserted, it was just as reasonable to believe that immediate creation occurred periodically as to assume that it had happened only once. John P. Gulliver, one of the more theologically conservative members of Andover Theological Seminary in the late nineteenth century, expressed the view of many of Darwin's opponents within the American Protestant community when in 1884 he confessed his inability to understand "what important gain to science, or to thought, it is, to go beyond the evidence of facts in the affirmation of natural causes."[14]

In truth, Protestants who cited scientific objections to the transmutation hypothesis were at least as strongly influenced by extra-empirical considerations as evolutionists. Both their standards of proof and their defense of the acceptability of supernaturalism as a mode of explanation were strongly informed by assumptions concerning the role of God in the natural world that had become deeply embedded in the orthodox Christian world view. But many Protestant critics could not— or would not—discern this and flatly denied the relevance of religious considerations to their opposition to transmutation.[15]

Still, attacks on the scientific credentials of the transmutation hypothesis played a less central role in the Protestant assault on the hypothesis after 1875. In part, this was because the scientific community's endorsement of the theory of organic evolution significantly altered the perspective from which such arguments were evaluated. For all the bravado some religionists displayed in denigrating the authority of scientific opinion, the American Protestant intellectual community had traditionally relied quite heavily on it. Prior to 1875, most of the arguments that the clergy and theologians employed to show that the theory was groundless had been advanced by scientists as well; they were thus "scientific" arguments in every sense of the word. Not only did they seem to constitute an "objective" and theologically neutral line of attack against the theory of organic evolution, but they also served to attest to a close alliance between Christianity and science. Once natural historians themselves embraced the theory of organic evolution, however, it required a confidence—or an audacity—that most nonscientists lacked to advance objections to it based on analysis of data relating to the natural world. Moreover, such objections may well have painfully reminded the clergy and theologians that the ideological gap between themselves and the scientific community was widening. The abandonment of "scientific" modes of argumentation was also doubtless at least partly a manifestation of disenchantment with science as a mode of interpreting phenomena. It is impossible to be very precise about the level of such disenchantment or to specify the number of people affected. But if an eminent scientist like Frederick A. P. Barnard could be sufficiently dismayed by the irreligious tenor of the theory of organic evolution to lament that "if this, after all, is the best that science can give me, give me then, I pray, no more science," it is not unreasonable to assume that other Protestants with less of a stake in scientific inquiry found the conversion of scientists to the transmutation hypothesis an occasion to ignore the opinions of scientists—and with them the data of science itself. Religionists who remained intimately involved in the dialogue over the scientific merits of the hypothesis tended to be those who were most inclined to accept the verdict of scientists.[16]

Consequently, only a small minority of Protestant intellectuals who opposed Darwinism did so primarily on the basis of arguments drawn from natural history. These holdouts characteristically refused to consider at length the theological implications of the theory until it had been "undeniably established." In contrast to this group, most American religious intellectuals believed that the conversion of a large contingent of scientists to the theory required Christians to ponder more seriously its religious implications. On the basis of their analysis, many Protestants concluded that their initial suspicions had been entirely warranted, their worse suspicions justified. In principle, these thinkers were willing to acknowledge that the theory of organic evolution could not be rejected simply "on account of any consequences to faith or morals which its reception involves." But they emphasized that because "of those consequences, terrible in their significance, we cannot wisely concede that it is true until it brings to its support that which is now lacking—overwhelming proof." And because they still believed that the truths of nature accorded with the truths of Christianity, they were confident that such proof would never be forthcoming. Insofar as they employed "scientific" arguments against Darwinism at all, most did so to reinforce a position they had chosen on theological grounds. In the remainder of this chapter the most contentious points at issue between the theory of organic evolution and conventional formulations of Christian doctrine will be surveyed.[17]

In 1882, Yale's president, Noah Porter, reported that his survey of the cultural landscape had convinced him that "multitudes are drifting into the half-formed conviction that the reasons for faith seem one after another to be dissipated by the advance of science and culture." In the late nineteenth century this assessment was widely shared, prompting an enormous body of literature dedicated to defending belief in the existence of God. Much of this literature was still predicated on the argument from design. Francis Patton, professor of the relations of philosophy and science to the Christian religion at Princeton Theological Seminary, expressed a common conviction when he wrote that "religious life would experience a very serious shock if it were to be shown that the teleological argument is worthless."[18]

From this perspective, some Protestants argued that the Darwinian hypothesis, which challenged the assumption that adaptation was the work of a divine Designer, threatened the very foundation of the apologetic enterprise. Charles Hodge's son Archibald, himself a professor of theology at Princeton Seminary from 1878 until his death in 1886, concurred with his father in believing that in Darwin's theory "the universe and its order is referred to Chance, teleology is impossible, theism stripped of its most effective evidence." Francis Bowen, continuing the campaign against Darwinism he had initiated in 1860, maintained that Darwin's attempt to reduce speciation "to a blind mechanical process" was precisely "the pepper which made the dish palatable" to proponents of scientific naturalism such as T. H. Huxley. Benjamin Tefft, a Methodist clergyman who confessed to having been "for many a day captivated by Mr. Darwin's rhetoric," declared that Darwinism was "a scheme essentially atheistic." The Unitarian L. J. Livermore acknowledged that Darwin's theory did not preclude individuals from believing in God, but he observed that it "tears out the richest and most explicit pages in the theist's book of heavenly knowledge, [and] changes what to the eye of faith is the clearest and most edifying scripture into a hotchpotch of semi-arabesque scrawls."[19]

With the publication of the three-volume *Life and Letters of Charles Darwin* in 1887, apprehensions about the corrosive impact of the Darwinian hypothesis on theism seemed to receive dramatic confirmation. Prior to the appearance of this work, many Christians who condemned Darwinism as subversive to belief in God had acknowledged that Darwin himself paid at least lip service to theism. Darwin's letters and autobiographical reflections, however, suggested that his exclusion of supernatural design from the organic world had ultimately destroyed his own religious convictions. Reviewing Darwin's *Life and Letters*, Benjamin B. Warfield, an erudite controversialist serving as Archibald Hodge's successor as professor of theology at Princeton, noted that as

Darwin had worked out the details of his theory, "God became an increasingly unnecessary and therefore an increasingly incredible hypothecation." The inference, Warfield believed, was clear: Darwin's "doctrine of evolution directly expelled his Christian belief." Warfield, who had briefly embraced Darwinism and flirted with the idea of doing graduate work in science, conceded that atheism did not necessarily follow from acceptance of the transmutation hypothesis, but he understandably viewed the desiccation of Darwin's religious beliefs as an ominous portent. The contrast between the potential for spiritual disaster residing in the transmutation hypothesis and the apologetic virtues of the traditional argument from design could hardly have been more vivid.[20]

Nor did Darwin's experience seem unique. A Methodist critic declared that "there is probably not an intelligent atheist in Christendom who does not claim Darwinism as the clincher to his argument." In 1893 W. J. Wright, a professor of metaphysics at Westminster College in Missouri, reported that the theory of organic evolution had undermined many individuals' belief in the existence of God. In contrast, he asserted, the period prior to publication of the *Origin of Species* had been one in which scientific discussion of the organic world "seemed always on the side of design and contrivance" and "an atheistic view of nature seemed impossible."[21]

Much, though certainly not all, of this concern about the damaging effect of the transmutation hypothesis on arguments for the existence of God was directed specifically against the Darwinian form of the hypothesis. Many of the other objections to the theory of organic evolution, however, were not limited to conceptions of it that emphasized the role of natural selection in the evolutionary process. In the judgment of many Protestant thinkers during the last quarter of the nineteenth century, the implications of the general theory of organic evolution were antithetical to "the whole system of truth, for the revelation of which the Scriptures were given to men." John Earnest, for example, submitted that the biblical and evolutionary accounts of natural history "have not only nothing in common, but are so absolutely antagonistic to, and destructive of, each other, that they cannot occupy one mind at the same time." Critics who chose to elaborate on this position maintained that the theory of organic evolution undermined the biblical conception of supernatural intervention in the natural order, challenged the biblical conception of the drama of salvation, and contravened the ethical principles embedded in the Christian Gospel.[22]

God's concern for His creation was central to the world view embodied in the Scriptures. Many of the doctrines attesting to that concern—the Incarnation and Resurrection, the efficacy of prayer, miracles, and the divine inspiration of the biblical authors—depended on God's having periodically intervened in the natural order in ways that defied natural law. The Methodist clergyman Jacob Todd of Philadelphia observed that if the universe disclosed nothing more than "a God whose hands are tied by law, . . . religion would only be an empty name." The Episcopal clergyman J. MacBride Sterrett was similarly blunt: "the supernatural is at the beginning, middle, and is to be at the close of the Christian dispensation. Christianity is supernatural—from above nature, or it is nothing."[23]

Belief that God had periodically intervened in the world did not logically entail the doctrine of special creation. There were, however, cultural pressures to relate the two. In an era in which American Protestant intellectuals felt besieged by opponents of supernaturalism, the doctrine of the special divine creation of individual species appeared to be a crucial source of "objective" evidence that God actively and personally intervened in the world. As such, it served to reinforce the credibility of other alleged instances of providential intervention. The Baptist clergyman George W. Samson gave voice to a common assumption when he observed in 1877 that "a Divine interposition to give such a revelation as man needs, is certainly in the line of those interpositions which have given origin to new species of plants and animals."[24]

Notwithstanding their insistence that natural laws simply described the way God chose to operate the universe, in practice many Protestant thinkers tended to regard natural agencies as an alternative to divine activity. This interpretation was predicated at least in part on an interpretation of causal agency that had become increasingly dominant in the Protestant community during the first three quarters of the nineteenth century. By 1860 most religious thinkers assumed that natural laws were intelligible descriptions of the orderly operation of "secondary" agencies. The behavior of these agencies was determined by the properties the Creator had imposed on matter. To be sure, Protestant intellectuals emphasized that matter was incapable of self-determination. They also stressed that while science could describe *how* matter behaved, it could not really explain *why* it acted as it did. Nevertheless, although they continued to affirm that the operation of secondary agencies was governed by divine purpose and that finite entities were constantly preserved "in being and vigour" by divine *concursus*, they assumed that natural phenomena possessed real power. Leonard Woods, Andover's Abbot Professor of Theology, gave expression to the prevailing view when he reasoned that just "because there is only one *supreme* cause it does by no means follow that there are no subordinate causes." On the contrary, he contended, God had established "many subordinate causes, . . . all having a measure of efficiency." A similar position prompted Charles Hodge to maintain that in the ordinary course of affairs, "the agency of God neither supersedes, nor in any way interferes with the efficiency of secondary causes." If finite entities could not act independently of God, they were nevertheless empowered to act. This view, which was partly a reflection of scientists' own interpretation of natural phenomena and partly the manifestation of a reaction against pantheism, implied that there was a sharp distinction between the natural and the supernatural.[25]

From this dualistic perspective, each extension of the realm of secondary cause further reduced the number of periodic supernatural interpositions in nature that most strongly attested to the existence of an active and personal Creator. To many proponents of that conception of the Deity, it seemed all too clear that "in proportion as order becomes complete, and the forces through which it is secured [become] fundamental, the mass of men cease to be greatly impressed by it." For this reason, many Protestants sought to adduce as much evidence as they could for supernatural intervention in the natural world. Efforts to resolve all cosmic phenomena into chains of natural causes and effects conjured up in their minds the specter of deism and smacked of a none too subtle assault on the concept of providential activity. The Congregational clergyman John Todd of New Haven, Connecticut, thus warned that "the representation that 'God sustains all relations through law,' takes away from us that immediate personal communion with God, which is the believer's greatest comfort."[26]

With each advance of science in bringing phenomena within the domain of natural law, the doctrine of special creation acquired greater apologetic significance. It is therefore not surprising that many Protestants expressed concern that the theory of organic evolution seriously undermined the credibility of the biblical God Who acted in nature and history. Not only did it remove the origin of species from the realm of immediate supernatural activity, but it also cast doubt on other alleged instances of "direct divine intervention" that were even more central to Christianity. A Methodist critic, for example, wondered "with what consistency can a reasoner scout the idea of 'special creation' and then tamely accept a 'special' incarnation and a 'special' resurrection of the Incarnate?" W. J. Wright observed that "if special creation is inadmissable, much more so, in consistency, are the miracles of Christ. But the proof of Christianity is suspended upon his moral and physical miracles, and he is himself the greatest of miracles."[27]

Noting that a theory that relied on "the necessary operation of laws or forces inherent in things themselves" was antithetical to belief in divine Providence, many Protestants who opposed the theory of organic evolution during the last quarter of the nineteenth century arraigned it as a dangerous example of "materialistic science." Benjamin Tefft, for example, charged that Darwin's "sole business" lay in attempting to demonstrate that new species could have arisen by means of "material principles . . . without the supposed intervention of a God." Other thinkers continued to make the familiar—and increasingly inaccurate—observation that the most conspicuous and tenacious support the transmutation hypothesis had received came from individuals who hailed it as a naturalistic alternative to supernatural creation.[28]

Most religious thinkers who were hostile to Darwin's work assumed that it was based on the same philosophical animus as Herbert Spencer's. Although some opponents of the transmutation hypothesis mistakenly credited Darwin with providing Spencer with his chief inspiration and source of ideas, and others no less erroneously regarded Darwin as a Spencerian who had chosen to focus his energies on establishing the scientific validity of biological evolution, most of them appear to have been aware that Darwin's conception of evolution differed from that of Spencer. Most also believed, however, that Darwin and Spencer shared a hostility to the supernatural, and for them this common ground was far more important than any difference that might have separated them. The intimate association of evolution and naturalism in the minds of many Protestant thinkers prompted Jesse B. Thomas, the nationally renowned pastor of Brooklyn's First Baptist Church of Pierrepont Street, to report in 1884 that the term "evolution" itself, "as popularly defined, implies the automatic working out of results through solely natural forces, without extraneous interferences."[29]

For Christians, of course, the most theologically pertinent instances of supernatural intervention lay not in the natural world but in God's interactions with human beings. And for them, the fundamental record of those interactions was contained in the Bible. In the judgment of many Protestants, challenges that the transmutation hypothesis posed to the veracity of the biblical narrative constituted its most dangerous and alarming feature.

No issue appeared to demonstrate more dramatically the conflict that existed between the theory of organic evolution and the Scriptures than the origin of humanity. Few nineteenth-century American Protestant intellectuals insisted upon "days" of creation that were only twenty-four hours long or an age of the earth that was less than six thousand years. On the other hand, during the last quarter of the nineteenth century, a sizable number of Protestant thinkers held that "any theory which assumes that man was not created by a special act of God, having no Cause, in the scientific sense of the term, . . . and assumes that woman was not *subsequently* created by a similar act, cannot be reconciled with the Bible." The theory of organic evolution was predicated on the assumption that the human species was the product of the same natural processes that accounted for the appearance of other plants and animals. The inference was thus clear: "Evolutionism and the scriptural account of the origin of man are irreconcilable." This was a serious charge indeed. Whereas natural historians characteristically assumed that the descent of the human species from other animals was a corollary of the theory of organic evolution, many Protestant intellectuals, convinced that "the Bible account of the creation of man is the basis of the whole Christian system of faith," regarded it as a radical threat to the validity of Christian anthropology.[30]

The central issue at stake in the controversy over human origins was the doctrine that God had created human beings in His image. This doctrine served as the foundation for a number of convictions that were central to the Christian's understanding of reality. One of the most important of these was that the attributes of human personality were clues to comprehending the nature of God. Indeed, Mark Hopkins, the eminent professor of moral philosophy at Williams College, insisted that "all true conceptions of God, so far as man is in his image, must be anthropomorphic." The vigorous assault that Herbert Spencer and other prominent thinkers were making on the legitimacy of ascribing anthropomorphic attributes to God only highlighted the importance of affirming that human beings shared "the same generic nature" as God.[31]

The doctrine that the human species had been created in the image of God could also be interpreted to suggest an alternative, equally compelling formulation of the relationship between God and humanity. D. D. Wheedon, the editor of the *Methodist Review*, articulated this formulation when he asserted that Christian anthropology affirmed "not so much that God is anthropomorphic, as that man is *theomorphic*." This perspective grounded the belief that God sustained a special redemptive relationship with the human species. This belief, in turn, provided a basis for the claim that each individual was an "heir of immortality" and a rationale for assuming that natural history should be interpreted anthropocentrically, as an unfolding drama in which the divine-human encounter held center stage.[32]

To some Protestant intellectuals, it was obvious that the doctrine that human beings had been created in God's image was irreconcilable with the claim that they were "but one remove above the brute." These thinkers believed that the choice confronting individuals concerned about the origin of the human species was clear: "whether man was evolved out of an ape by natural law, or was created by immediate divine agency, in 'the image of God.' " This way of posing the issue was largely a function of their assumption that the most decisive evidence that humanity was *"kindred with God"* was its *"kingship over nature."* The fact that human beings possessed unique mental and moral attributes, they believed, was what set them "in a rank above all other creatures on this globe." The theory of organic evolution undermined this belief by blurring the distinctions between the human species and other animals and by implying that the human species was simply the most recent "link in a chain of organic being."[33]

Critics drew inferences from the evolutionary conception of human descent that were as alarming as they were predictable. A Unitarian commentator held that the transmutation hypothesis implied that it was not "allowable for him [man] to ascribe the acquired attributes of his nature to Deity." Another critic, reminding his readers that "the hope of immortality has always rested on the theory that there was an infinite gulf between the nature of man and that of the lower animals," observed that the hypothesis threw a "great pall" over human aspirations for eternal life. Other Protestant thinkers warned that the hypothesis actually constituted an implicit challenge to the veracity of human knowledge itself. Darwin's *Life and Letters* furnished many of these thinkers with grounds for apprehension. Readers of that work discovered that Darwin was beset by the "horrid doubt" that "the convictions of man's mind, which has been developed from the mind of lower animals, are of any value or at all trustworthy." Darwin brought himself—and doubtless many of his readers—up short by asking, "Would any one trust in the convictions of a monkey's mind, if there are any convictions in such a mind?" This passage prompted Benjamin B. Warfield to suggest that the "strong acid" of such reasoning, if consistently applied, would corrode faith in the veracity of all human convictions. John William Dawson agreed, noting that Darwin's position exemplified the "depth of unscientific and unspiritual degeneration, into which the mind may be thrown by the excessive pursuit of evolutionary ideas."[34]

One of the critics who proved most relentless in calling his readers' attention to the dangerous epistemological implications of the transmutation hypothesis was Noah Porter. Porter's attitude toward the evolutionary hypothesis defies easy classification. By profession, he was an enthusiastic partisan of scientific investigation. Indeed, he once suggested in a sermon at the Yale chapel that "science, rightly considered, is as much a necessity in the Kingdom of God as is the so-called Christian church." But Porter was not willing to accept every idea simply because it was put forward in the name of science, and he made it clear that evolution was a concept that merited careful scrutiny. Although he grudgingly endorsed a narrowly circumscribed, "scientific" version of organic evolution, he devoted most of the considerable attention he gave to the evolutionary hypothesis to emphasizing how philosophically lethal it could be when accepted in its popular forms.[35]

As late as 1886 Porter was confidently proclaiming that "Darwin's doctrine is perfectly consistent with theism." He defended this view on the grounds that "Darwin himself asserted his belief in an intelligent Creator." His reading of Darwin's *Life and Letters*, however, apparently impelled him to change his mind. In his 1888 review of that work he upbraided Darwin's position as a "theory of atheistic evolution." Porter did not need Darwin's reflections, however, to convince him that "intellectual self-reliance and trustworthiness fail to be provided for by the theory of evolution." In 1879 he warned his readers that if, as evolutionists commonly implied, the human mind were simply a "temporary development" of natural forces, this would destroy the basis for confidence in human thought. This would have the effect of undermining science itself. Noting that scientific analysis itself was the fruit of human thought, he acidly observed that "if we do not assert for man and the thinking of man its appropriate authority, then science itself should bow off the stage."[36]

A small number of Protestants perceived in the evolutionary hypothesis another, no less fundamental, threat to the exalted status of humanity. These thinkers charged that the theory that the human mind had evolved from other, "lower" animals was based on the materialistic assumption that "spirit is a mechanical function of matter." Actually, although Darwin had long envisioned the mind in materialistic terms, he was reluctant to commit himself publicly to this position, and in the *Descent of Man* he maintained that efforts to discern the origin of "mental powers" were "hopeless." Notwithstanding such reticence, a few

Protestants insisted that a materialistic view of the human mind was part of the "essential logic" of the theory of organic evolution; others noted that it was entirely congruent with the philosophical thrust of the theory. But on one point, all could agree: the doctrine that human beings had been created in God's image could not be reconciled with a materialistic conception of mind. In large measure, what drove these thinkers to connect a materialistic conception of mind with the transmutation hypothesis was a conviction that the philosophical animus behind evolution was a determined hostility to the idea of fundamental ontological discontinuities within nature. This animus, which could be clearly perceived in the work of Herbert Spencer and T. H. Huxley, was profoundly uncongenial to the dualistic view of the world embedded within the fabric of liberal and evangelical theology alike. To most American Protestant intellectuals, a radical distinction between mind and matter was central to a correct understanding of reality. The notion that the elements of consciousness were nothing more than "attributes or concomitants of certain well-balanced, organized, complex physical conditions" not only implied that human intellectual and moral conceptions were products of a finite, mortal structure but also buttressed belief in "a fatalism more unbending than Grecian Philosophy ever dreamed of." Accordingly, Protestants who believed that there was an intimate connection between the concept of human evolution and a naturalistic conception of psychology inevitably found the former idea utterly unacceptable.[37]

Humanity's kinship with God was the most fundamental element of Christian anthropology that appeared to be threatened by the evolutionary conception of the descent of the human species, but it was not the only one. Many Protestants also failed to see how the scriptural affirmation of "the original·righteousness of our first parents, their fall and that of their posterity through a single act of disobedience, and the subsequent provisions of the economy of grace in which Adam's representative character is presupposed, can be accounted for except by believing in the special creation of Adam and Eve." By the last quarter of the nineteenth century, members of the American Protestant intellectual community differed sharply in their interpretation of the meaning and implications of the biblical story of Adam's act of disobedience and subsequent "Fall." Nevertheless, many of them could agree that the scriptural account of early human history was the linchpin of a proper understanding of the introduction of sin in the world, its transmission from one generation to another, and the need for the divine grace they believed was incarnate in Jesus. These thinkers were not inclined to look favorably upon any theory that regarded the human being as "an improved ape, rather than a fallen spirit."[38]

Actually, Darwin himself was not unsympathetic to the idea of human degeneration. Noting that human progress was "no inevitable rule," he had acknowledged in his *Descent of Man* that "many nations, no doubt, have fallen away in civilisation, and some may have lapsed into utter barbarism." He suggested, too, that the appearance of reason in humanity was actually accompanied by a decline in virtue. The "semi-human progenitors" of the human species, Darwin asserted, "would not have practiced infanticide or polyandry; for the instincts of the lower animals are never so perverted as to lead them regularly to destroy their own offspring or to be quite devoid of jealousy." On the other hand, the theory of organic evolution was irreconcilable with the view of orthodox Protestants that the entire human species had suffered a wholesale "degradation" in response to the single sinful act of an individual. Darwin thus affirmed that "progress has been much more general than retrogression." Moreover, his contention that "man has risen, though by slow and interrupted steps, from a lowly condition to the highest standard as yet attained by him in knowledge, morals and religion" was impossible to square with the notion that prior to the Fall, humanity had enjoyed a special, untarnished intimacy with the Creator. It is little wonder, therefore, that many Protestant intellectuals assumed that acceptance of human evolution would "necessitate giving up the doctrine of the fall."[39]

One of the most incisive analyses of the theological implications of the scenario of human development implied in the transmutation hypothesis was presented by John T. Duffield, an ordained Presbyterian clergyman who had been elected professor of mathematics at the College of New Jersey in 1854 and professor of mechanics and mathematics in 1862. A gifted and dedicated teacher, Duffield published little prior to 1878, when his article "Evolutionism, Respecting Man and the Bible" appeared in the *Princeton Review*. Duffield averred that he had little sympathy with individuals who sought to accentuate differences between scientists and theologians. He also believed, however, that it was imperative that Christians consider whether *"evolutionism, as it respects man,"* comported with the scriptural exposition of the scheme of redemption.[40]

Duffield was convinced that it did not. Even "in the least objectionable form in which it can be stated," the transmutation hypothesis was "irreconcilable with what the Scriptures teach as to man's original and present spiritual condition." Duffield noted that the Bible taught that as a result of Adam's sin, "the moral history of the race, *apart from supernatural influence*, has been constantly and only a retrogression, and not a progression, a descent and not an ascent." By contrast, the evolutionary model of human development implied that "whatever might be called *sinful* in man's nature or conduct, whether when in his original lowest estate, or at any subsequent stage of his ascent, was but a necessary incident to a condition of progressive and hence incomplete, development." The effect of this vision, he observed, was to make sin "*normal*—the legitimate result of the law of his being." By thus implying that supernatural redemption was wholly unnecessary, the theory contradicted the "central idea of the religion of the Bible."[41]

A more complex, though no less censorious, assessment of the way in which the theory of organic evolution related to the doctrine of the Fall appeared in the *American Church Review* in 1881. The author of the piece, F. D. Hoskins, was not a well-known figure within Episcopal circles, but he was representative of many Protestants in citing the Fall as one of those "facts" that were "of everlasting meaning and necessity" to Christians. Hoskins insisted that the historicity of the Fall was inconsistent with Darwinism. In support of this contention, he proceeded from the unwarranted but commonly held assumption that the theory of organic evolution was irreconcilable with "notable instances of decline and degeneration" in organisms. He then reasoned that if, as the Bible suggested, a "Fall" had occurred in which "man exchanged a good environment, the Garden of Eden, for a bad environment, the world," humanity should have become extinct. This had obviously not happened. Hence, if Darwinism were correct, "either the Fall did not take place, or if it did happen and had any ethical significance, that significance has been exaggerated in the old Hebrew myth." To the Christian, Hoskins believed, neither of these alternatives was theologically acceptable.[42]

Proponents of the historicity of the Fall brought forward several arguments designed to show that the data of natural history were inconsistent with the idea that the human species had originated as a "savage" not much different from the ape. Some held that there was "no credible account of savages evolving a civilization." In contrast to many proponents of the transmutation hypothesis, who regarded the presence of "primitive" tribes in their own day as living monuments to the stages of social evolution, a number of its critics concurred with John William Dawson, who suggested that contemporary "savages" were "more likely to be degraded races, in 'the eddy and backwater of humanity,' than examples of the sources from which it flowed." Hoskins concurred, insisting that "competent philologists" had discovered "signs of the primitive character of the simple worship of *one* God; and that polytheism was the confusion of this simple conception, and therefore a religious degradation." "Degenerationism" was also embraced by Mark Hopkins, who held that the absence of cruelty to females, cannibalism, and numerous other practices of savage peoples among all other animals suggested that these peoples were in some ways "degraded below the brutes." Hopkins maintained that the most reasonable inference was that savages had not arisen from other animals but had instead been victims of "a development downwards."[43]

Proponents of degenerationism were more concerned with refuting the evolutionary hopothesis than with establishing connections between savagery and the Fall. Several other arguments they advanced during the last quarter of the nineteenth century were more explicitly designed to establish the historicity of the Fall. John William Dawson, for example, held that the biblical narrative was entirely congruent with the evidence of natural history. In his *The Origin of the World* (1877), Dawson suggested that humanity had originated in an area populated by "a group of creatures adapted to contribute to his [man's] happiness, and having no tendency to injure or annoy." This area was Eden. Had it not been for man's "fall from innocence," Dawson surmised, this idyllic environment "would have gradually encroached on the surrounding wilderness," and the "happy and peaceful reign" of humanity would have "extended at least over all the temperate regions of the earth." The Fall altered the scenario; God now allowed the grimmer features of the wilderness to "invade his Eden." Other proponents of the historicity of the Fall appealed to evidence from cultural history in support of their position. Hoskins, for example, invoked references from widely disparate cultural traditions attesting to "a golden age, which mankind has lost," in opposition to what he regarded as the evolutionary paradigm of "slow, unbroken advance."[44]

That issues relating to humanity's encounter with the divine were central in the critical response of American Protestant thinkers to the transmutation hypothesis was also graphically illustrated in their discussion of its ethical implications. It is hardly surprising that this issue should have elicited a great deal of attention; ethics played a central role in most nineteenth-century Protestants' understanding of the Christian gospel. John Bascom, who had left his Williams College professorship in 1874 to become president of the University of Wisconsin largely because this move afforded him the opportunity to teach moral philosophy, expressed the view of many Christians when he declared in 1881 that "religion is not so much the foundation of morals, as morals the foundation of religion." Other thinkers believed, as Robert Lewis Dabney put it, that God's desire "to furnish a stage for the existence and action of reasonable moral beings" constituted His "true end" in creating the world.[45]

During the nineteenth century, the datum from which most Protestant thinkers in the United States proceeded in discussing moral philosophy was that human beings felt obligated to act in accordance with their conceptions of virtue. Although these thinkers found themselves confronted with a growing body of evidence suggesting that all human beings did not totally agree in their moral judgments, they remained convinced that the capacity all human beings possessed for moral judgment and a universal sense of duty implied the existence of a "law" of love that was to govern their relationships to each other and to God. In turn, the existence of this law, which Protestants believed had been clearly laid down in the Scriptures and could be confirmed by consulting the testimony of human consciousness, implied that the Creator of the world was also a Moral Governor. There was some disagreement among Protestant ethical theorists as to whether moral law was normative simply because the divine Lawgiver had prescribed it or whether He had prescribed it because it was intrinsically right, but most of them could agree that moral law was immutable, that it was the expression of the essential righteousness of God, that obedience to it was virtuous and disobedience was sinful, and that virtue would be rewarded and wicked conduct punished, either in this world or in the next. [46]

Charles Darwin forced ethical philosophers to grapple with a cluster of new considerations. His view of the origin and development of humanity's "moral sense" was predicated on the idea that morality was a form of adaptive behavior enabling some social groups to triumph over others. If he believed that the principle of the "golden rule" rather than either selfishness or pleasure "lies at the foundation of morality," he did so because he believed that it had proved useful in groups' struggle for survival, not because he assumed that the principle embodied the will of a divine Moral Governor. By placing the human moral sense within an evolutionary framework, he undercut the reasoning that supported belief in a divinely sanctioned moral law. Though he did not explicitly deny the existence of such law, it played no role in his discussion of the origins and substance of ethical principles. For Darwin, human moral standards derived from peoples' perceptions of "the general good or welfare of the community." He acknowledged that a few moral conceptions had been regarded as virtues and vices by virtually every culture, but he maintained that the presence of different conditions had generated widely different patterns of behavior. Just how different he believed these behavioral patterns could conceivably be was suggested by his statement that "if, for instance, to take an extreme case, men were reared under precisely the same conditions as hive-bees, there can hardly be a doubt that our unmarried females would, like the worker-bees, think it a sacred duty to kill their brothers, and mothers would strive to kill their fertile daughters; and no one would think of interfering."[47]

Of the numerous other expositions of moral theory that were based upon evolutionary postulates, the most well known in the United States was that of Herbert Spencer. Unlike Darwin, who was content simply to establish the continuity between the moral sense of human beings and the attributes of other animals, the more philosophically inclined Spencer aspired to show that ethical behavior was the capstone of an evolutionary process that was universal in scope. To this end, he published an article outlining his views on ethics in 1871. An extended discussion of his moral philosophy finally appeared in 1879 with the publication of his *Data of Ethics*.[48]

Spencer began by noting that in an increasingly secularized society, a growing number of people could no longer accept the idea that moral precepts were grounded on divine authority. This made it necessary to show that moral conceptions could be separated from religious dogma. Spencer endeavored to accomplish this task. Like Darwin, he believed that the roots of human moral conduct could be found in other animals. Unlike Darwin, however, he was not satisfied with describing how human moral conceptions had arisen; he was also committed to defining acceptable moral precepts. Essentially, his moral philosophy was a utilitarianism that employed evolutionary principles in its defense. Moral conceptions, he argued, were based not on the dictates of "a supernaturally-given conscience" but on the "accumulated experiences of Utility, gradually organized and inherited" during the course of many generations.[49]

Spencer assumed that, like all other behavior, moral conduct was adaptive activity. Because he believed that an organism's place within the evolutionary hierarchy was determined by the degree of success it enjoyed in adapting to its environment, he concluded that good conduct was "the relatively more evolved conduct." In developing this idea, he placed less emphasis than Darwin on the question of mere biological survival in the shaping of moral conceptions and argued that in those animals in which behavior was more highly evolved, good conduct included an extrabiological dimension involving the creation of "a surplus of agreeable feeling." The scope of ethics was therefore quite broad, encompassing "all conduct which furthers or hinders, in either direct or indirect ways, the welfare of self or others."[50]

Spencer believed that moral behavior was explicable in terms of a pleasure-pain calculus. Conduct, he wrote, was "good or bad according as their aggregate effects increase men's happiness or increase their misery." Spencer refused, however, to define pleasure and pain in a narrowly egoistic manner. Rather, he maintained that the struggle and competition that punctuated the lives of lower species had gradually given way during the course of evolution to activities in more complex organisms that were characterized by "co-operation and mutual aid." Though intense struggle among individuals had persisted during the early history of humanity, within civilized nations altruistic impulses had become dominant, and pleasurable moral activity had become identified with conduct that contributed to the welfare of the social group. Men and women relinquished "immediate and special good to gain distant and general good."[51]

From Spencer's perspective, the existence of a divinely created conscience was not a necessary condition of moral behavior. He conceded that social and religious sanctions and other forms of external coercion had led individuals to feel obligated to restrain themselves from acting immorally, but he speculated that the adaptation of the human species to the welfare of society would continue to improve in the future, and these restraints would no longer be necessary. The sense of obligation would ultimately simply disappear.[52]

In spite of the fact that Darwin and Spencer differed rather significantly in their approach to ethical questions, they both addressed such questions from a naturalistic perspective. Neither Spencer nor Darwin ascribed the human conscience to a transcendent source. Both held that moral impulses were not radically different in kind from attributes found in other animals. Both devoted a good deal of attention to the question of how moral conceptions had originated and developed, and they both envisioned human moral conduct as behavior enabling individuals to adapt to environmental imperatives and social pressures rather than as behavior that conformed to a moral law possessing universal and objective validity. In view of these similarities, it is not surprising that Protestant intellectuals rarely differentiated the ethical implications of Darwinism from those of Spencerianism in their discussion of "evolutionary ethics."

Many American religious thinkers charged that the evolutionary interpretation of human morality served to reduce the "great mystery of 'the voice of God in man' to a faculty of mere prudential wisdom." In justifying this allegation, one churchman observed that "conscience, if developed from the social instincts of inferior animals, must be regarded as having its genesis in selfishness, in the desire to secure the greatest good to the community, or in a regard to the highest happiness of the largest number, no other sources of moral principles existing in animals." To many members of the American Protestant intellectual community, which had long raised its voice in opposition to utilitarian accounts of ethical behavior, the association of evolutionary ethics with "pure utilitarianism" was sufficient to brand it as heretical.[53]

A number of Protestants who inveighed against the transmutationists' explanation of the origin of the human moral sense held that it tended to ignore the presence of a necessary component in any truly moral action: the sense of obligation. This motive for ethical behavior, they argued, was radically different in kind from other feelings. It therefore could not be derived from sympathy, calculations of pleasure and pain, or similar prudential considerations. This position prompted John Bascom to scorn the notion that conscience was "a transmitted susceptibility to public opinion." In reality, he maintained, individuals who were most captive to public opinion were precisely "those least ruled by conscience." Indeed, the most "notable victories of conscience have been over communities." For Bascom and numerous other critics, it seemed obvious that the presence of a sense of duty in humanity was explicable only if "there is in the very condition of our nature a law of righteousness, which we recognize with ever-growing clearness as of Him who gave us life and to whom our obedience is due." If evolutionists were successful in convincing people to abandon this view in favor of the notion that the sense of duty was actually nothing more than a sophisticated psychological elaboration of utilitarian considerations, morality would lose its imperative quality. "Morals cease to be authoritative," Francis Patton submitted, "when right and wrong resolve themselves into questions of utility, and are compared to the instincts of the retriever."[54]

The claim that moral precepts were simply adaptive instruments in the evolutionary process rather than divinely sanctioned principles also evoked criticism. To many Christians, this claim implied that the end of human conduct was the same as that for other organisms—physical well-being—and that virtue was simply behavior that was useful to that end. Notwithstanding Darwin's emphasis on the feeling of responsibility for the welfare of the group and Spencer's stress on the evolution of altruistic impulses, some Protestant thinkers expressed concern that acceptance of a theory that denied "the essential value of human nature as the image and partaker of the Divine" would lead to conduct significantly different from that enjoined by Christ. In justifying this position, these critics reminded their readers that the Christian defined both the source and the end of true virtue as "a state of consciousness variously and imperfectly described as peace with God, spiritual happiness, or blessedness, consciousness of Divine approval, and so on, but a state that has as its outward badge an independence of all physical conditions." Christian conduct, they noted, was not always conducive to survival or pleasure. The very essence of such conduct, personified in the lives of saints and the deaths of martyrs, was "disinterested, sincere, and self-sacrificing."[55]

Conversely, the kind of behavior enabling organisms to survive and prosper was not necessarily that which had been enjoined by Christ. One critic of "Scientific Ethics," noting that strength and brutality were frequently rewarded in the organic world, insisted that "it is a mistake to suppose that I am forbidden, by nature's laws, to take the life of a member of the race to which I happen to belong, if I choose to do so, any more than is the porpoise or the playful panther. Still harder is it to show that, by nature's laws, a man may not appropriate his neighbor's goods or indulge and gratify his appetite whenever and wherever he chooses to find the means." An examination of human history led the Lutheran clergyman C. A. Stork to espouse a similar point of view. "The most successful races," he submitted, "have not always been the most moral." Distilling in a few sentences many of the prejudices of his age, Stork remarked that the Chinese "are the most persistent of nations, the most successful in reducing the business of making the most of this world to an art; and yet they are not remarkable in the way of morals. So, too, the Jew has always been the toughest and the most unsocial of races. The Roman beat the world in success, but he was the incarnation of selfishness." Even when evolutionists advocated behavior initiated in the name of benefiting others, some critics asserted, they were not espousing Christian values; they were simply expressing approval of the idea of "living for one's self contemplated in a magnifying mirror."[56]

These critics were aware that neither Darwin nor Spencer had affirmed the ethical value of harsh struggle or endorsed conduct antithetical to that espoused by Christians, but they attributed this reticence to the personal character of these evolutionists rather than to the logical implications of their theories. A number of Protestants issued dire predictions about the moral consequences of basing behavior upon the postulates of evolutionary ethics. If survival ever became generally accepted as the appropriate standard of conduct, the Reformed clergyman John B. Drury warned, "the Christian virtues of self-denial, thoughtfulness for others, care for the infirm, the destitute and the aged; of meekness and patience, and forbearance, must, under such evolution be soon eliminated." Other critics suggested that by endorsing the position that the human being was little more than a brute, evolutionists encouraged him to act like one. Noah Porter, for example, warned that the masses would be "quick to receive a philosophy that teaches them that the right of the strongest is the only right which Nature sanctions, and trains them to infer that, therefore, capital and civilization and culture and religion are all outrages against the scientific view of man." Some Protestants, in fact, were inclined to attribute the violence, rapaciousness, and dishonesty that seemed all too prevalent in the American social and political environment to the appeal of the "Pig philosophy" that was evolutionary ethics. Without fixed moral principles that were established and sanctioned by a divine Moral Governor, society was a ship without an anchor. From this vantage point, a sizable number of Protestant thinkers concurred with the Boston Congregational clergyman Joseph T. Duryea when he declared in 1884 that "the theory of evolution cannot furnish a principle of ethics which either Scripture or the moral judgment of man will approve. . . . The ethics of the life and teachings of Jesus Christ are not the ethics of evolution."[57]

From 1875 to 1900, critics of the transmutation hypothesis within the American Protestant intellectual community succeeded in making a strong case for the irreconcilability of that hypothesis with the prevailing formulations of Christian theology. The work of these critics set the agenda for Protestants who sought to show that it was possible to embrace the theory of evolution without abandoning the Christian world view. The theological issues that elicited the most attention from opponents of the theory of organic evolution—the existence of God and His relationship to the world, the status of divine revelation, the origin, nature, and early history of the human species, and the validity of Christian ethics—were precisely those that figured most prominently in the work of Protestants who sought to sanctify the theory of evolution in the name of Christianity.

5

"Canst Thou by Searching Find Out God?": The Protestant Evolutionists' Defense of Theism

THE scientific community's endorsement of the theory of organic evolution prompted many American Protestant intellectuals to follow suit. Some of these thinkers had initially been quite critical of the theory. John B. Drury, a (Dutch) Reformed clergyman from Ghent, New York, exemplified the kind of conversion that many thinkers experienced during the late nineteenth century. As late as 1875, Drury rejected the Darwinian hypothesis as a threat to the fundamental tenets of Christian theology. By 1883, however, his views had changed. He continued to complain that the hypothesis had been exploited by opponents of Christianity for the purpose of undermining Christianity, and he termed the notion that only causes "capable of scientific analysis" were responsible for speciation an "unscientific and pure assumption." He conceded, however, that scientific investigation "renders it probable that things and beings are what they are by some process of gradual modification." Concurrently, he altered his position concerning the theological implications of the transmutation hypothesis; when recognized as "only an instrument or method of God, it ceases to be antagonistical to faith and religion."[1]

During the last quarter of the nineteenth century, most Protestant intellectuals in the United States who participated in the public dialogue about the religious implication of the transmutation hypothesis attempted to show that it was possible to endorse the theory of organic evolution while remaining faithful to the Christian world view. These thinkers differed, however, in both the theological perspectives they brought to this task and their interpretations of precisely what acceptance of the transmutation hypothesis entailed. Many Protestants regarded the hypothesis as grounds for initiating significant reformulations of Christian theology or as justification for revisions they favored on other grounds. Others were less enthusiastic about the idea of theological revision. The interpretation of the theory of descent by modification that some of these thinkers were willing to countenance was so limited, the range they accorded the evolutionary process so attenuated, that the primary justification for applying the appelation "Protestant evolutionist" to them is simply that they thought of themselves as adherents of the theory. Even these thinkers, however, found themselves altering their theology in significant ways in the wake of the controversy generated by the transmutation hypothesis.

Most American Protestant intellectuals assumed that scientists were the most reliable interpreters of natural history. These thinkers participated in the growing tendency of educated Americans to confer cultural authority on "experts." Like other nonscientists, they found themselves increasingly overwhelmed by vast quantities of data and sophisticated theoretical constructs. Though they were aware that even a casual examination of the history of science was sufficient to reveal the fallibility of scientists' judgments, most Protestant intellectuals nevertheless believed that people "incur greater danger of doing violence to truth by rejecting the general verdict of science than by devoutly accepting it." If they remained convinced that nature was a revelation of God, they were equally convinced that scientists were its most able expositors. Applying this reasoning to the history of life, they concluded that the scientific community's conversion to the transmutation hypothesis was sufficient reason for Christians to come to terms with the concept of organic evolution.[2]

These Protestants were also aware that they were living in an age in which many literate Americans honored modern science above other sources of wisdom. In such an age, they urged, it was imperative that Christians show that their faith could be reconciled with the scientific community's judgment. Any appearance of conflict between science and theology would be disastrous to the cause of religion. This concern received clear expression in the work of James Thompson Bixby. After receiving Harvard Divinity School's first B.D. degree in 1870, Bixby served as pastor in two Unitarian churches before becoming a professor of religious philosophy at the Unitarians' Meadville Theological School in 1878. From 1883 to 1885 he studied in Germany, receiving a doctorate from Leipzig. Upon his return to America, after briefly serving a church in Ann Arbor, Michigan, he became pastor of the Yonkers, New York, Unitarian Church, a position he held from 1887 until his retirement in 1903.[3]

Many of Bixby's numerous books and articles were devoted to mediating between science and religion. The crux of his position can be discerned in his *Similarities of Physical and Religious Knowledge*, a work he published in 1876. Noting that science enjoyed enormous prestige in modern culture, he concluded that "the future of Religion would be vastly more sure and prosperous if she could make science an ally instead of a rival." Two years later, Bixby reaffirmed this position, warning that "war between Christianity and science means injury to the cause of the former, even more than that of the latter."[4]

The numerous American Protestants who concurred with this view regarded the scientific community's acceptance of the theory of organic evolution as a clear signal that it was time for Christian apologists to do likewise. To these thinkers, attacks on the theory motivated by "mistaken religious zeal" posed a more serious threat to spiritual life than did the theory itself. Such attacks, they warned, would only give substance to the charges of individuals intent on equating religion with obscurantism and drive thinking people "over the precipice of infidelity." The proper task of the Christian thinker was not to rail against the transmutation hypothesis in the name of pre-Darwinian theological formulations but "to seek how to co-ordinate his essential faith" with it.[5]

That these thinkers assumed such a coordination possible was a measure of their confidence that valid theories concerning the natural world would accord with the insights of Christian theology. Noting that previous scientific advances had left Christian faith intact, they argued that there was no reason to assume that the theory of evolution would have a different effect. To them, it seemed clear that "whoever is afraid of science does not believe in God."[6]

These intellectuals were aware, however, that scientists' endorsement of the theory of organic evolution had generated doubts about the legitimacy of theism. Accordingly, in the last quarter of the nineteenth century, Protestant evolutionists devoted a good deal of attention to the task of showing that the transmutation hypothesis could be filled "full of God." They emphasized that although some transmutationists rejected the Christian world view, the fact that many scientists who endorsed that hypothesis had retained their belief in God demonstrated that there was no logical connection between commitment to an evolutionary interpretation of life and unbelief. Whereas the origin of species was a scientific question, the existence of God was a philosophical problem; and proficiency in science did not necessarily qualify an individual to render an accurate verdict on philosophical issues. From this perspective, they reasoned that in evaluating the work of Darwin, it was necessary "to distinguish between his personal belief and the views which logically follow from his scientific positions." The task confronting Christian apologists was to "rescue" the theory from "a wrong interpretation of it by men who have not been made infidels by evolution, but have illegitimately used evolution to support their infidelity."[7]

No aspect of this rescue effort was more fundamental than showing that the transmutation hypothesis was consistent with belief in God. During the last quarter of the nineteenth century the efforts of Asa Gray and James McCosh to reconcile the transmutation hypothesis with theism were frequently cited and even more frequently imitated by Protestants seeking to show that evolution could be viewed simply as the method God had employed in creating species. Most of these thinkers were not content, however, simply to "reconcile" the concept of transmutation with theism. They also sought to allay fears that the theory of organic evolution undermined the grounds for believing in God. It is simply not true, as a number of historians have suggested, that there was a wholesale abandonment of natural theology by Protestants who endorsed the evolutionary hypothesis. To the contrary, some Protestant evolutionists advanced arguments intended to demonstrate that an evolutionary interpretation of the origin of species was adequate only if placed within a theistic framework. Others attempted to develop additional arguments that would be just as effective as the traditional argument from design.[8]

Apologists commonly held that the very existence of the contingent, finite entities composing the cosmos afforded justification for postulating the existence of a divine First Cause. Most of them also believed, however, that this argument did little to establish the existence of the Christian Deity. After all, even many opponents of the Christian world view had conceded "the existence of something behind matter and force as its [sic] foundation." To most Protestant apologists, the real desideratum was an argument affording grounds for asserting that the First Cause was also intelligent and benevolent.[9]

Most of these thinkers continued to believe that the argument from design was best suited to perform this task. Several versions of this argument were popular during the late nineteenth century. Many Protestant evolutionists remained convinced that organisms presented "the most striking marks of design and contrivance." For these thinkers, the key to apologetics lay in showing that the course of organic evolution made sense only if it had proceeded "under the guidance of a superintending mind."[10]

Many of the Protestants who adopted this approach focused on the problem of variability. The assertion that what required explanation was not the *survival* but the *arrival* of the fit became a popular slogan among defenders of the faith. Many insisted that accidental variations arising by "the method of trial and error in all directions" could not accomplish the task "of steadily conducting life to higher variations and more perfect organization." It was far more reasonable, they argued, to believe that the course of organic evolution was governed by "a directing mind."[11]

In defending this position, which Asa Gray had been espousing since 1860, apologists made a point of emphasizing the criticisms of Darwin's theory of natural selection. Although they credited Darwin with having placed the theory of organic evolution on a firm foundation, and although they characteristically used the term "Darwinism" in referring to that theory, many of them pointed out that most scientists themselves were convinced that variability was less "random" and that natural selection played a more subordinate role in the evolutionary process than Darwin had originally suggested. Some noted, too, that even Darwin eventually conceded that his original formulation of the evolutionary hypothesis required revisions. Of central importance in this regard, they believed, was his admission that species tended "to vary in the same manner." Some commentators, dismissing Darwin's assertion that this tendency would be attributed to natural causes, reasoned that such "concessions rob Darwinism of its sting."[12]

A number of historians have noted that American Protestant thinkers characteristically repudiated "orthodox" Darwinism, and they have attributed their opposition to theological considerations. It is certainly true that Darwin's particular account of the mechanics of evolution was uncongenial to the apologetic requirements and doctrinal commitments of most Protestant intellectuals. To assume, however, that Protestants who rejected the Darwinian interpretation of evolution in favor of alternative evolutionary models did so for no other reason than "the basic lack of consonance between Darwinism and their theology" is to overlook the fact that the preponderance of opinion among scientists themselves during the late nineteenth century was opposed to the notion that Charles Darwin had presented a sufficient explanation of the evolutionary process. The same respect for the expertise of scientists that led Protestant evolutionists to endorse the transmutation hypothesis also seemed to justify their emphasis on the inadequacy of Darwin's evolutionary mechanism. Even Protestants who opposed the Darwinian model of evolution for theological reasons could find in the scientific community's discussion ample justification for subscribing to the theory of organic evolution while resisting Darwin's explanation of how transmutation had occurred. The arguments that apologists constructed on the basis of modified versions of the transmutation hypothesis may or may not have been philosophically cogent, but they were basically in accordance with patterns of evolutionary thought accepted by the nineteenth-century scientific community. Indeed, it would be closer to the truth to suggest that Protestants who accorded random variation and natural selection the predominant creative role in transmutation did not understand the prevailing temper of evolutionary science in the late nineteenth century.[13]

Apologists who grappled with the theological implications of natural selection characteristically denied that it constituted an adequate explanatory substitute for God. Noting that the term referred not to an entity but simply to a "generalized expression for the processes and the results of the whole interplay of living things on the earth with their inorganic surroundings and with each other," they maintained that only a divine "coördinating power" could account for the concatenation of forces and events giving rise to "the infinite variety of organic adaptations" that had made their appearance during the course of natural history. Andrew Preston Peabody was only one of numerous Protestant evolutionists who argued that "the very idea that blind, automatic nature, without a controlling will, could have blundered through these myriads of transformations with any show of success or regularity, bears absurdity on its face." To Protestants who held this view, natural selection was only a phrase describing the method by which the Deity had populated the world with organisms adapted to the conditions of their existence.[14]

No feature of the history of life appeared to supply more compelling grounds for retaining a teleological interpretation of the world than the direction of the evolutionary process. J. Lewis Diman, a Congregational clergyman who in 1864 accepted the chair of history and political economy at Brown University, observed in his 1880 Lowell lectures in Boston that "what strikes us most forcibly in the natural world is not simply the fact of development, but the fact that this development has been progressive, and that it proceeds in accordance with an orderly method, a method which results in the constant formation of more highly organized species." Noting that natural selection involved the convergence of many disparate and constantly changing environmental factors, Diman insisted that it was inconceivable that the "long series of favorable conditions" making progressive evolution possible was the product of "the blind working of mechanical forces."[15]

The "progressionist" interpretation of the history of life was consonant with the long-held belief of natural historians that a general advance in organic forms had occurred. Darwin's own view of the relationship between evolution and progress was equivocal. Adaptation rather than progression was the key to his view of evolution, and he professed to being unable to assign a clear meaning to the terms "high" and "low" in discussing species. Moreover, his conviction that the variations that had appeared during the course of the history of life were not necessarily related to the needs of organisms precluded him from assuming the existence of an "innate tendency to progressive development." Nevertheless, he frequently employed both progressionist language and normative judgments when discussing the evolutionary process. A representative example of such lapses can be found in the concluding passage of the *Origin of Species*, where Darwin declared that "from the war of nature, from famine and death, the most exalted object which we are capable of conceiving, namely, the production of the higher animals, directly follows."[16]

Whatever Darwin's position, most American Protestant evolutionists tended to equate evolution with progressive development. If they were not intent on demonstrating that the history of life disclosed the existence of a single line of advance, they did maintain that "the dominant classes became successively higher, and the whole organic kingdom successively greater and more highly organized." This interpretation lent support to their teleological conception of natural history. Persuaded that "progress means purpose," most Protestant evolutionists believed that the progressive development of life implied that "the course of events is tending away from some commencement toward some finality."[17]

These thinkers were quite willing to concede that the mere existence of variation and natural selection did not entail the progressive development of life. This was precisely what sustained their conviction that evolution had been directed by God. For if "in the nature of things there is no more reason for improvement than for deterioration," it seemed obvious that the reason for evolutionary progress lay "in some original, fundamental, all-inclusive design." This implied, apologists concluded, that the ultimate "ground of the world's progress" was God.[18]

While the organic world remained central in some expositions of the argument from design, in others it was only one source of data attesting to the existence of a "vast, all-embracing plan of existence." Thinkers who advanced this broader argument for the existence of God held that the very fact that the natural world was suffused with sufficient pattern and order to be comprehended in terms of intelligible "laws" implied that it was the work of a divine Creator and Governor. The ubiquity of order in the universe, these apologists insisted, was not logically necessary; instead of cosmos, there might well have been "a perpetual chaos, a chronic anarchy of discordant elements, incapable of stable organization." Nor could such order be attributed to the operation of natural laws. Indeed, the very fact that the universe behaved in accordance with such laws, which were merely descriptions of orderly processes, was precisely what required an explanation. Defenders of the faith emphasized that there were thus only two possible explanations for order, chance and creative Intelligence. The former they found absurd. Convinced that "chance produces nothing definite and orderly," and that "order is invariably conjoined with intelligence," they insisted that "that which is intelligible has intelligence in it." They therefore concluded, as R. S. MacArthur, the pastor of New York City's Calvary Baptist Church, put it in 1888, that "back of law is the Lawgiver; back of the observed order of the development is the Ordainer. There stands God!"[19]

This argument was not new. Nor was its appeal entirely limited to Protestant evolutionists. It is nevertheless true that Christians who were most inclined to assume that "the more law, the more God, the more mystery, wonder, awe, and trust" were also most easily able to believe that the origin of species could be described in terms of an intelligible natural process. Conversely, Protestants who felt obliged to concur with the scientific community's verdict on the transmutation hypothesis were naturally drawn to the argument that this hypothesis, far from undermining the credibility of God's existence, actually reinforced it by widening the scope of lawlike activity. Frederic Gardiner, a professor of Old Testament studies at the Berkeley Divinity School (Episcopal) in Middletown, Connecticut, thus commended the theory of organic evolution for establishing "a closer analogy" between the history of life and other realms of natural history.[20]

Many who shared this view valued the organic world less as a peculiarly fruitful source of manifestations of design than as an integral component of an evolutionary conception of the entire universe. Indeed, religionists who had nothing but contempt for Herbert Spencer's attempt to "reconcile" science and religion by invoking the existence of an Unknowable were quite willing to concur with his position that all natural phenomena could be described in terms of an intelligible process of evolutionary development. James McCosh, for example, upbraided Spencerianism as "the most confused and baseless metaphysics to be found in the history of speculation," but this did not stop him from enjoining his readers to

look upon evolution as we do upon gravitation as a beneficent ordinance of God. Gravitation is a law of contemporaneous nature, binding the bodies in space. Evolution is a law of successive nature, binding events in time. The two are powerful instruments in giving a unity and consistency to the world, and in making it a system compacted and harmonious, admired by the contemplative intellect.[21]

One of the most enthusiastic exponents of cosmic evolution was Joseph Le Conte. In 1850, after completing studies at the College of Physicians and Surgeons in New York, Le Conte became a member of the first class of Harvard's Lawrence Scientific School. There, he became a protégé of Louis Agassiz. In 1869, having served as a professor of natural history at Oglethorpe University, the University of Georgia, and the University of South Carolina, he accepted a position at the new University of California.[22]

Le Conte was a competent geologist, but it was primarily his numerous books and articles designed to accommodate Christianity to modern science that earned him distinction within American culture. By the early 1870s, he had come to believe that a neo-Lamarckian interpretation of the transmutation hypothesis offered the best account of the history of life. But in Le Conte's world view, organic evolution was only one instance of a developmental "law" that encompassed all natural phenomena. "In evolution," he wrote in 1881, "we reach the one infinite all-embracing design, stretching across infinite space and infinite time, which includes and predetermines and absorbs every possible separate design. There is still design in every object, but no longer a separate design, only a separate manifestation of one infinite design." Here was unity of plan with a vengeance.[23]

By the time of Darwin's death in 1882, a sizable majority of Protestant intellectuals in the United States who addressed the problem of relating the theory of organic evolution to Christian apologetics had convinced themselves that the theory "does not touch the great truths of natural theology nor can it touch them, except as it gives us new materials with which to prove them." A world that evolved, no less than one punctuated by periodic special creations, implied that the cosmos was "enlightened by intelligence, directed by choice and impelled by will." Many evolutionists, in fact, insisted that the origination of species by means of an intelligible process suggested "a more worthy conception of an infinite Designer, than an infinity of separate interferences."[24]

Such confident professions notwithstanding, the period from 1875 to 1900 witnessed a growing interest in apologetic strategies not predicated on analysis of natural phenomena. Several considerations contributed to this interest. One was the desire to insulate belief in God from the vicissitudes of scientific investigation. Even Christians who believed that the theory of organic evolution left natural theology intact perceived that their efforts to establish this claim focused attention on the formal status of the arguments themselves rather than on God. Moreover, it seemed apparent that for all of their efforts to refurbish the argument from design in the light of the transmutation hypothesis, apologists had failed to convince a number of earnest individuals to accept theism. Defenders of the faith ran aground of the "strange fact" that for many men and women, "to learn how a thing is done weakens faith in any design in its doing." By 1890, James McCosh was prepared to concede that although "those of us who believe in God on other grounds may trace in the development of Nature evidence of his wisdom and goodness," no "argument from Evolution" was capable of "furnishing the primary proof of the existence of God." Others, aware of "the doubt which has been temporarily cast upon the external arguments for the being of God," considered it only prudent to try to devise other, more compelling arguments for belief. Finally, there was a growing sense among Christian apologists that the traditional arguments for the existence of God simply did not inspire people to worship the Christian Deity. Notwithstanding his belief that the natural world witnessed to the existence of God, John W. Chadwick, the pastor of Brooklyn's Second Unitarian Church and the author of a biography of Charles Darwin, rejected the idea that contemplation of the external world constituted the wellsprings of religious belief. The real "foundation of religion," he declared, "is laid in human nature, in the great primal instincts of the soul."[25]

After 1875 an increasing number of Protestant intellectuals came to believe that the testimony of human consciousness constituted "a profounder and more spiritual source" of evidence for God's existence than arguments from the external world. For exponents of this view, the approach of several German theologians proved to be a valuable resource. Although the New England Transcendentalists and a number of other theologically heterodox individuals had borrowed enthusiastically from German theology earlier in the century, most defenders of the faith had resisted the speculations of German thinkers as dangerously subjective. After 1875, however, the changing theological climate led more and more Protestant thinkers to draw on the views of German theologians.[26]

Apologists were particularly attracted by the work of Friedrich Schleiermacher. Schleiermacher had contended that the primary source of humanity's apprehension of God was its feeling of dependence on an absolute Creator rather than inferences drawn from study of the natural world. One of the first influential expressions of Schleiermacher's influence on American apologetics was *The Religious Feeling* (1877), the first of numerous influential works written by Newman Smyth. In 1877, Smyth, who spent most of his career as pastor of the First Church of Christ (Congregational) in New Haven, Connecticut, was serving as pastor to the First Presbyterian Church in Quincy, Illinois. A graduate of Andover Theological Seminary, he was one of a growing number of Americans who studied theology in Germany. There, in "a season of quiet study of modern German thought," he arrived at the conclusions that appeared in *The Religious Feeling*. Smyth credited the insights of German theology with sustaining his own faith. They had also proved "useful in conversation with friends whose scientific studies had both brought them into unwilling doubts concerning those spiritual truths which give to life its real value, and, at the same time, thrown the prevalent proofs of religion out of all relation to their habits of mind."[27]

Like most American Protestant thinkers, Smyth found nature "wonderfully suggestive of God." But although he did not entirely discount traditional arguments for God's existence, he urged that the preoccupation of apologists with formal arguments from the external world was wrongheaded; they should instead direct greater attention to the "inner manifestation" of God in the human soul. Smyth termed this manifestation the "religious feeling," which was, "in its simplest form, the feeling of absolute dependence."[28]

Like Schleiermacher, whom he credited with "having led the thought of his age into the true way of approach towards God," Smyth held that the feeling of dependence was the "perennial source of religion, opened afresh in every new-born soul." This feeling, he maintained, implied the existence of an Unconditioned Cause on Whom humanity was dependent. Noting that human beings' feelings of dependence were as universal, constant, and ineradicable as their sensations of natural phenomena, he insisted that it was no less reasonable to believe that God was the Source of the former than to believe that an external world was the source of the latter. "Scientific and religious knowledge," Smyth averred, "stand or fall together, with the trustworthiness of our mental faculties. We cannot with logical consistency be toward the one half of our consciousness infidels, and toward the other half believers."[29]

During the last quarter of the nineteenth century, many other American Protestant apologists, convinced that "feelings are facts, and as such have evidentiary value," made the data derived from religious experience an important component in their defense of theism. In formulating their arguments for God's existence, most joined Schleiermacher and Smyth in emphasizing humanity's feeling of dependence, but this was not the only datum of experience cited in justification of belief in God. James C. Parsons, for example, submittted that "even as men know that there is an outward world, because they have perceived it, so men know there is a God because they have communed with him." Others asserted that the feeling of obligation to act virtuously attested to the existence of a righteous moral Governor to Whom human beings were responsible.[30]

It was certainly possible to support such claims without subscribing to the transmutation hypothesis. In practice, however, virtually every Protestant who was especially enthusiastic in using the varieties of religious experience to prove God's existence interpreted the history of life from an evolutionary perspective. This correspondence is hardly surprising, for it was Protestants who endorsed the theory of organic evolution who were most intent on devising new apologetic strategies. In turn, the argument most frequently advanced to justify the ontological significance of religious experience had a distinctly evolutionary cast. The Reverend George B. Stevens of Buffalo, New York, succinctly summarized this argument in 1881, when he maintained that, "as thirst implies the existence of water to quench it, so the sense of dependence and the longing of the soul after God, which are natural to man, imply the existence of their object." Implicit in this reasoning was the assumption that if an attribute had no "correlative" in the nature of things, it would possess no survival value and would not persist. Nothing was clearer than the fact that the religious sentiment had survived; it was virtually universal among human beings. The conclusion therefore seemed unassailable: the Object of that sentiment actually existed.

This argument was specious; a belief could be useful without being true. Nevertheless, in a period marked by the growing prestige of evolutionary modes of thought, it acquired an aura of scientific respectability.[31]

Unlike many of Schleiermacher's Continental disciples, Protestant apologists in the United States who advanced arguments based on human religiosity typically emphasized that the evidence derived from religious experience was "not intended to supersede the other evidences, but to supplement and enrich them." Newman Smyth, for example, suggested that nature's witness to the Deity could be appreciated fully only by individuals who apprehended God through the religious consciousness. "First thinking myself through God," he asserted, "I am able also to think nature through God; I begin to understand its development and order, to discern a sufficient reason for its existence, and to feel the pulse of a unifying principle of life in its ever-changing activities." Other apologists, taking the opposite tack, argued that the traditional arguments for the existence of God based on the natural world lent credibility to the testimony of human consciousness.[32]

If Protestant evolutionists remained convinced that there was abundant evidence of the existence of a wise and powerful Deity, most also recognized, as George P. Fisher, professor of ecclesiastical history at Yale, put it, that "it is one question whether there is an arrangement; it is another question whether that arrangement is merciful or not." The latter question was central to the development of a theism that could be meaningful for Protestants who shared Fisher's concerns. R. S. MacArthur, for example, observed that "the true ground of the worship of God is not his omnipotence but his goodness. Mere almightiness might bend the knee, but it could not secure the reverent love of the heart." Theodore T. Munger, pastor of the United Church in New Haven, Connecticut, and a prominent figure in liberal theological circles, drew a connection between the issue of God's beneficence and humanity's conviction that life is worth living. "So soon as one begins to doubt the goodness of God, or to suspect ever so vaguely that God is not infinitely good," Munger declared, "one begins to doubt if life has much value." In view of such considerations, a number of Protestant thinkers who endorsed the transmutation hypothesis assumed the burden of showing that its "method is not unworthy of God."[33]

The problem of theodicy, always perplexing to Christians, was never more theologically troublesome than in the nineteenth century. By 1800, a variety of social, cultural, and intellectual factors had combined

to heighten the sensitivity of many individuals to suffering and to en-
hance the position of sensitivity and compassion within the Western
hierarchy of values. These developments fostered and were in turn influenced by alterations in the pattern of Christian thought. During the
nineteenth century, the conviction that it was possible to draw inferences from the attributes of human beings to the attributes of God led
to a gradual softening of the image most American Protestants had of
the Deity. It also meant, however, that by 1875, numerous members of
the Protestant intellectual community in the United States had come to
believe that "the principles which govern the conduct of a righteous
God must be principles which approve themselves to the consciences
of righteous men." This belief helped to counter the indictment that
Christianity was a morally repugnant vision of reality, but it also served
to highlight the problem of sustaining belief in a benevolent Deity in a
world so full of pain and woe. Elizabeth Stuart Phelps, the author of a
series of popular religious novels, thus declared in 1881 that "the benevolence of the Creator, it is safe to assert, was never so thoughtfully
questioned by such numbers of human beings as it is to-day."[34]

It was in this cultural environment that a number of Protestants attempted to justify the evolutionary ways of God to man. This was not
an easy task. As long as apologists discussed only adaptive variations,
they could make an impressive case for God's wisdom and benevolence. But these thinkers were committed to the position that the Creator was ultimately responsible for all variations. Darwin's view of
evolution implied that during the history of life a multitude of organisms had been driven to the wall. Indeed, struggle between fit and unfit variations was a precondition of organic evolution. Suffering and
death, long a stumbling block for Christian apologists, became an integral component in speciation. Even interpretations of the evolutionary process that minimized the role of natural selection and lowered
the number of "failures" recognized the reality of a struggle for existence that made nature a grisly spectacle "of perpetual carnage where
innocence and weakness are sacrificed to gratify the greedy maw of
power." This view prompted the neo-Lamarckian Joseph Le Conte to
obseve that "what we call evil is not a unique phenomenon confined to
man, and the result of an accident, but must be a great fact pervading
all nature, and a part of its very constitution." If, as apologists commonly claimed, the evolutionary process confirmed God's wisdom, the
mechanics of that process raised difficult questions concerning His
goodness.[35]

It was contemplation of "the clumsy, wasteful, blundering, low, and horribly cruel works of nature" that more than anything else drove Charles Darwin to question the existence of a Christian Deity. In the *Origin of Species*, he had suggested that "we may console ourselves with the full belief, that the war of nature is not incessant, that no fear is felt, that death is generally prompt, and that the vigorous, the healthy, and the happy survive and multiply." Darwin himself, however, did not ultimately find this perspective sufficiently consoling to sustain his belief in a God of "unbounded" goodness. By the end of his life, whatever "grandeur" he continued to find in the evolutionary process had become divorced from moral considerations. The more he thought about "the sufferings of millions of the lower animals throughout almost endless time," the more psychically and intellectually difficult it became for him to believe in the God of Christianity. In the end, he found it more psychically satisfying simply to abandon that belief.[36]

Darwin had clearly pinpointed a difficulty for individuals who analyzed the transmutation hypothesis from a Christian perspective. On the face of it, therefore, it might seem odd that the difficulty of reconciling the transmutation hypothesis with belief in a benevolent God was rarely voiced by Protestants who rejected that hypothesis. A closer examination, however, suggests that critics may well have been reticent about raising the question because they realized that the doctrine of special creations was similarly vulnerable. However species had originated, the fossil record made it abundantly clear that many of them had become extinct. The idea that God had apparently periodically created species only to destroy them lent little support to the Christian's conviction that "the highest law of the universe is Love." Moreover, it was apparent to unbiased observers that individuals within a species were differentially adapted to their circumstances. The doctrine of special creation was unable to account for this fact in a manner capable of confirming belief in divine benevolence. Asa Gray had made this point in 1860. If the advocate of special creation "insists that green woodpeckers were specifically created so in order that they might be less liable to capture," he observed, "must he not equally hold that the black and pied ones were specifically made of these colors in order that they might be more liable to get caught?"[37]

Many creationists were therefore impelled to confess that it was simply impossible to demonstrate that each and every facet of the organic world bore witness to the goodness of the Deity. Such considerations enabled American Protestant evolutionists to assert that "no difficulty arises on the theory of development, which does not meet us on the theory of the immediate creation of every new individual and species."

In a period in which the question of God's benevolence had become acute, however, some Protestant evolutionists sought to do more than simply establish the parity of transmutation and special creation. They urged that the evolutionary hypothesis actually disclosed clues that could be helpful in grappling with the problem of theodicy.[38]

In the judgment of a few Protestants, the process of organic evolution testified to the existence of the God of John Calvin. The first sustained discussion of this position appeared in the work of George Frederick Wright. Wright, a prolific writer and hardy controversialist, was an avid participant in the dialogue concerning the relationship between science and religion. A graduate of Oberlin Theological Seminary in 1862, he served as pastor of the Congregational Church at Bakersfield, Vermont, until 1872, when he became one of an eminent circle of Congregational theologians residing in Andover, Massachusetts. In 1881 he returned to Oberlin. There, he taught New Testament language and literature until 1892, when he became the occupant of a chair in the Harmony of Science and Revelation that had been especially endowed for him. From 1883 until his death in 1921 he also edited the *Bibliotheca Sacra*.[39]

An amateur geologist of some repute, Wright was an early proponent of the transmutation hypothesis. From 1875 to 1880 he published a series of articles on the relationship between Darwinism and Christianity. In one of these articles, published in 1877, he considered how "the apparent failures and imperfections of nature" might be reconciled with the Christian's belief in "the power, wisdom, and goodness of its Designer." Wright conceded, even insisted, that human beings were incapable of fully comprehending God's rationale for creating each organism, but he suggested that "it may reasonably be supposed that it is of more account to God's creatures as a whole that the universe be capable of interpretation, and that the method of God in his works be manifested, than that any amount of temporary good should occur during the earlier stages of the process of development." God, in short, had had the human quest for intelligibility in mind when He created the world.[40]

Three years later, when he concluded his series with an article defending Darwin's right to "shelter himself behind Calvinism from charges of infidelity," Wright again addressed the problem of theodicy. Wright maintained that "if Calvinism is a foe to sentimentalism in theology, so is Darwinism in natural history." Neither in the theory of evolution nor in Calvinism did one find "absolute perfection in each individual." That organisms had been forced to the wall was no more inconsistent with the goodness of God than was the existence of sin in the world. If one viewed God's plan of salvation and the evolutionary process from the same perspective, it became clear that just as "the reprobation of the wicked may come in as a circumstance subsidiary to the general ends of the moral system that is created," so the suffering of animals had to be viewed in terms of "the requirements of the general scheme."[41]

James McCosh adopted a similarly tough-minded approach to the problem of theodicy. The evolutionary process, he emphasized, offered a salutary rebuff to that saccharine sentimentalism that saw the world as "all sunshine and hope—all grafitification and gayety." Like many of his forebears, who had regarded the struggle and death of organisms as a prefiguration of the Fall, McCosh submitted that the "groanings and travailings" in the struggle for survival represented "an anticipation of the grand battle between ignorance and light, between sin and salvation, in the present era of our earth's history."[42]

Christians who, like Wright and McCosh, believed that the doctrines of Calvinism accorded with belief in an infinitely benevolent Creator were unlikely to view the struggle and death of organisms as especially problematic. Relatively few Protestant evolutionists, however, hewed to a rigorously Calvinist line in their approach to theodicy. By the last quarter of the nineteenth century, though many Protestant thinkers continued to subscribe to a theological persuasion at least nominally Calvinistic, most of them had abandoned Calvinism's harsher elements. Human initiative rather than divine foreordination increasingly became central to the understanding most of them had of the dynamics of salvation. Some Protestants, to be sure, remained faithful to strict Calvinism, but few of them endorsed the transmutation hypothesis. The great majority of Protestant evolutionists belonged to the ranks of Christians who were moving most quickly and determinedly away from Calvinist dogma. For them, the doctrine of election was a "theodicy [that] failed just where it was most needed." The argument that the theory of evolution was no more inconsistent with the benevolence of God than the Calvinist scheme of redemption therefore begged the very question at issue.[43]

These thinkers were aware that it was impossible to demonstrate that the fate of each individual or even each species bore witness to the goodness of the Creator. The strategy they employed in confirming God's benevolence was quite different. Largely eschewing discussion of the mechanics of the evolutionary process, they chose instead to focus on its progressive direction and beneficient outcome. This strategy enabled them to concur with the neo-Lamarckian paleontologist A. S.

Packard, Jr., who submitted in 1880 that "the very idea of evolution implies optimism and points to the Infinite Goodness."[44]

Many Protestant intellectuals who shared this conviction emphasized that from an evolutionary perspective, the struggle and death of individuals during the course of natural history was not simply an inexplicable brute fact but a "necessary condition of all progress." Pain, struggle, and death were omnipresent but not purposeless. In nature, as in human life, sacrifice played a central role in the divine plan. This position received clear expression in the work of Asa Gray. In his "Evolutionary Teleology," Gray submitted that the theory of evolution showed that the profligacy and competition so apparent in the organic world were instrumental to the progressive development of life. "Without the competing multitude," he reminded his readers, "no struggle for life; and without this, no natural selection and survival of the fittest, no continuous adaptation to changing surroundings, no diversification and improvement, leading from lower up to higher and nobler forms." John Fiske took a similar position. In 1874 Fiske had argued that the ascription of goodness to God was unwarranted on the grounds that the course of evolution had been "attended by the misery of untold millions of sentient creatures for whose existence their Creator is responsible." By 1885, however, Fiske had altered his view. Though he continued to affirm that "Nature is full of cruelty and maladaptation," he expressed confidence that the progress disclosed in the evolutionary process was sufficient to demonstrate that "God is in the deepest sense a moral Being." Joseph Le Conte went even further, contending that the "good effect" of the survival of the fittest was "just in proportion to its pitilessness."[45]

Le Conte was only one of a number of Protestants who believed that the ends of the evolutionary process justified the means. Once it was remembered that this process had culminated in the appearance of humanity, he suggested, it became obvious that what had appeared to be evil when attention was focused on the individual organism struggling for its life was actually "a *good* in disguise." Other Protestants reasoned that by showing that earlier organisms, even nature's misfits, were not simply gratuitous whims of the Creator, to be obliterated at His pleasure, but integral elements in the evolutionary process, the transmutation hypothesis more clearly vindicated the benevolence of God than did the doctrine of special creation. This reasoning prompted the Presbyterian clergyman Joseph Van Dyke to suggest that "the new teleology may prove more successful than the old."[46]

Some Protestant evolutionists were not convinced that this approach really resolved the problem of theodicy. Even if pain and struggle redounded to a beneficent end, the question of why God had employed a means of populating the world that entailed wholesale slaughter, a means that involved "not a single tear of pity," remained unanswered. Borden Parker Bowne, a professor of philosophy at Boston University and an avid Christian apologist, cautioned that "the fancy that evolution in any way diminishes the Creator's responsibility for evil is really somewhat infantile." To defend the beneficence of transmutation by concentrating on the progress that resulted from the evolutionary process, he observed, "does not meet the question why this progress might not have been accomplished at less cost of toil and struggle and pain." In Bowne's view, individuals who based their judgment of God's character on an assessment of the universe alone would be forced to conclude that He was either indifferent, morally imperfect, or limited in power. Brooklyn's popular clergyman Henry Ward Beecher, though an ardent evolutionist, was similarly discomfited. Contemplation of the fit, he observed, was "a poor consolation to any man asking, 'Why were there any weak? Why were they not all strong to begin with?'" Beecher concluded that God's rationale for this system was "a mystery that can be solved only in the life beyond." Even Joseph Le Conte was forced to conclude that the natural world was "a revelation especially of the intellectual character of Deity, and only imperfectly of his moral nature." Though these thinkers could take some comfort in believing that the transmutation hypothesis provided more satisfactory clues to "the dark riddle of physical evil" than the notion of arbitrary special creations, they, like the Calvinists, were forced to conclude that God's purpose ultimately lay beyond humanity's ken, that "neither in Nature nor in Providence are His ways like our ways." A wholly adequate appreciation of God's benevolence, they argued, required that the testimony of God's works be supplemented with the testimony of His Word. For these Protestant evolutionists, belief in the infinite goodness of an omnipotent God did not really spring from contemplation of nature; indeed, some of them may have expressed their faith in this doctrine in spite of their estimate of natural history.[47]

Most Protestant intellectuals regarded discussion of God's existence and nature as only a prelude to analysis of His relationship to the world. Christians believed that God was not simply Creator and Governor of the universe but a personal Father Who actively participated in the affairs of His creation. The doctrine of special creation had nicely accorded with, even reinforced, this view. Protestants who rejected this doctrine in favor of the evolutionary hypothesis were thus driven to reconsider "the living question of our times"—God's relationship to the world—and to formulate new answers to this question.[48]

The theory of organic evolution played an important role in forcing Protestant thinkers who accepted it to reassess the relationship between nature and the supernatural. Not every Protestant evolutionist was willing to concur with Joseph Le Conte, who asserted that the doctrine of special creation was "the *last* line of defense for the supporters of supernaturalism in the realm of Nature." But virtually all of them recognized that a theory implying that the production of species was no more a series of miraculous events than the orbits of the planets around the sun significantly altered the terms in which supernaturalism could be discussed. Apologists had been deprived of the most compelling evidence they had been able to marshal for the reality of periodic "special" divine interventions in the natural world.[49]

A minority of Protestant evolutionists attempted to make the best of this altered state of affairs by emphasizing the remaining lacunae in scientific explanation. Such gaps, they argued, required the intervention of a supernatural Deity. These thinkers typically accepted the conventional assumptions that natural phenomena possessed "essential properties" enabling them to act as "secondary causes" and that natural laws were descriptions of the behavior of those phenomena. Because they ascribed to God the responsibility for creating and sustaining the efficacy of "mediate" causes, they denied that the discovery of natural causes was antithetical to supernaturalism. Still, they remained convinced that there was a fundamental ontological distinction between the natural and the supernatural. Many of them, clearly uneasy about the notion that God always worked by means of natural agencies, continued to emphasize that some events—in particular, the origin of matter, life, and mind—required infusions of "fresh creative energy" from the realm of the supernatural. Thinkers who applied this reasoning to the transmutation hypothesis characteristically held that although the hypothesis implied that the "primal creative act" had occurred "farther back in the line of development" than Christians had previously believed, this did not obviate the need for a supernatural act endowing the original "germs" of life with the power to evolve subsequent species. Some emphasized, too, that because science had failed to discover a natural cause of variability, it was perfectly reasonable to ascribe variation to the creative agency of God.[50]

Most Protestant evolutionists in the United States came to believe that the restriction of supernatural agency in nature to those events that had so far eluded scientific analysis was profoundly unsatisfactory. The theory of organic evolution played a profound role in leading them to reach this conclusion. By employing natural phenomena to account for the origin of species, it drastically narrowed the realm of events that appeared to be intelligible only if they were regarded as the product of "special" supernatural fiat. But it was not simply the content of the transmutation hypothesis that fostered unhappiness with the traditional understanding of the relationship between nature and the supernatural. The hypothesis itself dramatically reinforced the growing sense that "one after another, the wonderful phenomena and events of the past, which were supposed to be the result of supernatural causes, have been accounted for in the natural sequence of physical law." By the late nineteenth century, many Protestants assumed that scientists would "enlarge the boundaries of natural knowledge indefinitely." It is therefore not surprising that there was a good deal of concern that the effect of confining divine agency to events lying outside the range of scientific discourse might well be to promote an attenuated conception of divine activity not unlike that of the deists. Henry Churchill King, professor of theology at Oberlin Theological Seminary, felt moved to warn his readers that "for its own sake, theology can remain satisfied no longer with the old, inconsistent view of a virtual independence of the world in the larger part of it, and of direct dependence on God at certain points only, where we cannot yet trace the process of God's working."[51]

Theologically, dissatisfaction with suggestions that God's immediate activity was limited to "crises" within natural history was reflected in an increased emphasis on the doctrine of divine immanence. The doctrine itself was not new. From the very outset of the Reformation, Protestants had maintained that God was immanent within, as well as transcendent over, His creation. Still, it was not until the last quarter of the nineteenth century that a sizable number of American Protestant thinkers, committed to retaining the presence of divine agency in the natural world and convinced that the assumption that the scope of immediate divine activity was limited to events within natural history that defied scientific description would lead to spiritual disaster, made the immanentist conviction that "God is ever present and working in nature" the "guiding conception of philosophical theology."[52]

Nothing more clearly indicated the determination of immanentists to heighten humanity's appreciation of the ubiquity of divine activity than their resistance to the conventional view that God had endowed natural phenomena with causal efficacy. In place of this idea, now pilloried as "the materialism of theology," many Anglo-American Protestant intellectuals sought to substitute the idea that God was "the efficient cause and constant mover of all things." Proponents of this radical formulation of divine immanence, aware that granting God a monopoly on causal agency involved no alteration "in the *appearance* of things," made no attempt to construct a formal proof of their position. They did emphasize, however, that there was no way to validate empirically the causal efficacy of matter. This fact, of course, had been a prominent plank in the platform of David Hume. But whereas Hume had used this idea to undermine belief in causal necessity, some of his successors within the American Protestant intellectual community employed it to suggest that the assumption that matter possessed the power to act was unwarranted and that "all efficiency is volitional."[53]

Protestants who affirmed that the source of all causal activity was God denied that efforts to extend the realm of scientific analysis represented a threat to the Christian world view. Instead they found it entirely appropriate that science should attempt to extend its mode of analysis to heretofore uncharted territory, on the grounds that "the agency of God in creation can never be negatived or obscured, but only more clearly revealed, by the unveiling of the processes by which He works." Science and theology, immanentists urged, were complementary ways of interpreting the same data. Whereas the mission of *describing* the behavior of natural phenomena belonged to science, the task of truly *explaining* it fell to theology.[54]

Because an immanentist conception of God's role in the world gave free rein to scientific investigation, it is not surprising that many of the most outspoken proponents of that conception in the late nineteenth century were scientists of a religious bent. One of the most able of these was Joseph Le Conte. In his *Religion and Science*, published in 1873, Le Conte made certain statements that suggested that he was unwilling to abandon altogether the notion that mediate causes possessed a certain efficacy. For example, he based his defense of the argument from design on the claim that the argument for a divine Designer "is no less necessary if direct action be one degree removed, two degrees removed, three degrees removed, a thousand degrees, a million degrees removed, or even if removed to infinity." By 1881, however, Le Conte was no longer willing to countenance any mode of reconciliation that would relegate God's "direct action" to the past. The forces activating the natural world, he now maintained, were not "independent, efficient, self-acting agents" but "the ever-present, all-pervading, ever-acting energy of Deity."[55]

A number of other pious scientists reached similar conclusions. In 1877 the well-known geologist Alexander Winchell made it clear to readers of the *Methodist Quarterly* that his assessment of the religious implications of the transmutation hypothesis was considerably more optimistic than that which he had enunciated in 1863. Winchell now held that just as science was incapable of disclosing "the nature of causal efficiency" at the origin of life, it was similarly incapable of demonstrating that "which manifests itself at every term of the series." For Winchell, it seemed abundantly clear that "the hypothesis of evolution authorizes the believer in imminent [*sic*] divine power to posit such power in every term of the evolution." The geologist William North Rice was similarly convinced that "a true philosophy must recognize the immanence of God and his immediate efficiency in all natural processes." And Herbert W. Conn, a professor of biology at Wesleyan who distinguished himself in bacteriological research, maintained that evolution made it "necessary to assume the constant action of [divine] power underneath nature." Although Asa Gray frequently used the terms "physical cause" and "secondary cause" in describing natural phenomena, he professed ignorance as to the precise nature of such causes and the way in which they were "connected and interfused with first cause." Moreover, from the very outset of his efforts to reconcile Darwinism and Christianity he made it clear that he was prepared to countenance the idea that efficient causation was "the constant and orderly immediate action of an intelligent creative Cause." In 1887, he suggested that a "fuller recognition of Divine Immanence" would enable Christians to resolve the problem of relating God to a world ever more responsive to the probing inquiries of the scientist.[56]

During the 1880s and 1890s, a growing number of nonscientists also reached the conclusion that God's "will and his power are the only real forces in nature" and that natural law was simply "the divine mode of action which God prescribes to himself." From this perspective, they regarded evolution as simply the means God had employed in creating species. The appearance of new organisms from time to time, they believed, showed that "the immanent God has not exhausted himself." It is perhaps not surprising that this position found favor among religious thinkers such as John Fiske, who coupled a desire to defend a recognizably Christian conception of the Deity with enthusiasm for the cosmic philosophy of Herbert Spencer. But Protestants who scorned what they believed to be the vacuous affirmations of Spencerian metaphysics also gravitated toward a "God-intoxicated" view of natural phenomena. Just how pervasive this position proved to be is suggested by the fact that by 1898 Augustus Hopkins Strong, the president of the Baptists' Rochester Theological Seminary and a theologian not given to enthusiasm for radical departures from orthodoxy, was prepared to affirm that, with the exception of the human will, "the will of God is the only real force in nature" and that matter was "conceivable only as the energizing of an intelligible and personal will."[57]

The thrust of immanentism, as the clergyman James Douglas of Pulaski, New York noted, was "opposed to dualism in all its forms, whether religious or philosophical." Although Protestants who interpreted the Creator's role in the world in a more radically immanentist manner were more interested in demonstrating that the universe was grounded, guided, and sustained by Spirit than in speculating about the precise ontological status of matter, they commonly found themselves joining the numerous other Anglo-American intellectuals who in the late nineteenth century gravitated toward philosophical idealism. Borden Parker Bowne, the leading spokesperson in the late nineteenth century for an influential form of idealism that became known as personalism, maintained that "religiously there is no difference between idealistic theism and immanent theism." Other immanentists were less explicit in supporting idealism. Nevertheless, in ascribing all causal efficacy to God, these thinkers were in effect according all power in the cosmos to intelligent Spirit rather than to matter.[58]

For thinkers who embraced this position, the terms "natural" and "supernatural" connoted differing angles of vision rather than meaningful ontological categories. If the status of the supernatural became problematic in a world so fully describable by natural processes, the status of the natural was no less so in a world in which all causal efficacy resided in God. By extension, at the hands of immanentists the line between the miraculous and the ordinary became obscure. For those who chose to retain the orthodox definition of "miracle" as "an event, in the external world, brought about by the immediate efficiency, or simple volition of God," natural history became a procession of one miracle after another. Alternatively, those who thought of miracles simply as "extraordinary" acts of God envisioned them not as occurrences "above or outside of nature" but merely as "another class of divine operations." From an immanentist perspective, whether human beings chose to label phenomenal activity "natural" or "supernatural" seemed little more than a question of semantics.[59]

Not everyone was enamored of this radical formulation of immanentism. Some Protestant intellectuals expressed concern that in blurring the distinction between nature and the supernatural and affirming the pervasive presence of God in the world, immanentists were flirting with pantheism. One of the most vociferous opponents of the immanentist position was George Frederick Wright. In 1888 Wright warned that the radical formulation of the doctrine of divine immanence "easily degenerates into pantheism." Miracles could retain theological significance, he suggested, only if God had placed the forces by which natural phenomena ordinarily acted within those phenomena themselves. By 1895 Wright had become even more hostile to immanentism. In a terse article entitled "Bad Philosophy Going to Seed," he charged that "in abolishing the doctrine of second causes and resolving everything into the direct acts of God," immanentists were repudiating the "barriers between the natural and the supernatural" on which belief in the freedom of the will and a realm of existence beyond the natural world rested.[60]

Wright articulated the position of a number of intellectuals who saw pantheism lurking in the shadows of immanentism. A preoccupation with God's immanence, they warned, tended to undermine consciousness of His transcendence. It was the latter view that grounded the claim that the Deity was a "Being with whom we can sympathize and enter into conscious relations, . . . who can be to us a ruler, a judge, a friend, a father." That there was no logical incompatibility between embracing this view and affirming His ubiquitous presence in natural processes some critics of immanentism were prepared to concede. Nevertheless, at least some of them concurred with the Reverend John Tunis of Cambridge, Massachusetts, in believing that, in practice, "the employment of the Immanent God generally leads to leaving aside the personal God."[61]

Immanentists who responded to these criticisms took pains to point out that in affirming God's omnipresent activity, they were taking a position that was fully consonant with the scriptural vision of God as a Reality in Whom all things live and move and have their being. They hastened to assure their readers that the attribution of all causal activity to God did not imply that this was His only activity. Christians were therefore quite justified in simultaneously affirming the immanence and the transcendence of God. The charge of pantheism appeared to these thinkers to be nothing more than "a theological bugbear . . . to frighten the would-be-orthodox." It was not "the risk of concealed pantheism" but "the denial of the divine in nature and history, the refusal to believe in a *living God*," George Trumbull Ladd wrote in 1880, that constituted the real problem facing Christianity. For his part, Joseph Le Conte announced that he was quite content to call the position he espoused "Christian pantheism," but he stressed that his was not a pantheism that "sublimates the personality of the Deity into all-pervading unconscious force, and thereby dissipates all our hopes of personal relation with him."[62]

Le Conte believed that he could infer the personality of God from the presence of personality in the human species, which he viewed as the culmination of the evolutionary process. Like other immanentists, he also held that the elements of goodness and intelligence manifest in the universe were sufficient grounds for inferring that God was "an Infinite Personality." There was a subtle but significant difference, however, between maintaining that God possessed personality and affirming that He sustained a personal relationship with His creatures, and it was at this point that both proponents of immanentism and Protestant evolutionists who drew a more rigid distinction between nature and the supernatural found themselves face to face with a serious problem. Philosophical schemes that invoked the Deity as an explanatory hypothesis elicited little piety from nineteenth-century Christians. Bordon Parker Bowne, in fact, asserted that, however important the use of theism to account for the behavior of natural phenomena might be to the metaphysician, it was bereft of any real "religious function." The roots of piety lay in humanity's conviction that God maintained an ongoing providential relationship with His creatures. This conviction prompted George P. Fisher to observe that "theism signifies not only that there is a ground or cause of all things, . . . but also that the Cause of all things is a Personal Being." To Fisher it seemed obvious that "it is in the deviation of nature from its ordinary course that the personal agency—the justice, the mercy, the benevolent purpose of God—is revealed." Protestants who committed themselves to the theory of organic evolution had endorsed a description of a large class of such deviations in terms of an intelligible natural process. In so doing, they were sanctioning a sharp reduction in the number of instances of "special" providence within the natural world.[63]

Recognizing this, a few suggested that the kind of "deviations" necessary to sustain belief in God's personal interest in His creation could be found within the evolutionary process itself. Francis H. Johnson, one of a number of Congregational theologians residing in Andover during the late nineteenth century who assessed the religious implications of the evolutionary hypothesis, credited evolution with showing that nature was not a machine that operated in accordance with "mere routine and exact repetition" but a constantly changing mosaic of phenomena moving teleologically toward a preordained end. Whatever uniformity pervaded the cosmos, he maintained, was "the uniformity of an orderly mind of infinite resources." The lesson Johnson drew from evolution was that God "works not forever with the same means and intruments, but continually with higher organisms adapted to higher results."[64]

Most Protestant evolutionists approached the problem of divine providence from a different vantage point. Although they commonly insisted that it was not unreasonable to suppose that God occasionally acted in a special, miraculous manner, they assumed that the course of scientific investigation precluded the possibility of advancing a compelling argument for the frequent manifestation of such activity during the course of natural history. Accordingly, they largely abandoned discussion of special providence in the natural world in favor of a greater emphasis on "general" providence. The point of departure for this approach was implicit in Fisher's observation that "were the vision not clouded, the regular sequences of nature, its wise and beneficent order, would discover its Author, and call out emotions of love and adoration." Seeking to uncloud human vision, most Protestant evolutionists urged that the ubiquity of intelligible natural process testified to a more sophisticated conception of God's personal concern for His creatures than did the older view.[65]

In principle, the attribution of all causal efficacy to divine agency enabled radical immanentists to affirm that God periodically intervened in the natural world in an irregular manner. Their vision of the universe, however, precluded them from emphasizing such interventions. The same science that prompted them to limit causal efficacy to God also undermined the credibility of the notion that He acted in what could be construed as a capricious manner. Accordingly, immanentists sought to minister to humanity's desire for a "near God" by emphasizing that omnipresent divine activity attested far more decisively than sporadic interventions to God's ceaseless commitment to and involvement with His creation.[66]

The minority of Protestant evolutionists who adamantly insisted upon the efficacy of "secondary" causes and limited God's immediate activity to the gaps that remained in scientific explanation focused almost entirely on the doctrine of "general" providence. These thinkers continued to uphold the concept of supernatural intervention in the natural world and concurred with George Frederick Wright in believing that "no theory of evolution can be entertained which implies impassable limitations to God's spontaneity in manifesting himself to our most deeply implanted wants." Nevertheless, most of them also joined

Wright in assuming that divine "spontaneity" was most commonly displayed in God's interaction with human beings rather than within the "irrational creation."[67]

By 1875, most Protestant evolutionists had convinced themselves that the world disclosed by science made theological sense only if intelligible, lawlike processes were seen as witnesses to the providential concern of a God Whose will was immutable. In this connection, many Protestant evolutionists placed a great deal of emphasis on the familiar claim that intelligible events enabled God's children to interpret the cosmos. This ability afforded them intellectual gratification, a clearer apprehension of the wisdom of God, and assistance in their efforts to make their way in the world. This claim was not utterly irreconcilable with the idea that God had occasionally intervened in the world in an unusual manner, but it was clearly difficult to square with the idea that the order of nature was frequently abrogated by "special" divine interpositions. It made more sense, most Protestant evolutionists believed, either to focus on general rather than special providence or to collapse the distinction altogether by asserting that through what James McCosh called a "pre-arrangement" of laws, God could accomplish special and individual purposes.[68]

The identification of providential activity with lawlike natural processes was consistent with the scientific world view and may well have been the only recourse available to Christians who were committed to the conclusions of modern science. On the other hand, it less vividly demonstrated God's willingness to respond to the needs of His creatures than did "the departure of nature from its beaten path." Joseph Le Conte may have been guilty of some exaggeration when he complained that "no sooner do we find out, in any work of Nature, *how* it is made, than we all say that it is not made at all; it made itself." But there is little question that a world describable by means of natural processes was a world in which belief in providence had little impact on the thought of individuals in their confrontation with nature. Some Protestant evolutionists were aware that a consciousness of God's providence was waning among educated men and women. Few appear to have recognized, however, that in abandoning a robust doctrine of special providence for a conception of divine providence that seemed more amenable to scientific discourse, they were adopting a position that did little to resist trends to view God more as a silent Partner than as a constant Companion.[69]

As Christians, Protestant evolutionists were convinced that God's encounter with humanity was of fundamental significance in any evaluation of divine activity. In discussing the encounter, many of these thinkers felt compelled to confront the implications of the transmutation hypothesis. Some of them envisioned the task of relating that hypothesis to the Christian world view in relatively conservative terms. These thinkers concentrated on convincing their readers that acceptance of the theory of organic evolution entailed few significant alterations in the formulation of Christian doctrines relating to the scheme of redemption. Others, though no less determined to place the transmutation hypothesis within the context of Christian theology, also sought to place Christianity within an evolutionary context. For these thinkers, it seemed obvious that "the one word, which more than all others has been a revolutionary call to modern thought, is the word Evolution." Accordingly, they made determined efforts to show that the concept of evolution was a fruitful way of describing not only the method by which God created new species but also the way in which He achieved His other purposes. The idea that evolution was, as the eminent clergyman Lyman Abbott put it, "God's way of doing things" became central in shaping the way in which these thinkers understood and explicated the Christian message.[70]

Protestants who viewed evolution as paradigmatic of all divine activity characteristically equated that process with gradual, continuous, and progressive development. This definition was broader, looser, and more teleological in thrust than the transmutation hypothesis really implied. Nevertheless, for many American Protestant intellectuals, the notion that evolution, broadly defined, constitued a compelling theological principle was fostered by acceptance of the theory of organic evolution. To be sure, the nebular hypothesis and uniformitarian geology had described natural phenomena in terms of evolutionary change prior to the publication of the *Origin of Species*. It was not until the scientific community endorsed the transmutation hypothesis, however, that a significant number of religious thinkers came to believe that the history of the natural world could best be understood in developmental terms. Many of these thinkers, persuaded that God acted in a rational, consistent manner, reasoned that "the larger the sweep of one great progressive method, the more probable does it become that the method is universal." From this perspective, they concluded that God's interaction with humanity could also be described within an evolutionary framework.[71]

6

"Where Is the Place of Understanding?": The Protestant Evolutionists and Religious Knowledge

DURING the last quarter of the nineteenth century, the theory of organic evolution provoked a great deal of discussion concerning the sources, function, and finality of religious knowledge. Of central importance in this discussion was the status of the Scriptures. From the very outset of the Darwinian controversy, it had been obvious that the transmutation hypothesis was irreconcilable with prevailing interpretations of the biblical narrative of creation. Accordingly, it was incumbent upon Protestant evolutionists to show that it was possible to embrace the new biology without abandoning belief in the veracity of the Bible.

Toward this end, some of these thinkers urged that the theory of organic evolution was no more subversive of Scripture than the Copernican hypothesis, the geological estimates of the age of the earth, and many other accepted scientific ideas. They reasoned that just as "modifications" in biblical interpretation had frequently been made in the past without jeopardizing "faith in the Bible as the word of God," so additional changes necessitated by acceptance of the transmutation hypothesis could be made without undermining belief in the essential truths recorded in the scriptural narrative. These Christians commonly resorted to the already familiar claim that because biblical interpretation was a fallible enterprise, it was unwise to reject ideas out of hand simply because they conflicted with the prevailing understanding of the Scriptures. Lewis E. Hicks, a prominent member of the Baptist church and a professor of geology at Denison University, warned that the subordination of science to biblical exegesis "has had and can have no other noteworthy result than to promote the growth of skepticism." Alexander Winchell's belief in the tentative nature of biblical interpretation prompted him to insist that "we shall stand higher at the court of heaven for respecting the verdict of our God-given intelligence, than for taking up arms in defense of a fallible interpretation, which dethrones intellect and insults the Author of all truth."[1]

Most Protestant evolutionists who grappled with the problem of relating the theory of organic evolution to the biblical narrative adopted one of two major approaches. One of these centered on reinterpreting the narrative to bring it into accord with the implications of the theory. The other involved an even more radical application of the notion that the Scriptures did not convey an accurate scientific account of natural history. The first approach, which was predicated on belief in the "remarkable flexibility" of biblical language, was most commonly favored by Protestant evolutionists who remained committed to the doctrine of the plenary inspiration of the Bible. Though convinced that God had "condescended" to a scientifically unsophisticated audience in using "popular language" in Genesis, they insisted that such language, when rightly interpreted, would contain nothing inconsistent with the conclusions of modern science.[2]

In keeping with this assumption, a number of Protestants sought to show that the order of creation described in Genesis corresponded to that disclosed by scientific investigation. One of the most popular expositions of this theme was presented by Arnold Guyot, a professor of physical geography and geology at Princeton. In 1884 Guyot published *Creation; or, The Biblical Cosmogony in the Light of Modern Science*, a book that elaborated a position he had been defending since 1840. Through a detailed comparison of the language of the Bible with the fruits of scientific inquiry, Guyot sought to demonstrate that the "outlines" of the order of creation discovered by modern science "were precisely those of the grand history of life given in the First Chapter of Genesis." He continued to regard the validity of the transmutation hypothesis as "an open question" but insisted that, however this issue was resolved, there was every reason to assume that the findings of science would continue to parallel the biblical narrative of creation.[3]

Many American scientists, theologians, and clergy shared Guyot's confidence. Some maintained that the supposed parallels between the testimony of the Scriptures and the verdict of science constituted evidence of the divine inspiration of the Bible. George Frederick Wright, for example, insisted that "no unaided human intellect could, in the period when the first chapter of Genesis was written, have framed a cosmogony with which modern science could find so little fault."[4]

Wright, like many other Protestants who remained committed to the conventional doctrine of the plenary inspiration of the Scriptures, believed that it was both possible and necessary to interpret the language of the Bible in accordance with the dictates of the transmutation hypothesis. During the 1870s and 1880s he emphasized that the lessons of the Scriptures differed fundamentally from the results of scientific inquiry. Applying this view to the question of creation, he reasoned that because the purpose of the narrative in Genesis was limited to affirming "the *fact of creation by Divine agency*," scientists were free to investigate the "*mode* of creation." Convinced that science had played an instrumental role in promoting a better understanding of the Bible, Wright urged expositors of the Scriptures to be flexible. "There is great loss," he concluded, "in unreasonably delaying the concessions which biblical interpreters must from time to time make to science." By the 1890s, however, Wright had become more aggressive in defending the plenary inspiration of the Scriptures. He continued to distinguish the truths of the Bible from those of science. The path to truth, he wrote in 1892, was akin to "a double-track road, in which the Bible, laden with its rich stores of spiritual truth, is on one, and science, with its accumulating treasures of material truth, is on the other, and no collision is possible except in case some nervous man ventures, without orders, to meddle with the switches." Now, though, he placed greater emphasis on the idea that the truths discovered by science were quite compatible with the biblical narrative of creation. Applying this reasoning to the transmutation hypothesis, he maintained that "the language of Genesis may properly be regarded as the language of theistic evolution." In support of this view, he proposed that the biblical phrase "let the earth bring forth" could be construed as an implicit avowal of organic evolution.[5]

Not all Protestant evolutionists were enthusiastic about Wright's approach to the problem of harmonizing the Bible with the insights of modern science. A growing number of them, in fact, became skeptical of traditional modes of reconciliation. In 1883 George P. Fisher noted that "the progress of natural science has taught in repeated instances, and taught impressively, that the traditional views taken of the Scriptures contain error." He did not infer from this, however, that exegetes were to revise their interpretations of biblical passages to bring them into accord with the findings of science. On the contrary, Fisher was convinced that constant reinterpretation of the Scriptures, far from enhancing their credibility, would have precisely the opposite effect. "No course could be better adapted to excite a general distrust of Scripture," he declared, "than that of making a stand at one point after another, only to beat a retreat at the first regular onset of the assailant." What was needed was "some new canon of interpretation . . . which places the reader of the Bible above the reach of these rude disturbances of his belief."[6]

Although the growing reluctance of Protestants to countenance the periodic revision of biblical texts to bring them into harmony with the latest discoveries of science was at least partly a product of their recognition that "the earnest world is getting tired of this business of reconciliation," it would be a mistake to assume that it was inspired by nothing more than an assessment of effective apologetic tactics. It was also a product of the growing conviction that an unprejudiced comparison of the biblical narrative with the findings of science revealed significant inconsistencies rather than close agreement. In reality, William North Rice submitted, "the biblical writers show in general no indication of any knowledge of nature superior to that possessed by other men of their time."[7]

The theory of organic evolution played an important role in fostering discontent with the assumption that the language of the Scriptures could be reconciled with the disclosures of modern science. To be sure, the transmutation hypothesis was only one of an increasingly long series of scientific conceptions inconsistent with a literal interpretation of the narrative of creation set down in Genesis; indeed, many thinkers were doubtless receptive to the theory of evolution because they had already become disillusioned with efforts to find scientific truth in the Bible. But for other Protestant intellectuals, the evolutionary account of the history of life proved to be the final straw in destroying the credibility of efforts to show that the author of Genesis "had the science of the nineteenth century in his brain."[8]

Many thinkers found it quite difficult to break with traditional methods of harmonizing science and the Bible. In the work of Theodore T. Munger, this difficulty was manifest. In his well-known essay "The New Theology," which the most discerning student of American liberal Protestantism has termed a "manifesto" of that movement, Munger devoted seven pages to outlining his view of the proper approach that Christians should take to the Scriptures. These pages embodied many of the confusions and inconsistencies that often attend significant conceptual change.[9]

Munger called for "a more natural way" of interpreting the Scriptures in which students would read them "as literature, yet with no derogation from their inspiration." He denounced the "inconsistency" of the traditional conception of theology, which "slowly gives up the theory of verbal inspiration, but retains views based on verbal inspiration." The New Theology, by contrast, "does not regard the Bible as a magical book; it is not a diviner's rod." Notwithstanding this assertion, Munger slipped back into the familiar assumption that the Scriptures would be found to be harmonious with the contributions of modern scholarship. He thus reasoned that because the Bible was "a book to be constantly and freshly interpreted," the Christian confronted with apparent inconsistency was to "search the text to see if it will not bear a meaning, or rather does not contain a meaning,—indeed, was intended to convey a meaning that we have failed to catch,—consistent with ascertained facts." Though Munger insisted that this approach "does not reduce the Bible to a pliant mass," it is difficult to see precisely how it differed from the position held by those who subscribed to the doctrine of the plenary inspiration of the Scriptures.[10]

In the work of Newman Smyth, opposition to this traditional mode of reconciliation was clearer, but elements of the older view still remained. In his well-known *Old Faiths in New Light*, published in 1879, Smyth maintained that in affirming the law, order, and unity of the creation, the Bible better accorded with science than other ancient literary accounts of the origin of the world. Indeed, he insisted, the parallels between the disclosures of scientific investigation and the biblical account of incremental creation were so striking that if the narrative of creation in Genesis had been "some newly-developed remnant of Arabic literature, or a hieroglyphic just deciphered from some Egyptian monument," tough-minded naturalists such as Huxley, Tyndall, and Draper would hail the document "as a remarkable anticipation of some of the chief results of modern science." On the other hand, Smyth was dubious about the arguments that believers in plenary inspiration such as George Frederick Wright found so compelling. He thus rejected on principle the idea that the author of Genesis had been inspired to describe processes "far in advance of the knowledge of men living at that particular time." He also refused to employ the "coincidences" between the testimony of the Bible and that of modern science to defend the divine inspiration of the Scriptures, because he believed that neither of these sources of knowledge was necessarily infallible. By the time he wrote his *Recollections and Reflections* in 1926, he had come to view efforts to reinterpret the Bible to bring it into line with Darwinism and other scientific theories as "artificial" and "precarious" ways of dealing with the relationship between science and the Scriptures.[11]

Many Protestant intellectuals were more decisive than Munger and Smyth in dissociating themselves from conventional modes of reconciling science and the Bible. Just how radical an alteration in thought their rejection of these modes often involved can be seen in the work of the well-known (German) Reformed clergyman William Rupp. In 1874 Rupp had warned that the theory of evolution conflicted with "the whole spirit and genius of the Bible." Convinced that "science can never hope successfully to explore and explain the mysteries of the world of matter, or the mysteries of the world of mind unless she suffers herself to be guided by the torch of supernatural revelation," he rejected the transmutation hypothesis. By 1888, however, Rupp had radically altered his position. Noting that the theory had won the support of scientists, he now sought to show that it could be reconciled with Christianity. Toward this end, he insisted that the Bible was "a book purely of religious teaching, not of scientific, historical or philosophical information." This position prompted him to assert that attempts to "deduce the modern doctrine of evolution from the first chapter of Genesis" were untenable. Indeed, the notion that "the author of Genesis . . . was made unconsciously to utter ideas which he did not understand, and which men generally did not understand for thousands of years after, presupposes a view of inspiration that turns it all into magic."[12]

Rupp was only one of many American Protestant intellectuals in the late nineteenth century who insisted upon interpreting the familiar claim that the Bible was not intended to be a work of science in a radical manner. These thinkers continued to believe that the narrative of creation disclosed that God had created the natural world, but they denied that there was any reason to expect that narrative to accord with the conclusions reached by scientific investigators. For these Christians, consistency was irrelevant, "reconciliation" unnecessary.[13]

Not surprisingly, Protestants who opposed the idea that the biblical writers had conveyed an accurate account of natural history concluded that the doctrine of biblical infallibility was untenable. Many, in fact, concluded that it represented "a constant impediment to the progress of truth." Commitment to biblical inerrancy, they believed, forced believers either to reject the disclosures of science or to adopt disingenuous interpretations of the Scriptures. The harsh treatment accorded the transmutation hypothesis by many proponents of the doctrine of plenary inspiration all too clearly exemplified the former danger. The latter was no less disastrous to the cause of Christianity. Newman Smyth thus warned that "treating the Bible as a mere collection of oracular texts" would, by making it necessary to strain the meaning of biblical passages to bring them into accord with the conclusions of modern thought, "put in jeopardy belief in the very fact of revelation" that the doctrine of divine inspiration was designed to justify. Henry Ward Beecher was even more acerbic, laying "all forms of dishonest reasoning" in relating the Bible to science at the door of the doctrine of scriptural infallibility. Convinced that "evolution compels the rejection of the verbal and plenary inspiration of the Sacred Scripture," Beecher concluded that "the logical outcome" of that view of inspiration was "superstition on the one hand, and infidelity on the other."[14]

The conflict between science and the Scriptures was not the only source of opposition to the doctrine of biblical infallibility. No less important was the notion that significant conceptual development could be discerned within the pages of the Bible. During the last quarter of the nineteenth century, an increasing number of Protestant intellectuals maintained that the Scriptures recorded a "serial history" of changing ideas concerning God, ethical precepts, and many other important religious conceptions. These thinkers denied that the presence of significant conceptual change within the Scriptures impugned either the sanctity or the value of the Bible as a source of theological insight. God's method of revealing Himself to humanity, they reasoned, was akin to the procedure of a "father who gives a picture-book to his son when he is an infant and bestows upon him a library of learned volumes when he becomes a man." Nevertheless, they were aware that a developmental conception of biblical revelation was impossible to square with any meaningful concept of biblical inerrancy.[15]

The intellectual odyssey that often occurred before Protestants arrived at this view of the Scriptures is exemplified in the life and thought of William Newton Clarke. Clarke graduated from Hamilton Seminary in 1863 and held a number of Baptist pastorates before becoming professor of New Testament interpretation at the Baptist Theological School in Toronto in 1883. In 1890, three years after returning to the pastoral ministry in Hamilton, he accepted election to the Hamilton Theological Seminary's J. J. Joslin Professorship of Christian Theology.[16]

Clarke's pastoral experience made him especially sensitive to the theological unrest of his age. He recognized that the problematic status of the Bible was the focal point of much of this unrest, and in 1909 he published an autobiographical account of the development of his own thoughts regarding this question. He recalled that in the 1860s, he was, like most Americans, "a firm biblicist" who "looked upon the Bible as so inspired by God that its writers were not capable of error." He therefore rejected the theory of evolution, though he confessed to having had "a kind of dim suspicion that perhaps the question was not one that could be finally disposed of in that way." In the 1870s, suspicion yielded to conviction. Intensive biblical study convinced Clarke that there were inconsistencies in the way that different biblical authors had viewed the same idea. His doubts about scriptural inerrancy were reinforced by his awareness that humanity's understanding of the Bible was imperfect. If God had really provided man with an "infallible standard," Clarke reasoned, "he should and would, have insured to us the power of understanding it perfectly." This was not the case. By the 1880s, Clarke had concluded that "what was needed was a different conception of the whole matter from beginning to end." He thus adopted a radically altered view of the Scriptures: the Bible "contained old forms of truth that were long ago superseded by truth in higher forms, and the Bible itself contains the record of that superseding."[17]

The ever-growing number of American Protestant intellectuals who repudiated the doctrine of biblical infallibility emphasized that it was not the words of Scripture but its authors who had been divinely inspired. The Bible contained the Word of God and was thus an important source of truth, but this did not mean that every passage in the Bible was inerrant. A representative statement of this position was offered in 1888 by the Unitarian clergyman Robert Collyer, who became pastor of the Church of the Messiah in New York City in 1879 after a distinguished pastoral career in Chicago: "the fine wheat is there; so is the chaff: the fair flowers, so are the weeds, the pure gold, so is the dross and refuse and the slag of holy and unholy fires long burnt out." This position, some Protestants argued, was not new; the Reformers had recognized the presence of error in the Scriptures. It was actually Christians who insisted upon equating orthodoxy with subscription to the doctrine of biblical infallibility who were guilty of heretical innovation.[18]

If opponents of biblical infallibility could agree that "certain classes of mistakes" could be found in the Scriptures, they differed in their assessments of the nature and significance of these mistakes. Some expressed confidence that error was limited to the "inessential" passages of the Scriptures. A typical exposition of this position was presented by Lewis French Stearns. Stearns had studied theology at Princeton Seminary, Berlin and Leipzig, and Union Seminary in New York, and after short stints as a Presbyterian minister in Norwood, New Jersey, and a professor of history and belles lettres at Albion College, he accepted a call to the chair of systematic divinity at the Congregationalists' Bangor Theological Seminary. Until his untimely death at the age of forty-five he strove tirelessly to show that new insights gleaned from science and history could be expressed within traditional theological categories.[19]

Stearns denied that the validity of Christianity rested on the infallibility of the Scriptures. Indeed, he argued, it was impossible to find justification even in the Bible itself for the claim that it was inerrant. Convinced that "the Scriptures are the setting, but they are not the jewel," he insisted that it was imperative to "distinguish the revelation from its record." However, though he recognized the presence of "human imperfection and human error" in the Bible, he denied that this undermined its validity as a source of revelation. On the contrary, he remained convinced that the biblical authors had been "so directed by the supernatural influence of God's Spirit as to give us the perfect rule of faith and life."[20]

A similar view was espoused by Frank Hugh Foster, Professor of Biblical and Systematic Theology at the Pacific Theological Seminary (Congregational) in Oakland, California, and an enthusiastic evolutionist. Foster denied that the Scriptures were infallible, but he accepted a conception of biblical inspiration involving a "union of the writers of the Bible with God through his Spirit which enabled them to teach without error, and in the best manner for the permanent instruction of mankind, those things which they intended authoritatively to teach, viz., all ethical and religious things necessary to the salvation and sanctification of men." From Foster's perspective, the fact that the biblical writers had been inspired did not imply that everything they wrote was inerrant. In theory, this approach made it possible to embrace both the central religious affirmations of the Scriptures and the conclusions of modern science.[21]

The work of Stearns and Foster attests to the continued appeal of strong conceptions of scriptural authority even among many Protestants who could no longer subscribe to biblical inerrancy. There was a major problem, however, with the claim that the teachings of the Scriptures constituted the perfect rule of faith. Proponents of this position were able to present no clear criteria by which the lessons that the biblical authors intended to teach could be distinguished from those that they did not. It is a telling comment on the difficulty they faced that Foster was forced to concede that "the actual extent of inspiration" in scriptural testimony could be determined only "by an appeal to facts." This admission begged the very point at issue and vitiated confidence that one could assume that the teachings of the Bible were reliable.[22]

The difficulties attending efforts to demarcate an area of biblical inerrancy led an increasing number of American Protestant intellectuals to dismiss that concept, however circumscribed, as unacceptable. William North Rice, for example, observed that "inspiration is not omniscience." In Rice's judgment, it was perfectly reasonable to affirm that the biblical authors "were under the special influence of the Divine Spirit" without assuming "that their opinions were always just, their arguments always conclusive, or their knowledge of facts always accurate." James Morris Whiton, the erudite pastor of the First Congregational Church of Newark, New Jersey, echoed Rice: "If men blunder, though God made them, why may not a book blunder, though God made it, if he made it by men?"[23]

Proponents of this position recognized the presence of a quite substantial "human" component in the Scriptures. Because human beings were fallible, these thinkers reasoned, the doctrine of scriptural inerrancy was untenable. Joseph Le Conte expressed a view that became increasingly popular among Protestant intellectuals when he asserted that "revelations to man must of necessity partake of the imperfections of the medium through which it comes. As pure water from heaven, falling upon and filtering through earth, must gather impurities in its course differing in amount and kind according to the earth, even so the pure divine truth, filtering through man's mind, must take imperfections characteristic of the man and of the age."[24]

During the late nineteenth century, opponents of the doctrine of biblical infallibility commonly emphasized that the substance of the scriptural narrative was informed by the cultural milieu in which the biblical authors had composed their work. The conceptual development disclosed in the Scriptures, they believed, was not simply the result of God's condescension to the people to whom He had revealed Himself; it also stemmed from the fact that the "messengers of revelation were of the people, limited by their conditions, and bound under the burdens of their own generation." In support of this position, many Protestant intellectuals appealed to evidence derived from the "higher" criticism of the Bible. During the nineteenth century, a number of German biblical critics, unwilling to limit their inquiries to problems of textual translation, began to analyze the Scriptures by means of the same methods as those that were employed in assessing other historical texts. Some Americans became familiar with this historical approach to the Scriptures through their reading of *Essays and Reviews*, but it was really only after 1880 that a large number of American Protestants, many of whom had studied theology in Germany, began to appropriate the methodology and conclusions of the higher criticism. These thinkers urged that it was necessary to "read every Scripture in its own light, and interpret it in view of its own surroundings, and in its place in the gradual development of the Bible."[25]

Virtually all of the outspoken advocates of higher criticism in the United States also endorsed the theory of organic evolution. This dual commitment was not coincidental. Both the higher criticism of the Bible and efforts to account for the history of life in evolutionary terms were products of the increasing fascination with the problem of historical change that pervaded the West in the nineteenth century, and both enterprises relied on the concept of gradual development in describing such change. Moreover, the substantive content of higher criticism and the transmutation hypothesis were mutually reinforcing. The idea that the narrative of the creation in Genesis was a function of the time and place in which it had been written lessened the force of objections to the theory of evolution based on its incompatibility with scriptural language. Conversely, the fact of such incompatibility lent credibility to the higher critics' claim that the language and even the thought forms of the biblical writers were shaped by their cultural environment.[26]

For opponents of the doctrine of biblical infallibility, there was little problem accommodating the theory of organic evolution to the Scriptures. They simply denied that the narrative of the creation in Genesis constituted a valid historical account of natural history. These thinkers remained convinced that the Scriptures conveyed truths that were essential to an understanding of the divine scheme of redemption, but they rejected the notion that these truths required Christians to reject the transmutation hypothesis.

The role that the theory of evolution played in Protestants' discussion of epistemological problems during the late nineteenth century extended beyond its function in goading many of them to reassess their positions regarding the nature and scope of biblical authority. It also provided, albeit often in indirect and subtle ways, a mode of comprehending reality that proved useful in grappling with problems attending the abandonment of conventional views of biblical revelation. The remaining pages of this chapter will be devoted to an analysis of these problems and the way in which insights derived from the theory of evolution figured in attempts to resolve them.

For most American Protestant intellectuals, the question of biblical authority was subsumed in the larger problem of religious knowledge. Many concluded that it was necessary to recast the doctrines of revelation and inspiration to make them more credible and more relevant to a generation for whom radical conceptual change had come to appear commonplace. This recasting, which frequently involved the use of the concept of evolution as a source of insight into the nature of God's communication with man, altered the role of the Bible in Christian theology.

Many religious thinkers in the late nineteenth century maintained that the scope of divine revelation extended well beyond the Scriptures. It actually included "everything that makes God known to men, and everything that is made known of him." In this spirit, Samuel Harris, the distinguished Dwight Professor of Systematic Theology at the Yale Divinity School, defined revelation as "the action of God revealing himself in the constitution and course of nature, in the constitution and history of man, and preeminently in Christ reconciling the world unto himself, and in the Holy Spirit who comes to abide with us forever."[27]

This broad vision of revelation was most apparent in the work of Protestants who emphasized the immanence of God in His creation. This is hardly surprising. A. V. G. Allen, a professor of church history at the Episcopal Theological School in Cambridge, Massachusetts, observed in 1882 that the heightened awareness of God's immanence "has given a new meaning and value to outward nature, and it has lent sanctity to all that concerns man in his history and development." From an immanentist perspective, it seemed inconceivable that God's communication with humanity had been confined to a few ancient documents. William Newton Clarke thus declared that "when one thinks of the living God, near to his human creatures and the same forevermore, it cannot be that he has given man no word of revelation from himself since it [the Bible] was finished." It seemed far more reasonable to assume that God used all the data of human experience as vehicles through which to communicate with humanity. This position prompted Myron Adams, a Congregational clergyman who believed that all events could be placed within the framework of an evolutionary process energized and directed by an immanent Deity, to submit that revelation, far from being an "abnormal thing," was "involved in the very constitution of man and nature."[28]

During the last quarter of the nineteenth century, the notion that nature was "God's oldest Testament" continued to play an important role in the way that many American Protestant intellectuals conceived of divine revelation. It was this notion that prompted Henry Ward Beecher to ask, "if to reject God's revelation of the Book is infidelity, what is it to reject God's revelation of himself in the structure of the whole globe?" In itself, of course, the idea that it was possible to glean spiritual truth from analysis of the cosmos was not new. But whereas Protestant thinkers during the first three quarters of the nineteenth century had characteristically drawn a distinction between "natural" theology and "revealed" theology, late-nineteenth-century proponents of a broadened view of divine revelation found that distinction untenable.[29]

Most proponents of a broad vision of divine revelation were convinced that human history was the preeminent instrument of divine revelation. God, they believed, was "indwelling in the historical process and conducting it to its conclusion." The conviction that God was implicated in the history of the human race had long held an important place in Christian theology. In the late nineteenth century, however, many Protestant thinkers placed great emphasis on the idea that not only the events recorded in the Scriptures but the entire course of human history represented a vehicle of divine revelation. Thomas Howard MacQueary, an Episcopal clergyman from Canton, Ohio, who espoused a radically immanentist and evolutionary interpretation of divine activity, presented a characteristic expression of this position when he submitted that "all History, rightly understood, is also a Bible."[30]

During the 1880s and 1890s, an ever-increasing number of Protestants resisted the notion that it was necessary to confine one's examination to the past when looking for God's communication to humanity. Determined to create "a more living theology," they drew on the thought of Schleiermacher and other German theologians, as well as on the work of Anglo-American thinkers, in support of the idea that every human being possessed a faculty—variously termed the spiritual, religious, and Christian consciousness—that could serve as a vehicle of divine revelation. Individuals who made themselves receptacles of "the utterance of God," they asserted, were capable of arriving at a sizable number of spiritual insights, including the conviction of sin and the experience of forgiveness, redemption, and regeneration.[31]

Exponents of this position, which constituted one of the central motifs of liberal theology in the late nineteenth century, maintained that in contrast to knowledge obtained "through the natural processes of human thought, research and experience," communications from God to the human consciousness were frequently immediate and apprehensible through the feelings rather than through the cognitive faculties.

Like those who pointed to the "religious feeling" as an argument for the existence of God, these Christians insisted that feelings were not simply subjective, idiosyncratic emotions but legitimate sources of religious truth. They held that "in religion there are other correspondences of truth to fact than those which are purely intellectual and evidential." The spiritual insights of individuals who had opened themselves to receive "a special impression of the Divine thought and will" were no less valid than those gleaned from nature and history. Some even insisted that knowledge derived from "conscious experience, sanctified imagination, and the best Christian sentiment" was more compelling than that grounded on inference and argument.[32]

Protestants who assumed that an adequate comprehension of God's communications to human beings required an examination of nature, history, and the human consciousness conceived of divine revelation as a continuous process of "communion between the Supreme Spirit and subordinate spirits during the entire history of their relations." Concomitantly, the idea that God revealed Himself in an "abrupt or arbitrary way" seemed less plausible than the idea that He had manifested Himself by means of a gradual process of spiritual enlightenment. As William Newton Clarke put it, "revelation is not a lightning-flash: it is rather like the dawn, brightening into the full day."[33]

These believers acknowledged that spiritual truth itself was immutable, but they were convinced that God had dispensed that truth to humanity by means of "a continuous process, adjusted to the developing reason of man." The ability of human beings to grasp spiritual truth was a function of the general level of their knowledge and sensitivity: "Too much light would have rather dazzled and blinded than illumined and led." God therefore guided human beings in the understanding of His divine scheme "slowly, from age to age."[34]

Many Protestant intellectuals employed this notion of progressive revelation to account for the conceptual development that occurred within the pages of the Scriptures. Noting that the Bible was "a historical growth," Newman Smyth suggested that "at no time was its word of prophecy too far advanced for the people to follow it, if they would."[35]

Other thinkers applied similar reasoning to the broader conception of divine revelation. One of the most articulate expressions of this issue was presented by George Trumbull Ladd. Ladd graduated from Andover Theological Seminary in 1869, held Congregational pastorates in Edinburgh, Ohio, and in Milwaukee, and taught mental and moral philosophy at Bowdoin College before moving to Yale in 1881. A prolific writer, he published numerous works dealing with a wide variety of issues in philosophy, theology, and psychology. These works, which were characteristically interpretive syntheses of the views of others rather than original investigations, reflected the direction taken by many thinkers who were intent on accommodating Christianity to modern culture.[36]

Ladd's interest in revelation and inspiration found expression in a series of articles beginning in the late seventies and in a two-volume study, *The Doctrine of Sacred Scripture*, published in 1883. In these works he maintained that religious knowledge was "the result of a process of unfolding." Though he emphasized that both God and the truth were immutable, he held that as a result of man's limited but growing capacity for apprehending spiritual truth, "revelation is given to us in the form of development."[37]

Ladd's conviction that divine revelation "must be historic, evolutionary," was widely shared in the late nineteenth century. It seems clear that some Protestants valued this conception of revelation largely because it offered them a means of affirming the kind of sustained concern of the Deity for His creation that had been rendered problematic by modern science. Francis H. Johnson thus declared in 1885 that the fact that "new light, so coördinated with the intellectual and moral needs of men, does find its way into the world from time to time is one of the strongest evidences for the existence of a living God who watches over the destinies of men and educates them."[38]

In the judgment of many Protestants, revelation and inspiration were united by an "organic and vital relation." Whereas the former referred to the divine communication itself, the latter denoted the power God gave human beings to apprehend His message. Many Protestants who adopted a broad conception of revelation held similar views of divine inspiration. Ladd, for example, maintained that though the biblical authors were "the organs of a specific divine self-revelation," the inspiration they had received was not "specifically different" from that of individuals who had received subsequent revelations. Newman Smyth adopted a similar position, suggesting that "the inspiration of the prophet is not an anomaly, but in accordance with the nature of man."[39]

Some Protestant evolutionists also suggested that inspiration, like revelation, should be viewed in developmental terms. In their judgment, humanity's apprehension of the divine had gradually evolved, and they attributed this evolution at least in part to inspiration. Elizabeth Stuart Phelps enunciated this position in 1882 when she wrote that "what we call inspiration is a growth. It unfolds with history and like history. It is subject to evolution, like the race."[40]

Still, for all the rhetoric emphasizing the necessity for a gradual revelation of spiritual truth, the notion that an omnipotent God had revealed Himself and His will fully and clearly in an inerrant book was not patently absurd. It was not the imperatives of logic but the appeal of evolution as a paradigm of divine activity that encouraged many Protestant intellectuals to reject this notion. The fact that the most outspoken proponents of the developmental conception of religious knowledge were also characteristically avid supporters of the transmutation hypothesis was not simply coincidental. Underlying this link was the assumption that the means by which a consistent Deity revealed Himself to human beings resembled those that He employed in other realms of His activity. Henry Stimson, the pastor of the Manhattan Congregational Church, clearly articulated this assumption in 1900: "Everywhere there is one law, everywhere there is development, because God is wise as he is loving, and has no reason to change a method he has once adopted." This view led Stimson to reason that a gradual evolution of religious ideas more closely conformed to God's chosen mode of operation than the traditional assumption that the Bible "came complete from the hand of God." David Hill, the president of Lewisburg University (later Bucknell), adopted a similar position. Noting that "all nature reveals development," Hill reasoned that "it would be anomalous, indeed, if we did not find it in a revelation designed for men of different attainments and different consequent needs."[41]

Not every Protestant evolutionist attributed belief in a gradual, continuous, and progressive process of divine revelation to endorsement of the scientific theory of evolution. The Andover Theological Seminary professor George Foot Moore, for example, suggested that although that theory had been enormously influential, the view that God had gradually revealed Himself in the historical process owed at least as much to developments within historical studies as to science. Other thinkers regarded developmental conceptions of revelation as grounds for accepting evolution in the natural world. Samuel Harris, for example, endorsed the theory of organic evolution in part because he believed that an evolutionary method of creation accorded "with the theological truth that the historical revelation of God has been progressive according to the capacity of an age to receive it." The rather sparse explicit discussion of the relationship between developmental views of revelation and the evolutionary hypothesis, however, suggests that more often the influence ran in the other direction. Protestants such as Lewis French Stearns, who espoused the notion that the evolutionary process was periodically punctuated by special, supernatural creative acts, argued that this method had similarly been employed in His process of gradual revelation. By contrast, Protestant evolutionists who abandoned the notion that divine activity in nature was "local, special, and transitory" in favor of the idea that God characteristically effected His purposes by means of a gradual and continuous process found it eminently reasonable to suppose that divine revelation was a similarly "God-directed and God-impelled evolution" that "has not proceeded by arbitrary, unconnected leaps, but is a continuous river of light and life, flowing through the ages with a constantly increasing fulness of development."[42]

Toward that end, they often drew explicit connections between the scientific theory of evolution and developmental conceptions of religious knowledge. Newman Smyth, for example, noted that "the same powers of development, the same law of evolution, seem to have been followed, alike, in nature and in the Bible." Similarly, in his autobiographical *Recollections*, published in 1909, the eminent Congregational clergyman Washington Gladden recalled that he, like many other Christians, gradually came to perceive that God's revelation had occurred by "a continuous process" that paralleled His "work of creation."[43]

Broadened, developmental conceptions of revelation and inspiration may have been congenial to the spirit of modern science, but they raised troublesome questions about the role of the Bible in Christian theology. The idea that God had gradually and continuously revealed Himself and His will through a variety of vehicles blurred the distinction between "sacred" and "secular" history. It was thus vulnerable to the charge that it impugned the idea that the Scriptures were a special source of spiritual insight. If the Bible, which itself manifested conceptual development, represented only a few chapters in the continuing saga of God's communication with humanity, why should it be singled out as peculiarly canonical? And if the state of religious knowledge was a function of time and culture and God had progressively revealed Himself, what value remained in a book almost two thousand years old?

Some Protestant evolutionists feared that the characterization of all religious truth as divine revelation and all perception of such truth as inspiration might foster disrespect for the Bible. This apprehension was manifested in the work of Lewis French Stearns. Although Stearns denied that the Bible was inerrant, his conviction that the Scriptures remained "the rule of faith and practice" for Christians prompted him to reserve the term "revelation" for the biblical message. "God," he asserted, "has made no new revelations." Moreover, although Stearns acknowledged that divine inspiration was considerably broader than simply scriptural inspiration, he held that the "special and supernatural influence of God's spirit in the men who composed the biblical books" was fundamentally different from "that gracious illuminating power of the Holy Spirit granted to Christians in all ages."[44]

In theory, the idea that revelation was restricted to the Bible was quite different from the view that God had gradually revealed Himself and His will by means of a variety of instruments. In practice, however, this difference proved minimal. A large area of agreement obtained between proponents of the two positions. In the first place, although Stearns and others resisted the idea that God continually imparted *new* revelations to humanity, they nevertheless held that "God reveals himself to every soul." Moreover, those who limited their use of the term "revelation" to the Bible were no less convinced than those who adopted more catholic and evolutionary views that human beings had become increasingly cognizant of spiritual truth. Stearns, for example, acknowledged that history displayed a "line of progress in theology" resulting from a clearer apprehension of "the unchanging truth of the ages, the truth of the Bible, the truth of Jesus Christ." The Congregational clergyman Asher H. Wilcox of Norwich, Connecticut, similarly insisted that although the Bible was the fount of all Christian wisdom, human beings continued to grow in their understanding of it.[45]

For their part, the overwhelming majority of Protestants who believed that revelation was continuous and progressive continued to cling tenaciously to the idea that the Bible was, as William Newton Clarke put it, "a unique book, uniquely previous." These thinkers assumed that the divine truth disclosed in other realms of human experience only supplemented the revelation contained in the Bible. If "we do not look for evolution to produce greater poets than Homer, Dante, Milton, and Shakespeare," Lyman Abbott argued, it was no less reasonable for defenders of "the evolution of revelation" to assume that the Bible was a special and fundamental source of spiritual truth.[46]

This continued faith in the singular value of the Bible was understandable. The Christian gospel was above all else an interpretation of how God had acted in history, and it was the Scriptures that recorded the salient events relating to the divine-human encounter. Moreover, the Bible remained even for Protestants who rejected its inerrancy an invaluable repository of humanity's experience of "the reality and energy of God's redeeming grace in human history."[47]

The zealous commitment of virtually all Protestants to the centrality of the scriptural message ensured that even those who considered revelation to be continuous and progressive would confine their perceptions of "progress" within a perimeter determined by what they viewed as the essential tenets of the biblical record. Such conservatism cannot be attributed simply to a failure of nerve. Given their conviction that God was consistent, they found it entirely reasonable to believe that although the Deity had continuously and progressively revealed Himself to humanity, "the essential truths of Christianity have not been changed nor been superseded." For these religious thinkers, it seemed obvious that "the man who wakes each morning with the feeling that everything is still an open question is so much too much of a Protestant that he does not deserve to be called a Christian at all." Hence, they concluded, whatever headway humanity made in apprehending the divine, "the bed-rock of the Scriptures" would remain secure.[48]

Still, for those who coupled rejection of biblical infallibility with "progressive" conceptions of religious knowledge, the Bible's role in Christian theology changed significantly. Although Protestant evolutionists still maintained that the Scriptures contained "truth which no age could outgrow," most also denied that the Bible "settles all disputed points and clears up all mysteries off-hand." Unlike more conservative Christians, they did not look upon the Scriptures as "a book of statutes with external sanctions" or as "a treatise of systematic theology." David N. Beach, a liberal Congregational clergyman serving in Minneapolis, argued that the Bible's value lay less in the knowledge it imparted than in the capacity it possessed for "enkindling the soul, enlightening the eyes, and challenging man's whole being." From a doctrinal perspective, he suggested, the Scriptures were only a point of departure for "the blazing of a path out toward the never-to-be-overtaken horizon of enlightenment and growth."[49]

Belief in the eternal significance of the experiences recorded in the Scriptures appeared to ensure the Bible's preeminence. On the other hand, Protestants who coupled a commitment to the sanctity of biblical revelation with the conviction that divine revelation was a gradual, progressive process did not assume that the presence of an idea in the Scriptures was sufficient to establish its truth. Instead they argued, as Myron Adams put it, that "the Bible is a growth, and therefore has come according to the law of vital growths; it has its abiding elements, and its elements of transition and change." For these thinkers, theology was valid only insofar as Christian theologians were successful in their efforts to "pluck the rose from the bush, and leave the bush."[50]

Protestants who denied that doctrinal claims could be evaluated simply by appealing to the Bible found it necessary to devise principles that would enable them to distinguish the permanent truths of Christianity from the more transient human expressions of those truths. Noting the perplexity experienced by many Christians in the face of the "puzzling intricacies" of modern thought, Frank Hugh Foster urged that "this is a time when the sifting of truth from error, the separation of the essential and the non-essential, and the exhibition and proof of the eternal, divine verities of our faith, are needed as never before."[51]

Amidst the turmoil attending the abandonment of the doctrine of biblical infallibility, one anchor remained as a virtually universally accepted source of religious authority: the life and teachings of Jesus. Newman Smyth expressed the common sentiment of American Protestant intellectuals when he asserted that "Christ came as the most perfect possible impartation and revelation in human form of the very life of God with the world and in the world; and all that God had been graciously doing and becoming in history, as well as teaching and saying, reaches its perfect result, bears its final fruit, in the Son of man." This conviction prompted even the most outspoken opponents of biblical inerrancy to affirm that theological propositions could be tested by appealing to the authority of Jesus. Charles Briggs, a Union Theological Seminary professor whose militant progressivism provoked conservative members of the Presbyterian church to initiate heresy proceedings against him, offered a representative statement of this position: "The authority of Jesus Christ, to all who know Him to be their divine Savior, outweighs all other authority whatever. A Christian man must follow His teachings in all things as the guide into all truth."[52]

The claim that Jesus possessed special sanctity was one that could be held only on faith. Protestants who advocated a rigorous testing of biblical statements recognized that it was not possible to reduce the entire corpus of Christian theology to demonstrable propositions, and they reminded their readers that neither science nor any other important realm of human endeavor was bereft of mystery, paradox, and the need for faith. On the other hand, few were entirely comfortable with the idea of depending on mere "belief," and they sought to minimize its role in Christian theology. Most of them espoused what they considered to be a more rigorous approach to doctrine, an approach that relied on the experiential verification they associated with scientific investigation. Their commitment to this approach rested at least in part on their conviction that literate Americans were inclined to turn a deaf ear to appeals to faith and authority. Charles W. Eliot, a chemistry professor whose ascendancy to the presidency of Harvard in 1869 was itself testimony to the increasing prestige of science, observed in 1883 that the scientific method had yielded such striking results that within "the educated world," at least, "no other method of inquiry now commands respect." Most Protestant evolutionists were themselves persuaded that the term "unscientific" was "justly synonymous with *untrustworthy*." The Reverend James G. Roberts of Brooklyn urged that "the only way that the student of theology can escape from the perplexities of doubt, and arrive at a calm certainty in his convictions and conclusions is that he shall do as the natural scientist has done before him." Echoing this view, David N. Beach called on Christians to submit themselves "without reservations to the inductive process."[53]

In itself, of course, commitment to an "inductive theology" was neither new nor limited to partisans of modern science. But whereas Charles Hodge and other conservative Protestants assumed that the sole object of theological investigation was the testimony of the Scriptures, Roberts and others believed that it was necessary to bring all the data of human experience to bear in formulating Christian doctrine. If they remained convinced that the Bible was the foundation of the Christian message, they also believed that it was necessary to employ the "alembic of reason" in evaluating its testimony. Joseph Le Conte, for example, held that because "there is, and in the nature of things there can be, *no test of truth but reason*," it was necessary to "try all things, even revelations, by this test." Similarly, Henry Ward Beecher insisted that the Scriptures "have authority only concurrently with educated human reason and rational moral sense." "On any other supposition," he declared, "the church becomes a temple, the Bible an idol, and priests and theologians the despotic interpreters of its meaning."[54]

These thinkers regarded scientific and historical inquiry, which had played an integral role in convincing them that the Bible was an amalgam of permanent spiritual insights and transient human ideas, as essential to Christian theology, "purifying its faiths and guiding its reverences." They also recognized, however, that such inquiry was incapable of furnishing the kind of data necessary to evaluate many of the doctrines associated with Christianity. For this purpose, they believed, an appeal to the testimony of humanity's religious experience was required. Convinced that "spiritual things are spiritually discerned," they asserted that the religious consciousness was not only a source of religious truth but also an instrument of verification.[55]

In defending this position, Protestants commonly drew on the prestige of science by likening study of the contents of the Christian consciousness to the procedure of the scientist. W. R. Benedict, a Baptist clergyman and member of the faculty at the University of Cincinnati, suggested that "for a man to reason inductively he must reason experimentally; for him to reason experimentally he must bring his *entire nature* to bear on truths that affect the whole of his nature." In the same spirit, James T. Bixby argued that "a complete science should take note, not only of the verifications of physical doctrines, in physical experience, but of these equally strong verifications in spiritual experience of spiritual truths."[56]

One of the most intelligent expositions of the idea that religious experience should play a central role in evaluating the claims of Christian theology appeared in an article by George Harris published in the *Andover Review* in 1884. Harris, who graduated from Andover Theological Seminary in 1869, had served as pastor to Congregational churches in Auburn, Maine, and Providence, Rhode Island, before returning in 1883 to Andover Seminary as professor of Christian theology. He remained in this position until 1899, when he left Andover to become president of Amherst College.[57] It was Harris's view that "all statements and interpretations of truth, to be accepted, must commend themselves to the Christian consciousness." Although he acknowledged the primacy of scriptural testimony, he believed that religious experience offered a "scientific" means of rescuing the permanant corpus of Christian truth in the Bible from the thought forms and language in which the spiritual experiences of the biblical authors had become encased. By providing a standard against which to measure the testimony of the Bible, he asserted, the data of religious experience provided a means "of distinguishing that which is not and that which is Christianity." Harris reminded his readers that this was not a new idea; it was merely a "revival of one of the essential principles of Protestantism."[58]

During the late nineteenth century, some proponents of the value of religious experience maintained that it held real promise of liberating Christians from "servile dependence on tradition and blind idolatry of the past." Others emphasized that experiential data were invulnerable to conceptual revisions resulting from new advances in science and history. Lewis French Stearns, for example, held that once "the evidence of Christian experience has been given its proper place, the way is opened for the fullest and freest investigation of the historical and critical questions relating to the Bible." Christians who fearfully resisted "the full and free examination of biblical questions," he opined, "are generally those who are without the evidence of Christian experience, or those who having it at their disposal will not use it." Applying a similar line of reasoning in connection with the transmutation hypothesis, the well-known clergyman Lyman Abbott held that "if there has been wrought into the soul a personal sense of divine sonship, a consciousness of sin in falling away from it, and a hope of restoration to it through God's love coming down from above and bringing new life, no scientific theories of either man's origin or man's development will impair this spiritual life or prevail against it."[59]

Although the use of religious experience to evaluate Christian doctrine appeared on the surface to be a rather straightforward approach, it was actually quite problematic. In the first place, not all individuals shared the same religious experience. Hence, the notion that religious experience enabled individuals to discern the permanent truths of the Scriptures came perilously close to sanctioning the idea that "every Christian makes his own Bible." Moreover, the variety of religious experience seemed to undermine the claim that an examination of religious consciousness constituted a scientific means of verifying Christian doctrine. Whereas the data of natural science and history were, in theory, at least, available to all investigators, the subjective experience of one individual was not necessarily like that of another.[60]

Protestants who grappled with this difficulty offered two ways of "objectifying" religious experience, neither of which was wholly free of difficulty. Some argued that genuine religious experience, like valid scientific inference, was independently verifiable by a host of "experimenters." The way to avoid allowing individual "idiosyncrasies" to serve as the criterion for religious truth was to rely on a consensus among believers. Lyman Abbott, expressing a view that the influential American philosopher Charles Saunders Peirce was elaborating at some length during the late nineteenth century, urged that this was wholly in accordance with the established practice of science. Though he defended the "trustworthiness of spiritual experience," he insisted that "no individual may take his own consciousness as an ultimate authority in religion, as no man takes his own observation and his conclusions thereon as an ultimate authority in science. He must reach the truth in the one case by a careful study of the observations and conclusions of scientifically minded men; in the other by a not less careful study of the spiritual experiences of spiritually minded men." Because proponents of this position were Christians, they assumed that religious experience would vindicate the Christian view of the human condition. Accordingly, the consensus they relied upon for validating religious truth was the "agreeing experience of Christian believers throughout the ages and in our own time."[61]

Even if the premise that Christians enjoyed a privileged ability to adjudicate claims based on the testimony of the religious consciousness were accepted, history indicated that a "common" Christian consciousness could not be obtained. Unanimity among believers was the exception, furious theological controversy the rule. The few Protestant evolutionists who grappled with this problem were content—or perhaps forced—to invoke the opinions of "the most enlightened and pious men in all Christendom" as "the court of ultimate appeal in all questions touching the meaning of the Scriptures and the statements of Christian doctrine." They offered no prescriptions, however, either for identifying these Christians or for ascertaining the truth should their views happen to clash.[62]

More important in fortifying the confidence of Protestants that it was possible to verify theological doctrines by means of religious experience without sanctioning an anarchic epistemology was the assumption that veridical testimony from the individual's religious consciousness would conform to the essential truths recorded in the Bible. Harris, for example, insisted that "the function of the Christian consciousness is not exercised apart from the Bible nor apart from Christianity." Stearns suggested that Biblical testimony served as a useful corrective to the "one-sidedness" of an individual's religious experience. But this position, by making the Bible the criterion for the validity of religious experience, brought its advocates full circle and effectively nullified the role of experience as an instrument for verifying biblical testimony.[63]

The source of this circular reasoning lay in the assumption that because God was the source of both biblical and contemporary religious experience, the two would perforce be "organically united." However uncomfortable Protestant evolutionists might have been with faith, however hearty their endorsement of "scientific" modes of analysis, in the end their epistemology was strongly conditioned by the conviction that "with all the shakings and overturnings of the times, there remain things which not only *are* not, but *cannot* be shaken." Few of these thinkers favored radical theological innovations. There is no reason to assume that they were being disingenuous when they gave such titles to their works as *Progressive Orthodoxy* and *The New Orthodox Theology of To-day.* Because they were convinced that there was "an unshaken and immoveable rock of divine truth" embodied in the Christian gospel, they assumed that the essential tenets of Christianity would accord with all other truth and endure all advances in spiritual understanding. From this perspective, they reasoned that bringing the verdict of science, history, and religious experience to bear on the formulation of Christian theology would result not in the overthrow but in the purification of doctrine.[64]

Proponents of this view believed that the crucible in which outworn, transient human elements in theology were stripped from the permanent divine truths they sought to express was the historical process. Many of these Protestants expressed this idea in terminology derived from the evolutionary hypothesis. George Harris, for example, termed Christianity "the survival of the fittest religion." Frank Hugh Foster, asserting that "history tests doctrines by their power of survival," submitted that "evolution has brought order out of confusion, marking out the historic course of development, distinguished between the essential and the non-essential, the nascent and the mature, the voice of the individual and the voice of the church, and has thus enabled us to employ the history of doctrine as one of our most efficient allies in the defence, and one of our most instructive teachers in the unfolding, of Christian truth." Noting that "a pre-requisite for the survival of anything in this world is its serviceableness," the Unitarian Edward J. Young felt entitled to conclude in 1886 that "Christianity stands this test successfully." Other Protestant intellectuals used the test of survival in defending individual beliefs. Newman Smyth thus suggested that "the religious consciousness is not outgrown but persists; and the fact that it survives, shows that it is fit to survive."[65]

The use of natural selection as a principle for evaluating the truth of religious claims, which is yet another indication of the great resonance the concept of evolution had for many American Protestant intellectuals, was specious. It rested on an ambiguous use of the concept of "fitness." For the evolutionary biologist, attributes survived because they were useful. Even if natural selection were applicable to doctrine—itself a dubious proposition—this would suggest only that beliefs that had "survived" either were or had once been useful; it would not demonstrate their truth. Of course, a true doctrine might very well be useful, and vice versa. But the relationship was not logically necessary. Nor was this the only difficulty attending the use of natural selection in evaluating the validity of doctrine. In a period in which secularism appeared to be making steady advances on a religious view of the world, it was rather incautious, to say the least, to make survival the test of truth. Finally, the use of survival as a standard for assessing doctrinal validity opened the way to a rather circular type of reasoning. Doctrines that people chose to reject for any reason whatsoever would not survive; their demise could then be offered as proof of their falsity. Moreover, the idea that rejected doctrines were invalid would have undermined another idea that many Protestant evolutionists were committed to: that it was necessary to recover truths that had supposedly been obscured during the course of history.

The conviction that the essential truths of the Christian message had been underwritten by God, coupled with the belief that the insights yielded by science, historical research, and religious experience were to be viewed as disclosures from God, led Protestant evolutionists to assume both that no doctrinal formulation that was clearly in conflict with the results of modern thought was really essential and that many of their doctrinal tenets would survive in the battle between different versions of reality. But whereas their commitment to biblical revelation imposed limits on the doctrinal change they would countenance, their commitment to the testimony of modern thought convinced them that a number of the doctrinal formulations associated with orthodoxy should be rejected as products of a cruder, more "primitive" stage in man's evolving apprehension of divine truth. Theological revision, these thinkers urged, was imperative.[66]

Underlying the argument that it was necessary to test doctrines against the testimony of science, historical scholarship, and the Christian consciousness was a conviction that the elaboration of man's spiritual understanding was "human, and changes with human thought." For thinkers who endorsed this view theology, "the rational and systematic interpretation of the facts of Divine Revelation," became, as James G. Roberts put it, "as really human and fallible, as any other science." Many Protestant intellectuals reasoned that because creedal statements, like all human productions, were expressed in the language and the intellectual categories of the period and culture in which they were composed, they were at least in part idiomatic reflections of "the spirit of an age." Because one historical epoch differed from another, theology was in a constant state of flux. Indeed, the history of Christian thought was "strewn with outworn creeds and obsolete decrees of councils."[67]

Many Protestant intellectuals found it meaningful to place this view within an evolutionary perspective. Doctrinal formulations, these thinkers urged, were like species in that they were mutable "growths" that "follow laws of development." And like species, they thrived to the degree that they were adapted to the environment. When they ceased to express adequately the experiences of a given culture they became moribund and either yielded to doctrines that more satisfactorily conformed to humanity's perception of truth or became petrified obstructions to faith and insight. From this perspective, a sizable segment of the American Protestant intellectual community concluded that unbending adherence to a fixed and unchanging "orthodoxy" was a formula for spiritual suicide—"theologizing must always go on." This perspective prompted Newman Smyth to assert that it was necessary to assess doctrines periodically to ascertain whether "there is anything which can justly be subjected to the charge of being a hindrance to spiritual faith among thoughtful and honest minds."[68]

Nothing seemed more obvious to many Protestant thinkers in the late nineteenth century than the incompatibility of many of the prevailing doctrinal formulations with the age in which they were living. This view prompted the Episcopal clergyman Francis A. Henry to lament in 1884 that "traditional dogma has lost its hold upon this generation, and day by day the young and active-minded are leaving the home of their early faith." Daniel Curry, editor-in-chief of the *Methodist Review*, voiced a similar concern two years later: "The formularies of doctrine which have come down to us from the past, although they were so precious to those by whom they were once cherished, no longer satisfactorily express the theological conceptions of the best minds of Christendom." The crying need of the day, these thinkers urged, was theological "reconstruction."[69]

This position, though punctuated by a sense of urgency, was also informed by a conviction that "the widening dissent of our time from the old theology is an impressive sign of deepening spiritual insight." As in their discussions of natural history, Protestants who discussed the "evolution of doctrine" characteristically equated such evolution with progress. Convinced that humanity's understanding of religious truth gradually became clearer and more accurate, they viewed theology as "a progressive science." Augustus Jay DuBois, a professor of civil engineering at Yale's Sheffield Scientific School and a frequent participant in the dialogue on science and religion, offered a representative statement of this view when he observed in 1894 that "doctrines of theology, like theories of science, have their day, and give place to better."[70]

Protestants who embraced evolutionary conceptions of Christian doctrine were confident that they had corrected a number of theological errors. But if they believed that their understanding of Christianity was superior to that of their predecessors, their position implied that many of their own views would eventually be superseded by positions more consonant with new discoveries of truth. Noting that current theology "is relative to our day," M. Stuart Phelps, a professor of mental and moral philosophy at Smith College, reasoned that "future ages will reject many an error now preached as true from our pulpits,—just as they will reject many a mistake now taught in our laboratories,—and will formulate whole realms of new truths which, revealed to-day, would be incomprehensible mysteries." The denial that Christianity was "a definite, completed revelation" led to the exhilarating conclusion that "the age of inspiration has not perished" and that "all of revelation that has gone before is but as seed for the future." It also bred, however, a tentative approach to doctrine. However confident these thinkers may have been that the essential elements of Christianity would endure, the logic of their views precluded them from specifying precisely what these elements were.[71]

The contribution of the concept of evolution to the erosion of doctrinal certainty was profound. Recognizing this, George Foot Moore observed that "the domination of the intellect by the idea of development makes the claim of finality put forward by Christianity the greatest difficulty in the way of its acceptance." Many Protestants grappled with this difficulty by drastically pruning the list of doctrines they were prepared to defend as essential. Others argued that there was no more reason to despair about the future of the fundamental doctrines of Christianity than to fear for the fundamental ideas of science. In view of the biological revolution that had occurred before their very eyes, however, it is questionable whether this position engendered much security.[72]

However they chose to respond to the problems attending an evolutionary conception of Christianity, Protestants who embraced that conception were forced to concede that religious knowledge was more fluid and less certain than Christians had traditionally believed. There were, however, compensations. Christians could simultaneously endorse intellectual progress and the concept of divine revelation. Doctrinal revision could now be justified as a step toward progress and legitimated on evolutionary grounds.

7

"What Is Man, That Thou Art Mindful of Him?": The Protestant Evolutionists and Christian Doctrine

THE theory of organic evolution played an important role in shaping the way in which most Protestants who endorsed that theory discussed the Christian scheme of redemption. As in their analysis of the concept of divine revelation, Protestant evolutionists differed sharply in their assessments of the doctrinal implications of the transmutation hypothesis. Some of them held that this hypothesis entailed few significant alterations in the formulation and defense of the central categories of Christian theology. Others insisted that "to admit the truth of evolution is to yield up the reigning theology." Even for these thinkers, however, theological revision was limited by a commitment to the basic lineaments of Christian theology. Moreover, it is apparent that in some cases, at least, American Protestants who defended doctrinal restatements in the name of fidelity to insights furnished by the theory of organic evolution were actually using evolutionary language primarily as a polemical device to help justify the abandonment of formulations of dogma that they found desirable on other grounds.[1]

The resistance of Protestant evolutionists to interpretations of the transmutation hypothesis that required the radical reformulation of doctrines they perceived to be essential to the faith became abundantly clear in their discussions of the origin and nature of humanity. These thinkers could agree that it was unnecessary to accept the Bible's description of the origin of humanity as literally true. Evolutionists who remained committed to the doctrine of the plenary inspiration of the Scriptures held that the biblical account of human creation could be interpreted in evolutionary terms. George Frederick Wright, for example, maintained that when the Bible reported that God had created humanity from the dust of the ground, "it is no perversion of the language to

174

refer it to dust that had already been incorporated into some lower form of organization." Some proponents of this approach held that acceptance of the evolutionary hypothesis was consistent with the belief that all human beings had descended from a single ancestor. Others maintained that the term "Adam" should be reinterpreted to denote the entire human race. Underlying such differences in interpretation, however, was the common conviction that the biblical narrative could be harmonized with the dictates of the transmutation hypothesis.[2]

Protestant evolutionists not wedded to belief in plenary inspiration abandoned the idea that the biblical narrative presented an accurate historical account of human creation. The import of the story, these thinkers argued, lay in its claim that God had created the human species, not in its description of the manner in which He had done so.[3]

Though Protestants who subscribed to the transmutation hypothesis attached no importance to a literal account of the biblical narrative of human creation, they remained convinced that the idea that human beings had been created in God's image was of fundamental significance. Indeed, the idea that the human species had been created in the image of God was at least as fundamental for Protestants who endorsed the transmutation hypothesis as it was for those who opposed it. For many Protestant evolutionists, humanity possessed the kind of "inherent sanctity" that in an earlier age had appeared to reside in the Bible, the creed, and the church. The commitment most of them shared to the value of the "religious consciousness" as an instrument for ascertaining religious truth was predicated on the assumption that human beings enjoyed a special divine birthright. Protestant evolutionists also recognized that however useful the natural world might be in attesting to the existence of a divine Designer, it was human nature that most effectively attested to the fact that this Designer possessed attributes that showed that He was a loving and personal Father. Elaborating this view, Samuel Harris contended that God could have revealed His love, righteousness, moral perfection, and benevolence only to "finite beings who are reason or spirit like himself." From this perspective, he concluded that humanity was "the organ for the deepest and truest revelations of God."[4]

The special link between God and humanity also seemed to justify the hope of immortality. Noting that human beings had inherited their "godlike nature and powers" from their heavenly Father, Lewis French Stearns held that this bequest conferred upon them an "infinite value" entitling them to "participate in the divine eternity." "All arguments for immortality," George Harris maintained, "are eventually reduced to this one argument of kinship with God."[5]

Given the central role that the doctrine that humanity had been cre-

ated in God's image played in their theology, it is not surprising that
many American Protestant evolutionists felt compelled to grapple with
the claim that human beings had descended from lower animals. Because there appeared to be little at stake in discussions of the origin of
the human body, most of these thinkers conceded that humanity's
physical frame was the product of a divinely governed process of evolution. Aware of the clear affinities between the anatomical characteristics of human beings and those of other primates, they acknowledged
that it would be inconsistent to accept the evolution of other species
while rejecting the evolution of the human body.[6]

The origin of human personality evoked more disagreement. Like
critics of the evolutionary hypothesis, Protestant evolutionists assumed
that personality was the "crowning attribute of man" and the locus of
his "immortal spirit." A succinct summary of this position was offered
by William Rupp: "God is a person, a self, a being that thinks, and
wills, and loves, and is good, and holy and just. And these qualities, in
a finite form, man has in common with God. He possesses the faculty
of reason, and will, and sensibility; he has the power of self-determination, which makes him a free moral agent, responsible for his actions
and capable of sin as well as of righteousness." Whatever other issues
may have divided partisans of the transmutation hypothesis, they
could agree that personality attested to a special link between God and
the human species.[7]

Protestant evolutionists who believed that natural history required
the periodic supernatural intervention of God typically maintained
that the evolutionary model "breaks down when it comes to man's
higher nature." Drawing upon the testimony of Alfred Russel Wallace,
James Dwight Dana, and other scientists, they held that the elements
composing human personality were "too numerous and too peculiar to
have come in by slow increments." It was far more reasonable, they
concluded, to ascribe the appearance of humanity's intellectual, moral,
and religious attributes to a miraculous act of creation.[8]

An increasing number of Protestant evolutionists, persuaded that
"the whole order of the universe, so far as we know it," was the product
of evolution, came to believe that there was no reason to assume that
God had employed a different method in creating human personality.
Because they were convinced that the manner in which human beings
had been created was unrelated to their nature and status, they were
adamant in their insistence that there was nothing in the evolution of
human intellectual, moral, and spiritual attributes "to shake one iota of
the faith." Augustus H. Strong, for example, urged that "the biological

solution does not exclude the theological." "That man is the offspring of the brute creation," he asserted, "does not prevent him from being also the offspring of God." The more theologically liberal Theodore T. Munger went even further, insisting that "our attempts to separate ourselves from the previous creation are reflections upon God's handiwork."[9]

Protestant evolutionists who adopted this position adamantly denied that an evolutionary interpretation of human origin undermined the status of the human species. Some of them noted that the view of the origin of humanity gleaned from a literal interpretation of the Bible was not calculated to inspire thoughts of human dignity. Lyman Abbott thus quipped that he would " 'as soon have a monkey as a mud man for an ancestor.' " Others reasoned that "it is no more derogatory to man's dignity to have been, at some former period, an ape than to have been that red lump of mere flesh which we call a human infant." Still others maintained that the nature of the human species was a different issue than its origin. The University of Michigan philosopher George Sylvester Morris, for example, declared in 1876 that "whatever his historical or natural antecedents, yet man is, all the same, just what he is and is known to be; and the lower animals remain, none the less, mere brutes, separated from their head by an impassable gulf."[10]

Protestants who ascribed the orgin of the human species to evolutionary descent proceeded from the conviction that humanity bore the image of God. And like Christians who attributed the origin of humanity to a miraculous act of creation, they believed that the elements attesting to the special relationship between God and human beings resided in the fact that the human species possessed attributes—self-consciousness, reason, the moral sense, free will, and religiosity—that were different in kind from those of all other animals.[11]

The determination of these thinkers to defend the claim that the human species was radically different from other animals while simultaneously embracing the transmutation hypothesis was exemplified in their treatment of the orgin of humanity's moral sense. Protestants who endorsed Darwin's efforts to derive the human conscience from the social instincts nevertheless insisted that the sense of duty motivating human conduct was fundamentally different from the utilitarian considerations that determined the behavior of other animals. Francis H. Johnson, for example, argued that because natural processes were divinely ordained, there was nothing heretical in the affirmation that humanity's sense of duty had "come into the soul by a natural process." He denied, however, that this belief implied that experiences of pleasure and pain had "been transformed into the ideas of right and wrong, and that the feelings of *ought* and *ought not* have grown out of the compulsions that nature and society have brought to bear upon us when we have transgressed their laws." He conceded that pleasure and pain were often the consequences of behavior and sometimes even "co-öperate[d] with conscience to secure obedience to its commands," but he insisted that to assume that the motive for moral behavior was the desire to secure pleasure and to avoid pain was not to acknowledge the moral sense but "to abolish it."[12]

Most Protestants who employed the evolutionary hypothesis to describe the origin of humanity were convinced that not only the conscience but numerous other elements of human personality were different in kind from any attributes that could be found in other animals. That the roots of such elements could be found in nascent form in other animals and had arisen in humanity by a process of evolution did not alter the fact that the human species was unique. Theodore T. Munger, for example, observed in 1886 that "a flower is a flower only by refusing to be a leaf, though it comes about by differentiation from a leaf. So conscience or reverence may have come about by evolution through brute qualities, but they become themselves only by ceasing to be what they were. They get their real and essential nature from the mind that is behind—*in, cum et sub*—the whole process."[13]

The tenacity with which Protestant evolutionists held the view that humanity enjoyed a special kinship with God doubtless helps to account for the fact that these thinkers devoted relatively little attention to the relationship between mind and brain. Those who did address this issue reached differing conclusions, but they agreed that the attributes of human personality reflected those of the Deity. This appeared to be sufficient reason to dismiss as unwarranted the concerns about the trustworthiness of human mental faculties that so beset Darwin.[14]

In defending the claim that it was possible to endorse the transmutation hypothesis even while continuing to affirm that the differences between human characteristics and the attributes of other animals were differences of kind rather than degree, a number of Protestants maintained that evolution was actually a more "paroxysmal" process than Darwin and his followers had suggested. This saltatory conception of the evolutionary process was not essential to a "theistic scheme of transmutation," but it certainly facilitated the reconciliation of belief in the uniqueness of the human species with an evolutionary description of the origin of that species. It also greatly narrowed the analytical gap that separated Protestants who viewed the human species as the product of evolutionary descent and those who ascribed the origin of humanity to a special act of supernatural creation. The discussion of Reverend Anson P. Atterbury, a New York clergyman who affirmed the immanent presence of God within the evolutionary process, suggested the way in which the views of Protestant evolutionists converged on the subject of the magnitude of difference between human beings and other animals. Attributing the origin of the human mind to "a peculiar exercise of divine power," Atterbury argued that there was "something so essentially different . . . in the spiritual life of man from mere animal life," that the most reasonable inference to be drawn was that "the immanent God exerted His will differently, additionally and permanently" in creating humanity. This mode of reasoning prompted George Frederick Wright to observe in 1900 that "it is difficult to tell the difference between the paroxysms of evolution and the creative acts of the older theories."[15]

Actually, though the doctrine that "man alone is a *child of God*" clearly implied that the human species was superior to other organisms, it did not logically entail the view that human attributes were different *in kind* from those of other animals. That so many Protestant evolutionists insisted on maintaining that view attested to their inability to believe that a creature possessing an immortal soul differed from other animals only in degree. It also attested to their conviction that the clearest warrant for the claim that human beings were "above nature, while of nature," resided in their possession of attributes different in kind from those of other animals.[16]

In affirming that human beings were radically distinct from other organisms, Protestant evolutionists made it clear that they were no more willing than critics of the transmutation hypothesis to accept the notion that the human species was merely another cog in the evolutionary hypothesis. In fact, most American Protestant evolutionists continued to adhere to an anthropocentric interpretation of natural history. This interpretation was not easy to reconcile with the recognition—already well under way by the time the *Origin of Species* was published—that the fossil record disclosed the existence of numerous branches of development rather than a single line culminating in the appearance of the human species. Nor was it easy to square the conviction that there was a determinate, final goal in natural history—the appearance of humanity—with a theory based on the notion that the organic world disclosed continuous, ongoing change. Anthropocentrism was not even a legitimate deduction from the doctrine that human beings had been created in God's image. The narrative of creation in Genesis affirmed that God regarded all His work as "good." This implied that all created beings possessed an intrinsic value, not that they were simply "the scaffolding preparatory for man." These considerations notwithstanding, many Protestant evolutionists inferred from their belief that human beings enjoyed a special relationship with the Creator that the appearance and development of humanity constituted the goal of the evolutionary process. In turn, their belief that "man is the chief object of the creative energy" led a number of Protestant evolutionists to assert that "the globe was created for man as a house is created to serve the family."[17]

Many Protestant evolutionists based their anthropocentric interpretation of the transmutation hypothesis on the claim that the God Who directed the evolutionary process intended that the human species should constitute the end of creation. William Rupp, for example, reasoned that "if we assume that the cause of the world is a personal, intelligent Being, then it is as easy to believe in the realization of a predetermined plan or design in connection with the idea of evolution as in connection with the idea of instantaneous creation." Far from being "merely a process of transformation or change," evolution was actually an "ascending process" implying "an ideal of perfection, which, when reached, will bring the process to rest." This ideal was "man, the crown of the creation."[18]

John Fiske insisted that anthropocentrism was implicit within the transmutation hypothesis itself. Fiske, who had been villified throughout the 1870s for not giving sufficient weight to the cosmic significance of humanity, had come to believe by the mid-1880s that the human species was "different in kind from all other creatures" and that the idea that this species was "a mere local incident in an endless and aimless series of cosmical changes" was "at bottom neither more nor less than Atheism." In two series of lectures delivered to the Concord School of Philosophy, during the summers of 1884 and 1885, he sought to make amends for what he had come to view as a "shortcoming" in his earlier work: "an imperfect appreciation of the goal toward which the process of evolution is tending." This goal, he announced, was "the creation and perfecting of Man."[19]

In his *The Destiny of Man viewed in the Light of his Origin* (1884), Fiske attempted to show that an anthropocentric view of natural history received stronger support from the theory of evolution than from the doctrine of special creation. He argued that nothing in the latter doctrine, which implied that "man was suddenly flung into the world by the miraculous act" of God, precluded the possibility that the Deity would "at some future moment, by a similar miracle, thrust on the scene some mightier creature in whose presence Man would become like a sorry beast of burden." Darwin's theory, on the other hand, implied that "there was to be no further evolution of new species through physical variation." Henceforth, "the dominant aspect of evolution" would occur through "the progress of Civilization." In effect, the theory of organic evolution thus succeeded in placing the human species where the pre-Copernicans had tried to place it: "in the centre of the physical universe."[20]

Many scientists, including Charles Darwin and Alfred Russel Wallace, believed that it was reasonable to assume that significant physical change had ceased within the human species itself. There was nothing in the evolutionary account of natural history, however, to justify Fiske's contention that "it is impossible that any creature zoölogically distinct from Man and superior to him should ever at any time exist upon the earth." Nevertheless, numerous Protestant evolutionists joined Fiske in asserting that with the advent of the human species, the focus of evolutionary development shifted from biology to human culture and society.[21]

Although this assertion was impossible to prove, Protestant evolutionists could make a plausible case for the proposition that a gradual process of development could be discerned in the annals of human history. Joining the chorus of secular thinkers who interpreted the past as a record of progress, they concurred with Anson P. Atterbury, who declared in 1889 that "each successive generation is, in those spiritual respects which produce outward civilization, an advance upon the preceding."[22]

If, however, a number of Protestant thinkers were convinced that the "civilized" portion of the human race had traveled on an "ascending pathway from the first," they recognized that all groups had not progressed at an equal rate. Like many other intellectuals in the late nineteenth century, Protestant evolutionists assumed that the range of contemporary societies represented various stages of historical development and that the cultures of contemporary "savages" were comparable to the primitive cultures of prehistoric tribes. Atterbury, for example, found it reasonable to suggest that "the South African savage is merely an undeveloped American citizen."[23]

The inference most Protestant evolutionists drew from the differential rate of progress among human societies was that the development of civilization was contingent on the adoption of a determinate set of values: the moral precepts embodied in the Christian gospel. The culmination of human evolution, they believed, would occur when all human beings ordered their lives in accordance with these precepts. In this spirit, the Lutheran theologian Milton Valentine contended that "in the adjustment of moral beings, beings endowed in finite measure with the attributes of God, to moral law, which is the expression of God's nature and will, the conditions are laid for the realization at the top-most point in the evolutionary ascent of *God-likeness.*" From this perspective, Protestant evolutionists regarded moral behavior as both the basis of, and the standard by which to measure, human social and cultural development.[24]

Many proponents of the view that "personal and social morality advanced towards an ideal which is more or less distinctly seen, and which is realized progressively," were convinced that it was possible to discern in human progress the providential activity of God. Newman Smyth, for example, held that "man's conscience and its education through centuries of history are the work of God, or nothing is." The Methodist apologist B. F. Cocker agreed, submitting that "to the eye of the observant and conscientious student of all history, whether secular or ecclesiastical, there are undeniable evidences of the presence of Intelligence, disposing and collocating the conditions of human progress and directing humanity toward a nobler civilization."[25]

If Protestant evolutionists believed that "the spring of human progress is not in man but in God," many of them also believed that the means God had employed to secure the triumph of good over evil were embodied within the evolutionary process. These thinkers maintained that in human society, the precepts of Christian morality constituted the standard for judging "fitness." Charles Loring Brace, a founder of the New York Children's Aid Society who retained a lively interest in moral and theological issues, argued that "if the Darwinian theory be true, the law of natural selection applies to all the moral history of mankind, as well as to the physical. Evil must die ultimately as the weaker element, in the struggle with good." Myron Adams applied this reasoning to the social organism, submitting that "that society is most fit which is most Christlike." In support of this view he appealed to history. The record of the past, he asserted, revealed that "the relatively superior, in respect of mildness and reasonableness, has been gradually supplanting the inferior and fiercer."[26]

In reality, the belief that goodness would prevail over evil did not derive from the evolutionary hypothesis. Christians had always found spiritual purpose in the historical process, and they believed that the ultimate triumph of goodness was in accordance with the will of God. But evolution did provide a powerful idiom in which to express that faith. It is worth noting that even Protestant evolutionists who did not explicitly equate moral goodness with fitness commonly employed the term "evolution" to describe the progress of the human species.

One of the reasons that Protestant evolutionists linked progress to the evolutionary process was that the establishment of such a connection provided ostensibly scientific grounds for hope in continued improvement in the quality of human civilization. Their discussions of progress were not simply celebrations of past triumphs; they were also expressions of dissatisfaction with the present state of affairs. That there was still ample room for moral development in even "Christian" societies appeared to be obvious from the most casual reading of the daily newspapers. For many Christians the future, interpreted from an evolutionary perspective, offered consolations that were unavailable in the present. Thomas Howard MacQueary thus asserted that "if Evolution did not commend itself to our minds on any other ground, it ought to commend itself by the rainbow of hope which it flings across the dark clouds of sin and suffering which lower in our moral skies."[27]

The faith Protestant evolutionists shared that goodness would ultimately emerge victorious over evil prompted some of them to insinuate that progress was an inevitable corollary of human evolution. Edward Drinker Cope, for example, maintained that "the Creator of all things has set agencies at work which will slowly develop a perfect humanity out of his lower creation, and nothing can thwart the process or alter the result." Myron Adams enunciated a similar view in discussing social progress. "He may enjoy a serene confidence in the continued march of social improvement," Adams remarked, "who has discovered in evolution the mode of the creation of a Wise and Beneficent Creator."[28]

Most Protestant evolutionists were leery, however, of accepting any interpretation of human evolution that undermined belief in the freedom of the will. Cope himself allowed that human beings were free to refuse to realize their potential, but his simultaneous affirmation of a "necessitarian" view of the progress of the race entangled him in hopeless contradiction. Most Protestant evolutionists who discussed human progress were more successful than Cope in resisting the temptation to affirm that progress was predetermined and certain. These thinkers were quite willing to equate goodness with fitness, but they reasoned that this favorable "variation" would be preserved only if it actually appeared in the lives of individuals. This, in turn, was dependent on free moral choice. Just as past progress was due to people's ordering their behavior more closely in accordance with God's moral precepts, so future progress was ultimately contingent on the moral choices of human beings. Accordingly, they rejected the notion that there were "laws" of social development that made human progress inevitable.[29]

If, however, few Protestant evolutionists regarded progress as inevitable, many believed that it was cumulative. The concept of the inheritance of acquired characteristics, which was quite popular among biologists in the late nineteenth century, found a receptive audience among Protestants in the United States who endorsed the transmutation hypothesis. This was doubtless at least in part because it underscored the significance of moral choices. If, as many Protestant evolutionists believed, individuals transmitted their moral proclivities to succeeding generations, then it seemed reasonable to conclude that "the virtue of one generation is the gain of the next." William Newton Clarke thus felt entitled to declare that humanity was "a slowly rising race, with a native tendency to outgrow faults." At the same time, Protestants who adopted this position could continue to affirm that each individual retained both the freedom and the responsibility to make moral decisions. In this way, they managed to couple their belief in the freedom of the will with a reasoned defense of their faith in the continued progress of the human race.[30]

For most Protestant evolutionists, Christian morality was not simply the key to human progress; it was also an integral component of Christian theology. Not all of these thinkers joined Henry Ward Beecher in believing that "religion is simply Right Living." Most of them did assume, however, that "the cause of theology and morals is one."[31]

In view of the central role that Christian morality played in the world view of Protestant evolutionists, many understandably found it imperative to reply to the charge that the ethical implications of the transmutation hypothesis were inconsistent with Christian moral philosophy. Few issues, in fact, received more attention from these thinkers than the relationship between evolution and ethics. And few issues more clearly showed how decisively their understanding of the implications of the theory of organic evolution was shaped by their commitment to doctrinal tenets they believed to be central to Christianity.

The overwhelming majority of Protestants who endorsed the theory of organic evolution were no less convinced than those who did not that the basis of valid ethical standards was a moral law that humanity "did not make and cannot alter." The essence of such law, which they believed was most clearly embodied in the Christian gospel, was not an unchanging code of rules but the principle of love. This unconditional principle was predicated on belief in the sanctity of human personality and the conviction that the perfection of the individual was to be realized through loving relationships with others.[32]

Not all peoples, of course, subscribed to Christian moral philosophy. On the contrary, historical research and anthropology revealed the existence of widely different moral codes. This fact impelled a number of Protestant evolutionists to acknowledge that "there is no table of commandments written upon the heart." These thinkers continued to believe that the human conscience conferred upon all human beings the capacity for distinguishing right from wrong, and some joined Francis H. Johnson in believing that "the fundamental principles of the highest morality" were "dimly shadowed forth in the least developed conscience." Few, however, regarded the conscience as an infallible source of insight as to the content of moral conceptions.[33]

During the last quarter of the nineteenth century, a number of Protestants concluded that by examining the variegated moral landscape through evolutionary lenses, it was possible to make sense of the data while remaining faithful to Christian moral philosophy. These thinkers reasoned that the fact that more "primitive" peoples did not adequately grasp moral law was no more shocking than the fact that they were unaware of the existence of natural laws. Like other learned behavior, valid conceptions of right and wrong were the product of "an evolution which has had historical stages." But in contrast to those evolutionists who were content to ascribe the disparate moral codes manifested over time and in various cultures to differing estimates of the kind of conduct that would contribute to group welfare, proponents of the theory of evolution within the Protestant community interpreted them as manifestations of "a forereaching towards perfect morals which is in conformity with the ways of God." Far from impugning the sanctity of humanity's moral sense or demonstrating the legitimacy of moral relativism, the existence of moral codes differing from that embodied in Christianity underlined the need to "educate conscience" in the Christian gospel.[34]

If Protestant evolutionists responded favorably to the idea that the concept of evolution was useful in describing the history of human morality, most rejected the claim of Darwin, Spencer, and other transmutationists who maintained that utility constituted "the governing principle of human conduct." They adamantly denied, in fact, that moral conceptions could be reduced to utility. These thinkers believed that it was reasonable to assume that a benevolent Designer had ensured that virtuous behavior would be of the "highest utility" *sub specie aeternitatis*, but they denied that moral conduct always contributed to survival, pleasure, or other mundane utilitarian ends. On the contrary, the moral imperative often required individuals to act in a manner that was antithetical to such ends. Noting that Christians believed that "there are things better than living, and other things worse than dying," Borden Parker Bowne declared that "the law of righteousness must never be abandoned, though the fagots be gathered and the instruments of torture be spread." Conversely, Protestant evolutionists asserted, behavior that might be considered useful from a narrowly practical perspective was not always good; on the contrary, a consistent application of utilitarian principles was a formula for moral chaos and would result, as Francis H. Johnson noted, in an "evolution downward." To illustrate this point, Bowne suggested that although it might well be true that society would function more smoothly if efforts to improve the lot of the "idle and mischievous classes" were replaced by a program in which the members of those classes were exterminated, such a program would be antithetical to the "sacredness of personality" that lay at the heart of Christianity.[35]

These considerations served to reinforce the conviction that the ultimate basis of morality was a law that placed human beings "under the government of a personal God who would have us holy because he is holy." They also prompted Protestants who endorsed the transmutation hypothesis to insist that an understanding of God's plan for the world required individuals "to hear what morality says to evolution as well as what evolution says to morality." These Protestants argued that nothing in the theory of organic evolution necessitated acceptance of a philosophy that would "reduce the moral law to a name." In subscribing to utilitarianism, they reasoned, Darwin and Spencer were making philosophical rather than scientific judgments.[36]

Some Protestants who attempted to dissociate the transmutation hypothesis from utilitarianism held that the human species developed standards of behavior that were quite different from considerations motivating the behavior of other species. James McCosh, for example, submitted that the appearance of the human species was marked by the emergence of moral considerations that were different in kind from the principle of pleasure that characterized the highest behavioral end of other animals. James T. Bixby agreed, suggesting that although "experiences of utility may have preceded moral ideas and led up to them, it by no means follows that these experiences of the useful have *produced* the moral ideas."[37]

Other Protestant evolutionists sought to disjoin the theory of evolution from utilitarian ethics by claiming that although the origin of some moral conceptions might be found in the kind of utilitarian considerations described by Darwin and other evolutionists, this was irrelevant to the more fundamental question of the validity of these conceptions. One of the most trenchant discussions of this position was presented by James Hervey Hyslop, a psychologist who later became prominent as an advocate of psychical research. Though Hyslop subscribed to the theory of organic evolution, he denounced what he saw as a prevalent tendency to venerate the theory "as the 'open sesame' of all mysteries." After completing work for his Ph.D. under G. Stanley Hall at Johns Hopkins in 1887, he published a series of articles opposing that tendency.[38]

Hyslop's resistance to the claim that the transmutation hypothesis provided the key to moral philosophy was largely a function of his conviction that description could not be equated with prescription. Though he acknowledged that the "historical method" employed by proponents of evolutionary ethics had disclosed that primitive moral conceptions were often rooted in utilitarian considerations, he insisted that the origin of moral ideas was irrelevant to the central problem of moral philosophy, "the meaning and validity of moral conceptions after they had been acquired." In solving this problem, Hyslop insisted, the transmutation hypothesis was useless.[39]

If, however, Protestant evolutionists could agree that it was possible to endorse the transmutation hypothesis while rejecting utilitarianism in favor of a moral philosophy grounded on belief in the existence and sanctity of a transcendent moral law, they reached differing conclusions concerning the nature of the relationship between evolution and ethics. In their discussion of this issue, which reached its peak in the late eighties and nineties, two positions garnered roughly equal support. One of these was that the transmutation hypothesis was irrelevant to moral philosophy. The other was that it actually reinforced the dictates of Christian ethics.

Adherents of the former position characteristically emphasized the disjunction between the moral and the natural worlds. Even before T. H. Huxley made his celebrated attack on the deduction of ethical norms from natural processes in his Romanes lecture of 1893, a number of American Protestant evolutionists were arguing that moral imperatives could neither be inferred from nor verified by the mechanisms at work in the larger cosmic order. For thinkers who held this position, the transmutation hypothesis, far from establishing greater continuity between humanity and the rest of the organic world, actually drove a wedge between them and helped make the distinction between human beings and other creatures more vivid. Moral law, these thinkers asserted, was not a "product of evolution" but "a transcendental reality that awaited man's appearance."[40]

One of the most able statements of this position was presented by the young John Dewey. Though Dewey was to convert to ethical naturalism less than a decade later, in 1887 he remained convinced that "whatever exiles theology makes ethics an expatriate." In seeking to show that ethics was intelligible only from a theological perspective, he argued that the evolutionary mechanisms that accounted for the origin of the human species were incapable of providing an "ideal end" of human conduct. Evolutionists who interpreted moral behavior teleologically as an effort to further the end of the evolutionary process, he asserted, were laboring under a fundamental misconception; in reality, "nature has no end, no aim, no purpose."[41]

It was Dewey's contention that insofar as the natural world related to moral activity at all, it compounded rather than mitigated the problems of ethical theorists who would take their cue from nature. Those who ascribed the idea of concern for others to the recognition of the desirability of mutual protection, he charged, were guilty of begging the question. "The existence of an identity of interests and the more or less conscious recognition of it," he maintained, was precisely what the evolutionary process could not explain. Wherever one looked, the evolutionary mechanism could be seen to operate "by rivalry, by struggle, by gaining a good at the expense of others, by differentiation of interests, by stronger weapons of attack, by superior methods of defense, by multiplying so that others are crowded out." Clearly, therefore, something other than "physical evolution" was required to account for an ethical ideal that stressed "harmony, unity of purpose and life, community of well-being." This something was divine purpose.[42]

During the last quarter of the nineteenth century, many other American Protestant evolutionists were similarly intent on showing that valid—by which they meant Christian—ethical norms could not be derived from "the vast carnival of slaughter" pervading "animated nature." Unwilling to impugn the benevolence of God, they emphasized the amorality of the natural world. Because transmutation had resulted in a "progressive" series of life forms that culminated in the emergence of human beings, these thinkers felt justified in viewing the evolutionary process as beneficent. Still, they emphasized that this process was bereft of any "law of mercy or of justice" capable of serving as a guide to human conduct. Only because proponents of "evolutionary ethics" had already presupposed the existence of Christian moral principles were they able to devise an ethical philosophy that had a semblance of viability.[43]

Some of these thinkers emphasized that the use of survival of the fittest as a norm of behavior would sharply circumscribe the boundaries of altruism. The Christian's belief in the value of personality, they maintained, implied that the proper end of conduct was the promotion of all human life, not simply the survival of the fittest. Theodore T. Munger, for example, urged that "Christianity teaches not that the strongest only survive but also the weak. Indeed Christianity is not itself except it teaches this. Its inmost principle, its entire significance, is the salvation of the weak." Similarly, James McCosh, noting with alarm that the doctrine of the survival of the fittest had fostered complacency in some missionary circles regarding the prospect of the extinction of "inferior races," invoked "the spirit of Him who stood by the weak against the strong" to justify his claim that the true "disciple of Christ recognizes as brothers and sisters the lowest specimens of humanity, whether found in pagan lands or in the lowest sinks of our cities."[44]

If many Protestant evolutionists emphasized the inadequacy of the survival of the fittest as an acceptable goal of conduct, some were no less concerned that the competitive struggle designed to ensure that outcome led to behavior that was "not even an approximation to the ideal." Competitive struggle itself, these critics charged, involved "a flat contradiction to the law of love" lying at the center of the gospel. Whereas the very function of Christian morality was to restrain "natural" impulses, to "stand by right, and not by might," the principle that "might makes right" would have the effect of reducing society to a competitive jungle. The individuals who would survive in such a jungle, J. H. Hyslop warned, would be those who were "bad and strong enough to disregard the rights of others."[45]

Like critics of the transmutation hypothesis, Protestant evolutionists who were intent on demonstrating that the transmutation hypothesis was incapable of serving as a foundation of ethical behavior were captivated by the idea that the evolutionary process entailed competitive struggle. Although the discussion of many of the ardent proponents of the theory of organic evolution lent some credibility to this idea, it is nevertheless true that Darwin, Spencer, and other proponents of "evolutionary ethics" had acknowledged that cooperation and altruism also played an important role in human behavior in "civilized" societies. The tendency of many Protestant evolutionists to ignore or to dismiss such concessions may have been the result of the fact that they, like Dewey, believed that the willingness of individuals to participate in groups for cooperative purposes was the very phenomenon the evolutionary hypothesis could not explain. It may also have stemmed from the fact that many Darwinians retained the idea of struggle among groups in their analysis of human evolution. The Christian world view was no less irreconcilable with the idea of struggle among groups than with the idea of struggle within a group. Whatever the reasons, Protestant evolutionists who tended to equate evolution with struggle generally agreed that the foundation of legitimate ethical principles was to be found not in natural processes but in "reverence for an ideal above the laws of nature." This ideal imposed limits on the operation of the evolutionary mechanism.[46]

Other Protestant intellectuals in the United States adopted a quite different view of the relationship between evolution and ethics. In contrast to religious thinkers who argued that "evolution has not materially changed the basis of reasoning upon ethical questions," these intellectuals maintained that it was possible to "find in evolution itself a solid basis for morals." Proponents of this position, who were typically among that group of Protestant evolutionists who believed that an immanent Deity had employed a consistent method in accomplishing His creative purposes, believed that it was only reasonable to assume that God had grounded Christian ethical precepts within the very fabric of reality. As Washington Gladden put it, "surely our ethical doctrine must be in harmony with the nature of things. The teaching that leaves a bottomless chasm between what is natural and what is right confounds our reason." Convinced that the natural world derived its chief significance as a theater for the human moral drama, they concluded that "nature is favorable to goodness."[47]

Protestants who insisted that "morals are not the contradiction of natural processes" commonly argued that altruism was no less "natural" than selfishness. Drawing upon the work of such thinkers as Herbert Spencer and Henry Drummond, a Scottish theologian whose *Ascent of Man* (1894) made the phrase "struggle for the life of others" one of the theological catchphrases of the nineties, these thinkers held that the evolutionary mechanism comprehended more than egoism and competitive strife; it also included the existence of a "law of love for others." This "higher moral or spiritual law," they maintained, modified and limited the egoistic impulses and motivated individuals to strive for "the survival and improvement of *all*."[48]

Exponents of this position concurred with Francis H. Johnson, who maintained that "striking instances of fidelity to communal as distinguished from individual interests" had been "exhibited on a great scale by the lower animals." In higher species, these thinkers maintained, the communal impulse became progressively more dominant. Even in the human race, egoism continued to play a role in determining conduct. This was as it should be: "there is morality in self regard as well as in sympathy." Still, the human species possessed the capacity for placing love of others on a par with, or even above, love of self, thus enabling them to obey Jesus' commandment to "love thy neighbor as thyself." When human beings responded to their best impulses, they found it to be a moral "necessity for the strong to help and defend the weak." Obedience to these impulses, which they identified as divine moral law, established human beings as "fit." As George Harris put it, "immorality is a disease which makes men unfit to survive. Morality is natural selection and makes man fit to survive."[49]

In an age given to justifying its dogma by appealing to science, it is not surprising that some thinkers chose to emphasize that the theory of organic evolution confirmed the teachings of Jesus that "the law of altruism" was "the only law under which is possible the evolution of mind and soul." The idea that "the welfare of one and of all is bound up together" was embedded within the evolutionary process also played an important role in fostering the elevation of "social Christianity" to a privileged place among the categories of theological analysis. An emphasis on the significance of altruism as a component of evolution carried no implication as to whether love was to be manifested in personal or institutional forms. Moreover, the value of attending to the needs of others had been an element of Christian theology long before promulgation of the transmutation hypothesis. Nevertheless, the notion that the "solidarity of life" was a legitimate inference from the evolutionary hypothesis lent a hard edge of realism to demands that Christians apply the tenets of their faith to the social order. In this connection, Washington Gladden observed that "when we urge that good-will must be inseparably joined with self-regard in all our industrial and social enterprises, they cannot answer that the counsel is visionary; for we can show them that it has been the law of all life from the beginning."[50]

The principle of evolution was occasionally brought to bear on the problem of how social reform could best be effected. The clergyman S. R. Calthrop, for example, suggested that "the Central Lesson we have got to learn from this sublimely slow process of Evolution is that the Amelioration of Human Society is of necessity a process of growth." Such statements, however, were uncommon. This may have been because most Protestants in the United States believed that the idea of revolutionary social change was so appalling that defense of gradualism was unnecessary. It may have also stemmed from a recognition that the concept of evolution was none too clear in its implications. A saltatory view of the evolutionary process, after all, could be rendered consistent with more revolutionary visions of reform. Whatever the reason, Protestants who placed human morality within an evolutionary framework rarely cited the idea of evolution in defending their positions regarding the appropriate pace of social change.[51]

The issues on which American Protestant evolutionists differed in their assessment of the relationship between evolution and Christian ethics were considerably less significant than those on which they agreed. Protestants who placed ethical behavior within an evolutionary context were no less convinced than those who did not that "morality, as we know it, came into the world in connection with man" and that the ultimate basis of morality was a moral law ordained by God and clearly revealed in the Christian gospel. Moreover, though they embedded the law of love within the evolutionary process, they recognized that human beings often used the freedom they possessed to disobey that law. Such disobedience, they believed, constituted the very essence of sin. Accordingly, they joined other Christians in affirming that a recognition of the reality of sin and the need for redemption was fundamental to an understanding of the human condition.[52]

The transmutation hypothesis played an important role in the way in which many Protestant intellectuals who endorsed that hypothesis described the Christian scheme of redemption. A few of these thinkers sought to show that it was possible to endorse the hypothesis while retaining commitment to orthodox views of sin and salvation. Most of them, however, held that acceptance of the transmutation hypothesis required alteration in prevailing doctrinal formulations, and they enlisted the theory in the cause of theological revision. For some, the theory of organic evolution acted as a stimulus for doctrinal reassessment; for others, it proved useful in legitimating changes that had been prompted by other considerations.

On no theological issue was the theory of organic evolution refracted in more multifarious ways than in discussions of the Fall. A minority of Protestant evolutionists maintained that it was possible to retain belief in the historicity of the Fall while endorsing the transmutation hypothesis. John Cotton Smith, an Episcopal clergyman who served as rector of the Church of the Ascension in New York from 1860 until 1882, noted that the transmutation hypothesis implied that "degeneration" as well as progress had occurred during the history of life. The biblical narrative of the Fall merely recorded the fact that this tendency had manifested itself in the moral order as well as in the physical world. A similar argument was advanced by George Frederick Wright. Wright defended his belief that Darwinism was compatible with the affirmation of the Westminster Catechism that "man was made in the beginning upright, but fell from his first estate," by reminding his readers that the Darwinian hypothesis was not "a theory of invariable and progressive development," but allowed for instances of "degradation." Sin, which he defined as "a maladjustment of the soul to the conditions of its best existence," seemed to Wright to be an instance of such degradation. Moreover, he maintained, "the Darwinian doctrine of heredity" provided "illustrative analogies" with "the Calvinistic doctrine of the spread of sin from Adam to his descendants."[53]

Among the American Protestant evolutionists who affirmed the compatibility of the transmutation hypothesis with the historical authenticity of the Fall was John Thomas Gulick, a Christian missionary to the Far East and an amateur naturalist held in high regard by professional scientists. Gulick insisted that the idea that "man has risen above all the other animals" by means of evolution accorded with the claim that "he has fallen below the condition in which he commenced his career as man." In support of the latter proposition, he submitted that the human species was unique in violating the dictates of its natural instincts and conscience alike. "There is no dictate of nature or reason," he observed, "that is not dishonored by some community of men." Gulick spurned the notion that barbaric behavior was nothing more than a concomitant of social and cultural conditions; many of "the very worst fiends" had been raised in civilized society. Moreover, he argued, there was a universal propensity among human beings to separate themselves from God by allowing "self-seeking motives" to govern their behavior. These moral phenomena suggested that "a fall of some kind" had occurred.[54]

By the last quarter of the nineteenth century, an ever-increasing number of American Protestant intellectuals could no longer view the biblical narrative of Adam's transgression and subsequent penalty as "authoritative history." In 1880 William Hayes Ward, the superintending editor of the weekly *Independent*, estimated that "perhaps a quarter, perhaps a half of the educated ministers in our leading Evangelical denominations" were persuaded that "the story of the creation and fall of man, told in Genesis, is no more the record of actual occurrences than is the parable of the Prodigal Son." The theory of organic evolution con-

tributed to the erosion of belief in the historicity of the Fall by undermining the credibility of the idea that all human beings had descended
from a single progenitor who was created in a state of moral perfection.
No less important, it gave Protestants who considered the idea that God
had condemned all human beings because of the transgression of one
individual to be an outrageous indictment against the character of the
Deity justification for asserting that the orthodox conception of the Fall
was as scientifically untenable as it was morally reprehensible. Indeed,
some Protestants regarded the corrosive impact of the transmutation
hypothesis on the conventional interpretations of the Fall as one of the
salient reasons for applauding that hypothesis.[55]

One of the most outspoken critics of the doctrine of the Fall was
Minot J. Savage. The son of poor and pious parents, Savage spent his
early years in Maine. At the age of thirteen, after enduring six weeks of
the "horror and fear of hell," he joined the Methodist church. After
graduating from Bangor Theological Seminary in 1864, he was ordained in the Congregational church and served short stints as a missionary in California and a pastor in the Congregational Church in
Framingham, Massachusetts, before moving in 1869 to Hannibal, Missouri. There he succeeded in developing the largest Congregational
church in the state.[56]

Savage recalled that as early as 1870, he had become "an earnest out-
and-out evolutionist and Darwinian." Indeed, he boasted of being the
first individual in either Europe or the United States "who, while occupying a pulpit, in the regular course of his pulpit ministrations,
frankly accepted evolution and Darwinism, and frankly attempted to
reconstruct religious and theologic thinking and theory, and bring
them into accord with this newer and higher revelation of God." Savage's conversion to Darwinism, along with his studies in biblical criticism and history, led him to believe that fundamental creedal revision
was imperative. Convinced that Congregationalism provided an un-
promising forum for such revisions, Savage accepted a call in 1873 to
the Third Unitarian Church of Chicago. A year later he moved to Boston, where he assumed pastoral duties at the Church of the Unity and
carried on his campaign against orthodoxy.[57]

One of the central objects in this campaign was the doctrine of the
Fall. This is not surprising, for Savage believed that this doctrine was
fundamental to the orthodox vision of redemption: "there is not an orthodox church on the face of the earth that was not organized for the
one express purpose of saving man from the supposed effects of the
fall. There is not one single doctrine in the plan of salvation that would
have been dreamed of, had not men first believed in the fall."[58]

Convinced that the orthodox interpretation of the gospel was calculated to "outrage the sense of justice of any intelligent and unbiassed mind," Savage prized the transmutation hypothesis for the ammunition it supplied opponents of that interpretation. In a collection of sermons published in 1876 as *The Religion of Evolution*, he called upon Christians to repudiate the doctrine of the Fall, not because "it does not please our thought, or because we have chosen to take up with some new-fangled notion," but because the evolutionary hypothesis had "absolutely proved" that "humanity has never fallen." By 1892, when his *The Irrepressible Conflict between Two World-Theories* appeared, Savage predicted that the theory of organic evolution, which postulated "the *ascent of man*, instead of the *fall of man*," would lead "every intelligent and honest man" to abandon belief in the doctrine of the Fall.[59]

Less theologically radical than Savage but no less critical of orthodox formulations of the Fall was Henry Ward Beecher. The seventh living child of a family rivaled in talent and intellect only by the Adams and James clans, Beecher was the most popular—and controversial—clergyman of his age and one of the most powerful preachers in American history. Like his eminent father, Lyman, Henry regarded himself as an evangelical Calvinist, but he placed his rhetorical and polemical skills in the service of a theology that was far more uncompromising in its hostility to orthodoxy than anything his father would have countenanced. A lonely, melancholy child, he was at once captivated and terrified by the "alleviated" version of Calvinism he heard from his father. By the time he graduated from Lane Seminary in 1837, he had made God's love the cornerstone of his theology. After spending two years in Lawrenceburgh, Indiana, Beecher became pastor of the Second Presbyterian Church in Indianapolis, where he preached for eight years. In 1847 he accepted a call to the newly organized Plymouth Congregational Church in Brooklyn. There he conducted his ministry for more than forty years.[60]

In 1867 Beecher indicated that he was determined "to secure for the truths now developing in the sphere of Natural Science a religious spirit & harmonization with all the cardinal truths of religion." Even more pronounced in his preaching, however, was the exploitation of the concepts and rhetoric of modern scientific investigation to justify theological departures from orthodoxy. His professed hatred of religious controversy did little to inhibit him from assailing theological positions that he regarded as antithetical to his own. Nor, in contrast to Savage, was he reluctant to attack orthodoxy from the pulpits of churches that continued to subscribe to orthodox formulations of Christian doctrine.[61]

In 1882 Beecher commended the transmutation hypothesis for providing relief "from some of the most disgraceful tenets of theology," tenets involving an "impious and malignant representation of God and his government." No doctrine was more repugnant to Beecher than that of the Fall, which he regarded as the very foundation of orthodox Christianity. The suggestion that all mankind was implicated in the transgression of one individual, he fumed, was "repulsive, unreasonable, immoral, and demoralizing." Not only did it portray God's treatment of Adam in terms that were unworthy of even human standards of parenthood, but in holding that God had transmitted Adam's corruption to the rest of the human race, the orthodox doctrine of the Fall implied that "the business of God for ten thousand years . . . [had been] to produce infinite sin and suffering."[62]

Beecher denied that the Fall was an essential element of Christian theology. It was rather "a bastard belief of the Jews, grown up, with other glosses and absurdities of Pharisaic theology, outside of scriptural authority or teaching." In the Old Testament, he noted, discussion of the Fall had been limited to the story in Genesis. Jesus had referred neither to the Fall nor "to any malign stream of tendencies" that had supposedly derived from it. Even the Apostle Paul had not really affirmed the historical or theological import of the Fall; he had merely "allud[ed] to it as a theory familiar to his readers."[63]

For his own part, Beecher, who interpreted the narrative of the Fall in Genesis as nothing more than "a poem" expressing "the earliest notions of the origin of the Human Family," believed that the doctrine of the Fall was not only monstrous; it was also untenable. In defense of this view, he invoked the theory of organic evolution. That theory, he argued, "weighs fatally against the commonly accepted view of the Fall of Man in Adam" by establishing that human beings "had their start by the Divine decree, at the lowest point; and the method of creation is, working up from zero, higher and higher in degree."[64]

Most Protestant thinkers who endorsed the transmutation hypothesis, though similarly convinced that the biblical story of Adam's transgression was not to be interpreted as a historical event, were more concerned than Beecher and Savage with showing that it conveyed important truths about the human condition. These thinkers reached differing conclusions as to just what these truths were. In grappling with this problem, many of them drew upon considerations they derived from the theory of evolution. Their discussion offers additional evidence of the determination of Protestant evolutionists to ground the transmutation hypothesis within a recognizably Christian frame of reference even while using it to sanction theological revision.

Some participants in the dialogue over the meaning of the Fall urged that it should be interpreted not as an event that had occurred in the past but as an allegory of every individual's experience. From this perspective, theories concerning the origin and early history of the human species were simply irrelevant to the real meaning implicit in the biblical account of Adam's transgression. One of the most avid partisans of this position was the Congregational clergyman Lyman Abbott. Abbott, who was licensed to preach in 1859, served several pastorates before being invited to succeed Henry Ward Beecher at Brooklyn's Plymouth Congregational Church in 1887. His national prominence, however, rested less on his preaching than on his roles as author, lecturer, and editor of the *Christian Union* (which changed its name to *Outlook* in 1893). A prolific writer, Abbott published a number of articles and two well-known books, *The Evolution of Christianity* (1892) and *The Theology of an Evolutionist* (1897), designed to show that the theory of evolution rendered orthodox views of sin and salvation untenable. Among doctrines that were most in need of revision, he believed, was the Fall. Like Beecher, Abbott denied that the orthodox interpretation of this doctrine was central to the teachings of the Scriptures. This did not mean, however, that the story of the Fall was meaningless. "Every broken resolve, every high purpose lowered, every sacrifice of reverence to sensual desire, of conscience to passion, of love to greed or ambition or wealth," he declared, "is a fall." This view prompted him to reason that "the story of every individual, the story of the race, is a story of successive falls and restorations." Abbott suggested that the clergyman would be well advised to concentrate on "awakening in the consciences of his hearers a personal sense of their own sin and fall" and to leave "severly alone" historical questions relating to the dawn of human history.[65]

Some Protestants were readier to assume that the meaning of the Fall was bound up with elements relating to humanity's past. For George Harris, the "Scriptural truth" conveyed in the biblical story of the Fall was that "man made wrong choices very early, say, at the beginning, and that those choices brought many evils upon him." Others maintained that the story yielded other insights that received confirmation and illumination from the transmutation hypothesis.[66]

Francis H. Johnson advanced one of the most rigorous and provocative statements of this view. In 1887 he credited the evolutionary interpretation of the origin and early history of humanity with disclosing an element in the story of the Fall that was frequently overlooked: "the dawning of a moral sense in man." Whereas the traditional interpretation of the biblical narrative had focused on Adam's decision to reject the promptings of that sense, an interpretation informed by "the principles of evolution" would also emphasize that the ability of human beings to make sinful choices was contingent upon the evolutionary development of the moral consciousness in the human species. Because he was convinced that "the knowledge of good and evil was also the beginning of salvation" and "the first step toward the rescue of the spiritual possibilities of the soul," he felt justified in arguing that the Fall was "an incident in the elevation of the creature to a higher grade of existence." This analysis led Johnson to conclude that "evolution brings distinctly before us the important fact that what we have been in the habit of emphasizing as the *Fall* was a result of the *rise* of man; and that the rise is by far the more important aspect of this great crisis." What made it so important was that it implied that sinfulness was an inevitable concomitant of the creation of a moral being in God's image and thus "relieves us of the conception of a God whose purposes were thwarted by the willfulness of his creatures."[67]

Johnson's position received a mixed review. Theodore T. Munger, Minot Savage, and a few other Protestant evolutionists judged it to be a useful way of interpreting the Fall. Other Protestants were less enthusiastic. Lyman Abbott, for example, argued that individuals who, like Johnson, described the Fall as "a step upward" were guilty of confusing "the obstacles to progress with the progress which they hinder and delay." A similar belief led Lewis French Stearns to insist that humanity's sinful "abuse of his freedom" was yet another "break" in a process of gradual, progressive development. Other readers detected in Johnson's position a casual, even self-congratulatory, attitude toward humanity's rebellion against God. At the very least, his interpretation implied that sin was a "natural" feature in the evolution of human personality, "unavoidable and therefore blameless or nearly so." Not surprisingly, some thinkers believed that this view reflected an inadequate appreciation of the heinousness of sin.[68]

Of far greater popularity was the view that the transmutation hypothesis confirmed the traditional doctrine that sinful proclivities were transmitted from one generation to the next. Calvinists like George Frederick Wright were not the only Protestants who were enamored of the idea that human generations were bound together in a web of sin. Many of the same Protestant evolutionists who repudiated the notion that Adam's guilt had been "imputed" to his progeny regarded the inheritance of acquired characteristics as a mandate for adopting a position that bore striking similarities to "the doctrine which the old theologians strove to express under the name of original sin." These Christians held that individuals in the dawn of human history had distorted and perverted their wills through evil moral choices and had then passed on their "predispositions to the wrong" to their descendants. A representative statement of this view was presented by William Rupp. Rupp believed that the doctrines of Adam's "federal headship" and the "imputation of sin" were "monstrous." Nevertheless, he suggested that, although it was simply impossible to account for why primitive human beings had chosen to disobey the will of God, once this decision had been made, "the doctrine of evolution in its *law of heredity*" revealed how sinfulness "could become persistent in the race."[69]

However they chose to interpret the Fall, Protestant evolutionists could agree that sinfulness was an affliction that beset all human beings. Awareness of that grim reality prompted Henry Ward Beecher to observe sardonically that "we need not be afraid of getting rid of original sin, because we can get all the actual transgression that the world needs to take its place." Beecher joined many other American Protestant intellectuals in believing that an evolutionary interpretation of human origins yielded insights into the nature of sin. These thinkers held that sinful behavior resulted from the willful decision of human beings to subordinate their "better and nobler impulses" to other, more "primitive," impulses they had inherited from their brute ancestors. For some of them, such a decision involved the refusal to rise from the animal to the spiritual. For others, such as Lyman Abbott, this view seemed to suggest that sin was simply immaturity. Accordingly, they described sin as a "fall," a reversion to animality. But on one issue they could agree: "brutishness lies in the very roots of human beings." This led the Baptist theologian L. C. Barnes of Pittsburgh, Pennsylvania, to suggest that "original sin is more original than we should ever know except for the light of evolution."[70]

Some Christians who discussed sin from this vantage point insinuated that the "animal" elements of human character were inherently evil. John Fiske, for example, equated human progress with "throwing off the brute-inheritance" and declared that the ultimate end of human life on earth was the creation of a character that was "so transformed that nothing of the brute can be detected in it." It would be a mistake, however, to assume that Fiske's statement typified the position of most Protestant evolutionists. To affirm that the brute-like qualities that had been passed down to humanity were themselves evil was to hold that the human species had been created with a nature that was inherently

flawed. This was a position that few Christians were prepared to sanction. Accordingly, most Protestant evolutionists who described the connection between sinfulness and "animalism" concluded, as William
Newton Clarke put it, that "it is not so much the brute in man that is
sin, as it is the preference of the man for the brute rather than for the
spirit, or the yielding of the spirit to the brute." This was a subtle distinction, but it was important, for it enabled proponents of the evolutionary hypothesis to acknowledge that brute-like impulses played a
useful role in human life even while insisting that they must be subordinated to spiritual ones. Joseph Le Conte thus maintained that "true
virtue consists, not in the extirpation of the lower, but in its subjection
to the higher."[71]

In suggesting that human beings were guilty of allowing their "animal" appetites to overcome their better natures, Protestant evolutionists were employing insights gleaned from the theory of organic
evolution to lend credibility and substance to a view that had played a
prominent role in the Christian analysis of sin since the Apostle Paul
had reflected on the struggle between the spirit and the flesh. It is probably not surprising that in the late nineteenth century, when middle-
class Americans contemplated the agressive and sexual passions of humanity in a spirit of horrified fascination, this theme received a good
deal of attention. But most Protestant evolutionists recognized that
however valuable humanity's evolutionary heritage might be in providing an intelligible analytical framework for discussing some sins, it
could not account for all varieties of sinfulness. George Harris, though
conceding that many sins were due to "physical desires" prompted by
humanity's "animal instincts," observed that "some injustice is done
our humble ancestors when all human iniquities are fathered upon that
which they have bequeathed to us." It was his contention that many of
the most grievous human sins—"revenge, pride, falsehood, selfish ambition"—were due not to animal impulses but to perversions of the
very intellectual and spiritual attributes that distinguished human
beings from other animals. William Newton Clarke similarly acknowledged that "the brute in man is the source of much of the evil that we
observe," but he emphasized that "the spirit has subtle and dangerous
sins of its own, in the life that lies above the realm of the brute." Indeed,
he argued, "the higher part of man has capabilities of moral evil far
greater than the brute element ever possessed."[72]

Nor did the ascription of human sinfulness to the persistence of
hardy animal impulses exempt God from responsibility for the prevalence of sin and its resultant guilt. A number of Protestants held that by

showing that sinfulness "arises from the very method of the divine creation," they had demonstrated that orthodox Protestants had been "right as to the fact of man's universal sinfulness," but "wrong as to the cause of it and of the nature of it." The revised view of sin, however, did not actually render God any less responsible for sin and guilt than the explanation that ascribed them to the "terrible theory" of the transgression of Adam. Of course, whereas imputationist explanations implied that human beings were condemned to sin by virtue of being Adam's progeny, Protestants who attributed sin to the struggle between the animal and the spiritual within human beings could place the blame on humanity's free choice. Theodore T. Munger thus declared that "man himself is a free actor, sinking backward into brute conditions, or rising into the divine life of which he has become conscious." For Munger and other Protestant evolutionists, life was a drama in which each individual was constantly confronted with the necessity of choosing either to manifest the godlike attributes of his "essential humanity" or to succumb to the lower passions of his "inherited animality." If, however, human beings were really able to control their own destinies, the idea that they sometimes subordinated their higher impulses to their lower ones became simply a heuristic device to describe a category of sinful activity. It could not be used, as many Protestants sought to use it, as an *explanation* of the ubiquity of sin. On the other hand, if sin was inevitable, God, as the creator of humanity, remained responsible for it.[73]

Whereas the evolutionary perspective did little to resolve the problem of the prevalence of sin, it played a more significant role in shaping the way in which its adherents commonly thought about the "sinfulness" of sin. For all the controversy concerning the causes and nature of sin, most of these thinkers agreed that what made an action sinful was that it precluded individuals from realizing their essential nature as creatures created in the image of God. As such, they believed, it was a "maladaptive" action. This view led many of them to liken sin to biological "degeneration" in that it involved a "departure" from the kind of creature that God had intended the human species to be. Minot Savage was not always representative of American Protestant intellectuals in the theological positions he espoused, but when he maintained that the human being who allowed his "animal" nature to gain mastery over him "falls back into a position worse than that of the animal, by as much as he is capable of something higher," he articulated an opinion that was widely shared. Many Protestant evolutionists tended to place far more emphasis on the idea that sin was an "unnatural" failure of an

individual to conform to his essence as a child of God than on the idea
that it constituted a heinous desire to place self above God. George
Harris, for example, chose to stress that the deplorable aspect of humanity's sinful "transgression of God's law" was that it contravened
"the laws of his [man's] own constitution." If Harris acknowledged that
such sinfulness resulted in "alienation from God," he found the chief
manifestation of this alienation in the fact that human beings became
"restless and unhappy." To be sure, many proponents of this view
could heartily agree with William Newton Clarke when he observed
that the revolt against human nature involved in sin was also a revolt
"against God as the God of nature." Still, it is difficult to avoid the conclusion that by emphasizing that sin was a maladaptive act that precluded human beings from realizing their potential rather than an
offense against divine sovereignty, Protestant evolutionists, often un-
wittingly, ratified and even accentuated a tendency to focus on humanity rather than on God that had been growing increasingly strong for
more than a century.[74]

A few Protestant evolutionists attributed sin to ignorance. These
thinkers reasoned that the remedy for sin resided in greater knowledge
of the divine moral law. When the human being "gets wise enough to
know that obeying the divine laws must always be for his good," Minot
Savage asserted, "then the whole force of self-interest even will be
turned toward doing right." In the course of evolutionary progress, he
maintained, humanity would come to recognize that obedience to the
moral law was in accordance with their best interest. At that time, "the
pang of pain following a breaking of one of these finer laws of thinking
and feeling will be as keen and real as is now the burning that follows
the putting of a finger into the fire."[75]

Savage's position was not popular. Most Protestant evolutionists believed that the primary cause of sin was not a lack of knowledge but a
perversity of will that led individuals to choose to ignore or to disobey
the "known law." The remedy for such perversity lay not in knowledge
but in regeneration. Concomitantly, they reasoned that "development
will cure crudeness; but only redemption will cure sin."[76]

This did not mean, however, that Protestant evolutionists minimized
the role of knowledge in the redemptive process. On the contrary, they
assumed that knowledge of the moral law was a necessary condition
of true virtue and that the growth of such knowledge was a desideratum. Nor did they believe that the concept of evolution provided no assistance in comprehending the nature of salvation. Many of them
assumed, in fact, that the scheme of redemption could be truly

understood only by appropriating insights and language derived from the theory of evolution.

The same anthropocentric assumptions that fostered the conviction that the emergence of the human species represented the goal of the history of life also led many Protestant intellectuals to regard the redemption of humanity as the ultimate goal of human history. Opponents of the theory of evolution and Protestant evolutionists who believed that God occasionally intervened in the natural world in pursuance of His purposes tended to assume that history was periodically punctuated by special redemptive acts. Those who believed that the evolutionary process constituted the paradigm for divine activity, on the other hand, characteristically regarded evolution as "a steady process by which God accomplishes the uplift of the race."[77]

The dynamics of the redemptive process was only one of the issues relating to the plan of salvation that provoked heated controversy within the American Protestant intellectual community in the last quarter of the nineteenth century. The role that the concept of evolution played in these controversies was subordinate but not insignificant. Most Protestants who endorsed the transmutation hypothesis were proponents of theological revision. The revisions they espoused were not always an outgrowth of their commitment to the theory of evolution. Many, however, found the insights they gleaned from that theory to be useful in defending and expressing their doctrinal reformulations.

No issue was more important in any Christian interpretation of the scheme of redemption than soteriology. The vast majority of Protestant intellectuals could agree that Jesus played a preeminent role in the redemptive process. Differences arose, however, when they discussed the precise nature of that role. Most Protestant evolutionists were among that sizable group of Christians who subordinated the significance of Jesus' death to the import of his life and teachings. Members of this group charged that orthodox views of the Atonement, which regarded the crucifixion of Jesus as a "ransom," or penalty, designed to salvage the honor of God or to satisfy the imperatives of divine justice, were predicated upon a barbaric, even blasphemous, conception of God. A proper understanding of soteriology, they urged, would emphasize the role of Jesus in bringing about a more adequate comprehension of God and His will for humanity.[78]

Thinkers who shared this view of the agency of Jesus characteristically placed special emphasis on the ethical precepts contained in his teachings and expressed in his life. The meaning embedded in the doctrine of the Atonement, they reasoned, was God's hatred of sin. It was the office of Jesus to show human beings how to escape the bondage of sin and to be the kind of creatures God intended them to be. In this connection, they noted that Jesus had placed morality at the very center of his vision of spirituality. As the Congregational clergyman George A. Gordon of Boston's Old South Church put it, "it is with the moral character of God, the moral order of the world, the moral condition and hope of man, the moral nature of his own mission, and the transcendent moral effect in history of his own career, that the mind of Christ is incessantly and absorbingly occupied."[79]

Many Protestants who emphasized that ethics was central to the Christian message held that Jesus had inaugurated a new era in the moral life of humanity. H. H. Peabody, a Baptist clergyman from Rome, New York, offered a representative statement of this position when he asserted in 1898 that in conforming to God's will, Jesus "put Himself under the law of moral evolution, and became the culminating feature of its divine order." Francis H. Johnson, persuaded that the moral law was most clearly embodied in the life and teachings of Jesus, maintained that "the moral history of man naturally divides itself into two great epochs: that which antedated the incarnation of the Savior of the world, and that which is subsequent to it." George Harris agreed, calling Jesus "the most potent force in the progress of the race."[80]

Protestants who adopted this view of the role of Jesus in the scheme of redemption maintained that he was not only "humanity's consummate flower" but also God incarnate. Thinkers who emphasized the immanent presence of God in all creatures denied that the ontological distinction between Jesus and humanity was absolute. Lyman Abbott, for example, maintained that "the divinity of man is not different in kind from the divinity in Christ." On the other hand, they acknowledged that Jesus was unique among human beings in completely bringing his human nature into unity with the divine.[81]

In discussing how "the fulfillment of all that we know best of both God and man" could have been personified in a single individual, some Protestant intellectuals found it useful to resort to evolutionary modes of analysis. Jesus, they asserted, was a divinely-ordained "variation," a "new type" in the evolutionary process. This conviction prompted John Coleman Adams, a Universalist clergyman occupying a pastorate in Brooklyn, to assert that Jesus could be placed within "the chain of evolution." Similarly, John Cotton Smith praised Jesus as "the highest and final expression" of human evolution.[82]

Evolutionary rhetoric also functioned in discussions of the special role that Jesus played in the redemptive process. John Coleman Adams, for example, maintained that Jesus had initiated "a new epoch in the evolution of life. . . . He comes to humanity, the first-born of its new, its spiritual men." As "the possibility of the human race made real," Jesus served as both a model for humanity to emulate and a standard by which they could measure their spiritual condition. The Methodist theologian B. F. Cocker gave voice to this conviction when he observed that "the idea of man is the teleological principle of the world, the idea of Christ is the teleological principle of humanity." A similar view prompted Lyman Abbott to call Jesus "the secret of spiritual evolution." Persuaded that "Christ comes, not merely to show divinity to us, but to evolve the latent divinity which he has implanted in us," Abbott concluded that "the consummation of evolution, the consummation of redemption" would occur only when "the whole human race becomes what Christ was."[83]

Most proponents of this position closely associated the imitation of Christ with redemption. In itself, they reasoned, the death of Jesus was not sufficient to ensure the salvation of humanity. Forgiveness and reconciliation with God were contingent upon repentence, which they equated with abandoning a life of sin in favor of obedience to the commandments of Jesus.[84]

In common with all Christians, these Protestants were convinced that the weakness and perversity of the human will made it impossible for human beings to repent without divine assistance. God provided such assistance, they believed, by using His Spirit to awaken human beings to a sense of their sinfulness and enable them to conform to His will. Protestants who sanctioned the notion of periodical supernatural intervention in the natural world regarded this assistance as another class of such events. Immanentists, on the other hand, maintained that it further attested to the presence of the Deity within each human being.[85]

If the initiative for regeneration came from God, this did not mean that human beings were altogether passive in the process. "Grace," Lyman Abbott observed in 1897, "is not an easy bestowment of virtue on an unstruggling creature, but such aid as is necessary to inspire the courage of hope and give assurance of victory." Abbott was one of a number of Protestants who maintained that in the human species, the struggle for existence that characterized all God's creation took place within the soul of each individual. Human life, they held, was the scene of a "perpetual battle" between good and evil. In conducting this battle, men and women were responsible for responding to God's gracious initiative and for using the power God conferred upon them in resisting temptation. With every success they enjoyed in this endeavor, the impulses they possessed for acting in accordance with the precepts of the gospel became stronger and more vigorous.[86]

Partisans of this view believed that regenerate individuals attained a character dominated by the principle of love and a state of holiness characterized by intimate communion with God. By patterning their lives after Christ, Henry Ward Beecher wrote, men and women were drawn "out of their own selfishness, their own passions and appetites, into a higher regimen, and on to a nobler platform, where their upper nature should recognize God, and enter into communion with him, and feel the whole interchange of the Divine nature moving into theirs." Persuaded that regeneration enabled individuals to approach the "perfect ideal of humanity," many Protestants noted that it was both a "new birth" enabling men and women to participate in the achievement of the goal of human evolution and a restorative process in which they became the kind of creatures God intended them to be when He had created the human species.[87]

Most proponents of this view maintained that regeneration was not a dramatic, sudden event but a gradual process of purification and spiritual growth. This view antedated the publication of the *Origin of Species*. Still, there seems to be no reason to doubt Lyman Abbott's contention that the popularity of this idea owed more to "the doctrine of evolution in its application to the spiritual life" than to Horace Bushnell's notion of "Christian nurture." Commitment to an evolutionary view of regeneration helped at least some Protestants to make sense of the fact that not all believers could claim a determinate conversion experience or a sudden, radical change of character. In turn, the gradual nature of regeneration could be interpreted as vindication of the claim that evolution was the method God employed in all His cosmic activity.[88]

For Christians, regeneration culminated in eternal life. Protestants who discussed immortality frequently acknowledged that science was incapable of providing decisive evidence concerning the validity of that doctrine, but many of them employed evolutionary language and arguments ostensibly derived from the concept of evolution in discussing life beyond the grave. At least some of these thinkers, aware that the scientific theory of organic evolution had been advanced to account for the development of species rather than individuals, attempted to justify using the idea of evolution in discussing individual destiny by suggesting that with the appearance of human beings, the focus of the evolutionary process shifted not only from the zoological to the psychic and social arenas but also "from a race development to a personal development." Vida D. Scudder, a pious Episcopalian who became a well-known settlement house worker, presented a representative statement of this position when she proposed that with the appearance of the human species "nature, having apparently perfected her type, now devotes her energies to the development of the individual." Such development, many Protestants suggested, could not reach fruition during the course of an individual's life on earth. Accordingly, they reasoned, "belief in individual immortality is the legitimate sequence [*sic*] of faith in the law of Evolution."[89]

Some Protestant evolutionists, convinced that all events could be placed within an evolutionary framework, were content simply to assert that immortality was an instance of "the great law of the survival of the fit." Everlasting life, these thinkers believed, was the reward individuals received for resisting temptation and aligning their lives with the spiritual environment. Other Protestants advanced arguments designed to show that insights gleaned from the theory of evolution sustained the credibility of the doctrine of immortality. Two such arguments were especially popular during the late nineteenth century. One of them was predicated on the familiar claim that the transmutation hypothesis implied that the attributes of organisms that survived were adapted to "external realities." On the basis of this claim, some apologists insisted that the "hopes and longings" of human beings for immortality afforded grounds for inferring the reality of such a destiny. The other argument proceeded from two assumptions deeply embedded in the world view of Protestant evolutionists: that the evolutionary process was guided by an intelligent and benevolent Designer and that the development of the human species was the ultimate goal of God's creative activity. When the theory of evolution was viewed through the prism of these assumptions, it seemed to suggest that the spirit of at least some human beings would persist after death. This view prompted Joseph Le Conte, who believed that "all evolution has its beginning, its course, its end," to assert that "without spirit-immortality the cosmos has no meaning." For Le Conte and a number of other Protestant evolutionists, this consequence was utterly absurd.[90]

These arguments were unlikely to convince anyone who was not already committed to the doctrine of life after death. Belief in immortality was no more a legitimate inference from the idea of evolution than was a disbelief in that doctrine. More than anything else, the effort to relate immortality to evolution provides additional evidence of how influential the latter concept was in the minds of its adherents in the American Protestant intellectual community.

During the last quarter of the nineteenth century, the theory of organic evolution played a protean role in theological analysis. Not only did it impel Protestants who endorsed that theory to show that it could be reconciled with a Christian understanding of the divine-human encounter, but it also provided many of them with a concept and a vocabulary—evolution—that appeared to be central to a more adequate comprehension of the scheme of redemption. In retrospect, it is apparent that the vast majority of Protestant evolutionists were quite cautious in their approach to the transmutation hypothesis. Both their affirmation that the human species was different from other organisms and their insistence that the moral law embodied in the gospel possessed special sanctity were inconsistent with the spirit of that hypothesis and derived from their commitment to Christian theology. Their use of evolutionary rhetoric in discussing other doctrines, such as immortality, similarly attests to their determination to employ the insights of evolution in defending traditional Christian dogma. Even their use of evolutionary ideas to justify theological reconstruction was frequently motivated by a distaste for orthodox Christianity that originated in considerations that had little direct relevance to the history of life. This is not to minimize the achievement of American Protestant evolutionists. It is rather simply to indicate that the basis of that achievement lay not in provoking radical changes in the way in which the drama of salvation was envisioned but in showing that the categories and doctrinal formulations of Christian theology to which they were committed could be expressed and defended in evolutionary terms. To believers who were acutely conscious of living in a culture that equated science with truth, this was achievement enough.

8

"*Get Thee Hence, Satan*":
Continued Opposition to the Theory
of Organic Evolution

NOT all Protestant intellectuals believed that the theory of organic evolution could be reconciled with Christianity. A sizable minority of them, convinced that the implications of that theory were antithetical to the Christian world view, remained committed to the doctrine of special creation. A few others, such as Archibald Hodge, acknowledged that evolution may have played some role in natural history but imposed such narrow limits on that role and devoted so much energy to attacking the philosophical tenor of the transmutation hypothesis that it seems unreasonable to place them in the camp of even the more conservative Protestant evolutionists. Though many critics of the theory of evolution recognized that Charles Darwin enjoyed "a more popular following, a more noisy proclamation, than has ever been accorded to any of the great philosophers of ancient or modern times," they regarded the religious issues at stake in the history of life as too vital to be decided on the basis of a popularity contest.[1]

Many historians have maintained that the determined opposition to the theory of organic evolution within the American Protestant intellectual community was primarily motivated by concern that it undermined the prevailing formulation of the argument from design. It is certainly true that much of the initial hostility to the Darwinian hypothesis was motivated by this concern. After 1875, however, few Protestants regarded the status of the argument from design as the major stumbling block to acceptance of an evolutionary account of the origin of species. Many special creationists, in fact, explicitly conceded that the transmutation hypothesis was compatible with the existence of God and teleological interpretations of the history of life. At least two considerations served to temper the initial apprehensions. First, by 1875, there was a good deal of support within the scientific community for revisions that appeared to reduce significantly the element of "chance" in the evolutionary process. Second, the discussion among Protestants who endorsed the transmutation hypothesis made it increasingly clear that apologists who could not square that hypothesis with the traditional argument from design had recourse to other persuasive arguments for the existence of God.[2]

Some historians have ascribed much of the animosity to the theory of organic evolution to the recognition of Protestant thinkers that it challenged the supremacy of "Baconian" induction and the legitimacy of their belief in the fixity of species. These challenges were real enough, and there appears to be little doubt that they prompted a few American religious intellectuals, such as George Ticknor Curtis and Thomas Hill, to oppose the transmutation hypothesis. On the face of it, however, neither Baconianism nor the fixity of species appears to have been sufficiently fundamental to the status of Christian theology to warrant Protestants' repudiation of the scientific community's verdict on the history of life. Recognizing this, the author of a recent study of the evolutionary controversy in England and America has suggested that the Protestant assault on the transmutation hypothesis was motivated by philosophical commitments that had little to do with Christianity at all.[3]

An examination of the literature assailing organic evolution indicates that most hostility to the theory during the last quarter of the nineteenth century was informed by a more manifestly religious concern. To most opponents of the evolutionary hypothesis within the American Protestant intellectual community, it appeared to be simply impossible to endorse the theory while remaining committed to the veracity of the Scriptures. It is significant that Charles Hodge, often cited by historians as representative of the religious opposition to Darwinism, placed his attack on the Darwinian hypothesis in his *Systematic Theology* within a section devoted to a survey of "Anti-Scriptural Theories" and emphasized in *What Is Darwinism?* that even if the theory of evolution could be harmonized with theism, it was manifestly irreconcilable with the testimony of the Bible.[4]

A recurrent pattern of reasoning can be discerned in the work of American Protestant intellectuals who rejected the theory of organic evolution. Most began with the claim that its implications were inconsistent with one or more passages that seemed to them to be central to the entire biblical message. These thinkers concluded that it was impossible to endorse the theory of organic evolution while simultaneously affirming that the Bible was a trustworthy vehicle of divine revelation. And because they regarded the Scriptures as the foundation of knowledge about the scheme of redemption, they characteristically equated an attack on the trustworthiness of the Bible with an assault on Christianity itself.[5]

Two indictments played a major role in the work of opponents of the theory of organic evolution. One of these was the charge that the thrust of the theory, which significantly reduced the scope of supernatural activity, was antithetical to the notion that God was a providential Being who had periodically intervened in the natural order in a manner that defied description in terms of natural law. To Protestants who advanced this allegation, it seemed obvious that both the message of the Bible and belief in the divine inspiration of the biblical authors depended on a supernaturalist conception of the Deity. This view led the popular and influential Brooklyn clergyman T. De Witt Talmage to warn that "the moment you begin to explain away the miraculous and supernatural, you surrender the Bible."[6]

Thinkers who shared this position expressed little enthusiasm for the radical formulation of the doctrine of divine immanence espoused by many Protestant evolutionists. They believed that the notion that the activities of God could be encapsulated within the framework of intelligible natural processes sustained belief in divine activity at the cost of a lively sense of God's sovereignty and providence. The Reverend D. E. Frierson of Anderson, South Carolina, gave voice to this concern when he charged that, while the effort "to enshrine deity in the archives of nature and give him a ubiquity in natural law . . . enthrones him as the symbol of natural law and universal agency, it denies to him the power of breaking the charm of awful continuity in which he has enwrapt himself." These thinkers did not deny that God was immanent within, as well as transcendent over, His creation, but like some Protestants who embraced the transmutation hypothesis, they asserted that an overweening emphasis on God's immanence veered perilously close to pantheism.[7]

The other major indictment advanced by opponents of the theory of organic evolution was that its implications were irreconcilable with "the sublime announcement of the first words of the Holy Bible" concerning the origin of species. Some exponents of this position called attention to the passage in Genesis affirming that God had created each organism "after its kind." The most impassioned rhetoric, however, centered on the origin of humanity. Indeed, some critics insinuated that they would have found it possible to accept the theory of organic evolution if they had not been convinced that it entailed the proposition that the human species had descended from lower forms of life. Opponents of the transmutation hypothesis commonly asserted that "the Bible stands or falls with the doctrine of a first man made man by the fiat of God." From this perspective, a clergyman from Fairfield, Iowa, informed readers of the *New Englander* that if the human species were the product of organic evolution, "then the Scriptures are in fatal error, not simply with regard to man's advent on the globe, but in all their doctrines concerning his original and present spiritual condition, the method of his recovery and his future destiny—that is their entire system of spiritual teaching, for which they were confessedly given, is at fault." The Methodist theologian Miner Raymond was equally blunt, warning that "if the origin of the race be found anywhere else than in the special creation of a single pair, from whom all others have descended, then is the whole Bible a misleading and unintelligible book."[8]

In spite of the fact that biblical concerns abound in the books and articles published by nineteenth-century Protestant intellectuals who rejected the transmutation hypothesis, most recent students of the history of the evolutionary controversy have either discounted their significance or denigrated the intellectual rigor of those who discussed them. It is difficult to avoid the conclusion that such assessments stem at least in part from the assumption that only the ignorant and uneducated could find merit in arguments based on biblical authority. This assumption has effectively precluded the recognition of the centrality of biblical arguments in the work of intellectuals who opposed the theory of evolution and the complexity of the reasoning that often underlay those arguments.[9]

The failure of historians to give sufficient weight to biblical considerations in fostering opposition to the transmutation hypothesis may also be attributable to two prominent features of the history of the relationship between science and the Bible. First, prior to the evolutionary controversy American Protestant intellectuals had consistently responded to scientific conclusions that were irreconcilable with prevailing interpretations of biblical passages by revising their biblical exegesis. Second, in the late nineteenth century many Protestant evolutionists insisted that the same logic that had led to previous reinterpretations could also be applied to the transmutation hypothesis. Recognition of these facts may well have encouraged students of the Darwinian controversy to dismiss expressions of outrage concerning the impact of the theory of organic evolution on the biblical message as ephemeral and anomalous. Neither of these considerations, however, is really relevant to the question of what generated opposition to the theory during the last quarter of the nineteenth century. It is rather necessary to examine the literature. Such an examination reveals that biblical considerations were paramount.

Still, the fact that past compromises were made and that not all Protestants found it impossible to reconcile the theory of organic evolution with the Scriptures does indicate that opponents of the theory were adopting a position that differed from that of their predecessors and their brethren within the American Protestant community. It is impossible to understand this position without reconstructing the position of most Protestants who rejected the transmutation hypothesis concerning the nature and source of religious knowledge. The following section is dedicated to that task.

Many Protestants who rejected the theory of organic evolution participated in the sustained analysis of epistemological problems that occurred within the American intellectual community during the last quarter of the nineteenth century. Emerging from this analysis was a commitment to strong views of biblical authority. Proponents of such views typically ascribed to biblical revelation three salient characteristics: completeness, inerrancy, and clarity. This position was not new, but most special creationists coupled their advocacy of it with a refusal to subscribe to the slogans that most of their predecessors had invoked to moderate its implications. The result was a more uncompromising notion of biblical authority that might usefully be termed Biblicism.

The idea that all the data comprising the "science" of Christian theology could be found in the Bible was of central importance to Biblicists. However greatly they may have valued nature as a witness to the power and glory of God, they found it both difficult to decipher and "dumb in response to the most pressing demands of the human soul." The Bible, they believed, suffered from neither of these deficiencies. This view led John L. Girardeau, who from his post as professor of didactic and polemical theology at the Columbia Seminary became one of the most influential voices of southern Presbyterianism, to submit in 1875 that the Scriptures "furnish as perfect a provision for the spiritual, as does nature for the physical, wants of man, and, therefore, exlude every other rule as unnecessary and superfluous." For Girardeau and many others, this proposition was the only one that was consistent with the venerable Protestant principle of *Scriptura sola*.[10]

The conviction that "the believer is never to go beyond the circumference of the Word in his search for truth" was inconsonant with the claim that revelation was a continuous, ongoing process. Girardeau thus acknowledged that doctrinal development could be discerned within the pages of the Bible itself, but he insisted that such development had ceased with the closing of "the canon of Scripture." Nor was the argument that religious experience was an essential epistemological instrument accorded a friendly reception. Many partisans of the view that the Scriptures were a sufficient source of knowledge concerning spiritual truth were not hostile to the idea of such experience, but they refused to equate it with the inspiration of the biblical authors. Convinced that the experiential element of Christianity was subordinate to the Scriptures, they maintained that the suggestion that it served as an independent source of truth was tantamount to acceptance of the heretical doctrine that each individual was his own Bible.[11]

Biblicists characteristically held that the Scriptures were also an infallible source of religious truth. These thinkers subscribed to a doctrine of plenary inspiration that ensured the absolute truth of each statement that the biblical authors made. Indeed, most of them assumed that the very function of divine inspiration was to assure "the high quality of infallibility" in the Scriptures. Noting that "the whole value of inspiration consists in placing the contents of revelation upon record with absolute certainty," Shadrach L. Bowman, dean of the Methodists' School of Theology at DePauw University, reasoned that "the denial of the characteristic of infallibility in supernatural inspiration means logically the denial of the correctness of divine revelation itself." From this perspective, the issue at stake in controversies relating to the truth of specific scriptural passages was not simply the status of specific moral and religious doctrines; it was the trustworthiness of the Bible as an authoritative repository of divine truth.[12]

Though few proponents of this view explicitly asserted that God had assured the inerrancy of biblical testimony by means of a process of "mechanical dictation," they did affirm that His inspiration extended to the very words that the biblical authors had employed. Accordingly, they rejected schemes for partitioning the Scriptures "into portions that are authoritative, partially authoritative, and not at all authoritative." Enoch Fitch Burr, for example, submitted that the notion that the scope of biblical infallibility was limited to "things moral and religious would, if fully understood and adopted by the people at large, completely destroy the authority of the Scriptures among them." Other church people assailed the view that the Bible was an amalgam of permanent and transient elements and that Christians in every age were charged with the task of drawing the line between them. This position, they charged, implicitly substituted the judgment of human beings for the authority of God's Word. For their part, it seemed clear, as Charles Hodge had put it in his *Systematic Theology*, that "complete havoc must be made of the whole system of revealed truth, unless we consent to derive our philosophy from the Bible, instead of explaining the Bible by our philosophy."[13]

Many proponents of scriptural infallibility emphasized that only the original, no longer extant, "autograph manuscripts," which recorded the actual testimony of the biblical authors, were wholly inerrant; the text available to nineteenth-century Christians contained certain "errors, interpolations, and corruptions." This claim, which was not new, was quite popular in the late nineteenth century, when the inerrancy of the Bible was affirmed with greater vigor than ever before. It would be a mistake, however, to assume that Protestants who espoused this position employed it as a way of explaining away all challenges to the veracity of the text. The same conviction that God had intended the Scriptures to serve as a complete and infallible source of divine truth that led these thinkers to affirm the inerrancy of the original autographs led them also to assume that subsequent errors in transcription were confined to trivial points and that "not one single doctrine has been thereby affected."[14]

Christians who embraced the doctrine of scriptural infallibility devoted a good deal of attention to the task of defending the veracity of biblical passages dealing with natural history. These thinkers conceded that God had not intended the Bible to be a scientific treatise, but they insisted that its discussion of the natural world contained no errors. Indeed, many of them believed that the veracity of the Bible depended on its inerrancy in describing natural history. The Methodist theologian Luther Tracy Townsend, who had emerged from a "period of personal skepticism" during his college days at Dartmouth in the 1850s with a vigorous and aggressive confidence in the infallibility of the Scriptures, asserted that the presence of "scientific errors" in the Bible would indicate "that the book is not in a special sense God's book, and therefore, its claims upon us are not supreme." A similar view was enunciated by the Episcopal clergyman G. T. Bedell. "If the facts are doubtful," he reasoned, "why not the dogmas? They stand on the same footing, have the same authority."[15]

Although this position would seem to ensure that any controversy between science and holy writ would involve high stakes, it is important to remember that prior to 1875, Protestants who affirmed the iner-

rancy of biblical testimony concerning natural history had characteristically muted the force of this claim by suggesting that the language
of the Scriptures was subject to erroneous interpretation. This position
enabled them to reinterpret biblical passages in accordance with the
conclusions of science while simultaneously maintaining that these
passages themselves were free from error. In the last quarter of the
nineteenth century, however, many Christians who espoused the doctrine of biblical inerrancy became quite resistant to the idea that the
Scriptures needed to be constantly reinterpreted. These thinkers reasoned that the Bible could serve as a repository of truth to all human
beings only if it was characterized by "clearness, and in all vital partic-
ulars simplicity." Although many of them acknowledged that the Scriptures contained certain "hidden truths" that had been disclosed only
after sustained exegetical effort, their interpretation of divine revelation led them to concur with Stuart Robinson, the pastor of the Second
Presbyterian Church in Louisville, Kentucky, and a well-known expo-
nent of conservative theology, who declared in 1879 that "to assume
that after eighteen centuries the substantial meaning of the Scriptures,
outside of unfulfilled prophecy, has not yet been reached, is in effect to
declare the revelation practically useless."[16]

Belief in the clarity of Scriptures was not new. The doctrine of the pri-
esthood of all believers was firmly entrenched within the Protestant
tradition, and throughout the first three quarters of the nineteenth century, the claim that this principle implied that the biblical message had
been revealed so clearly that it was not apt to be misinterpreted by even
the most untutored reader continued to be voiced. Prior to 1875, however, proponents of this view had characteristically compromised this
claim by applauding the work of scientists, historians, and biblical critics for shedding needed light on the meaning of scriptural passages.
During the last quarter of the nineteenth century, some Protestant
thinkers moved toward a more unqualified commitment to the perspi-
cuity of the Scriptures. Many of these thinkers continued to maintain
that the "anticipation" of modern scientific knowledge in the Bible was
evidence of the divine inspiration of the Scriptures. Moreover, at least
some of them continued to assume that God had accommodated the
message of the Scriptures to the people for whom that message was
originally intended. This implied that an investigation of the social and
intellectual environment in which the biblical authors lived might yield
dividends. These considerations notwithstanding, Biblicists increasingly gravitated toward a repudiation of the notion that a correct understanding of the Scriptures was contingent on the work of specialists

in scientific and historical inquiry. Luther Tracy Townsend, for example, asserted that "science, philosophy, archaeology, and all the correlated sciences, have added not one new fundamental truth to our theological knowledge, and have changed nothing." The Lutheran clergyman J. M. Cromer agreed, insisting that "a proper interpretation of God's word is not subject to the corrections of an advanced science." Cromer maintained that the advances Christians had made in understanding the Scriptures had occurred independently of developments in the secular arena. Hence, he urged, they had been *"as possible centuries ago as now."*[17]

It is difficult to avoid the conclusion that this emphasis on the clarity of the Scriptures was largely a reaction to the conclusions emanating from scientists, historians, and biblical critics. These conclusions would have demanded far more radical revisions in biblical interpretation than anything that had previously been countenanced. Recognizing this, a relatively small but growing contingent of American Protestant thinkers reasoned that "the only safe course is to take the Bible substantially as we find it."[18]

These Christians professed to have become quite "weary of those who claim to believe the Bible is from God, explain(?) away passage after passage, till the strongest words melt into a dim cloudiness, and there seems to be nothing so certain, nothing so fixed, that it may not be shifted to meet our logical exigencies." The periodic, seemingly endless, revision of biblical interpretation in response to the kaleidoscope of scientific opinion, they maintained, undermined confidence in the Bible as "a rule of faith." In contrast to some Protestants, who reasoned that the uncertainties attending biblical interpretation undermined the rationale for belief in an infallible text, Biblicists concluded that the infallibility of the text implied that scriptural interpretation was not as uncertain as some expositors had suggested.[19]

The unwillingness of these thinkers to countenance the strategy of altering the interpretation of the Scriptures to bring them into line with the conclusions of modern science placed them in the same camp with not only many Protestant evolutionists but also such infamous opponents of Christian theology as T. H. Huxley, who lost few opportunities to taunt the "army of 'reconcilers' " for endorsing the most tortured interpretations imaginable in an effort to show that the Bible could be reconciled to science. During the course of his lecture tour in the United States in 1876, for example, Huxley observed that "a person who is not a Hebrew scholar can only stand by and admire the marvellous flexibility of a language which admits of such diverse interpretations." But whereas Huxley and numerous Protestant evolutionists decided that the proper course of action was to abandon the doctrine of biblical infallibility, Protestants who remained committed to the doctrine concluded that God would not have provided humanity with an infallible Bible without making it possible for all human beings who could read the text to interpret it correctly.[20]

Proponents of this populistic concept of religious knowledge held that although human beings sometimes erred in interpreting passages of Scripture, the use of "common sense principles" would enable them to understand the truths recorded in the Bible. The true meaning of biblical passages, these Christians argued, was to be found in their "plain sense." Proponents of this venerable Protestant principle continued to subscribe to a nonliteral interpretation of some scriptural texts, but they insisted that the meaning of these texts was to be found "not in human authorities, but in the Word itself." Just as important, they reasoned that passages they perceived to be central to an understanding of the Christian message meant precisely what they said. Luther Tracy Townsend thus assailed the notion that Genesis presented nothing more than a "pictorial" account of creation on the ground that this view would imperil "the integrity of the whole record" by precluding interpreters from being able to ascertain "where the poetry of any part of the Bible ends and where the literal account begins."[21]

Protestants who embraced the view that the Scriptures were a complete, infallible, and perspicuous source of knowledge reasoned that the Bible was, as Edward D. Morris, professor of systematic theology at Lane Theological Seminary in Cincinnati, put it, "a supreme judge and arbiter, by which all controversies, decrees, opinions and doctrines of men, are to be examined and tested." They thus concluded that God's Word was the final court of appeal in evaluating interpretations of natural history generated by the scientific community. If they acknowledged that the Bible was not intended to convey a scientific account of the world, they all assumed that the Bible contained the "germs and elements of all true science" and that a correct understanding of the natural world would conform to the truths revealed in the Scriptures. The inference to be drawn, they maintained, was obvious: in cases of conflict between the conclusions of scientists and the testimony of the Bible, acceptance of the latter was the only reasonable course of action.[22]

A clear articulation of this position was presented by George D. Armstrong. Armstrong was not in principle opposed to the scientific enterprise. On the contrary, prior to becoming pastor of the First Pres-

byterian Church in Norfolk, Virginia, in 1851, he had served as professor of chemistry and mechanics at Washington College (Virginia). This
experience gave him credentials enabling him to assume a prominent
position within southern Presbyterian circles as an authority on the relationship between science and theology. He used this position to defend as vigorously as he could the infallibility of the biblical narrative.
Some indication of how closely he adhered to the "plain sense" of this
narrative can be gleaned from his declaration that "the garden of Eden
had as distinct a location as the city of Jerusalem." Not surprisingly,
Armstrong had little patience with hypotheses that he considered to be
inconsistent with the Bible. In 1888 he presented a succinct statement
of his position concerning the appropriate relationship between science
and the Bible: "where there is a conflict between a truth or doctrine
clearly taught in Scripture, and the generally accepted conclusions of
science, sound logic requires that we accept the former, and reject the
latter. God cannot err; science may err, in the present, as it often has in
the past."[23]

During the last quarter of the nineteenth century, many Biblicists
joined Armstrong in emphasizing the fallibility of scientific analysis.
Unlike proponents of modern science, who saw the changing pano-
rama of scientific thought as a testimony to the promise of the scientific
method, they tended to see it as a witness to the vacillation and error
inherent in a human discipline. Commenting on the "FICKLENESS OF SCI-
ENCE," one critic asserted that the history of scientific thought indicated
that "science is considerably unsettled and often in error; that the opinions current to-day, are, in a great many cases, not the opinions of a few
years to come." Biblicists also emphasized that the testimony of nature
was not as clear as that of the Scriptures. One writer, noting that "the
world abounds with things we can never [sic] know only upon testimony," attempted to convince his readers that in dealing with the
"great facts concerning man's origin and destiny," it was necessary to
rely on the testimony of the Bible.[24]

Proponents of strong conceptions of biblical authority inevitably regarded the theory of organic evolution as an untenable interpretation
of natural history. For many of them, in fact, that theory appeared to
be the most appropriate and compelling occasion imaginable for applying their views concerning the proper relationship that was to obtain
between science and the Scriptures. A representative statement of their
position can be seen in John T. Duffield's article "Evolutionism, Respecting Man and the Bible." Duffield acknowledged that the intent of
divine revelation was redemptive rather than scientific, and he was in-

clined to reject the notion that every passage relating to natural history was intended to be interpreted literally. He insisted, however, that many passages relating to the natural world were so central to the scriptural exposition of the scheme of redemption that it was impossible for individuals who believed in the divine inspiration of the Bible to concede that they were "untrustworthy" without undermining the authority of biblical revelation. To illustrate his point, Duffield alluded to the narrative of human creation. The Bible's teaching on this subject, he contended, was, "as to extent, explicitness, and importance, wholly different from its teaching concerning the structure of the solar system, or the length of a creative day." In fact, he argued, the doctrine that human beings had been specifically created was no less "distinctly and conclusively" taught than the divinity of Jesus. For Duffield, the inference was clear: "If the teaching of the Bible on this subject can be regarded as an open question, then none can assert with confidence what it teaches on any subject."[25]

Some Protestants who shared Duffield's assessment of the transmutation hypothesis continued to assert that they would alter their attitude toward the hypothesis if it was supported by "overwhelming proof." It is apparent, however, that their conviction that the theory of organic evolution was irreconcilable with the testimony of the Scriptures precluded them from accepting anything short of the actual observation of transmutation as sufficient proof of the theory's merits. John Duffield thus appraised the likelihood that the theory would someday be proved as comparable to the prospect that mathematicians would eventually establish that two plus two equaled five. W. J. Wright agreed, concluding that an evaluation of the merits of the idea that human moral and mental faculties had arisen by means of a process of evolution presented little difficulty: "As this contradicts Scripture it cannot be true."[26]

A number of Biblicists made a point of repudiating the notion that Christians who possessed no special scientific training had no right to evaluate scientific opinions. To accept that exclusionary principle, an indignant Francis Patton declared, "would be to allow that the theist repeats his creed and says his prayers under scientific sanction." Persuaded that Christian apologists were to seek relentlessly "to expose the absurd fallacies continually put forward in the name of science, but utterly unscientific," they continued to assert that true science attested to the cogency of the doctrine of special creation. If many scientists dissented from this conclusion, John Moore asserted, "so much the worse for them." For Moore and other Biblicists, the scientific·community's endorsement of the theory of organic evolution was evidence not of the theory's validity but of the proclivity of scientists to leap to unwarranted conclusions. Commenting on the tendency of scientists to substitute conjecture for facts, Stuart Robinson charged that "science has become as speculative and as prolific of metaphysical theories as the most insane metaphysician could wish. The most distinguished scientists, leaving their proper calling, . . . mistake their gossamer metaphysical theories for the hard, substantial facts of their science." Partisans of this position, convinced that much that paraded under the banner of science was arrant nonsense, thus agreed with Jesse B. Thomas when he declared in 1884 that "to recast a theological system to the pattern of a shifting and precarious biological hypothesis is madness."[27]

For Protestants who embraced the view that the Bible was a complete, infallible, and clear record of divine revelation, theology appeared to be a profoundly conservative enterprise. These thinkers insisted that the notion that doctrinal formulations were contingent on cultural factors specific to the time and place in which they were formulated represented an implicit denial of the immutability of biblical revelation. Persuaded that the Scriptures were the source of all valid theological ideas, Biblicists held that the task of the theologian was limited to explicating the meaning "implicitly contained" in them. Theological discourse was to be evaluated by only one criterion: "whether it is true to the Scripture." This view prompted Francis Patton to declare sarcastically that "a creed is not like a coat, made to fit the wearer and accommodate his taste."[28]

Although these conservative Protestant intellectuals applauded all efforts to bring creeds and other doctrinal positions "into closer approximation to the changeless and everlasting Word," their conception of biblical revelation made them quite leery of the concept of theological progress. Luther Tracy Townsend, for example, submitted that "the writers of the Bible advanced so far into the field of pure theology, and revealed so much, that, from the nature of the case, theology cannot discover an essentially new truth, and cannot in this respect be a progressive science." Lamenting what he perceived to be the "demand of the times" for theological development, John L. Girardeau insisted that "the doctrine of Scripture, if rightly apprehended by the individual mind, or rightly expressed in a church-creed, admits of no substantial development. It is a completed product of the divine intelligence. . . . nothing can be added to it and nothing taken from it." Some Protestants inferred from their belief in the essential clarity of Scripture—and doubtless, too, from their assessment of the doctrinal innovations advocated by partisans of the New Theology—that most theological change actually signified declension. Henry Darling, a Presbyterian clergyman who from 1881 to 1891 served as president of Hamilton College in Clinton, New York, thus invoked Tertullian's maxim that "what is first is true, what is more recent is false." A similar view prompted Charles Hodge to boast that "Princeton has never been charged with originating a new idea."[29]

Although numerous observers of the American religious landscape in the late nineteenth century testified that most Christians in the United States subscribed to the doctrine of biblical infallibility that grounded this conservative theological perspective, Biblicism received explicit support from only a minority of Protestants who discussed scriptural authority in the books and religious quarterlies published during the last quarter of the nineteenth century. Unfortunately, the kind of detailed biographical information that would make it possible to arrive at accurate generalizations concerning the personal and social characteristics of these Biblicists does not exist. The information that is available suggests that many of the most outspoken partisans of this position were Presbyterians who subscribed to the "Princeton theology," but a minority of thinkers in the other mainline Protestant denominations also supported this position. It would appear, too, that although ardent Biblicists could be found in every geographical region in the United States, a slightly disproportionate number of them resided in the southern and border states. This was doubtless due in large measure to the strength of Princeton Seminary's influence in those regions, but it may have also been at least partly the result of the fact that the commitment of clergy and theologians to the epistemological priorities of modern culture was most attenuated in regions further from the levers of cultural power within American society.[30]

Proponents of Biblicism were rarely explicit in delineating the process of thought that prompted them to espouse the idea that the Scriptures constituted a complete, inerrant, and clear source of religious knowledge. In retrospect, however, it seems clear that their decision to renounce the compromises and ambiguities that had typified discussion of divine revelation prior to 1875 in favor of a more "muscular belief" in biblical authority reflected the same quest for certainty that motivated other thinkers in the late nineteenth century to look to science, the "expert," or the life and teachings of Jesus. That these Protestants looked to the Scriptures for certainty was both a function and a measure of their confidence that a gracious Deity had not set His children adrift without providing them with an "ultimate standard of authority as to religious truth." Persuaded that the Bible was the vehicle God had chosen to supply such a standard, they reasoned that the message of the Bible was far more indubitable than any conclusions that had been reached by means of human efforts.[31]

The fervor with which some Protestants defended the centrality of the Bible in understanding the nature of reality was heightened by their conviction that they were living in an era in which this belief was being subjected to sustained assault. The higher criticism of the Bible, which presupposed that the message of the biblical authors was fundamentally conditioned by the culture in which they composed their work, played a fundamental role in fostering this conviction. No less important was the work of scientists. From the very outset of the scientific revolution, some Cassandras within the Protestant community had warned that science bred an arrogance and single-mindedness that was antithetical to the kind of humility necessary to attain a proper understanding of spiritual truth. By 1875, many Protestants who contemplated the views of scientists against the backdrop of the militant campaign that outspoken proponents of scientific naturalism had been waging against the Christian world view during the third quarter of the nineteenth century were convinced that these concerns had been justified. The "tendency of scientific men to throw suspicion over the trustworthiness of the Bible," they charged, was one of the most pronounced features of their age. This assessment grounded a litany of complaints about the philosophical tenor of modern science. "Between 'infidelity' and 'science,'" the Universalist S. A. Gardner asserted in 1883, "there is a relationship which is utterly wanting between 'science' and the church." F. H. Kerfoot, a theologian in the Southern Baptist Seminary in Louisville, Kentucky, agreed, warning that the "so-called Scientific Spirit . . . seems unwilling to accept the peculiar and proper evidence that the Bible is a revelation from God."[32]

The scientific community's conversion to the theory of organic evolution was of fundamental importance in convincing many Protestants that it was an untrustworthy guide to natural history. Some opponents of the theory, noting that "God's anvil has worn out many a hammer," entertained the hope that the scientific community would see the light and consign the theory of evolution to the slag heap of discarded hypotheses. A few thinkers even believed that there were signs that enthusiasm for the transmutation hypothesis among scientists was waning. Most were more pessimistic. These critics attributed scientists' acceptance of the theory of evolution not simply to a mistake in judgment but to a determination "to put the evidence of a divine revelation out of the circle of admissible data of reasoning." In reality, most scientists had declared their independence from biblical dogma long before 1875. Still, the scientific community's endorsement of the transmutation hypothesis held a special symbolic significance. Because that hypothesis appeared to strike so clearly at the very heart of the biblical message, proponents of Biblicism regarded the favorable response of scientists to it as a more forcible indication than any previous episode in the history of the relationship between science and Christian theology that scientists were unwilling to accept the hegemony of the Bible in assessing the nature of reality. It may have also suggested that the result of compromise was simply demands for further concessions. Finally, it served as a warning that scientists could not be entrusted with science.[33]

Partisans of Biblicism continued to insist that they had no quarrel with true science, which they believed would "maintain a respectful attitude to Scripture." They also insisted, however, that the role of scientists should be strictly limited to the task of compiling and classifying "visible and tangible" data. A correct interpretation of those data, they argued, required an understanding of the Scriptures. This position, as a number of historians have noted, involved a "Baconian" conception of the scientific enterprise. Underlying their continued commitment to this position, however, was not simply an abstract allegiance to a given philosophy of science but a belief in the centrality of the Bible in understanding the basic framework of natural history.[34]

The conversion of scientists to the theory of organic evolution, which occurred at roughly the same time that the higher criticism of the Bible was attaining prominence in many circles, engendered a garrison mentality among Biblicists, a posture toward the modern world that has become recognizable in the twentieth century as fundamentalism. From all appearances, evolutionists and higher critics were "combining their forces in the attack on Evangelical Christianity." In response to this assault, a number of Protestants concluded that it was time to nail the colors to the mast. Beset on all sides by challenges to their faith, they reasoned that Christians faced a starkly simple alternative: "to give up or make a stand."[35]

Protestants who rejected the theory of organic evolution frequently pointed out that the vast majority of Christians who believed in the veracity of the plain sense of the Bible remained committed to the doctrine of special creation. They were also acutely aware, however, that not all Protestant thinkers shared their assessment of either the transmutation hypothesis or scriptural authority. Indeed, by 1896, Luther Tracy Townsend was prepared to acknowledge that Protestant intellectuals who remained committed to the idea that the biblical narrative of creation was a valid historical statement were a small, beleaguered minority. The explanation that members of this minority characteristically proffered for the rapid growth of support for the theory of evolution was that many ostensible believers were guilty of giving "that infallibility to secular science which alone belongs to the theology of the Bible." In this spirit, J. M. Cromer charged that "the fear of scientific criticism is greater than the desire to be loyal to the Scriptures." S. A. Gardner agreed, attributing the "almost complete revolution" that had occurred among Protestants in their attitude toward the evolutionary hypothesis to the fact that "Mount Science overshadows Mount Sinai." Convinced that the transmutation hypothesis was patently irreconcilable with the truths embedded in the Bible, these thinkers reasoned that no one could serve those two masters. The fact that so many Protestant intellectuals endorsed the theory of organic evolution was instrumental in convincing many Biblicists that erosion from within posed as great a danger to the Christian faith as assaults from beyond the border. Accordingly, special creationists devoted almost as much of their attention to denouncing the views of Protestant evolutionists as they did to attacking the work of outspoken opponents of Christianity.[36]

The lengths to which some of these thinkers were prepared to go in attacking "accommodating concessionists" who sought to reconcile Christianity with the transmutation hypothesis can be seen in the dismissal of James Woodrow from Columbia Theological Seminary. Woodrow had begun his college teaching career in 1853, when he became professor of natural science at Oglethorpe University in Milledgeville, Georgia. He took an immediate leave of absence, and after taking graduate courses under Louis Agassiz at Harvard, he transferred to the University of Heidelberg, where he received a Ph.D., summa cum laude, in 1856. He refused an offer to lecture at Heidelberg and chose instead to return to Oglethorpe. There he studied theology privately and was ordained in 1860. The next year he became Columbia Seminary's first Perkins Professor of Natural Sciences in Connexion with Revelation. In 1869 he also became professor of science at South Carolina College (now the University of South Carolina). From 1861 to 1885 he served as editor of the *Southern Presbyterian Review*, and from 1865 to 1893 he published the weekly *Southern Presbyterian*.[37]

Woodrow was not theologically radical. Throughout his career he adhered to the plenary inspiration of the Scriptures, and he apparently
had no difficulty believing the biblical story that Joshua had made the
sun stand still. He also believed, however, that science was one of
God's chosen vehicles for making Himself known, and he scored those
whom he thought guilty of "denouncing as atheistic what every reasonable man must believe." In 1873 Woodrow had taken the offensive
against Robert Lewis Dabney, whose villification of the tenor of modern
science seemed to Woodrow to be unfair and dangerously divisive. The
tone of this polemic suggests that Woodrow was prone to the kind of
self-righteousness commonly associated with his more famous
nephew, Woodrow Wilson. It is not difficult to understand why he
made numerous personal enemies during the course of his life.[38]

Woodrow insisted that the Scriptures made no definitive statement
as to how the world had been created, but even as late as 1881, it is not
clear that he actually subscribed to the transmutation hypothesis.
By the late seventies, however, rumors of his acceptance of the hypothesis had begun to circulate. Finally, at the May 1884 meeting of the
Alumni Association of Columbia Theological Seminary he acceded to
repeated requests that he make manifest his precise position regarding
evolution.[39]

Woodrow began by confessing that he had "modified" his views
concerning the theory of evolution, and he devoted a large part of his
speech to discussing the evidence supporting it. He clearly recognized,
however, that his listeners were primarily interested in the problem of
how that hypothesis related to the scriptural account of creation, and
he dealt at length with this issue. He affirmed his belief in the "absolute
inerrancy" of the Holy Scripture but reiterated his long-held position
that "the Bible does not teach science; and to take its language in a scientific sense is grossly to pervert its meaning." He likened comparisons
of the Bible and science to comparisons of two different scientific dis-
ciplines, such as astronomy and zoology. The task was thus to demonstrate not harmony but simply the absence of contradiction.[40]

Woodrow observed that the Bible was quite vague in its discussion of
the way that God had created species and insisted that nothing in the
narrative contradicted the view that "having originated one or a few
forms, he [God] caused all the others to spring from these in accordance with laws which he ordained and made operative." He acknowledged that the scriptural account of the origin of man was somewhat
"more detailed." He insisted, however, that the statement that man
was created "of the dust of the ground" need not be interpreted liter-

ally, and he concluded that "there would seem to be no ground for attributing a different origin to man's body from that which should be attributed to animals." On the other hand, he continued to affirm that the Scriptures clearly taught that the human soul had been "immediately created." He also recognized that there were "insurmountable obstacles in the way of fully applying the doctrine of descent" to the creation of the first woman.[41]

Woodrow's assessment of the theological implications of the transmutation hypothesis was clearly quite moderate. Nevertheless, one individual who was at the meeting recalled that there was some question as to whether Woodrow would even receive the customary vote of thanks from the Alumni Association. In the ensuing months, as reports of his address became more widely disseminated, many Presbyterians in the South expressed outrage that Woodrow was inhabiting a chair in one of their theological seminaries and demanded his resignation. This demand, a compound of personal animosity, fear about the prospect of future financial support for the seminary if Woodrow remained, and belief that his views were decisive steps on the road to infidelity, resulted in a long series of synod trials and other confrontations between Woodrow and his opponents. Finally, in 1886 the Woodrow case came before the General Assembly of the Presbyterian Church. A committee appointed by the Assembly and chaired by the staunchly anti-evolutionist George D. Armstrong returned a majority report affirming

that the Scriptures, as truly and authoritatively expounded in our "Confession of Faith" and "Catechisms," teach—

That Adam and Eve were created, body and soul, by immediate acts of Almighty power, thereby preserving a perfect race unity;—

That Adam's body was directly fashioned by Almighty God, without any natural animal parentage of any kind, out of matter previously created from nothing;—

And that any doctrine at variance therewith is a dangerous error, inasmuch as in the methods of interpreting Scripture it must demand, and in the consequences which by fair implication it will involve, it will lead to the denial of doctrines fundamental to the faith.

The General Assembly voted overwhelmingly, 137 to 13, in favor of this report. In December 1886 the Board of Directors of Columbia Theological Seminary, responding to a directive from its four governing synods, dismissed Woodrow from his chair.[42]

Alexander Winchell suffered a similar fate at the Methodists' Vanderbilt University in 1878. In 1875 Winchell agreed to travel each year from Syracuse, where he was a professor of geology, to Vanderbilt to lecture for twelve weeks on zoology and historical geology. A convinced Christian evolutionist, he had struggled for years to reconcile his belief in the transmutation hypothesis with biblical doctrines relating to the origin of the human species. In 1878 he published *Adamites and Preadamites*, a work in which he argued that "Adam" referred only to the white race, which had "descended from a common stock with the Negro," whom he termed "preadamic" man. This view clearly implied that "Adam" was not the parent of all men, but Winchell insisted that God had intended both the Fall and the Atonement to "operate retroactively." Hence, the preadamic races of man were exempt from neither the consequences of the Adamic Fall nor the fruits of Christ's atonement.[43]

Winchell also devoted a section of this work to a defense of the theory of organic evolution. He urged that if it was reasonable to believe that the different races of man had descended from a common stock, it was equally reasonable to accept "the derivative origin of organic forms in general." Although he conceded that the absence of hard evidence left the question of whether the human species had evolved from other animals "quite open," his work left the impression that he believed the human body to be a product of the evolutionary process. Winchell took the position that "it is absolutely immaterial whether God created man by a fiat instantly, or by a fiat derivatively."[44]

To many believers, Winchell's view of the early history of the human race seemed manifestly irreconcilable with the biblical scheme of redemption. It is not clear whether the orthodox were more appalled by Winchell's acceptance of the theory of evolution or by his espousal of preadamitism. But in 1878, within a day after Winchell had delivered a commencement address entitled "Man in the Light of Geology," Vanderbilt abolished his lectureship. The *Popular Science Monthly* editorialized that this action suggested just how desperately in need of education the Tennessee Methodists really were. The Tennessee Conference offered a different interpretation:

This is the age in which scientific atheism, having divested itself of the habiliments that most adorn and dignify humanity, walks abroad in shameless denudation. The arrogant and impertinent claims of this science, falsely so called, have been so boisterous and persistent that the unthinking masses have been sadly deluded. But our university alone has had the courage to lay its young, but vigorous, hand upon the mane of untamed speculation, and say: "We will have no more of this."[45]

Although the trials and dismissals centering on the theory of evolution attracted a good deal of publicity, there were actually relatively few such episodes. This is not altogether surprising. Once it became apparent that the scientific community endorsed the transmutation hypothesis, a majority of Protestants who discussed that hypothesis concluded that it was necessary to come to terms with it. It is therefore quite likely that a systematic effort to harass Protestant evolutionists by means of institutional mechanisms would have merely revealed how numerically weak the opposition to the evolutionary hypothesis among the leadership of the American churches really was. More important, a sustained campaign to expel evolutionists from seminaries and the pulpits might well have provoked internecine denominational hostility akin to, if not more severe than, that which had occurred over slavery. Finally, although the publicity given the Woodrow and Winchell dismissals may have deterred some Christians from taking a more outspokenly favorable position toward the transmutation hypothesis in regions where there was strong opposition to it, it may also have conferred a martyrdom upon the victims.[46]

The paucity of formal institutional proceedings does not mean, however, that opponents of the evolutionary hypothesis remained passive in the face of what they perceived to be the growth of "rationalistic skepticism" within the church itself. Denunciations of the "timid apologists" who urged compromise in the name of allegiance to modern science became commonplace in American theological discourse during the late nineteenth century. Henry Darling, for example, upbraided Protestant evolutionists for their "cowardly fear" and complained that those who altered their theological position "upon the incoming of every new theory in science" were adopting a strategy that "impairs the confidence of the people in the Sacred Scriptures as a rule of faith." Similarly nettled, Archibald Hodge declared that "the conduct of some weak christian apologists who hasten with super-serviceable zeal to abate the claims of revelation, and to adjust the doctrines of Christianity to the demands of the passing mode of thinking of the hour, surpasses all else in absurdity."[47]

The conviction of special creationists that the bland compromises sanctioned by theistic evolutionists eviscerated the faith of Christians was bound up with their antipathy to the New Theology. Though the work of G. F. Wright and a minority of other theologically conservative Protestants indicated that support for the hypothesis did not invariably lead Christians to espouse significant theological alterations, the embattled opponents of the transmutation hypothesis recognized that the "reconstruction" of theology advocated by proponents of the New Theology was "largely influenced and colored, if not actually dominated, by Evolution." Whereas many liberal Protestants valued evolutionary rhetoric for the credibility it conferred upon their position among some of the perplexed, thinkers who rejected the theory of organic evolution because they were convinced that it was irreconcilable with the Scriptures regarded the epistemological and doctrinal revisions espoused by most Protestant evolutionists as confirmation of their position. They had nothing but contempt for the claim that those revisions actually accommodated Christianity to the transmutation hypothesis. Jesse B. Thomas, for example, sarcastically observed that "when the Bible has been arbitrarily purged by 'rejecting' what one is compelled to reject by his 'belief in evolution,' it will be easy enough to 'reconcile' what remains." Convinced that the New Theology was tantamount to no theology, opponents of the evolutionary hypothesis warned that the work of skepticism was bearing evil fruit within the vineyard of the church itself.[48]

From this perspective, special creationists denounced as "foul libels" the charges that hostility to the theory of organic evolution was driving educated people away from the church. "If the age becomes infidel," one critic rejoined, "it will be the work of the Darwins, the Huxleys, the Du Bois Raymonds [sic], the Haeckels and their semi-Christian apologists." Another went even further, suggesting that the danger that the evolutionary hypothesis held for Christianity "does not arise from the bold, arrogant speculations of atheistic scientists, but, rather, from the smooth and polished theistic believers, and teachers of science, who hold to evolution theories."[49]

In repudiating a theory that had become fundamental to the research program and analytical framework of natural historians, special creationists were rejecting for the first time in American history a part of the established corpus of scientific thought. This rejection, which was both a reflection and a major cause of the growing hostility of these thinkers to modern culture, destroyed the alliance that had long persisted between the work of scientists and the claims of Christian theology. It would be difficult to exaggerate the significance of this decisive cutting of the Gordian knot. For well over a century Protestants had regarded the work of scientists as an invaluable source of ostensibly objective assistance in confirming some of the major elements of the Christian faith. The conversion of the scientific community to the theory of organic evolution convinced some Protestant intellectuals that the price of accepting its verdict was the abandonment of doctrines that were essential to Christianity. This conviction did not lead these Protestants to abandon their belief that natural history, rightly interpreted, attested to the validity of the Christian world view. Instead, it prompted them to maintain more insistently than ever before that it was necessary to differentiate the true lessons of science from the conjectures of its most renowned and devoted practitioners. This view was not necessarily untenable, but it was not widely shared. To most literate Americans, the "science" that special creationists espoused was a component of their polemic rather than an "objective" confirmation of it.

Conclusion

HENRY ADAMS once suggested that in all the "essentials" of human thought, "the American boy of 1854 stood nearer the year 1 than to the year 1900." Though Adams doubtless overstated the case, there is no question that the last half of the nineteenth century was a period of enormous, often convulsive, cultural change. The triumph of the theory of organic evolution was only one of a number of conceptual revolutions that occurred during this period. Still, if we are willing to credit the testimony of numerous observers, it is obvious that it was among the most decisive in driving educated men and women in the United States to reexamine many of their most fundamental assumptions.[1]

Protestant intellectuals were among those most profoundly affected by the conversion of scientists to the transmutation hypothesis. By 1900 it was obvious that the breach between members of the Protestant community who regarded that hypothesis as a threat to be resisted and those who viewed it as a truth to be reckoned with had become an abiding and conspicuous characteristic of American religious life. Protestant thinkers could unite in affirming that because the God of nature was also the God of grace, valid interpretations of the natural world would accord with the essential tenets of Christianity. They reached radically different conclusions, however, as to how that dictum applied to the transmutation hypothesis. A comparatively small but distinguished number of religious thinkers were convinced that it was impossible to embrace the theory of evolution without abandoning doctrines that were absolutely essential to Christian theology. This conviction drove them to infer that it was therefore inconceivable that the theory was true. Most Protestant intellectuals adopted a different view. Like most other literate Americans, these thinkers assumed that scientists were the most authoritative interpreters of the natural world. They regarded the scientific community's endorsement of the transmutation hypothesis as sufficient grounds for believing that it was a valid interpretation of the history of life. From this perspective, they reasoned that it was inconceivable that the transmutation hypothesis was irreconcilable with Christianity. The urgent task confronting Christians, they urged, was the "reconstruction" of theology in accordance with its dictates. During the course of their protracted discussion of numerous issues—God's relationship to the world, biblical interpretation, the origin and early history of the human species, the ethical precepts of Christianity, and the dynamics of sin and salvation—it became obvious that Protestant evolutionists did not approach this task from the same vantage point or with the same enthusiasm. A large minority of these thinkers insisted that it was possible to endorse the letter of the theory without making extensive revisions in the formulation of Christian doctrines. Most Protestant evolutionists adopted a less conservative view of their mission. They held that it was necessary not only to place the evolutionary hypothesis within a recognizably Christian framework but also to set the tenets of Christian theology within an evolutionary framework. Toward this end, they took the position that gradual, continuous, and progressive change was paradigmatic of the way that God had chosen to operate.

The controversy that occurred during the late nineteenth century between Protestant intellectuals who rejected the transmutation hypothesis and those who accepted it was a conflict not between scientists and theologians but between thinkers who embraced fundamentally different views of the nature and sources of truth and knowledge. Most critics of the hypothesis were convinced that the Bible constituted the vehicle by which a gracious God had chosen to provide the human race with a complete, inerrant, and perspicuous compendium of spiritual truth. These thinkers regarded any conflict between the ideas recorded in God's Word and the conclusions of scientists concerning God's works as a conflict between an infallible source of divine truth and the fallible views of human beings, and they angrily resisted efforts to confer upon science "the prerogative of dictating our faith." The suggestion that the arguments advanced by scientists in favor of the transmutation hypothesis were sufficient to establish the validity of a theory so patently at odds with the biblical message staggered their credence.[2]

Protestant thinkers who endorsed the transmutation hypothesis, on the other hand, believed that both the work of scientists and historians and the testimony of the human consciousness were vehicles of divine self-disclosure. They also believed that the "increasing power of intellectual perception and comprehension is accompanied, despite seeming exceptions, by a growth in the spirit." If they continued to accord the Bible a unique and exalted status, they did so because they believed that it recorded many of the salient events and experiences in God's ongoing relationship with humanity rather than because they believed it to be inerrant. Many proponents of this view charged that the notion that God had ceased revealing Himself to human beings was a manifestation of the "glaring conceit" that nothing of importance remained to be learned. For these believers, the theological enterprise was an ongoing process by which the insights entrusted to individuals in each generation were incorporated within the categories of Christianity.[3]

It was impossible by any mutually accepted set of rational criteria to resolve the problem of whether God had given humanity an infallible source of religious truth or whether He gradually disclosed Himself during the course of history. Moreover, both proponents and opponents of the theory of organic evolution could appeal to elements within the Protestant heritage to support their views of the proper sources of religious knowledge. Whereas Protestants who rejected the theory insisted that their position was dictated by the principle of *Scriptura sola*, those who subscribed to it maintained that they were adopting the only position that could sustain the traditional alliance between Protestant theology and the conclusions of modern science. The fact that neither Protestant evolutionists nor their opponents could offer a reasonable claim to exclusive rights on rationality or the Protestant tradition may well have intensified the acrimony that attended discussion of the transmutation hypothesis.[4]

The epistemological dispute among Protestant thinkers was a major constituent in a larger division within American culture during the late nineteenth century, a division between individuals who looked to venerable sources of authority for an understanding of the data of human experience and those who appealed to methods and theoretical concepts embodied in the work of scientists and other "experts." Adumbrations of this division can be perceived within the American Protestant community throughout the nineteenth century. Prior to 1875, however, most religious thinkers succeeded in convincing themselves that it was possible to harmonize the words of the biblical narrative with the conclusions of modern science. As long as all roads appeared to lead to the same destination, few believers developed clear, systematic positions concerning the nature and sources of spiritual truth. For numerous Protestants, however, the favorable response of natural historians to the transmutation hypothesis decisively disclosed the intellectual bankruptcy of the formulas that had long been employed in reconciling science and the Bible. To be sure, a small number of these thinkers were convinced that a judicious application of those formulas would once again serve the cause of peaceful coexistence between science and theology. The majority of commentators, however, concluded that it was simply not possible to endorse the theory of organic evolution without making fundamental alterations in the divisions of authority between science and the Scriptures. For these thinkers, the evolutionary controversy served as both a cause and an occasion for the clarification and articulation of epistemological priorities.

The verdict that American Protestant thinkers rendered on questions of epistemology was instrumental in determining the way in which they approached the problem of apologetics. Protestants who remained committed to the hegemony of the Bible in all areas of inquiry that came within its purview expressed concern that the categories of theology no longer played a decisive role in the manner in which many literate Americans described and understood the world. These thinkers attributed this development largely to the growing influence of science in shaping the pattern and dynamic of secular culture. For exponents of this view, the scientific community's conversion to the theory of organic evolution was of crucial symbolic significance, for it confirmed their fears that the scientific naturalism that had appeared in such aggressive guise during the third quarter of the nineteenth century had become the reigning perspective from which natural historians approached the world.

Protestants who rejected the theory of organic evolution were rejecting norms that were becoming increasingly powerful within American culture. These believers were aware of the enormous influence of science in general and the transmutation hypothesis in particular, but this served to foster and, in turn, reinforce a pessimistic assessment of the character of intellectual life in the United States. Their confidence in the validity of their own epistemological position, coupled with their conviction that truth was not subject to a vote, enabled them to confront opposition to their position in a spirit of self-righteousness. Convinced that the theory of organic evolution constituted a challenge to the foundations of the biblical message, they held that those who were adulterating the gospel in order to bring it into accord with the dictates of secular society were attempting to gain the world at the cost of their souls. The way to counter defections from biblical Christianity, they asserted, was to proclaim the faith once delivered to the saints. This perspective also prompted them to conclude that the proper response of Protestant thinkers to the scientific community's endorsement of the transmutation hypothesis was to stand at Armageddon and battle for the Lord.[5]

Protestants who valued the work of scientists for disclosing more clearly the process by which God had chosen to operate were similarly alarmed by the increasingly secular tenor of modern thought. They adamantly denied, however, that it was either necessary or legitimate to abandon the culture to unbelief, and they harshly denounced assaults on the theory of evolution. Persuaded that this theory embodied a truth that was applicable to theology as well as to the organic world, they reasoned that doctrinal formulations that were not well adapted to the cultural environment in which they appeared could not survive. Accordingly, they warned that failure to bring doctrinal formulations into alignment with the scientific thought of their age would drive thinking men and women away from Christian theology. Only by showing that the reconstruction of theology necessitated by the theory of evolution provided a more adequate comprehension of the divine-human encounter, they argued, could Christians hope to convince the reading masses to resist the blandishments of unbelief and accord to Christianity a central role in their understanding of reality.

Whether the efforts of these Protestants to reconcile Christian theology with the implications of the transmutation hypothesis resulted in an abandonment of Christianity, as many of their opponents alleged, is ultimately a theological rather than a historical question. It should be emphasized, however, that a few Protestant evolutionists, such as George Frederick Wright, were quite consciously conservative in their approach to theology. Moreover, even those proponents of "evolutionary theology" who were most ardent in their efforts to align the tenets of Christian dogma with the spirit of scientific thought continued to defend a number of doctrines, such as the radical difference between the human species and other animals and the uniquely normative character of Christian ethics, that were abandoned by evolutionists who did not share their commitment to Christianity. Finally, it is obvious that Protestants who accepted the theory of organic evolution were taking a position that was more in keeping than that of critics of the theory with the conventional wisdom of literate Americans. As a result, their efforts to bring doctrines into harmony with the dictates of the transmutation hypothesis may have enabled a large number of educated men and women to retain at least tacit allegiance to the Christian faith. It is certainly true that by 1900, many Protestant thinkers believed that they were justified in declaring victory in their war with unbelief. Borden Parker Bowne, for example, noted in 1887 that "the atheistic gust of recent years has about blown over." A primary reason for this triumph, many assumed, was that Christians had succeeded in showing that the transmutation hypothesis could be reconciled with their theology.[6]

If, however, these thinkers could congratulate themselves on showing that religious belief was credible, they were considerably less successful in showing that it was compelling or even interesting. In spite of the fact that church membership reached new heights, spiritual torpor remained a conspicuous feature of the late-nineteenth-century American cultural landscape. Lyman Abbott thus submitted that "the greatest foe to spiritual religion is neither heresy nor skepticism, but thoughtless indifference." A similar assessment led Bowne to couple his proclamation that atheism was "dead as a philosophy" with the warning that it continued to live on "as a disposition."[7]

A host of factors in the cultural milieu of the United States during the late nineteenth century contributed to the growing tendency among literate Americans to ignore the categories of Christian theology in interpreting their experience. It would be inaccurate to ascribe this state of affairs to the work of Protestant evolutionists. Still, it is important to note that the division of labor between science and theology that these thinkers sanctioned in an effort to justify their endorsement of the transmutation hypothesis did little to check the inclination of a large number of Americans to contemplate and discuss the behavior of natural phenomena without resorting to a theological vocabulary. Once they had endorsed the evolutionary theory of the origin of life, Protestants who believed that God's immediate activity was confined to events that lay beyond the reach of scientific analysis found themselves defending a very attenuated view of God's role in the universe. Such a view was unlikely to avert a shift in the location of intellectual energy from the sacred to the profane or the further desanctification of the natural world.

Protestant evolutionists who embraced a radical formulation of God's immanence in the natural world adopted a position that seemed, at least on the face of it, more conducive to sustaining a pious view of nature. Their effort to "reenchant" the world by affirming God's effusive presence in it was animated by a conviction that had been clearly enunciated by William Paley in 1802:

if one train of thinking be more desirable than another, it is that which regards the phaenomena of nature with a constant reference to a supreme intelligent Author. To have made this the ruling, the habitual sentiment of our minds, is to have laid the foundation of every thing which is religious. The world from thenceforth becomes a temple, and life itself one continued act of adoration.

The change is no less than this, that, whereas formerly God was seldom in our thoughts, we can now scarcely look upon any thing without perceiving its relation to him.

By ascribing every natural event to divine activity and thus "rendering all existence essentially sacred," immanentists were in effect making a "temple" of the world.[8]

It is difficult to ascertain precisely how successful this effort really was. Some literate men and women may well have been prompted by an immanentist conception of reality to adopt a more sacramental view of nature. On the other hand, the immanentist message also sustained, if it did not encourage, tendencies to find meaning and significance in the behavior of the entities composing the cosmos. Though the philosophical thrust of that message lay in the direction of showing that the sacred was embedded in natural phenomena, the message itself was quite compatible with expending a great deal of intellectual energy on determining the patterns and changes of those phenomena. It was all very well for proponents of immanentism to maintain that a comprehensive understanding of the natural world required individuals to recognize that whereas the description of a natural event was the task of science, it was necessary to look to the activities of an immanent Deity to explain that event. In practice, however, the differentiation of description from explanation suggested that the same event could be interpreted either scientifically or theologically. Though few educated Americans in the late nineteenth century were vociferous in ascribing to science an ability to explain the ultimate origin and activity of natural phenomena, many of them found the primary source of their fascination with and excitement about the natural world in the conclusions obtained by scientific investigation. Within the intellectual community itself, some individuals discovered that a disinterested investigation of the natural world provided emotional satisfactions akin to those that pious Christians had long derived from Christian theology.[9]

By 1900, much of the tension between science and theology was more insidious than the crude metaphor of "warfare" implies. The work of scientists had provided humanity with the opportunity to interpret the cosmos in intramundane terms, and many educated Americans were content to elaborate their descriptive accounts of natural phenomena while ignoring altogether the philosophical issue of ultimate explanation. Enamored of the empirically verifiable, "hard" fact, they derived little emotional and intellectual stimulation or engagement from a theophanous view of nature that could be defended only on the grounds that it was an accurate rendition of reality. Many, indeed most, of these Americans did not militantly deny the validity of the theistic approach to nature; they simply disregarded that approach.[10]

The difficulties Protestant evolutionists faced in combating spiritual indifference were compounded by the epistemological position that most of them adopted. These thinkers, most of whom tended to take for granted the cognitive superiority of science to the assertions of the biblical writers, concluded that their endorsement of the transmutation hypothesis was irreconcilable with belief in the inerrancy of the Bible and moved toward the position that the mere presence of a statement in the Scriptures was not in itself a sufficient warrant of its validity. Instead, they argued, it was necessary to test the veracity of each statement against the conclusions of scientific and historical investigation and the data yielded by the religious consciousness. Protestants who endorsed the theory of evolution were convinced that the essential tenets of Christianity could be confirmed only by subjecting them to such a test. But because the results of human inquiry and the testimony of religious experience changed from age to age, it was impossible to determine in advance which tenets of the faith would survive the next "reconstruction" of theology. Indeed, the revolution in scientists' position concerning the history of life served as a rather pointed lesson in how rapidly ideas and assumptions about the nature of reality could change.

Few Protestants explicitly acknowledged this problem, but their resistance to "dogmatizing" and their affirmation of the fallible nature of theology suggest that they implicity recognized that an open-ended view of religious knowledge precluded the possibility of determining in advance precisely where the limits to doctrinal revision lay. Their insistence upon the ongoing character of the theological enterprise was congenial, as many of them were quick to point out, to a "progressive" view of that enterprise. It also offered a way of engendering a kind of immediacy in the quest for meaningful doctrines. At the same time, however, it precluded them from affirming the doctrines and imperatives of Christianity with the kind of certainty that many people who found themselves living in a tumultuous period of social and intellectual change had come to hope for and expect from religion. For some of these individuals, science appeared to provide a more secure cognitive and emotional foundation than theology.[11]

Since 1900, significant changes have occurred in the way that the American Protestant intellectual community has grappled with the transmutation hypothesis. In the early twentieth century, Protestants of a liberal theological persuasion, enamored of Ritschlianism and increasingly overwhelmed by the complexities of modern science, subordinated discussion of such cosmic questions as God's relationship to the natural world to an analysis of the role of Christianity as a source of human values. Insofar as they discussed problems engendered by the theory of organic evolution at all, they characteristically employed patterns of reasoning that had been articulated by Protestant evolutionists during the last quarter of the nineteenth century. For most of them, however, the relationship between science and theology ceased to be a major source of interest.

Twentieth-century Biblicists have continued to regard the theory of evolution as one of the major emblems of modern culture's hostility to the Christian world view embodied in the Scriptures. In the past few decades, however, many of these Protestants have devoted an increasing amount of attention to a theme that, though never absent in their ruminations during the late nineteenth century, had been subordinated to more explicitly biblical considerations: the inability of the theory of organic evolution to account adequately for the data of natural history. These Biblicists have apparently concluded that the most effective way to widen the appeal of their position within American society is to assault in the name of "science" the evolutionary synthesis embraced by virtually all members of the scientific establishment.

The views that Protestant intellectuals have adopted toward the theory of organic evolution since 1900 are central to an understanding of the history of the relationship between science and religion in the twentieth century. Although a detailed analysis of these views lies beyond the scope of this volume, a cursory examination suggests that the stance of neither liberal Protestants nor Biblicists has succeeded in piquing interest in Christian theology within the intellectual community. This century appears to represent another stage in the long process by which the locus of cultural authority for many educated men and women has shifted from theology to science.

It is unlikely that any tactic religious thinkers could have employed would have prevented the elimination of theological discourse from scientific analysis. On the other hand, neither does there appear to be any reason to assume that scientific investigation should be considered the only, or even the preferred, approach to the natural world. Protestant intellectuals in the United States may not have made that assumption, but historical accuracy demands that we remember that for more than two centuries members of the Protestant community played an integral role in lending credibility and prestige to the scientific enterprise. Indeed, it is one of the ironies of history that after freeing themselves from the Catholic church's authority, Protestants increasingly found their own understanding of the relationship between nature and nature's God limited, even determined, by their affiliation with science. If the vocabulary and categories of Christian theology have become insignificant in shaping the way that many literate Americans comprehend the natural world, this is due at least in part to the inability of Protestant theologians and clergy to offer a convincing means of escaping the cultural consequences of that affiliation.

Notes

Index

Notes

Preface

1. Similar uses of the term "intellectual," can be found in D. H. Meyer, "American Intellectuals and the Victorian Crisis of Faith," in Daniel Walker Howe, ed., *Victorian America* (Philadelphia, 1976), p. 60; Edward A. Purcell, Jr., *The Crisis of Democratic Theory: Scientific Naturalism and the Problem of Value* (Lexington, 1973), p. x.

2. An extended indictment of historians' use of the "military metaphor" of warfare to describe the history of the relationship between science and religion can be found in James R. Moore, *The Post-Darwinian Controversies: A Study of the Protestant Struggle to Come to Terms with Darwin in Great Britain and America, 1870–1900* (Cambridge, 1979), esp. pp. 1–122. See also David C. Lindberg and Ronald L. Numbers, "Beyond War and Peace: A Reappraisal of the Encounter between Christianity and Science," *Church History*, 55 (1986), 338–354.

Chapter 1. "The Firmament Sheweth His Handywork"

1. W. C. Wilson, "Darwin on the Origin of Species," *Methodist Quarterly Review*, 4th ser., 13 (1861), 605. See also [J. A. Lowell], "Darwin's Origin of Species," *Christian Examiner*, 5th ser., 6 (1860), 449; [Samuel A. Eliot], "The Origin of Species," *North American Review*, 91 (1860), 528.

2. [Charles Darwin], *The Autobiography of Charles Darwin, 1809–1882, With original omissions restored*, ed. Nora Barlow (New York, 1958), pp. 46–49, 71–72, 76, 229.

My brief discussion of Darwin's life and thought hardly even begins to suggest the subtleties and complexities unraveled by students of his career. My analysis has been particularly influenced by the following works: Gavin de Beer, *Charles Darwin: Evolution by Natural Selection* (New York, 1964); Gertrude Himmelfarb, *Darwin and the Darwinian Revolution* (New York, 1959); Dov Ospovat, *The Development of Darwin's Theory: Natural History, Natural Theology, and Natural Selection* (Cambridge, 1981); Sylvan S. Schweber, "The Origin of the *Origin* Revisited," *Journal of the History of Biology*, 10 (1977), 229–316; Martin J. S. Rudwick, *The Meaning of Fossils: Episodes in the History of Palaeontology*, 2d ed. (New York, 1976); Sandra Herbert, "Darwin, Malthus, and Selection," *Journal of the History of Biology*, 4 (1971), 209–217; Robert M. Young, "Darwin's Metaphor: Does Nature Select?" *Monist*, 55 (1971), 442–503; Howard E. Gruber and Paul H. Barrett, *Darwin on Man: A Psychological Study of Scientific Creativity* (New York, 1974); Edward Manier, *The Young Darwin and His Cultural Circle: A Study of Influences Which Helped Shape the Language and Logic of the First Drafts of the Theory of Natural Selection* (Dordrecht, Holland, 1978); Michael Ruse, *The Darwinian*

Revolution: Science Red in Tooth and Claw (Chicago, 1979); Neal C. Gillespie, *Charles Darwin and the Problem of Creation* (Chicago, 1979).

3. [Darwin], *Autobiography*, pp. 76–77, 101, 118–119; Charles Darwin, *On the Origin of Species by Means of Natural Selection, or the Preservation of Favoured Races in the Struggle for Life* (1859; facsimile ed., Cambridge, Mass., 1964), p. 1; Darwin to A. R. Wallace, April 6, 1859, *More Letters of Charles Darwin*, ed. Francis Darwin and A. C. Seward (London, 1903), 1:118–119 (hereafter cited as *MLD*); *Charles Darwin and the Voyage of the Beagle*, ed. Nora Barlow (London, 1945), pp. 246–247; Darwin to Otto Zacharius, 1877, *MLD*, 1:367; Darwin to W. D. Fox, July 1835, *The Life and Letters of Charles Darwin, Including an Autobiographical Chapter*, ed. Francis Darwin (London, 1887), 1:263 (hereafter cited as *LLD*).

4. Darwin, *Origin of Species*, p. 1 (the phrase was John Herschel's). See also [Darwin], *Autobiography*, p. 119; Darwin to L. Horner, August 29 [1844], *MLD*, 2:117.

5. William Paley, *Natural Theology; or, Evidences of the Existence and Attributes of the Deity, Collected from the Appearances of Nature* (London, 1802), pp. 66–67, 1–19, 83, 579, 457–458, 473, 439, 444–446. See also Darwin to John Lubbock [November 15, 1859], in *LLD*, 2:219. The most useful study of the life and thought of Paley is D. L. Le Mahieu, *The Mind of William Paley: The Philosopher and His Age* (Lincoln, Nebr., 1976).

6. Darwin, *Origin of Species*, pp. 45, 82, 95, 102, 167, 170, 459; Young, "Darwin's Metaphor," pp. 449–450; de Beer, *Darwin*, pp. 86–90, 96–97.

7. Darwin to A. R. Wallace, April 6, 1859, *MLD*, 1:118. See also [Darwin], *Autobiography*, pp. 119–120; Young, "Darwin's Metaphor," pp. 448–449, 452–455, and passim. Few topics in the "Darwin industry" have aroused more heated discussion than the nature of the debt Darwin owed to Malthus. A useful brief discussion of the historiography is Manier, *Young Darwin*, esp. pp. 75–85, 190–192. See also Peter Vorzimmer, "Darwin, Malthus, and the Theory of Natural Selection," *Journal of the History of Ideas*, 30 (1969), 539.

8. Barry G. Gale, "Darwin and the Concept of a Struggle for Existence: A Study in the Extrascientific Origins of Scientific Ideas," *Isis*, 63 (1972), 327–331; Loren Eiseley, *Darwin's Century: Evolution and the Man Who Discovered It* (New York, 1958), pp. 201–202. For manifestations of Darwin's view in the *Origin of Species*, see, for example, pp. 84, 80–81, 459.

9. Darwin to J. D. Hooker [September n.d.], *LLD*, 2:39; Rudwick, *Meaning of Fossils*, p. 232.

10. Rudwick, *Meaning of Fossils*, pp. 232–233. Rudwick has pointed out that Darwin's work on barnacles also showed him that barnacles lost a number of organs and functions during the course of their life. Hence Darwin saw that "regression" could be as adaptive as "progression" and "that the same kind of Malthusian selective pressure must be causally responsible for *both* kinds of change." Ibid.

11. R. C. Stauffer, ed., *Charles Darwin's Natural Selection: Being the Second Part of His Big Species Book Written from 1856 to 1858* (Cambridge, 1975), pp. 5–10; [Darwin], *Autobiography*, p. 121; Darwin to Lyell, 18th [June 1858], *LLD*, 2:116.

12. For a useful discussion of Wallace's discovery of the theory of evolution by natural selection, see H. Lewis McKinney, *Wallace and Natural Selection* (New Haven, 1972). For the relationship between Darwin and Wallace prior to publication of the *Origin of Species*, see Barbara G. Beddall, "Wallace, Darwin and the Theory of Natural Selection," *Journal of the History of Biology*, 1 (1968), 261–323.

13. De Beer, *Darwin*, pp. 119–134, 150–156; Himmelfarb, *Darwin and the Darwinian Revolution*, pp. 238–241.

14. Darwin, *Origin of Species*, p. 82; [Darwin], *Autobiography*, pp. 120–121. See also de Beer, *Darwin*, pp. 151, 140; Darwin to Asa Gray, September 5 [1857], *LLD*, 2:124–125; Dov Ospovat, "Darwin after Malthus," *Journal of the History of Biology*, 12 (1979), 211–230; Janet Browne, "Darwin's Botanical Arithmetic and the 'Principle of Divergence,' 1854–1858," *Journal of the History of Biology*, 13 (1980), 68–89; Darwin to J. D. Hooker, June 8 [1858], *MLD*, 1:109. Dov Ospovat has made a persuasive case for the view that between 1844 and 1859 Darwin abandoned his theologically conditioned belief in perfect adaptation in favor of the idea that surviving organisms were only sufficiently well adapted to compete successfully with other organisms. Ospovat, *Development of Darwin's Theory*, pp. 170–211, esp. pp. 191–192.

15. Darwin to Baden Powell, January 18, 1860, in "Some Unpublished Letters of Charles Darwin," ed. Gavin de Beer, Royal Society of London, *Notes and Records*, 14 (1959), 52–53; Rudwick, *Meaning of Fossils*, p. 235; Darwin, *Origin of Species*, pp. 346–456.

16. Darwin, *Origin of Species*, pp. 177–179, 172–173, 279–311, 463–465; Rudwick, *Meaning of Fossils*, pp. 234–236.

17. Darwin, *Origin of Species*, p. 488 and the epigraphs opposite the title page; Edward Hitchcock, "The Law of Nature's Constancy Subordinate to the Higher Law of Change," *Bibliotheca Sacra and Biblical Repository*, 20 (1863), 522–523.

18. J. Haven, "Natural Theology," *Bibliotheca Sacra and Theological Review*, 6 (1849), 614–615; Edward Hitchcock, "Special Divine Interpositions in Nature," *Bibliotheca Sacra and American Biblical Repository*, 11 (1854), 796. See also E[zra] S[tiles] G[annett], "The Value of Natural Religion," *Christian Examiner and General Review*, 3d ser., 16 (1843), 296–298; James A. Lyon, "The New Theological Professorship of Natural Science in Connection with Revealed Religion," *Southern Presbyterian Review*, 12 (1859), 191; Frederick A. P. Barnard, Inaugural Address, *Proceedings at the Inauguration of Frederick A. P. Barnard, S.T.D., LL.D., as President of Columbia College . . .* (New York, 1865), pp. 61–62; John Brazer, "Review of the Argument in Support of Natural Religion," *Christian Examiner and General Review*, 3d ser., 1 (1835), 138–143; [Francis Bowen], "Brougham's Natural Theology," *North American Review*, 54 (1842), 113, 115, 123, 126.

The important role that Scottish common-sense realism played in shaping the perspective of the American intellectual community has been treated in a number of works. These include Sydney E. Ahlstrom, "The Scottish Philosophy and American Theology," *Church History*, 24 (1955), 257–272; Theodore Dwight Bozeman, *Protestants in an Age of Science: The Baconian Ideal and Antebellum American Religious Thought* (Chapel Hill, 1977); George H. Daniels, *American Science in the Age of Jackson* (New York, 1968); and Daniel Walker Howe, *The Unitarian Conscience: Harvard Moral Philosophy, 1805–1861* (Cambridge, Mass., 1970).

Much of the discussion of natural theology in the period prior to 1859 has focused primarily on Great Britain. Valuable treatments include Alvar Ellegård, "The Darwinian Theory and the Argument from Design," *Lychnos* (1956), pp. 173–192; John Hedley Brooke, "The Natural Theology of the Geologists: Some Theological Strata," in L. J. Jordanova and Roy S. Porter, eds., *Images of the Earth: Essays in the History of the Environmental Sciences* (Chalfont St. Giles, 1979), pp. 39–64; Peter J. Bowler, "Darwinism and the Argument from Design: Suggestions for a Reevaluation," *Journal of the History of Biology*, 10 (1977), 29–43. Useful treatments of natural theology in the United States can be found in Bozeman, *Protestants in an Age of Science*; Conrad Cherry, *Nature and Religious Imagination: From Edwards to Bushnell* (Philadelphia,

1980); E. Brooks Holifield, *The Gentlemen Theologians: American Theology in Southern Culture, 1795–1860* (Durham, 1978); Howe, *Unitarian Conscience*; Neal C. Gillespie, "Preparing for Darwin: Conchology and Natural Theology in Anglo-American Natural History," *Studies in History of Biology*, 7 (1984), 93–145; and Ronald L. Numbers, *Creation by Natural Law: Laplace's Nebular Hypothesis in American Thought* (Seattle, 1977). For a valuable discussion of the considerations underlying the increasing resort of American religious thinkers to the arguments of natural theology prior to the publication of the *Origin of Species*, see James Turner, *Without God, Without Creed: The Origins of Unbelief in America* (Baltimore, 1985), esp. pp. 7–170. There are also two quite useful unpublished dissertations that deal at length with this problem: John F. McElligott, "Before Darwin: Religion and Science as Presented in American Magazines, 1830–1860" (New York University, 1973), and John Arlo De Jong, "American Attitudes toward Evolution before Darwin" (State University of Iowa, 1962).

19. [Bowen], "Brougham's Natural Theology," p. 130.

20. Voltaire, "The Lisbon Earthquake," in *The Portable Voltaire*, ed. Ben Ray Redman (New York, 1949), pp. 560, 567. See also David Hume, *Dialogues Concerning Natural Religion, Philosophical Works of David Hume* (Boston, 1854), 2:436, 438, 481, 506, 509–519, and passim; Immanuel Kant, *The Critique of Judgment*, trans. James Creed Meredith (London, 1952), p. 374 (22–24).

21. [Samuel Harris], "The Harmony of Natural Science and Theology," *New Englander*, 10 (1852), 17; Anon., Review of *The Indications of the Creator; or, The Natural Evidence of the Final Cause*, by George Taylor, *Knickerbocker*, 39 (1852), 84–85. See also Anon., "The Study of Natural History as a School-Classic," *Knickerbocker*, 25 (1845), 290; J. Jay Dana, "The Religion of Geology," *Bibliotheca Sacra and American Biblical Repository*, 10 (1853), 506; Edward Hitchcock, "The Relations and Consequent Mutual Duties between the Philosopher and the Theologian," *Bibliotheca Sacra and American Biblical Repository*, 10 (1853), 177. For Charles Finney's favorable appraisal of science, see William G. McLoughlin, Jr., *Modern Revivalism: Charles Grandison Finney to Billy Graham* (New York, 1959), p. 120.

More extensive treatment of the essentially harmonious relationship between science and religion during the pre-Darwinian period include John Dillenberger, *Protestant Thought and Natural Science: A Historical Interpretation* (London, 1961), pp. 21–162, 207–218; Bozeman, *Protestants in an Age of Science*; Holifield, *Gentlemen Theologians*.

22. Hitchcock, "Relations and Consequent Mutual Duties," p. 177. See also Barnard, Inaugural Address, pp. 49–50; Brooke, "Natural Theology of the Geologists," pp. 45–47; John C. Greene, "Science and Religion" in Edwin S. Gaustad, ed. *The Rise of Adventism* (New York, 1974), pp. 50–57; Daniels, *American Science*, pp. 51-54. Robert M. Young has concluded in a number of articles that in Great Britain, too, science and religion were "part of a common intellectual context." See, for example, "Natural Theology, Victorian Periodicals, and the Fragmentation of a Common Context," in Colin Chant and John Fauvel, eds., *Darwin to Einstein: Historical Studies on Science and Belief* (New York, 1980), pp. 69–107.

23. [Orville Dewey], "Diffusion of Knowledge," *North American Review*, 30 (1830), 312; [Francis Bowen], "Chalmer's Natural Theology," *North American Review*, 54 (1842), 359. See also Anon., "The Bridgewater Treatises," *Southern Literary Messenger*, 5 (1839), 211; Dana, "Religion of Geology," p. 506; Anon., "The Personality of God, as Affecting Science and Religion," *Southern Presbyterian Review*, 14 (1861), 461–

462; Asa Mahan, *The Science of Natural Theology; or, God the Unconditioned Cause, and God the Infinite and Perfect, as Revealed in Creation* (Boston, 1867), p. 23n.

24. Edward Hitchcock, *Elementary Geology*, 8th ed. (New York, 1852), p. 302; Dana, "Religion of Geology," pp. 507–509, 514–515; Henry M. Harmon, "Natural Theology," *Methodist Review*, 4th ser., 15 (1863), 183–184, 204; Joseph P. Thompson, "Does Science Tend to Materialism?" *New Englander*, 19 (1861), 95–96; [G. W. Featherstonhaugh], "Geology," *North American Review*, 32 (1831), 475–476.

Paley continued to be very popular in America during the first half of the nineteenth century. See, for example, [A. P. Peabody], "Dr. Harris's Pre-Adamite Earth and Man Primeval," *North American Review*, 70 (1850), 401; F. W. P. G[reenwood], "Dr. Roget's Bridgewater Treatise," *Christian Examiner*, 3d ser., 2 (1836), 153; Wendell Glick, "Bishop [*sic*] Paley in America," *New England Quarterly*, 27 (1954), 347–349.

25. Stuart Robinson, "The Difficulties of Infidelity," in W. H. Ruffner, ed., *Lectures on the Evidences of Christianity . . .* (New York, 1851), p. 557. See also G[reenwood], "Roget's Bridgewater Treatise," pp. 138–140, 143; [Francis Bowen], "A Theory of Creation," *North American Review*, 60 (1845), 476–477; Benjamin W. Dwight, "The Doctrine of God's Providence, in Itself and in Its Relations and Uses," *Bibliotheca Sacra*, 21 (1864), 591–592; Ellegård, "Darwinian Theory," pp. 176–177; Daniels, *American Science*, pp. 179–181; Ospovat, *Development of Darwin's Theory*, pp. 7–22; Dov Ospovat, "Perfect Adaptation and Teleological Explanation: Approaches to the Problem of the History of Life in the Mid-Nineteenth Century," *Studies in History of Biology*, 3 (1978), 33–56; Bowler, "Darwinism and the Argument from Design," pp. 29-43; Anon., Editor's Table, *Harper's Monthly*, 16 (1858), 263; J[ames] W[alker], "Strauss-Durckheim's Natural Theology," *Christian Examiner and Religious Miscellany*, 4th ser., 25 (1856), 430; Anon., "Bridgewater Treatises," pp. 211, 216; George I. Chace, "Of the Existence and Natural Attributes of the Divine Being," *Bibliotheca Sacra and Theological Review*, 7 (1850), 331–334, 351; Hitchcock, "Special Divine Interpositions," pp. 785, 791; Anon., Review of *The Course of Creation*, by John Anderson, *Biblical Repertory and Princeton Review*, 24 (1852), 147–148, 150. A perceptive discussion of the difference between the conception of design as order and as purpose is Thomas McPherson, *The Argument from Design* (London, 1972).

26. The progressionist interpretation of natural history within the scientific community is ably treated in Rudwick, *Meaning of Fossils*, pp. 142–149, 181, 191–201; Peter J. Bowler, *Fossils and Progress: Paleontology and the Idea of Progressive Evolution in the Nineteenth Century* (New York, 1976); and Leonard G. Wilson, ed., *Sir Charles Lyell's Scientific Journals on the Species Question* (New Haven, 1970), pp. xxxi–xxxiii. For typical statements affirming this position, see [James Dwight Dana], "Sequel to the Vestiges of Creation," *American Journal of Science and Arts*, 2d ser., 1 (1846), 251; O[ctavius] B. F. F[rothingham], "Man and Nature in Their Religious Relations," *Christian Examiner and Religious Miscellany*, 4th ser., 19 (1852), 462; Hitchcock, "Special Divine Interpositions," p. 791; Anon., Review of *The Ancient World; or, Picturesque Sketches of Creation*, by D. T. Ansted, *Church Review and Ecclesiastical Register*, 1 (1848), 126; John O. Means, "Narrative of the Creation in Genesis," *Bibliotheca Sacra and American Biblical Repository*, 12 (1855), 333.

27. John Harris, *The Pre-Adamite Earth: Contributions to Theological Science* (Boston, 1849), p. 182; Hitchcock, *Elementary Geology*, pp. 284–285; Anon., Review of *Course of Creation*, pp. 147–148; L. W. Green, "The Harmony of Revelation and Natural Science: With Especial Reference to Geology," in Ruffner, ed., *Lectures on the Evidences*

of Christianity, pp. 463, 476–477. See also William G. Howard, "Mysteries of the Bible," *Southern Literary Messenger*, 6 (1840), 626; [John Brazer], "Essay on the Doctrine of Divine Influence," *Christian Examiner and General Review*, n.s. 12 (1835), 318, 323–325; Professor Durbin, "On the Omnipresence of God," *Methodist Magazine and Quarterly Review*, n.s. 2 (1831), 48–51; Horace Bushnell, *Nature and the Supernatural, as Together Constituting the One System of God* (New York, 1858), p. 207; Edward Hitchcock, *The Religion of Geology and Its Connected Sciences* (Boston, 1851), pp. 156, 166, 320, 340, 343–344, 364; [Francis Bowen], "Greenleaf and Strauss: The Truth of Christianity," *North American Review*, 63 (1846), 421; David Hume, *An Inquiry Concerning the Human Understanding, Philosophical Works of David Hume*, 4:124–150; [Oliver Stearns], "Rationalism in Religion: The Need and Purpose of Miracles," *Christian Examiner and Religious Miscellany*, 4th ser., 20 (1853), 258–259; T[homas] H[ill], "The Plurality of Worlds," *Christian Examiner and Religious Miscellany*, 4th ser., 22 (1854), 212; [Albert Barnes], "Readjustments of Christianity," *Presbyterian Quarterly Review*, 11 (1862), 89.

Though I think that James Turner has underestimated the commitment that the American Protestant intellectual community in the period prior to 1875 retained toward the doctrine of "special" providence within nature, their belief in special creations does not really negate Turner's claim that by the early nineteenth century, few Protestant thinkers expected to see instances of direct, "special" divine intervention in the natural world. Turner, *Without God*, pp. 38–43, 77–81.

28. F[rothingham], "Man and Nature," p. 456; A[ndrew] P. P[eabody], "The Bible," *Christian Examiner and General Review*, 3d ser., 15 (1842), 155; [D. Olmsted], "Thoughts on the Sentiment that 'The World was Made for Man,' " *New Englander,* 7 (1849), 17, 32–33); [?] Davies, "God Himself the Ultimate End of All Things," *Biblical Repertory and Theological Review*, n.s. 4 (1832), 94; James D. Dana, "Science and the Bible," *Bibliotheca Sacra*, 13 (1856), 116, 121; Dana, "Religion of Geology," p. 515. See also J[oseph] L[overing], "Somerville's Physical Geography," *Christian Examiner and Religious Miscellany*, 4th ser., 11 (1849), 74; Bushnell, *Nature and the Supernatural*, pp. 204–206; W[illiam] H. F[urness], "The Miracles of Jesus," *Christian Examiner and General Review*, 3d ser., 4 (1837), 290; Harris, *Pre-Adamite Earth*, pp. 270–272. Christians were initially resistant to the idea of extinction because they viewed it as an indictment of God's workmanship. Rudwick, *Meaning of Fossils*, p. 64; John C. Greene, *The Death of Adam: Evolution and Its Impact on Western Thought* (Ames, Iowa, 1959), pp. 5–8, 89.

29. George I. Chace, "The Realm of Faith," *Baptist Quarterly*, 5 (1871), 46; Henry Ware, quoted in F[rancis] P[arkman], "Ware's Inquiry," *Christian Examiner and General Review*, 3d ser., 14 (1842), 91; [Olmsted], "Thoughts on the Sentiment," p. 31. See also Dana, "Religion of Geology," p. 517; Hitchcock, *Elementary Geology*, p. 287.

30. [G. P. Marsh], "The Study of Nature," *Christian Examiner*, 5th ser., 6 (1860), 57–58; Josiah Parsons Cooke, *Religion and Chemistry* (1864; New York, 1880), p. 329. See also Tayler Lewis, *The Bible and Science; or, The World-Problem* (Schenectady, 1856), pp. 183, 326–330; John David Yule, "The Impact of Science on British Religious Thought in the Second Quarter of the Nineteenth Century," Ph.D. diss., Cambridge, 1976, pp. 164, 175, 212, 218, 230, 366, and passim; John Hedley Brooke, "Natural Theology and the Plurality of Worlds: Observations on the Brewster-Whewell Debate," *Annals of Science*, 34 (1977), pp. 222, 226–228, 281, 284; Herbert Hovenkamp, *Science and Religion in America, 1800–1860* (Philadelphia, 1978), pp. 48–49.

31. H. Alleyne Nicholson, "Life and Its Origin," *Presbyterian and Princeton Review*,

n.s. 2 (1873), 689; Edward Hitchcock, "The Connection between Geology and Natural Religion," *Biblical Repository and Quarterly Observer*, 5 (1835), 117–118. See also [Bowen], "Theory of Creation," pp. 438–439.

32. Milton Millhauser, *Just before Darwin: Robert Chambers and Vestiges* (Middletown, Conn., 1959), pp. 58–85. Both Millhauser and Gavin de Beer have suggested that the idea of transmutation, despite its rejection by the scientific community, was "in the air." Gavin de Beer, Introduction to [Robert Chambers], *Vestiges of the Natural History of Creation* (1844; rpt. New York, 1969), pp. 11–19, 22.

Montesquieu, Maupertuis, Diderot, Erasmus Darwin, Maillet, Lamarck, Geoffroy Saint-Hilaire, and a host of others have been cited as proponents of transmutation before Darwin. See, for example, Eiseley, *Darwin's Century*, pp. 27–56, 117–140; Greene, *Death of Adam*; and the essays in Bentley Glass, Owsei Temkin, and William L. Strauss, Jr., eds., *Forerunners of Darwin: 1745–1859* (Baltimore, 1968). For a perceptive treatment of one manifestation of the use of the concept of development in dealing with natural phenomena, see Numbers, *Creation by Natural Law*. Although I can agree with Numbers' suggestion (pp. 105–110, 123) that the nebular hypothesis, by widening the realm in which natural phenomena were described by reference to gradual development and natural agencies, lent credibility to applying similar principles to the origin of species, I think the issue is somewhat more complicated than he implies. In the short run, the success of the nebular hypothesis may have actually raised the stakes in the Darwinian controversy by further limiting the instances of direct supernatural intervention in nature. I address this issue, though without specific reference to the nebular hypothesis, in Chapter 4.

33. [Robert Chambers], *Explanations: A Sequel to the "Vestiges of the Natural History of Creation"* (London, 1845), pp. 175–177, 179. My discussion of Chambers' life and thought has been informed by Millhauser, *Just before Darwin*, and M. J. S. Hodge, "The Universal Gestation of Nature: Chambers' *Vestiges* and *Explanations*," *Journal of the History of Biology*, 5 (1972), 127–161.

34. [Chambers], *Vestiges*, pp. 152–156, 232–233, 184–185, 388. See also Charles Coulston Gillispie, *Genesis and Geology: The Impact of Scientific Discoveries upon Religious Beliefs in the Decades before Darwin* (Cambridge, Mass., 1951), p. 153; Millhauser, *Just before Darwin*, pp. 111–112.

35. [Chambers], *Vestiges*, pp. 197–198, 153–154, 147, 231, 213, 203–205, 222–223, 160–164, 359–360. See also Hodge, "Universal Gestation of Nature," p. 137.

36. [Chambers], *Vestiges*, pp. 160, 324–325, 388, 147, 232–233. See also Young, "Darwin's Metaphor," pp. 456–457. James Moore has noted that in the tenth edition of *Vestiges*, Chambers became more explicitly Lamarckian in his account of adaptation. He invoked an "impulse" that tended "to modify organic structures in accordance with external circumstances." Chambers continued to assert, however, that the impulse was a product of "the providence of God." James R. Moore, *The Post-Darwinian Controversies: A Study of the Protestant Struggle to Come to Terms with Darwin in Great Britain and America, 1870–1900* (Cambridge, 1979), pp. 143–144. To Darwin, Chambers' discussion of adaptation was no explanation at all. Darwin, *Origin of Species*, pp. 3–4.

37. [Chambers], *Vestiges*, pp. 361–386 (quotations on pp. 384, 377). In the second American edition of *Vestiges*, readers were informed by Chambers that "it does not, according to this view, appear necessary that God should exercise an immediately superintending power over the mundane economy." [Chambers], *Vestiges*, 2d American from the 3d London ed. (New York, 1845), p. 273.

38. [Albert Baldwin Dod], "Vestiges of the Natural History of Creation," *Biblical Repertory and Princeton Review*, 17 (1845), 531–533; Tayler Lewis, "Vestiges of the Natural History of Creation," *American Review*, 1 (1845), 527, 531, 536, 539, 541–542. See also Samuel D. Cochrane, "God's Positive Moral Government over Moral Agents, Additional to That Which Is Merely Natural," *Bibliotheca Sacra and American Biblical Repository*, 11 (1854), 257; Anon., Review of *Course of Creation*, p. 149; Dana, "Religion of Geology," p. 510; Hitchcock, *Religion of Geology*, pp. 293–294, 296; [Edward Strong], "Vestiges of Creation and Its Reviewers," *New Englander*, 5 (1846), 115; James D. Dana, "Science and the Bible. No. 3," *Bibliotheca Sacra and American Biblical Repository*, 14 (1857), 499; [Bowen], "Theory of Creation," pp. 438–439, 464.

39. William North Rice, "The Darwinian Theory of the Origin of Species," *New Englander*, 26 (1867), 633; Darwin, *Origin of Species*, pp. 470, 206, 420–422, 472; [Francis Bowen], "Darwin on the Origin of Species," *North American Review*, 90 (1860), pp. 475–476; D. R. Goodwin, "Darwin on the Origin of Species," *American Theological Review*, 2 (1860), 330; [Lowell], "Darwin's Origin," pp. 449, 462–464; J. Q. Bittenger, "Christian Miracles and Physical Science," *American Presbyterian and Theological Review*, n.s. 3 (1865), 33; Charles Bliss, "Darwin's Animals and Plants, Under Domestication," *Congregational Review*, 9 (1869), 461, 453–454. See also Ospovat, *Development of Darwin's Theory*, pp. 191–192 and passim; Anon., "The Reign of Law," *Biblical Repertory and Princeton Review*, 42 (1870), 58–59, 70; Harmon, "Natural Theology," p. 192; Hitchcock, "Law of Nature's Constancy," p. 522; Thompson, "Does Science Tend," pp. 86–88; Anon., "The Origin and Antiquity of Man: Darwin, Huxley, and Lyell," *American Quarterly Church Review and Ecclesiastical Register*, 17 (1865), 185; John Bascom, "Darwin's Theory of the Origin of Species," *American Presbyterian Review*, n.s. 3 (1871), 375; Edward H. Walker, "The Present Attitude of the Church toward Critical and Scientific Inquiry," *New Englander*, 19 (1861), 345–346; Edward F. Williams, "On the Origin of Species by Natural Selection, or the Preservation of Favored Races in the Struggle for Life," *Evangelical Quarterly*, 16 (1865), 22; W. A. Stearns, "Recent Questions of Unbelief," *Bibliotheca Sacra*, 27 (1870), 481; Anon., "Darwinianism," *American Quarterly Church Review*, 21 (1870), 529.

It may well be, as some historians have suggested, that in drawing "the first wrath of the critics," Chambers' work prepared the public for "a more able, scientific presentation of the subject." Eiseley, *Darwin's Century*, pp. 134, 139–140. But it also gave religious critics experience in attacking the transmutation hypothesis and a false sense of security.

40. Charles Hodge, *Systematic Theology* (New York, 1872–73), 2:13–33 (quotation on p. 16), 47–48; [Charles Hodge], "Discussion of Darwinism and the Doctrine of Development," in Philip Schaff and S. Irenaeus Prime, eds., *History, Essays, Orations, and Other Documents of the Sixth General Conference of the Evangelical Alliance, Held in New York, October 2–12, 1873* (New York, 1874), p. 320. Although there is still no fully adequate biography of Hodge's life and thought, a number of works treat various elements of his thought. These include John C. Vander Stelt, *Philosophy and Scripture: A Study in Old Princeton and Westminster Theology* (Marlton, N.J., 1978), esp. pp. 120–147; Jack Rogers and Donald McKim, *The Authority and Interpretation of the Bible: An Historical Approach* (New York, 1979), pp. 274–298; Ralph John Danhof, *Charles Hodge as a Dogmatician* (Goes, The Netherlands, n.d.); and Alexander A. Hodge, *The Life of Charles Hodge* (London, 1881).

41. Charles Hodge, *What Is Darwinism?* (New York, 1874), pp. 64, 168, 173, 176–177, 41–42, 47–48, 52–53, 70–71, 96, 119, 168–169, 174–175, 145–149, 27, 46, 174–177, 95. See also Hodge, *Systematic Theology*, 2:15–30.

Favorable treatments of Hodge's work include Anon., Review of *What Is Darwinism?* by Charles Hodge, *Baptist Quarterly*, 8 (1874), 558–559; Anon., Review of *What Is Darwinism?* by Charles Hodge, *Presbyterian Quarterly and Princeton Review*, n.s. 3 (1874), 558–559; Anon., Review of *What Is Darwinism?* by Charles Hodge, *Methodist Quarterly Review*, 4th ser., 26 [1874], 514–516; L. J. Livermore, "What Is Darwinism?" *Unitarian Review and Religious Magazine*, 3 (1875), 237–250.

42. My discussion of Gray is greatly indebted to A. Hunter Dupree, *Asa Gray: 1810–1888* (Cambridge, Mass., 1959), and to Dupree's introduction to Asa Gray, *Darwiniana: Essays and Reviews Pertaining to Darwinism*, ed. A. Hunter Dupree (1876; Cambridge, Mass., 1963). For Gray's religious views, see also Gray, *Darwiniana*, p. 5.

43. [Asa Gray], Review of *Explanations: A Sequel to the Vestiges of the Natural History of Creation, North American Review*, 62 (1846), 468, 470–472, 498–502, 504, 496.

44. [Asa Gray], "Review of Darwin's Theory on the Origin of Species, by Means of Natural Selection," *American Journal of Science and Arts*, 2d ser., 29 (1860), 180–184. See also American Academy of Arts and Sciences, *Proceedings*, 4 (May 1857–May 1860), 425.

45. [Asa Gray], "Darwin and His Reviewers," *Atlantic Monthly*, 6 (1860), 410–412, 416–418. See also [Gray], "Review of Darwin's Theory," p. 180. The three *Atlantic* articles were reprinted separately in 1861 at the request of Darwin as a pamphlet entitled *Natural Selection Not Inconsistent with Natural Theology*.

46. [Gray], "Darwin and His Reviewers," pp. 412–419, 424–425. See also American Academy, *Proceedings*, 4:414–415, 424–425. A more extensive discussion of Gray's attempt to reconcile Darwinism and design can be found in Dupree, *Asa Gray*, pp. 264–301.

47. Asa Gray to Darwin, March 31, 1862, *Letters of Asa Gray*, ed. Jane Loring Gray (1893; New York, 1973), 2:479–480; James McCosh, *The Religious Aspect of Evolution*, 2d ed. (New York, 1890), pp. viii–ix, 58; James McCosh, *Christianity and Positivism: A Series of Lectures to the Times on Natural Theology and Apologetics* (New York, 1871), pp. 8, 33, 81. See also James McCosh, "Religious Aspects of the Doctrine of Development," in Schaff and Prime, eds., *History, Essays, Orations, and Other Documents of the Evangelical Alliance*, p. 270.

The best biographical treatment of McCosh's life and thought is J. David Hoeveller, Jr., *James McCosh and the Scottish Intellectual Tradition: From Glasgow to Princeton* (Princeton, N.J., 1981). For Hoeveller's treatment of McCosh's view of evolution, see esp. pp. 202–211. McCosh's view of natural history in the period prior to 1859 is perceptively discussed in Moore, *Post-Darwinian Controversies*, p. 246.

48. Francis Bowen, "The Latest Form of the Development Theory [1860]," *Gleanings from a Literary Life, 1838-1880* (New York, 1880), p. 216.

49. Daniel R. Goodwin, "The Antiquity of Man," *American Presbyterian and Theological Review*, n.s. 2 (1864), 259. See also Anon., "Reign of Law," p. 70; Mahan, *Science of Natural Theology*, p. 314.

50. Ernest R. Sandeen has similarly suggested that no systematic theology concerning biblical authority existed in America prior to 1850. *The Roots of Fundamentalism: British and American Millenarianism, 1800–1930* (Chicago, 1970), pp. 106, 110. See also John C. Greene, *Darwin and the Modern World View* (Baton Rouge, 1961), p. 33.

51. Hodge, *Systematic Theology*, 2:153–166 (quotations on pp. 166, 157), 180–182; [Barnes], "Readjustments of Christianity," p. 32. The popularity of the doctrine of plenary inspiration among religious thinkers in the United States is discussed in Ira V. Brown, "The Higher Criticism Comes to America, 1880–1900," *Journal of the Pres-*

byterian Historical Society, 38 (1960), 194; Norman Maring, "Baptists and Changing Views of the Bible, 1865–1918, Part I," *Foundations*, 1 (1958), 60; David Edwin Harrell, Jr., *Quest for a Christian America: The Disciples of Christ and American Society to 1866* (Nashville, 1966), 1:26–28; George M. Marsden, "Everyone One's Own Interpreter? The Bible, Science, and Authority in Mid-Nineteenth-Century America," in Nathan O. Hatch and Mark A. Noll, eds., *The Bible in America: Essays in Cultural History* (New York, 1982), p. 89; and John D. Woodbridge, *Biblical Authority: A Critique of the Rogers/McKim Proposal* (Grand Rapids, Mich., 1982), pp. 119–140. Not everyone, of course, endorsed the doctrine of plenary inspiration. See, for example, J[ames] W[alker], "Dr. Palfrey on the Jewish Scriptures," *Christian Examiner and General Review*, 3d ser., 7 (1838), 111.

52. Hodge, *Systematic Theology*, 1:9–15 (quotation on p. 10), 1–3, 17. See also B[enjamin] B. Smith, "Theology a Strictly Inductive Science," *Literary and Theological Review*, 2 (1835), 90–91, 93–94; J. MacBride Sterrett, "Natural Realism; or, Faith, the Basis of Science and Religion," *Bibliotheca Sacra*, 31 (1874), 83; Bozeman, *Protestants in an Age of Science*, pp. 144–159.

53. [Matthew Boyd Hope], "Relation between Scripture and Geology," *Biblical Repertory and Princeton Review*, 13 (1841), 391. See also Anon., "Geology and Revealed Religion," *Knickerbocker*, 7 (1836), 441–442; [Mrs. John Ware], "Hugh Miller and Popular Science," *North American Review*, 73 (1851), 449; E. P. Barrows, "The Mosaic Narrative of the Creation Considered Grammatically and in Its Relations to Science," *Bibliotheca Sacra and American Biblical Repository*, 13 (1856), 744; Conrad Wright, "Rational Religion in Eighteenth-Century America," in *The Liberal Christians* (Boston, 1970), pp. 1–21; Rudwick, *Meaning of Fossils*, pp. 132, 169, 185–187; Walter Cannon, "The Uniformarian-Catastrophist Debate," *Isis*, 51 (1960), 38–39; Francis C. Haber, *The Age of the World: Moses to Darwin* (Baltimore, 1959), pp. 195–196, 199, 214, 255; Gillispie, *Genesis and Geology*, pp. 96, 122, 140–143.

54. [James Read Eckard], "The Logical Relations of Religion and Natural Science," *Biblical Repertory and Princeton Review*, 32 (1860), 580–583, 608, 605, 607; Hodge, *Systematic Theology*, 1:11, 17, 182–183; Goodwin, "Antiquity of Man," pp. 235–236. See also [Samuel Tyler], "Connection between Philosophy and Revelation," *Biblical Repertory and Princeton Review*, 17 (1845), 390–392; Anon., Editor's Table, *Harper's New Monthly Magazine*, 9 (1854), 548–551; James W. M'Lane, "Speculation and the Bible," *Bibliotheca Sacra*, 18 (1861), 339–342, 345–346; Anon., "The Sixth Day of Creation," *Boston Review*, 3 (1863), 69.

55. [Eckard], "Logical Relations," p. 580. See also John Laing, "An Open Letter to Professor Tyndall," *Presbyterian Quarterly and Princeton Review*, n.s. 4 (1875), 231; Hodge, *Systematic Theology*, 1:171; Conway P. Wing, "The Order of Nature and Miracles," *Methodist Quarterly Review*, 13 (1861), 181; A. F. Dickson, "The Knowledge of God, as Obtained from Scripture and from Nature," *Southern Presbyterian Review*, 13 (1860), 337, 348; Richard S. Gladney, "Natural Science and Revealed Religion," *Southern Presbyterian Review*, 12 (1859), 461; Goodwin, "Antiquity of Man," p. 235; M'Lane, "Speculation and the Bible," p. 342.

56. [Francis Bowen], "Lyell's Second Visit to America," *North American Review*, 69 (1849), 338. See also Gardiner Spring to Benjamin Silliman, quoted in Haber, *Age of the World*, pp. 260–263; Hodge, *Systematic Theology*, 1:570–571; [Tyler], "Connection between Philosophy," p. 388.

In his study of American journals and magazines from 1830 to 1860 John F. McElligott has noted that "the literal interpretation [of the Bible] was treated with unrestrained contempt by both the secular and religious press." McElligott discovered that "out of scores of articles on the subject in the periodical press, only two supported the position [literalism]." McElligott, "Before Darwin," pp. 292–298. See also Stanley M. Guralnick, "Geology and Religion before Darwin: The Case of Edward Hitchcock, Theologian and Geologist (1793–1864)," *Isis*, 63 (1972), 532.

57. [Strong], "Vestiges of Creation," p. 119; Goodwin, "Antiquity of Man," pp. 234–235. See also Dana, "Science and the Bible," p. 91; Hitchcock, "Relations and Consequent Mutual Duties," p. 194; [Ware], "Hugh Miller and Popular Science," p. 449.

The popularity of geology among members of the educated community was frequently noted by American writers. See, for example, Anon., "Geology and Revealed Religion," p. 441; Samuel Metcalf, "The Interest and Importance of Scientific Geology as a Subject of Study," *Knickerbocker*, 3 (1834), 226–228.

58. Moses Stuart, *A Hebrew Chrestomathy* (Andover, 1829), pp. 115–118. See also M. Stuart, "Critical Examination of Some Passages in Gen. I; with Remarks on Difficulties That Attend Some of the Present Modes of Geological Reasoning," *Biblical Repository and Quarterly Observer*, 7 (1836), 49–53, 79–82. An informative discussion of Stuart's career can be found in Jerry Wayne Brown, *The Rise of Biblical Criticism in America, 1800–1870* (Middletown, Conn., 1969), pp. 45–59.

59. Stuart, "Critical Examination," pp. 52, 49; Lewis, *Bible and Science*, pp. 15–16; Lyman Atwater, "Rationalism," *Biblical Repertory and Princeton Review*, 38 (1866), 345–346; Lyon, "New Theological Professorship," pp. 191–192; Hodge, *Systematic Theology*, 1:173, 573.

Among those most adamant in insisting on the right and ability of science to help determine the meaning of Genesis were a number of pious scientists, most notably Edward Hitchcock and James Dwight Dana. The mid–nineteenth century witnessed two celebrated controversies centering on the role of science in biblical interpretation. In the first, Edward Hitchcock assailed Moses Stuart's contention that biblical statements regarding natural history were not to be interpreted from a scientific perspective. To Hitchcock, this position was tantamount to suggesting that God had not ensured that the biblical authors had presented an accurate account of creation. To accept a position that made "physical statements in the Bible uninspired," he asserted, "is, in fact, to abandon all belief in inspiration." Edward Hitchcock, "The Connection between Geology and the Mosaic History of the Creation," *Biblical Repertory and Quarterly Observer*, 6 (1835), 270–271. Discussions of the controversy between Stuart and Hitchcock include Conrad Wright, "The Religion of Geology," *New England Quarterly*, 14 (1941), 335–353; Guralnick, "Geology and Religion before Darwin," pp. 529–543; and John H. Giltner, "Genesis and Geology: The Stuart-Silliman-Hitchcock Debate," *Journal of Religious Thought*, 23 (1966-67), 3–13.

In 1856 Professor Tayler Lewis of Union College, like Moses Stuart, castigated scientists for imposing their views on the meaning of the Bible. James Dwight Dana, offended by what he perceived to be Lewis' attack on science, upbraided Lewis for obscurantism, and offered a long, four-article treatment, "Science and the Bible," in the *Bibliotheca Sacra*, accompanied by a letter in refutation of Dana's position by Lewis. Both individuals, however, rejected literalism and agreed that the biblical writers did not employ scientific language. The controversy is discussed in Greene, "Science and Religion," pp. 61–66; Wright, "Religion of Geology," pp. 353–356; and Numbers, *Creation by Natural Law*, pp. 95–100.

60. Means, "Narrative of the Creation in Genesis," pp. 112–122 (quotation on 112), 86, 105, 105n. See also R[ufus] P. S[tebbins], "The Religion of Geology," *Christian Examiner and Religious Miscellany*, 18 (1852), 51–52, 54–58; Hitchcock, *Religion of Geology*, pp. 33–70, 472–473; E. P. Barrows, "The Mosaic Six Days and Geology," *Bibliotheca Sacra and Biblical Repository*, 14 (1857), 75–91;[Peabody], "Dr. Harris's Pre-Adamite Earth," p. 399; Dana, "Religion of Geology," p. 520; Denis Crofton, *Genesis and Geology; or, An Investigation into the Reconciliation of the Modern Doctrines of Geology with the Declarations of Scripture* (Boston, 1857), pp. 13, 33–47; Benjamin Silliman, "Consistency of Geology with Sacred History," in Robert Bakewell, *An Introduction to Geology*, 2d American from 4th London ed. (New Haven, 1833), pp. 439–458; Holifield, *Gentlemen Theologians*, pp. 99–100; Hovenkamp, *Science and Religion*, pp. 127, 135–136.

61. S[tebbins], "Religion of Geology," pp. 55–59; Means, "Narrative of the Creation in Genesis," pp. 113–116; Crofton, *Genesis and Geology*, pp. 20–21; Hitchcock, *Elementary Geology*, pp. 294–295; Holifield, *Gentlemen Theologians*, p. 99.

62. Barrows, "Mosaic Narrative of the Creation," pp. 744, 747; Heman Lincoln, "Development versus Creation," *Baptist Quarterly*, 2 (1868), 257–258. See also S[tebbins], "Religion of Geology," p. 59; Means, "Narrative of the Creation in Genesis," pp. 86, 88, 91–95; [Hope], "Relation between Scripture and Geology," p. 390; [Harris], "Harmony of Natural Science and Theology," p. 11; William W. Patton, "The Tendency of Scientific Men to Skepticism," *Methodist Quarterly Review*, 4th ser., 14 (1862), 558–559; Joseph P. Thompson, *Man in Genesis and in Geology; or, The Biblical Account of Man's Creation, Tested by Scientific Theories of His Origin and Antiquity* (New York, 1870), pp. v–vi; Samson Talbot, "Development and Human Descent," *Baptist Quarterly*, 6 (1872), 137–138; Anon., Review of *The Six Days of Creation*, by Tayler Lewis, *Church Review and Ecclesiastical Register*, 8 (1856), 617; [Ware], "Hugh Miller and Popular Science," p. 449; S. D. Hillman, "Alexander Von Humboldt and His Cosmos," *Methodist Quarterly Review*, 4th ser., 12 (1860), 414. Even John William Draper, who was inclined to view the history of thought as a series of conflicts between science and religion, acknowledged that geology had not encountered the same bitterness from theologians that astronomers had confronted earlier. John William Draper, *History of the Conflict between Religion and Science*, 3d ed. (1874; New York, 1875), p. 200. See also Wright, "Religion of Geology," pp. 356–357; De Jong, "American Attitudes toward Evolution," p. 128. As early as 1835 Benjamin Silliman noted in his diary that his attempts to reconcile science and religion were "equally acceptable to the wise and good of all religious denominations" and that his remarks on "delicate points" had been well received by Unitarians and the Orthodox alike. George P. Fisher, *Life of Benjamin Silliman* (New York, 1866), 1:347, 372.

63. [Dod], "Vestiges of the Natural History of Creation," p. 535; Hodge, *Systematic Theology*, 1:58–59. See also J[oseph] H[enry] A[llen], "Vestiges of Creation and Sequel," *Christian Examiner and Religious Magazine*, 4th ser., 5 (1846), 347; [Strong], "Vestiges of Creation," p. 115; [Matthew Boyd Hope], "Professor Bachman on the Unity of the Human Race," *Biblical Repertory and Princeton Review*, 22 (1850), 314–315; Anon., Editor's Table, *Harper's New Monthly Magazine*, 9 (1845), 548–551; Means, "Narrative of the Creation in Genesis," pp. 91–94.

64. The best account of scientific attitudes concerning the origin of the human race in America prior to 1859 is William Stanton, *The Leopard's Spots: Scientific Attitudes toward Race in America, 1815–59* (Chicago, 1960). See also Richard H. Popkin, "Pre-Adamism in Nineteenth-Century American Thought: 'Speculative Biology' and 'Racism,' " *Philosophia*, 8 (1978–79), 205–239.

65. For my discussion of Agassiz's life and thought I have drawn on Edward Lurie's excellent *Louis Agassiz: A Life in Science* (Chicago, 1960). Also helpful were Edward Lurie, "Louis Aggasiz and the Idea of Evolution," *Victorian Studies*, 3 (1959), 87–108; Edward Lurie, "Louis Agassiz and the Races of Man," *Isis*, 14 (1954), 227–242; and Ernst Mayr, "Agassiz, Darwin, and Evolution," *Harvard Library Bulletin*, 13 (1959), 165–194.

66. Jules Marcou, *Life, Letters, and Works of Louis Agassiz* (New York, 1895), 1:246–247; Louis Agassiz, *Introduction to the Study of Natural History* (New York, 1847), pp. 6, 53–54, 58; Louis Agassiz and Augustus A. Gould, *Principles of Zoology* (Boston, 1848), pp. 154, 180; Stanton, *Leopard's Spots*, pp. 100–102; Lurie, "Agassiz and the Races," p. 236.

67. L[ouis] A[gassiz], "The Diversity of Origin of the Human Races," *Christian Examiner and Religious Miscellany*, 4th ser., 14 (1850), 121–124 (quotation on p. 124), 128, 132, 136–137. See also L[ouis] A[gassiz], "Geographical Distribution of Animals," *Christian Examiner and Religious Miscellany*, 4th ser., 13 (1850), 204.

68. A[gassiz], "Diversity of Origin," pp. 110–111, 113, 117–120, 139.

69. A[gassiz], "Geographical Distribution," pp. 181, 184–185. See also A[gassiz], "Diversity of Origin," pp. 111–112, 134–136, 138.

70. George R. Gliddon, quoted in Stanton, *Leopard's Spots*, p. 162. Stanton has contended that the bond joining many polygenists together was a strain of anticlericalism and antibiblicism." Ibid., p. 193. For a fuller discussion of *Types of Mankind* and the responses it evoked, see ibid., pp. 161–173. In 1857 Agassiz wrote a brief introductory letter to *Indigenous Races of the Earth; or, New Chapters of Ethnological Inquiry* (Philadelphia, 1857), also authored by Nott and Gliddon. This letter was primarily concerned with rejecting the argument that language affinities constituted a valid basis for arguing for a single origin of the races of man. For discussion of this work and the responses to it, see ibid., pp. 174–180.

71. N. L. F[rothingham], "Men before Adam," *Christian Examiner and Religious Miscellany*, 4th ser., 15 (1851), 89, 85, 80–83, 88, 96. See also E. M. Wheelock, "Cosmogony," *Monthly Religious Magazine*, 26 (1861), 370; [L. J. Livermore], "The Origin of Man," *Christian Examiner*, n.s. 1 (1866), 66.

72. Thomas Smyth, *The Unity of the Human Races Proved to Be the Doctrine of Scripture, Reason, and Science* (New York, 1850), pp. 372–374, 378–379, 356–358, 363.

73. Albert Barnes, "The Relation of Christianity to the Present Stage of the World's Progress in Science, Civilization and the Arts," *American Presbyterian and Theological Review,* n.s. 3 (1865), 585; Anon., Editor's Table, *Harper's New Monthly Magazine,* 9 (1854), 549; Anon., Review of *The Types of Mankind*, by J. C. Nott and George Gliddon, *Church Review and Ecclesiastical Register,* 7 (1854), 443. See also [B. N. Martin], "The Original Unity of the Human Race—Pickering, Bachman, Agassiz," *New Englander*, 8 (1850), 548, 581.

74. Dana, "Religion of Geology," pp. 510–511. See also Edward Hitchcock, *Religious Truth, Illustrated from Science, in Addresses and Sermons on Special Occasions* (Boston, 1857), p. 219; A[llen], "Vestiges of Creation and Sequel," p. 344; J. D. Whelpley, "Sequel to the Vestiges of the Natural History of Creation," *American Review*, 3 (1846), 387; Lewis, "Vestiges," pp. 532–534.

75. Gladney, "Natural Science," p. 453.

76. Anon., "Origin and Antiquity of Man," pp. 197, 189–190. See also E. Nisbet, "Darwinism," *Baptist Quarterly*, 7 (1873), 76–77; Anon., "Synopsis of the Quarterlies and Others of the Higher Periodicals," *Methodist Quarterly Review*, 4th ser., 20 (1868), 124; Alexander Winchell, "Voices from Nature," *Ladies Repository*, 23 (1863), 390;

James B. Tyler, "Evolution in Natural History as Related to Christianity," *New Englander*, 30 (1871), 469; Frederic Gardiner, "Darwinism," *Bibliotheca Sacra*, 29 (1872), 252–253; Talbot, "Development and Human Descent," pp. 137-139; Hitchcock, "Law of Nature's Constancy," pp. 522–523; Lincoln, "Development versus Creation," p. 264; R. T. Brumby, "Relations of Science to the Bible," *Southern Presbyterian Review*, 25 (1874), 3.

77. Wilson, "Darwin on the Origin," p. 627; [Barnes], "Readjustments of Christianity," pp. 70–71. A number of historians have concluded that the initial response to the publication of *Essays and Reviews* (1860) provoked a greater initial outcry, at least in England, than the *Origin of Species*. See, for example, Josef L. Altholz, "The Mind of Victorian Orthodoxy: Anglican Responses to 'Essays and Reviews,' 1860–1864," *Church History*, 51 (1982), 186; Basil Willey, *More Nineteenth-Century Studies* (New York, 1956), p. 172. Although no detailed study of the American reaction to this work has been made, I have no reason to suspect that the American reaction was not similarly vitriolic. See, for example, [Francis Bowen], "The Oxford Clergyman's Attack on Christianity," *North American Review*, 92 (1861), 177–216; Walker, "Present Attitude," p. 342; Anon., "Recent Inquiries in Theology Examined," *American Quarterly Church Review and Ecclesiastical Register*, 14 (1861), 275.

78. Anon., "Reign of Law," p. 61; Goodwin, "Darwin on the Origin," p. 339. See also Lyon, "New Theological Professorship," p. 184.

Chapter 2. "Science, Falsely So Called"

1. Anon., "Darwinianism," *American Quarterly Church Review*, 21 (1870), 525; Austin Phelps, "The Oneness of God in Revelation and in Nature," *Bibliotheca Sacra and Biblical Repository*, 18 (1859), 841; J. M. Manning, "The Denial of the Supernatural," ibid., 20 (1863), 260; R. F. Fuller, "Radical Idolatry," *Monthly Religious Magazine*, 40 (1868), 78; Richard S. Gladney, "Natural Science and Revealed Religion," *Southern Presbyterian Review*, 12 (1859), 449; J. C. Koller, "Should Clergymen Study Natural Science?" *Quarterly Review of the Evangelical Lutheran Church*, n.s. 4 (1874), 597, 601; Donald Zochert, "Science and the Common Man in Ante-Bellum America," *Isis*, 65 (1974), 448–473; Margaret W. Rossiter, "Benjamin Silliman and the Lowell Institute: The Popularization of Science in Nineteenth-Century America," *New England Quarterly*, 44 (1971), 602–626.

2. Charles Lyell, *Principles of Geology* (London, 1832), 2:65; Charles Darwin to J. D. Hooker [1844?], *The Life and Letters of Charles Darwin, Including an Autobiographical Chapter*, ed. Francis Darwin (London, 1887), 1:333 (hereafter cited as *LLD*). See also Anon., "The Reign of Law," *Biblical Repertory and Princeton Review*, 42 (1870), 61; J. G. Wilson, "The Specific Unity and Common Origin of the Human Race," *American Theological Review*, 2 (1860), 633; [James Dwight Dana], "Sequel to the Vestiges of Creation," *American Journal of Science and Arts*, 2d ser., 1 (1846), 252–253; Edward Hitchcock, *The Religion of Geology and Its Connected Sciences* (Boston, 1851), pp. 286, 309–318, 321; Martin J. S. Rudwick, *The Meaning of Fossils: Episodes in the History of Palaeontology*, 2d ed. (New York, 1976), pp. 120, 149–153, 207–209, 227; David Hull, *Darwin and His Critics: The Reception of Darwin's Theory of Evolution by the Scientific Community* (Cambridge, Mass., 1973), pp. 15, 67–77; Barbara Beddall, "Wallace, Darwin and the Theory of Natural Selection," *Journal of the History of Biology*, 1 (1968), 281; William Coleman, *Georges Cuvier, Zoologist: A Study in the History of Evolution Theory* (Cambridge, Mass., 1964), pp. 142–164, 171–176; William Coleman, "Lyell and

the 'Reality' of Species: 1830–1833," *Isis*, 53 (1962), 325–338; Milton Millhauser, *Just before Darwin: Robert Chambers and Vestiges* (Middletown, Conn., 1959), pp. 121–131.

3. William North Rice, "The Darwinian Theory of the Origin of Species," *New Englander*, 26 (1867), 631–632; Edward A. Walker, "The Present Attitude of the Church toward Critical and Scientific Inquiry," *New Englander*, 19 (1861), 345; [Francis Bowen], "Darwin on the Origin of Species," *North American Review*, 90 (1860), 474, 477, 482, 485–486; D. R. Goodwin, "Darwin on the Origin of Species," *American Theological Review*, 2 (1860), 330; Anon., "The Origin and Antiquity of Man: Darwin, Huxley, and Lyell," *American Quarterly Church Review and Ecclesiastical Register*, 17 (1865), 173–174.

4. Louis Agassiz, "Methods of Study in Natural History," *Atlantic Monthly*, 10 (1862), 88; L[ouis] A[gassiz], "Contemplations of God in the Kosmos," *Christian Examiner and Religious Miscellany*, 4th ser., 15 (1851), 10–11, 2, 4, 6–7; Louis Agassiz, *Introduction to the Study of Natural History* (New York, 1847), pp. 6, 9. See also Louis Agassiz, *Methods of Study in Natural History* (Boston, 1863), pp. 42–43; Edward Lurie, "Louis Agassiz and the Idea of Evolution," *Victorian Studies*, 3 (1959), 93–94; Edward Lurie, *Louis Agassiz: A Life in Science* (Chicago, 1960), pp. 34–37, 50–52, 55–63.

5. [Louis Agassiz], "The Diversity of Origin of the Human Race," *Christian Examiner and Religious Miscellany*, 4th ser., 14 (1850), 113, 110. A more extensive discussion of Agassiz's view of species can be found in Mary Winsor, "Louis Agassiz and the Species Question," *Studies in History of Biology*, 3 (1979), 89–117.

6. Louis Agassiz, *Lake Superior: Its Physical Character, Vegetation, and Animals, Compared with Those of Other and Similar Regions*, with a Narrative of the Tour by J. Elliot Cabot (Boston, 1850), p. 145; Agassiz, *Introduction to the Study*, p. 25; Louis Agassiz, "Sketch of the Natural Provinces of the Animal World and Their Relation to the Different Types of Man," in J. C. Nott and George R. Gliddon, *Types of Mankind; or, Ethnological Researches* (Philadelphia, 1854), pp. lxxv–lxxvi. See also Ernst Mayr, "Agassiz, Darwin and Evolution," *Harvard Library Bulletin*, 13 (1959), 176.

7. Louis Agassiz, *Contributions to the Natural History of the United States* (Boston, 1857–1862), 1:106, 9, 11, 13–14, 16–17, 21, 51–52, 123, 127, 130, 8, 135; A[gassiz], "Contemplations of God," pp. 10–11, 5–6; Louis Agassiz, *Discours prononcé à l'ouverture des séances de la Société Helvétique des Sciences Naturelles, à Neuchatel, le 24 juillet, 1837*, reprinted in Jules Marcou, *Life, Letters, and Works of Louis Agassiz* (New York, 1895), 1:107 (my translation).

8. Agassiz, *Lake Superior*, pp. 144–145, 377; L[ouis] A[gassiz], "Geographical Distribution of Animals," *Christian Examiner and Religious Miscellany*, 4th ser., 13 (1850), 185.

9. Agassiz, *Contributions*, 1:135, 11.

10. Charles Darwin to Louis Agassiz, November 11 [1859], *LLD*, 2:215; Asa Gray to Joseph Hooker, January 5, 1860, ibid., p. 268. See also Charles Darwin, *On the Origin of Species by Means of Natural Selection, or the Preservation of Favoured Races in the Struggle for Life* (1859; facsimile ed., Cambridge, Mass., 1964), pp. 139, 302, 305, 335–336, 338, 449–450, 453.

11. [Louis Agassiz], "Professor Agassiz on the Origin of Species," *American Journal of Science and Arts*, 2d ser., 30 (1860), 142–144, 148–151. See also Lurie, *Louis Agassiz*, pp. 292–299.

12. [Agassiz], "On the Origin," pp. 148–149.

13. Ibid., pp. 144–147, 154.

14. Manning, "Denial of the Supernatural," p. 265; [Lyman Atwater], "Herbert Spencer's Philosophy: Atheism, Pantheism, and Materialism," *Biblical Repertory and Princeton Review*, 37 (1865), 267–268; Heman Lincoln, "Development versus Creation," *Baptist Quarterly*, 2 (1868), 270–274. See also A. F. Dickson, "The Knowledge of God as Obtained from Scripture and from Nature," *Southern Presbyterian Review*, 13 (1860), 349; W. C. Wilson, "Darwin on the Origin of Species," *Methodist Quarterly Review*, 4th ser., 13 (1861), 626; Anon., Review of *Methods of Study in Natural History*, by Louis Agassiz, *Atlantic Monthly*, 13 (1864), 132; Denis Wortman, "Resumé of the Geological Argument," *American Presbyterian and Theological Review*, n.s. 3 (1865), 617; [Chester Dewey], "The True Place of Man in Zoology," *Biblical Repertory and Princeton Review*, 35 (1863), 116; Edward F. Williams, "On the Origin of Species by Natural Selection, or the Preservation of Favored Races in the Struggle for Life," *Evangelical Quarterly Review*, 16 (1865), 18; J. H. Wythe, "Theories of Life," *Methodist Quarterly Review*, 4th ser., 26 (1874), 299; Charles Hodge, *What Is Darwinism?* (New York, 1874), pp. 160–161. Agassiz's role in retarding the early open espousal of evolution by older naturalists is discussed in Wesley R. Coe, "A Century of Zoology in America," in E. S. Dana, et al., *A Century of Science in America* (New Haven, 1918), pp. 410, 437; Burt G. Wilder, "Jeffries Wyman, Anatomist," in David Starr Jordan, ed., *Leading American Men of Science* (New York, 1910), p. 193.

15. Lurie, *Louis Agassiz*, pp. 306–312; George H. Daniels, *American Science in the Age of Jackson* (New York, 1968), p. 59.

16. Asa Gray to John Torrey, January 24, 1847, *Letters of Asa Gray*, ed. Jane Loring Gray (1893; New York, 1973), 1:345–346 (hereafter cited as *LG*); Agassiz, *Contributions*, 1:131. For Gray's growing antagonism to Agassiz, see A. Hunter Dupree, *Asa Gray: 1810–1888* (Cambridge, Mass., 1959), pp. 154, 224–229, 247–248.

17. Darwin to Gray, July 20 [1856], *LLD*, 2:79. See also Darwin to Gray, September 5 [1857], ibid., pp. 120–126; Dupree, *Asa Gray*, pp. 238–240.

18. Asa Gray, quoted in Dupree, *Asa Gray*, p. 250. See also pp. 239–250.

19. Gray to Hooker, January 5, 1860, *LG*, 2:455; [Asa Gray], "Review of Darwin's Theory on the Origin of Species, by Means of Natural Selection," *American Journal of Science and Arts*, 2d ser., 29 (1860), 156, 180, 170–179, 184.

20. [Asa Gray], "Darwin on the Origin of Species," *Atlantic Monthly*, 6 (1860), 109–110, 113.

21. [Asa Gray], "Darwin and His Reviewers," *Atlantic Monthly*, 6 (1860), 406–408.

22. J[effries] W[yman], "Review of the Monograph of the Aye-Aye . . ., by Richard Owen," *American Journal of Science and Arts*, 2d ser., 36 (1863), 296, 294; Frederick A. P. Barnard, Inaugural Address, *Proceedings at the Inauguration of Frederick A. P. Barnard . . .* (New York, 1865), pp. 73, 54. See also Hull, *Darwin and His Critics*, pp. 6–7, selections; Rudwick, *Meaning of Fossils*, pp. 236–239; Thomas Huxley, "On the Reception of the 'Origin of Species,' " in *LLD*, 2:184–186, 204; Edward Lurie, "An Interpretation of Science in the Nineteenth Century: A Study in History and Historiography," *Journal of World History*, 8 (1965), 696; Dupree, *Asa Gray*, pp. 309–311; Wilder, "Jeffries Wyman," p. 193.

Wyman and Gray were not alone in looking favorably upon the theory of organic evolution from 1859 to 1865. The prestigious physicist Joseph Henry wrote Gray that in his judgment, evolution was "the best working hypothesis which you naturalists have ever had." Henry, possibly because of the influence of his close friend Agassiz, possibly because of a hatred of controversy that he shared with Wyman, and in large measure because he believed that the biological issue was not one on which he possessed any special expertise, did not make his views public. Thomas Coulson, *Joseph Henry: His Life and Work* (Princeton, 1950), pp. 294–295. The Philadelphia anatomist Joseph Leidy also liked Darwin's work. Henry Fairfield Osborn, *Impressions of Great Naturalists* (New York, 1924), p. 139. For the entomologist Benjamin Walsh's support of Darwin's theory, see Edward J. Pfeiffer, "United States," in Thomas F. Glick, ed., *The Comparative Reception of Darwinism* (Austin, 1974), pp. 184–185. The zoologist William Keith Brooks was another early proponent of the theory. E. A. Andrews, "William Keith Brooks: Zoologist," *Leading American Men*, p. 431. The geologist William Barton Rogers expressed appreciation of the *Origin of Species* and skirmished with Agassiz at the Boston Society of Natural History over the implications of the fossil record. See William Barton Rogers to Henry Rogers, January 2, 1860, *Life and Letters of William Barton Rogers*, edited by His Wife (Boston, 1896), 2:19; Boston Society of Natural History, *Proceedings*, 7 (1859–1861), 231–252, 271–274. In May 1860 the mathematician Chauncey Wright also converted to Darwinism and testified in 1860 before the American Academy of Arts and Sciences that the structure of bee cells was a function of utilitarian considerations. C. Wright to Mrs. Lesley, February 12, 1860, *Letters of Chauncey Wright*, ed. James Bradley Thayer (Cambridge, Mass., 1878), p. 43; American Academy of Arts and Sciences, *Proceedings*, 4 (1857–1860), 432–433.

23. Wilson, "Darwin on the Origin," pp. 627, 614. See also Henry M. Harmon, "Natural Theology," *Methodist Review*, 4th ser., 15 (1863), 196. Works that have cited the Civil War and its aftermath as the reason for the relative lack of attention accorded Darwin's theory by American Protestant intellectuals include Sydney E. Ahlstrom, *A Religious History of the American People* (New Haven, 1972), p. 768; Richard Hofstadter, *Social Darwinism in American Thought*, rev. ed. (New York, 1955), p. 13; Frank Hugh Foster, *The Modern Movement in American Theology: Sketches in the History of American Protestant Thought from the Civil War to the World War* (1939; New York, 1955), p. 38; H. Shelton Smith, Robert T. Handy, and Lefferts A. Loetscher, *American Christianity: An Historical Interpretation with Representative Documents* (New York, 1963), 2:216.

24. Goodwin, "Darwin on the Origin," p. 327. See also Anon., "Synopsis of the Quarterlies and Others of the Higher Periodicals," *Methodist Quarterly Review*, 4th ser., 20 (1868), 123–124; [J. A. Lowell], "Darwin's Origin of Species," *Christian Examiner*, 5th ser., 6 (1860), 450; Noah Porter, "*The Sciences of Nature* versus *The Science of Man* [1871]," *Science and Sentiment, with Other Papers, Chiefly Philosophical* (New York, 1882), p. 71.

Few historians have appreciated the sophistication of the scientific objections that numerous religious thinkers advanced against Darwin's hypothesis. See, for example, Hofstadter, *Social Darwinism*, p. 25; Cynthia Eagle Russett, *Darwin in America: The Intellectual Response, 1865–1912* (San Francisco, 1976), p. 26.

A useful collection of responses to Darwin's theory from scientists and philosophers of science can be found in Hull, *Darwin and His Critics*. In the following section, I concentrate primarily on the objections advanced by members of the American religious community, though I also sometimes cite scientists who involved themselves in the discussion within that community.

25. Charles Darwin to Asa Gray, November 29 [1859], *More Letters of Charles Darwin*, ed. Francis Darwin and A. C. Seward (London, 1903), 1:126 (hereafter cited as *MLD*); Darwin to Joseph Hooker, February 14 [1860], ibid., pp. 139–140. See also

Darwin to Asa Gray, November 11 [1859], *LLD*, 2:217; Darwin to Gray, February 18 [1860], ibid., p. 286; Darwin to F. W. Hutton, April 20, 1861, *MLD*, 1:184. The literature on Darwin's views on scientific method is immense. See, for example, Neal C. Gillespie, *Charles Darwin and the Problem of Creation* (Chicago, 1979), pp. 54–63.

26. Asa Mahan, "Theism and Anti-Theism in their Relations to Science," in Randolph S. Foster et al., *Ingham Lectures on the Evidences of Natural and Revealed Religion* (Cleveland, 1872), p. 111; Randolph S. Foster, "Origin of Species: An Examination of Darwinism," in ibid., p. 89. See also Ransom Welch, "Admission of Philosophical Skepticism," *Bibliotheca Sacra*, 31 (1874), 638; Daniels, *American Science*, pp. 63–85, 100–101, 167–190; Theodore Dwight Bozeman, *Protestants in an Age of Science: The Baconian Ideal and Antebellum American Religious Thought* (Chapel Hill, 1977), pp. 3–31, 101–108; Alvar Ellegård, "The Darwinian Theory and Nineteenth-Century Philosophies of Science," *Journal of the History of Ideas*, 18 (1957), 362–393; Hull, *Darwin and His Critics*, pp. 16–29.

27. Anon., "The Origin and Antiquity of Man: Darwin, Huxley, and Lyell," *American Quarterly Church Review and Ecclesiastical Register*, 17 (1865), 344; [Bowen], "Darwin on the Origin," pp. 485–486. See also Wilson, "Darwin on the Origin," p. 619; Goodwin, "Darwin on the Origin," pp. 329–330; Anon., "The Evolution Hypothesis," *Southern Review*, 3 (1868), 415; Walker, "Present Attitude," p. 346; Anon., Review of *Origin of Species*, by Charles Darwin, *Methodist Quarterly Review*, 4th ser., 12 (1860), 338; I. C. K[nowlton], "The Human Race," *Universalist Quarterly and General Review*, 20 (1863), 354; Anon., Review of *Annual of Scientific Discovery*, ed. David A. Wells, *Methodist Review*, 4th ser., 16 (1864), 522; Anon., "Darwinianism," p. 528; J. S. Newberry, Address of the President of the Association, American Association for the Advancement of Science, *Proceedings*, 16 (1868), 11; Joseph P. Thompson, *Man in Genesis and in Geology; or, The Biblical Account of Man's Creation, Tested by Scientific Theories of His Origin and Antiquity* (New York, 1870), pp. 54, 82; Manning, "Denial of the Supernatural," p. 264; Lincoln, "Development versus Creation," p. 265; C. A. Stork, "Some Assumptions against Christianity," *Quarterly Review of the Evangelical Lutheran Church*, n.s. 3 (1873), 327–328; Howard Crosby, Introduction to John R. Leifchild, *The Great Problem: The Higher Ministry of Nature Viewed in the Light of Modern Science, as an Aid to an Advanced Christian Philosophy* (New York, 1872), n.p.; Charles Hodge, *Systematic Theology* (New York, 1872–73), 2:19–20; Daniels, *American Science*, pp. 121–122; Bozeman, *Protestants in an Age of Science*, pp. 3, 14–20.

28. [L. T. Townsend], *Credo* (Boston, 1869), p. 101n. See also Anon., "The Religion of Geology," *Bibliotheca Sacra and Biblical Repository*, 17 (1860), 680–681; Alexander Winchell, "Voices from Nature," *Ladies Repository*, 23 (1863), 387–389; Edward Hitchcock, "The Law of Nature's Constancy Subordinate to the Higher Law of Change," *Bibliotheca Sacra and Biblical Repository*, 20 (1863), 509–510, 524; Williams, "On the Origin of Species," p. 18; Julius H. Seelye, *A Criticism of the Development Hypothesis, as Held by Charles Darwin, Thomas Huxley, Alfred Russel Wallace, Herbert Spencer, and the New School of Naturalists* (New York, 1871), pp. 1–5; Anon., "The Idea of God," *Southern Review*, 15 (1874), 308; E. Nisbet, "Darwinism," *Baptist Quarterly*, 7 (1873), 81, 209, 211–213; Anon., Review of *Origin* [1860], p. 338; James D. Dana, *Manual of Geology: Treating of the Principles of the Science with Special Reference to American Geological History* (New York, 1874), p. 602; C. H. Hitchcock, "The Relations of Geology to Theology," *Bibliotheca Sacra*, 24 (1867), 371; E. P. Barrows, "Revelation and Inspiration," *Bibliotheca Sacra*, 25 (1868), 326–327; Rice, "Darwinian Theory," pp. 621–625; Samuel Adams, "Darwinism," *Congregational Review*, 11 (1871), 339, 342;

[Bowen], "Darwin on the Origin," pp. 484, 488–489; Anon., "Darwinianism," p. 532; Harmon, "Natural Theology," p. 189; Anon., "Origin and Antiquity of Man," pp. 185, 188.

29. Wilson, "Darwin on the Origin," p. 625; [Bowen], "Darwin on the Origin," p. 503; Anon., "Darwinianism," p. 527. See also Goodwin, "Darwin on the Origin," pp. 339–340; Lincoln, "Development versus Creation," pp. 265–266, 270; Rudwick, *Meaning of Fossils*, pp. 228–236.

30. Harmon, "Natural Theology," pp. 191, 193; Anon., "Origin and Antiquity of Man," pp. 190, 194–195, 177–182; Walker, "Present Attitude," p. 346; S. T. Frost, "Darwin and Domestication," *Harper's New Monthly Magazine*, 36 (1867), 61; Anon., "Huxley on Man's Place in Nature," *Boston Review*, 4 (1864), 375; Rice, "Darwinian Theory," pp. 625–626, 609; Charles Bliss, "Darwin's Animals and Plants, Under Domestication," *Congregational Review*, 9 (1869), 461, 455; [Albert Barnes], "Readjustments of Christianity," *Presbyterian Quarterly Review*, 11 (1862), 71; [Lowell], "Darwin's Origin," pp. 450–452; Lincoln, "Development versus Creation," pp. 267–268; Rudwick, *Meaning of Fossils*, p. 238. For a fascinating discussion of Darwin's tendency to employ anthropomorphic language in discussing natural selection and the complex role that this language played in affecting the fortunes of evolutionism, see Robert M. Young, "Darwin's Metaphor: Does Nature Select?" *Monist*, 55 (1971), 442–503.

31. Darwin, *Origin of Species*, pp. 133, 51–52, 111, 469; Francis Bowen, "The Latest Form of the Development Theory [1860]," *Gleanings from a Literary Life, 1838–1880* (New York, 1880), p. 206; Leonard Withington, "Analysis and Synthesis Both Necessary, in Their Proportion, to True Reasoning," *Bibliotheca Sacra*, 23 (1866), 622–623; Horace Bushnell, "Science and Religion," *Putnam's Monthly Magazine of Literature, Science, Art, and National Interests*, n.s. 1 (1868), 271. See also Chester Dewey, "Natural History," *American Theological Review*, 2 (1860), 510–511; Frederic Gardiner, "Darwinism," *Bibliotheca Sacra*, 29 (1872), 263–264; Anon., "Evolution Hypothesis," pp. 419–421.

32. Wilson, "Darwin on the Origin," p. 609; Rice, "Darwinian Theory," pp. 628–629, 631. See also [Bowen], "Darwin on the Origin," p. 478; Williams, "On the Origin of Species," p. 20; Hull, *Darwin and His Critics*, pp. 49–50.

33. Darwin, *Origin of Species*, pp. 245–278 (quotations on pp. 248, 245, 260, 264); Wilson, "Darwin on the Origin," pp. 609, 621; Rice, "Darwinian Theory," p. 629; Anon., Review of *Origin* [1860], pp. 337–338.

34. [Francis Ellingwood Abbot], "Philosophical Biology," *North American Review*, 107 (1868), 386–387; Rice, "Darwinian Theory," pp. 623–625. See also Goodwin, "Darwin on the Origin," p. 343; [Robert Lewis Dabney], "Geology and the Bible," *Southern Presbyterian Review*, 14 (1861), 270–271; Harmon, "Natural Theology," p. 192.

35. [C. C. Shackford], "Unity of Life," *North American Review*, 94 (1862), 152, 140; Hitchcock, "Law of Nature's Constancy," p. 522; Benjamin W. Dwight, "The Doctrine of God's Providence, in Itself and in Its Relations and Uses," *Bibliotheca Sacra*, 21 (1864), 625; [Bowen], "Darwin on the Origin," p. 476; Joseph P. Thompson, "Does Science Tend to Materialism?" *New Englander*, 19 (1861), 90, 97. See also Ebenezer Dodge, *The Evidence of Christianity, with an Introduction on the Existence of God and the Immortality of the Soul* (Boston, 1869), pp. xxviii–xxxi.

36. Darwin, *Origin of Species*, pp. 207–244 (quotation on pp. 210–211); [Bowen],

"Darwin on the Origin," pp. 489–491; Rice, "Darwinian Theory," pp. 627–628; Williams, "On the Origin of Species," pp. 19–20.

37. [Lowell], "Darwin's Origin," pp. 461–462; [Bowen], "Darwin on the Origin," pp. 491–492; Darwin to C. Lyell, June 6 [1860], *LLD*, 2:318.

38. Valuable treatments of the assault on the efficacy of natural selection include Peter J. Vorzimmer, *Charles Darwin: The Years of Controversy: The Origin of Species and Its Critics* (Philadelphia, 1970), and Alvar Ellegård, *Darwin and the General Reader: The Reception of Darwin's Theory of Evolution in the British Periodical Press, 1859–1872* (Göteborg, 1958), pp. 242–279.

39. [Henry Charles Fleeming Jenkin], "The Origin of Species," *North British Review*, 46 (1867), 286–293 (quotations on pp. 288, 293). For nineteenth-century biologists' view of blending, see Peter Vorzimmer, "Darwin and Blending Inheritance," *Isis*, 54 (1963), 371–390, esp. p. 373. For American Protestants' enunciations of the "swamping" argument before Jenkin, see, for example, [Bowen], "Darwin on the Origin," pp. 499–501; [Lowell], "Darwin's Origin of Species," pp. 450–451.

40. [Jenkin], "Origin of Species," pp. 294–305 (quotation on p. 301). For a perceptive discussion of Thomson's views, see Joe D. Burchfield, *Lord Kelvin and the Age of the Earth* (New York, 1975).

41. St. George Mivart, *On the Genesis of Species* (London, 1871), pp. 20, 241, 5, 225. The most complete account of Mivart's life and thought is Jacob W. Gruber, *A Conscience in Conflict: The Life of St. George Jackson Mivart* (New York, 1960). See also Vorzimmer, *Charles Darwin*, pp. 226–232.

42. Mivart, *Genesis of Species*, pp. 225, 20, 23, 50, 34, 38.

43. Ibid., pp. 136–143 (quotation on p. 143), 97–104, 128–133, 223–224, 23.

44. Ibid., pp. 60, 118, 144–187 (quotations are from pp. 176 and 186), 63–64, 67, 118, 103, 239, 224.

45. Attacks on the transmutation hypothesis that invoked the work of Jenkin, Kelvin, and Mivart include Samson Talbot, "Development and Human Descent," *Baptist Quarterly*, 6 (1872), 131; G. E. E., "Darwin's Descent of Man," *Religious Magazine and Monthly Review*, 45 (1871), 502–504; Anon., Review of *On the Genesis of Species*, by St. George Mivart, *Christian Quarterly*, 3 (1871), 410–411; J. B. Drury, "Darwinism," *Scribner's Monthly*, 10 (1875), 353, 356–357; Nisbet, "Darwinism," p. 207.

46. Darwin to A. R. Wallace, December 22, 1857, *LLD*, 2:109; Darwin, *Origin of Species*, p. 488. See also [Charles Darwin], *The Autobiography of Charles Darwin, 1809–1882, With original omissions restored*, ed. Nora Barlow (New York, 1958), p. 130; Howard E. Gruber and Paul H. Barrett, *Darwin on Man: A Psychological Study of Scientific Creativity* (New York, 1974), pp. 10, 20, 29–31, 176–257.

47. [Gray], "Darwin on the Origin," pp. 111–112; [Bowen], "Darwin on the Origin," p. 475. See also Goodwin, "Darwin on the Origin," pp. 334–335; Anon., "Review of *Origin*, [1860], p. 336; [Barnes], "Readjustments of Christianity," p. 69; Andrew P. Peabody, "The Bearing of Modern Scientific Theories on the Fundamental Truths of Religion," *Bibliotheca Sacra*, 21 (1864), 712–713.

48. Dewey, "True Place," p. 138.

49. Darwin called Lyell's work "a compilation, but of the highest class, for when possible the facts have been verified on the spot." Darwin to Joseph Hooker, February 24 [1863], *LLD*, 3:8. Useful discussions of the data relating to the issue of the antiquity of the human species include Francis C. Haber, *The Age of the World: Moses to Darwin* (Baltimore, 1959), pp. 272–287, and Kenneth P. Oakley, "The Problem of

Man's Antiquity," *Bulletin of the British Museum* (Natural History), Geological Series, 9, no. 5 (1964), 86–155.

50. Anon., Review of *The Geological Evidences of the Antiquity of Man*, by Charles Lyell, *North American Review*, 97 (1863), 292; L. Sternberg, "Geology and Moses," *Evangelical Quarterly Review*, 19 (1868), 149; R. Weiser, "Pre-Adamite Man," *Evangelical Quarterly Review*, 17 (1866), 229, 232; J. S. Jewell, "Geological Evidences of the Antiquity of Man," *Methodist Quarterly Review*, 4th ser., 21 (1869), 119; Anon., Review of *The Geological Evidences of the Antiquity of Man*, by Charles Lyell, *Evangelical Quarterly Review*, 15 (1864), 455; Anon., "Origin and Antiquity of Man," p. 534; Thompson, *Man in Genesis and in Geology*, pp. 98–107; Anon., "Heathen Views on the Golden Age, etc., Compared with the Bible," *Biblical Repertory and Princeton Review*, 42 (1870), 376; Hodge, *Systematic Theology*, 2:40; Bushnell, "Science and Religion," p. 270.

51. Charles Lyell, *The Geological Evidences of the Antiquity of Man* (Philadelphia, 1863), pp. 385–388 (quotation on p. 386). Similar statements by American thinkers include [Gray], "Darwin on the Origin," p. 114; K[nowlton], "Human Race," pp. 359–360. Few American religious intellectuals perceived that Agassiz's espousal of polygenism had been designed "to strengthen natural theology against the degrading materialism of the Darwinian doctrine" until long after the publication of the *Origin of Species*. Anon., "Agassiz on Provinces of Creation and the Unity of the Race," *Biblical Repertory and Princeton Review*, 41 (1869), 5.

52. Lyell, *Geological Evidences*, pp. 387–388. See also Daniel R. Goodwin, "The Antiquity of Man," *American Presbyterian and Theological Review*, n.s. 2 (1864), 257; Wilson, "Specific Unity," p. 633; Anon., "Origin and Antiquity of Man," pp. 188–189; Barrows, "Revelation and Inspiration," p. 317.

53. Darwin to T. H. Huxley [February?] 26, 1863, *MLD*, 1:239; Lyell, *Geological Evidences*, pp. 421, 423, 469, 505–506; Leonard G. Wilson, ed., *Sir Charles Lyell's Scientific Journals on the Species Question* (New Haven, 1970), pp. 458–459, 168, 427.

54. Lyell, *Geological Evidences*, pp. 504–505, 469, 472–473, 492–493. Lyell had long recognized that acceptance of transmutation involved the inclusion of man. See, for example, Wilson, ed., *Lyell's Scientific Journals*, pp. 238, 380–381. He also believed, however, that "man is of a higher dignity than were any pre-existing beings on the earth." Charles Lyell, *Principles of Geology; or, The Modern Changes of the Earth and Its Inhabitants* (London, 1830), 1:155. This belief made it impossible for him to accept the notion that the human species was merely another link in the chain of minute changes postulated by Darwin. For a more extensive discussion of the role that Lyell's views concerning the origin of humanity played in shaping his response to the transmutation hypothesis, see Michael Bartholomew, "Lyell and Evolution: An Account of Lyell's Response to the Prospect of an Evolutionary Ancestry for Man," *British Journal for the History of Science*, 6 (1973), 261–303.

55. Lyell to Darwin, March 15, 1863, *Life, Letters, and Journals of Lyell*, ed. Katherine Lyell (London, 1881), 2:365–366; Lyell to Darwin, May 5, 1869, ibid., p. 442; Lyell to Joseph Hooker, March 9, 1863, ibid., pp. 361–362; Lyell to Darwin, March 11, 1863, ibid., p. 363. For representative letters attesting to Darwin's dissatisfaction with Lyell's position, see Darwin to Lyell, March 6 [1863], *LLD*, 3:12; Darwin to Lyell, 12 [March, 1863], ibid., pp. 13–14.

56. Anon., "Origin and Antiquity of Man," pp. 506–507; [C. H. Hitchcock], "The Antiquity of Man," *North American Review*, 97 (1863), 474; Anon., "Origin and Antiquity of Man," p. 170. See also Anon., Review of *The Geological Evidences of the An-*

tiquity of Man, by Charles Lyell, *Atlantic Monthly,* 12 (1863), 128; Goodwin, "Antiquity of Man," pp. 243–244.

57. A perceptive discussion of Huxley's thought is James G. Paradis, *T. H. Huxley: Man's Place in Nature* (Lincoln, Nebr., 1978). A more conventional biographical treatment of Huxley is Cyril Bibby, *Scientist Extraordinary: The Life and Scientific Work of Thomas Henry Huxley, 1825–1895* (New York, 1972). I have also profited from R. Chalmers Mitchell, *Thomas Henry Huxley* (New York, 1900); Gertrude Himmelfarb, *Darwin and the Darwinian Revolution* (New York, 1959); and William Irvine, *Apes, Angels and Victorians: The Story of Darwin, Huxley, and Evolution* (New York, 1955).

58. Huxley, "On the Reception of the 'Origin,' " pp. 196–197, 187–189, 194–196; Huxley to Darwin, November 23, 1859, *LLD,* 2:231–232.

59. Thomas Huxley, "The Origin of Species [1860]," *Collected Essays by Thomas Huxley* (1893; New York, 1968), 2:78, 56-61, 75 (hereafter cited as *Huxley's Essays*).

60. Thomas H. Huxley, *Evidence as to Man's Place in Nature* (New York, 1863), pp. 71–73. See also Paradis, *T. H. Huxley,* pp. 118, 121–137; Mitchell, *Huxley,* pp. 129–135, 165.

61. Huxley, *Man's Place in Nature,* pp. 80–123, 157–158, 180–184 (quotations on pp. 115, 157–158, 123, 120).

62. Ibid., pp. 73, 123–129 (quotation on p. 123), 85–86.

63. Ibid., pp. 125–127.

64. [Barnes], "Readjustments of Christianity," p. 69; Phillips Brooks, "The Eternal Humanity [June 12, 1864]," *Sermons: Sixth Series* (New York, 1893), p. 315; Anon., "Huxley's *Origin of Species;* and *Man's Place in Nature,*" *New Englander,* 22 (1863), 592. See also Anon., "Huxley on the Origin of Species," *North American Review,* 97 (1863), 293; Anon., "Origin and Antiquity of Man," pp. 337, 342; Anon., "Huxley on Man's Place," p. 374.

65. [L. J. Livermore], "The Origin of Man," *Christian Examiner,* n.s. 1 (1866), 63–64, 61; Goodwin, "Antiquity of Man," pp. 254–255. See also Anon., "Origin and Antiquity of Man," p. 364; [Chester Dewey], "Man's Place in Nature," *Biblical Repertory and Princeton Review,* 36 (1864), 293; Lincoln, "Development versus Creation," p. 264; J[ames] D. D[ana], Review of *Evidence as to Man's Place in Nature,* by Thomas Huxley, *American Journal of Science and Arts,* 2d ser., 35 (1863), 453; [Hitchcock], "Antiquity of Man," pp. 464, 475; Winchell, "Voices from Nature," p. 388; K[nowlton], "Human Race," p. 355; Anon., Review of *Geological Evidences,* p. 129.

66. K[nowlton], "Human Race," p. 350. See also [Charles Hodge], "Diversity of Species in the Human Race," *Biblical Repertory and Princeton Review,* 34 (1862), 460; [Dewey], "Man's Place," pp. 284–285, 292; Anon., "Origin and Antiquity of Man," pp. 353–361; Harmon, "Natural Theology," pp. 199–200.

67. J. D. Dana, "On Man's Zoological Position," *New Englander,* 22 (1863), 283, 285–287. See also James D. Dana, "On the Higher Subdivisions in the Classification of Mammals," *American Journal of Science and Arts,* 2d ser., 35 (1863), 66–68. For a valuable discussion of Dana's part in the evolutionary controversy, see William F. Sanford, Jr., "Dana and Darwinism," *Journal of the History of Ideas,* 26 (1965), 531–546.

68. Darwin to Lyell [February 17, 1863], *MLD,* 1:236; Anon., "On Man's Zoological Position," *American Quarterly Church Review and Ecclesiastical Register,* 15 (1863), 291–305; [Hitchcock], "Antiquity of Man," p. 475. See also [Dewey], "Man's Place," p. 289; Thompson, *Man in Genesis and in Geology,* p. 46.

69. Dana, "On Man's Zoological Position," p. 287; Anon., "The Personality of

God, as Affecting Science and Religion," *Southern Presbyterian Review*, 14 (1861), 456. See also [Dewey], "True Place," p. 119; Harmon, "Natural Theology," p. 199.

70. [Dewey], "True Place," pp. 122–123; Dana, *Manual of Geology*, p. 573; Goodwin, "Antiquity of Man," p. 255; Thompson, *Man in Genesis and in Geology*, pp. 45–46, 74; Anon., "Origin and Antiquity of Man," pp. 363, 365; [Livermore], "Origin of Man," p. 64; Bowen, "Latest Form," pp. 221–226; Anon., "Agassiz on Provinces," pp. 9–10.

71. [Dewey], "True Place," pp. 124, 119, 128; James A. Lyon, "A Supernatural Revelation Necessary," *Southern Presbyterian Review*, 13 (1860), 327–328. See also Dana, "On Man's Zoological Position," p. 283; Harmon, "Natural Theology," p. 200; Barrows, "Revelation and Inspiration," p. 329; Thompson, *Man in Genesis and in Geology*, pp. 45, 74; [Hodge], "Diversity of Species," pp. 461–462, 464; Daniel Walker Howe, *The Unitarian Conscience: Harvard Moral Philosophy, 1805–1861* (Cambridge, Mass., 1970), p. 55; D. H. Meyer, *The Instructed Conscience: The Shaping of the American National Ethic* (Philadelphia, 1972), p. 45.

72. Dana, *Manual of Geology*, p. 574; K[nowlton], "Human Race," p. 351. See also [Hodge], "Diversity of Species," pp. 462, 464; Benjamin W. Dwight, "The Doctrine of God's Providence," *Bibliotheca Sacra*, 26 (1869), 320; Thompson, *Man in Genesis and in Geology*, pp. 45, 74–75; Seelye, *Criticism of the Development Hypothesis*, p. 8; P. A. Chadbourne, *Lectures on Natural Theology; or, Nature and the Bible from the Same Author* (New York, 1867), p. 19.

73. [Livermore], "Origin of Man," pp. 61–62; Herbert Spencer, *The Principles of Psychology* (London, 1855), pp. 485–486, 584; Edwin G. Boring, *A History of Experimental Psychology*, 2d ed. (New York, 1950), p. 240; Herbert Spencer, *An Autobiography* (New York, 1904), 1:546–552, 2:84–85. A useful discussion of Spencer's view of psychology can be found in Robert M. Young, *Mind, Brain and Adaptation in the Nineteenth Century: Cerebral Localization and Its Biological Context from Gall to Ferrier* (Oxford, 1972), pp. 150–196.

74. Darwin, *Origin of Species*, p. 488. See also Darwin to C. Lyell, October 11 [1859], *LLD*, 2:211; Robert M. Young, "The Role of Psychology in the Nineteenth Century Evolutionary Debate," in Mary Henle, Julian Jaynes, and John T. Sullivan, eds., *Historical Conceptions of Psychology* (New York, 1973), pp. 183–184; James H. Tufts, "Darwin and Evolutionary Ethics," *Psychological Review*, n.s. 16 (1909), 201.

75. [Thomas Huxley], "Huxley on the Relations of Man with the Lower Animals," *Natural History Review*, 1 (1861), 68; Lyell, *Geological Evidences*, pp. 493–495. See also Alfred Russel Wallace, "The Origin of Human Races and the Antiquity of Man Deduced from the Theory of 'Natural Selection,' " *Journal of the Anthropological Society of London*, 2 (1864), clxxxiii; J. P. Lesley, *Man's Origin and Destiny* (Philadelphia, 1867), p. 92; Kenneth Franklin Gantz, "The Beginnings of Darwinian Ethics, 1859–1871," University of Texas, *Studies in English* (1939), pp. 186–191.

76. [Dewey], "True Place," p. 129; [Dewey], "Man's Place," pp. 290–293, 279; Hitchcock, "Law of Nature's Constancy," p. 525; Bowen, "Latest Form," pp. 221–222; Rice, "Darwinian Theory," p. 626. See also Dana, "On the Higher Subdivisions," p. 65; [Charles Loring Brace], "Darwinism in Germany," *North American Review*, 110 (1870), 293–294; Anon., "Huxley on the Origin," p. 293; Anon., "Origin and Antiquity of Man," p. 347. Brief discussions of the dualistic view of mind and matter that obtained within the American Protestant intellectual community during the first half of the nineteenth century can be found in Howe, *Unitarian Conscience*, p. 41, and Bozeman, *Protestants in an Age of Science*, pp. 53–54.

77. [Alfred Russel Wallace], "Sir Charles Lyell on Geological Climates and the Origin of Species," *Quarterly Review*, 126 (1869), 391–394; Alfred Russel Wallace, "The Limits of Natural Selection as Applied to Man," *Contributions to the Theory of Natural Selection* (London, 1870), pp. 332–355. See also Wallace, "Origin of Human Races," pp. clviii–clxx. As Roger Smith has observed, because Wallace believed that all force was the product of "Will," there was no real inconsistency between his adherence to the mechanism of natural selection for species other than man and his belief in higher purpose. Roger Smith, "Alfred Russel Wallace: Philosophy of Nature and Man," *British Journal for the History of Science*, 6 (1972-73), 188–189.

78. [Brace], "Darwinism in Germany," p. 295; Anon., Review of *Contributions to the Theory of Natural Selection*, by Alfred Wallace, *Methodist Quarterly Review*, 4th ser., 22 (1870), 623; Hitchcock, "Law of Nature's Constancy," p. 525. See also Darwin to Wallace, April 14, 1869, in James Marchant, *Alfred Russel Wallace: Letters and Reminiscences* (New York, 1916), p. 199; Thomas Henry Huxley, "Mr. Darwin's Critics [1871]," *Huxley's Essays*, 2:173–179; Chauncey Wright, "Limits of Natural Selection," *North American Review*, 111 (1870), 298–303; Cyrus Thomas, "The Descent of Man and Sexual Selection in Relation to Sex," *Quarterly Review of the Evangelical Lutheran Church*, n.s. 2 (1872), 351; Gardiner, "Darwinism," pp. 279–282.

79. Useful discussions of sexual selection include Michael T. Ghiselin, *The Triumph of the Darwinian Method* (Berkeley, 1969), pp. 214–231, and Gavin de Beer, *Charles Darwin: Evolution by Natural Selection* (New York, 1964), pp. 219–221.

80. Charles Darwin, *The Descent of Man, and Selection in Relation to Sex* (London, 1871), 1:213, 206, 212, 32–33, 165, 198–199, 213. See also 2:389, 404–405.

81. Ibid., 2:386, 1:160, 200–201, 10–33, 186.

82. Ibid., 1:68. See also pp. 34–36, 46–65, 104–106, 2:390–396. As Howard E. Gruber has noted, whereas in the *Descent of Man* Darwin concentrated on showing that animals possess rudiments of many of man's mental faculties, in *The Expression of the Emotions in Man and Animals*, published a year later, he dealt with the surviving elements of animality in the human species. Gruber and Barrett, *Darwin on Man*, pp. 202–203. Because the latter work evoked little attention from American religious thinkers, I have not discussed it.

83. Darwin, *Descent of Man*, 1:70–71, 88–89, 2:391–392. A perceptive discussion of Darwin's view of the development of the moral sense can be found in Robert J. Richards, "Darwin and the Biologizing of Moral Behavior," in William R. Woodward and Mitchell G. Ash, eds., *The Problematic Science: Psychology in Nineteenth-Century Thought* (New York, 1982), pp. 43–64.

84. Darwin, *Descent of Man*, 1:71–99 (quotations on pp. 89, 85, 99), 106, 162–163.

85. Ibid., pp. 71–72, 104, 87–91. See also 2:390–394.

86. Ibid., 1:72–73, 91–92, 100–101, 86–87, 104, 106, 164–166, 173, 180. See also 2:392–393, 404. The idea that "approbativeness" was an important source of moral behavior had a long history prior to Darwin's work. See, for example, Arthur C. Lovejoy, *Reflections on Human Nature* (Baltimore, 1961), pp. 88–99, 156–193. A number of thinkers in the seventeenth and eighteenth centuries even suggested that the sense of approbativeness was unique to the human species. Ibid., pp. 129–151.

87. Anon., "Philosophy versus Darwinism," *Southern Review*, 13 (1873), 259. See also John Bascom, "Instinct," *Bibliotheca Sacra*, 28 (1871), 683; Thomas, "Descent of Man," p. 240; Talbot, "Development and Human Descent," pp. 140–141; Nisbet, "Darwinism," p. 204; A Learned Gorilla [Richard Grant White], *The Fall of Man; or,*

The Loves of the Gorillas (New York, 1871), Dedication; Anon., "Modern Atheism," *Southern Review*, 10 (1872), 145. Darwin himself admitted that the general argument he was making was not new. Darwin, *Descent of Man*, 1:3–4.

88. R. T. Brumby, "Gradualness Characteristic of All God's Operations," *Southern Presbyterian Review*, 25 (1874), 525; John Bascom, "Darwin's Theory of the Origin of Species," *American Presbyterian Review*, n.s. 3 (1871), 370–371; Nisbet, "Darwinism," pp. 205–206, 214; Anon., Review of *The Descent of Man and Selection in Relation to Sex*, by Charles Darwin, *Christian Quarterly*, 3 (1871), 408–409.

89. Bascom, "Darwin's Theory," pp. 372–373; Talbot, "Development and Human Descent," pp. 141–144; Anon., "Review of *Descent of Man*," pp. 408–409; James Freeman Clarke, "Have Animals Souls?" *Atlantic Monthly*, 34 (1874), 419; Nisbet, "Darwinism," pp. 206–207; Brumby, "Gradualness Characteristic," p. 525; Laurens P. Hickok, *Creator and Creation; or, The Knowledge in the Reason of God and His Work* (Boston, 1872), pp. 341–349; M. Charles Levegue, "The Sense of the Beautiful in Brutes," *Presbyterian Quarterly and Princeton Review*, n.s. 3 (1874), 134; Gardiner, "Darwinism," pp. 276–277; P. A. Chadbourne, *Instinct: Its Office in the Animal Kingdom, and Its Relation to the Higher Powers in Man* (1872; New York, 1883), pp. 207–209, 257.

90. R. B. Welch, "Faith—Its Place and Prerogative," *Presbyterian Quarterly and Princeton Review*, n.s. 1 (1872), 645; James A. Lyon, "The Contrast between Man and the Brute Creation Establishes the Divine Origin of the Scriptures," *Presbyterian Quarterly and Princeton Review*, n.s. 2 (1873), 726–727, 729–730; Thomas, "Descent of Man," pp. 360–363; Nisbet, "Darwinism," pp. 208–209; Chadbourne, *Instinct*, pp. 282–283, 307.

91. Gardiner, "Darwinism," pp. 270–271. See also Talbot, "Development and Human Descent," p. 144; Lyon, "Contrast between Man," p. 729; Anon., "The Origin of Species," *Southern Review*, 9 (1871), 705; Chadbourne, *Instinct*, pp. 272–275; Stork, "Some Assumptions against Christianity," p. 326; Nisbet, "Darwinism," pp. 207–208.

92. Anon., "Darwinianism," p. 532.

Chapter 3. "In the Twinkling of an Eye"

1. S. C. Bartlett, "The Present Attitude of Evangelical Christianity towards the Prominent Forms of Assault," *Bibliotheca Sacra*, 25 (1868), 182. See also Joseph Haven, "Place and Value of Miracles in the Christian System," *Bibliotheca Sacra*, 19 (1862), 328; J. E. Wells, "Law, Providence, and Prayer," *Bibliotheca Sacra*, 30 (1873), 595–596.

2. W. A. Stearns, "Recent Questions of Unbelief," *Bibliotheca Sacra*, 27 (1870), 469, 480; J. T. Tucker, "Natural and Supernatural," *Boston Review*, 6 (1866), 173. See also Haven, "Place and Value of Miracles," p. 328; A. D. Mayo, "The Impending Conflict of Christianity," *Religious Magazine and Monthly Review*, 44 (1870), 118; George P. Fisher, "The Conflict of Skepticism and Unbelief. First Article: The Questions at Issue," *New Englander*, 23 (1864), 129; A. B. M[uzzy], "The Great Issue," *Monthly Religious Magazine*, 39 (1868), 193; [Lyman H. Atwater], "Rationalism,"*Biblical Repertory and Princeton Review*, 38 (1866), 347–348; Tayler Lewis, "Nature and Prayer," *American Presbyterian Review*, 3d ser., 2 (1870), 208–209; T. W. Fowler, "Science and Immortality," *Popular Science Monthly*, 1 (1872), 28; F. A. Gast, "Modern Skepticism," *Mercersburg Review*, n.s. 8 (1874), 318–322; Wells, "Law, Providence, and Prayer," p. 595; Charles E. Hamlin, "The Attitude of the Christian Teacher in Respect of Sci-

ence," *Baptist Quarterly*, 6 (1872), 28–29; Stuart Robinson, "The Difficulties of Infidelity," in W. H. Ruffner, ed., *Lectures on the Evidences of Christianity* . . . (New York, 1851), p. 541; Charles Bliss, "Darwin's Animals and Plants, Under Domestication," *Congregational Review*, 9 (1869), 461; Richard S. Gladney, "Natural Science and Revealed Religion," *Southern Presbyterian Review*, 12 (1859), 450.

3. Andrew P. Peabody, "The Bearing of Modern Scientific Theories on the Fundamental Truths of Religion," *Bibliotheca Sacra*, 21 (1864), 711; James W. Thompson, "The Situation," *Monthly Review and Religious Magazine*, 43 (1870), 128; [James Read Eckard], "The Logical Relations of Religion and Natural Science," *Biblical Repertory and Princeton Review*, 32 (1860), 579. See also Edward Hitchcock, "The Law of Nature's Constancy Subordinate to the Higher Law of Change," *Bibliotheca Sacra and Biblical Repository*, 20 (1863), 536; F. E. Abbot, "Positivism in Theology," *Christian Examiner*, n.s. 1 (1866), 255; Joseph P. Thompson, "Does Science Tend to Materialism?" *New Englander*, 19 (1861), 95; A. F. Dickson, "The Knowledge of God as Obtained from Scripture and from Nature," *Southern Presbyterian Review*, 13 (1860), 351; Benjamin W. Dwight, "The Doctrine of God's Providence, in Itself and in Its Relations and Uses," *Bibliotheca Sacra*, 21 (1864), 620; William North Rice, "The Darwinian Theory of the Origin of Species," *New Englander*, 26 (1867), 608; E. F. Burr, *Pater Mundi; or, Doctrine of Evolution* (Boston, 1873), pp. 153–154; P. A. Chadbourne, *Lectures on Natural Theology; or, Nature and the Bible from the Same Author* (New York, 1867), p. 179; Ransom Welch, "Admissions of Philosophical Scepticism," *Bibliotheca Sacra*, 31 (1874), 638; J. C. Koller, "Should Clergymen Study Natural Science?" *Quarterly Review of the Evangelical Lutheran Church*, n.s. 4 (1874), 597–599; J. MacBride Sterrett, "Natural Realism; or, Faith, the Basis of Science and Religion," *Bibliotheca Sacra*, 31 (1874), 77; Hamlin, "Attitude of the Christian Teacher," p. 29; Samuel P. Sadtler, "Modern Science and Materialism," *Quarterly Review of the Evangelical Lutheran Church*, n.s. 4 (1874), 81–82; James T. Bixby, "Science and Religion," *Religious Magazine and Monthly Review*, 45 (1871), 333.

4. John Bascom, "Darwin's Theory of the Origin of Species," *American Presbyterian Review*, n.s. 3 (1871), 351; Francis Bowen, "The Latest Form of the Development Theory [1860]," *Gleanings from a Literary Life, 1838–1880* (New York, 1880), p. 230; [Robert Lewis Dabney], "Geology and the Bible," *Southern Presbyterian Review*, 14 (1861), 265, 271; Robert Lewis Dabney, "A Caution against Anti-Christian Science [1871]," *Discussions by Robert L. Dabney*, ed. C. R. Vaughan (Richmond, Va., 1892), 3:128–131; Robert Lewis Dabney, "The Caution against Anti-Christian Science Criticised by Dr. Woodrow" [1873], ibid., pp. 166–174. See also R. T. Brumby, "Relations of Science to the Bible," *Southern Presbyterian Review*, 25 (1874), 16; Elias J. Richards, "Sources of Divine Knowledge," *Presbyterian Quarterly and Princeton Review*, n.s. 2 (1873), 498; J. H. M., "Providence," *Religious Magazine and Monthly Review*, 50 (1873), 504–505; Augustus Woodbury, "Divine Providence," *Religious Magazine and Monthly Review*, 49 (1873), 27; S. W. Culver, "The Natural and the Supernatural—How Distinguished and How Related," *Baptist Quarterly*, 7 (1873), 367–368; Samuel Adams, "Darwinism," *Congregational Review*, 11 (1871), 358; J. B. Drury, "Darwinism," *Scribner's Monthly*, 10 (1875), 359; James W. M'Lane, "Speculation and the Bible," *Bibliotheca Sacra*, 18 (1861), 346–347; Stearns, "Recent Questions," p. 480.

5. [Samuel John Baird], "The Providential Government of God," *Biblical Repertory and Princeton Review*, 30 (1858), 329–330. See also [Oliver Stearns], "Rationalism in Religion: The Need and Purpose of Miracles," *Christian Examiner and Religious Miscellany*, 4th ser., 20 (1853), 259; Edward Hitchcock, "The Connection between Geology and Natural Religion," *Biblical Repository and Quarterly Observer*, 5 (1835), 121;

Edward Hitchcock, "Special Divine Interpositions in Nature," *Bibliotheca Sacra and American Biblical Repository*, 11 (1854), 796–797; Josiah Parsons Cooke, *Religion and Chemistry* (1864; New York, 1880), pp. 293–294; Alexander Winchell, "Voices from Nature," *Ladies Repository*, 23 (1863), 386; Thompson, "Situation," p. 128; Tucker, "Natural and Supernatural," pp. 173–174; Lewis E. Hicks, "Scientists and Theologians: How They Disagree and Why," *Baptist Quarterly*, 9 (1875), 63–64; Woodbury, "Divine Providence," p. 27; Orville Dewey, "Rights, Claims, and Duties of Opinion," *Christian Examiner*, 4th ser., 4 (1845), 101.

6. S. A. Ort, "The Controversy between the Theist and the Scientist," *Quarterly Review of the Evangelical Lutheran Church*, n.s. 4 (1874), 218; Samson Talbot, "Development and Human Descent," *Baptist Quarterly*, 6 (1872), 146. See also Frederic Gardiner, "Darwinism," *Bibliotheca Sacra*, 29 (1872), 288; J. H. Morison, "The Sadducean Tendencies of our Age," *Monthly Review and Religious Magazine*, 43 (1870), 541; Samuel Harris, "The Progress of Christ's Kingdom in Its Relation to the Spirit of the Present Age," *Bibliotheca Sacra*, 30 (1873), 299–300; Thomas Munnell, "Problem of the Supernatural," *Christian Quarterly*, 7 (1875), 338–339; Anon., "The Origin of Species," *Southern Review*, 9 (1871), 716; Robert Winthrop, *An Address to the Alumni of Harvard University* [1852], quoted in Russell Blaine Nye, *Society and Culture in America, 1830–1860* (New York, 1974), p. 239.

7. Thomas Huxley, "The Origin of Species [1860]," *Collected Essays by Thomas Huxley* (1893; New York, 1968), 2:52 (hereafter cited as *Huxley's Essays*); Thomas H. Huxley, "Mr. Darwin's Critics [1871]," *Huxley's Essays*, 2:147–149. Huxley's most celebrated encounter with the forces of religion, of course, was his reply to the bishop of Oxford, Samuel Wilberforce, at the Saturday "D Section" meeting of the British Association in June 1860. An entertaining treatment of this encounter can be found in William Irvine, *Apes, Angels, and Victorians: The Story of Darwin, Huxley, and Evolution* (New York, 1955), pp. 3–7. The most balanced view of the encounter is probably J. R. Lucas, "Wilberforce and Huxley: A Legendary Encounter," *Historical Journal*, 22 (1979), 313–330. A perceptive treatment of Huxley's confrontational posture toward religion can be found in James R. Moore, *The Post-Darwinian Controversies: A Study of the Protestant Struggle to Come to Terms with Darwin in Great Britain and America, 1870–1900* (Cambridge, 1979), pp. 58–68.

Suggestive evidence concerning Huxley's views on religion can be found in a set of letters Huxley wrote to Charles Kingsley in 1863. See Leonard Huxley, ed., *Life and Letters of Thomas Henry Huxley* (London, 1900), 1:238–244. Huxley declared that he could "not see one shadow or tittle of evidence that the great unknown underlying the phenomena of the universe stands to us in the relation of a Father—loves us and cares for us as Christianity asserts." Huxley to Kingsley, May 5, 1863, 1:241.

8. Huxley, "Origin of Species," pp. 58–59; Thomas H. Huxley, "The Genealogy of Animals [1869]," *Huxley's Essays*, 2:110, 113; Thomas H. Huxley, "Criticisms on 'The Origin of Species' [1864]," ibid., pp. 82–83; Thomas H. Huxley, "On the Physical Basis of Life [1868]," ibid., 1:154, 159, 164, 155; Thomas H. Huxley, "Biogenesis and Abiogenesis [1870]," ibid., 8:256; Letter from a New York Presbyterian, quoted in Daniel Coit Gilman, *The Launching of a University and Other Papers: A Sheaf of Remembrances* (New York, 1906), pp. 22–23 (the original was in italics). See also Huxley, "Mr. Darwin's Critics," pp. 162–163; Thomas H. Huxley, "Six Lectures to Working Men 'On Our Knowledge of the Causes of the Phenomena of Organic Nature' [1863]," *Huxley's Essays*, 2:471; James G. Paradis, *T. H. Huxley: Man's Place in Nature* (Lincoln, Nebr., 1978), pp. 90–94.

9. Herbert Spencer, *An Autobiography* (New York, 1904), 2:6–7, 57–58; Peter J. Bow-

ler, "The Changing Meaning of 'Evolution,' " *Journal of the History of Ideas*, 36 (1975), 106–112, 114; Herbert Spencer, "The Filiation of Ideas," in David Duncan, *The Life and Letters of Herbert Spencer* (London, 1908), pp. 535, 554–555; Herbert Spencer, *First Principles*, 4th ed. (New York, 1886), pp. i–ii. In the original edition of *First Principles*, Spencer's discussion of Darwin's work was confined to a footnote. Herbert Spencer, *First Principles* (London, 1862), p. 404n.

Useful studies of Spencer's life and thought include John David Yeardon Peel, *Herbert Spencer: The Evolution of a Sociologist* (London, 1971); Derek Freeman et al., "The Evolutionary Thought of Charles Darwin and Herbert Spencer," *Current Anthropology*, 15 (1974), 211–237; Elizabeth Flower and Murray G. Murphey, *A History of Philosophy in America* (New York, 1977), 2:528–535; Robert M. Young, *Mind, Brain and Adaptation in the Nineteenth Century: Cerebral Localization and Its Biological Context from Gall to Ferrier* (Oxford, 1972), pp. 150–196.

10. Spencer, *Autobiography*, 2:9; Herbert Spencer, "The Development Hypothesis [1852]," *Essays Scientific, Political, and Speculative* (New York, 1891), 1:6, 1–3. See also Spencer, *Autobiography*, 1:200–201, 448–449, 2:7, 194–199. A more extended attack on special creation can be found in Herbert Spencer, *Principles of Biology* (London, 1864), 1:333–345, 350–355.

Spencer's view of transmutation was different from that of Darwin. Of central importance, Spencer downplayed the role of natural selection. From 1840 on, Spencer believed in the inheritance of acquired characteristics. Peel, *Herbert Spencer*, pp. 141–153; Young, *Mind, Brain and Adaptation*, pp. 186–190.

Few scientists felt indebted to Spencer's views. Darwin, for example, believed that Spencer was a great philosopher, but he denied that he had profited from Spencer's work and remarked that "his deductive manner of treating every subject is wholly opposed to my frame of mind." [Charles Darwin], *The Autobiography of Charles Darwin, 1809–1882, With original omissions restored*, ed. Nora Barlow (New York, 1958), pp. 108–109; Darwin to C. Lyell, February 23 [1860], *The Life and Letters of Charles Darwin, Including an Autobiographical Chapter*, ed. Francis Darwin (London, 1887), 2:290 (hereafter cited as *LLD*).

11. Spencer, *Autobiography*, 2:9–14 (quotation on p. 9); Herbert Spencer, "Progress: Its Law and Cause [1857]," *Essays*, 1:10; see also pp. 35–38, 58–59.

12. Spencer, *First Principles* (1st ed.), pp. 216, 20–21, 46, 66. See also pp. 30–67, 234–235, 496.

13. Ibid., pp. 106, 20, 99, 17, 110, 123, 109, 107. See also pp. 99–103, 45–46, 250–258, 498–502.

14. [E. L. Youmans], "Purpose and Plan of Our Enterprise," *Popular Science Monthly*, 1 (1872), 114. Useful accounts of Youmans' life and thought include William E. Leverette, Jr., "E. L. Youmans's Crusade for Scientific Autonomy and Respectability," *American Quarterly*, 17 (Spring, 1965), 12–33; Charles M. Haar, "E. L. Youmans: A Chapter in the Diffusion of Science in America," *Journal of the History of Ideas*, 9 (1948), 193–213; and John Fiske, *Edward Livingston Youmans: Interpreter of Science for the People* (1893; New York, 1972).

15. [Youmans], "Purpose and Plan," p. 113; [E. L. Youmans], "The Conflict of Ages," *Popular Science Monthly*, 8 (1876), 494. See also [E. L. Youmans], "The Accusation Atheism," *Popular Science Monthly*, 11 (1877), 369; Leverette, "E. L. Youmans's Crusade," pp. 25–28.

16. [E. L. Youmans], "The Doctrine of Evolution," *Popular Science Monthly*, 2 (1872),

114–115; E. L. Youmans, "Herbert Spencer and the Doctrine of Evolution," *Popular Science Monthly*, 6 (1874), p. 42; Anon., "The Popular Science Monthly," *Scribner's Monthly*, 4 (1872), 775. Youmans observed that the religious press disliked *Popular Science Monthly*. E. L. Youmans to [Herbert Spencer], August 21, 1872, in Fiske, *Edward Livingston Youmans*, p. 303.

17. John Fiske, *Outlines of Cosmic Philosophy* [1874], *The Miscellaneous Writings of John Fiske* (Cambridge, 1902), 1:14, 31, 15, 19, 21–23, 31, 39–46, 133, 138–141, 168, 187, 269, 275, 4:174–175. The best study of the life and thought of John Fiske is Milton Berman, *John Fiske: The Evolution of a Popularizer* (Cambridge, Mass., 1961). See also H. Burnell Pannill, *The Religious Faith of John Fiske* (Durham, N.C., 1957), and Bruce Kuklick, *The Rise of American Philosophy: Cambridge, Massachusetts, 1860–1930* (New Haven, 1977), pp. 80–91.

18. Fiske, *Outlines*, 4:167, 2:373, 377, 411.

19. Ibid., 1:127–128, 4:180. See also Berman, *John Fiske*, pp. 38, 103–105.

20. Fiske, *Outlines*, 4:238, 178.

21. Ibid., 1:255, 19, 4:260, 227, 206, 167.

22. Ibid., 4:228–229, 226, 233–235, 245–247, 290, 1:260, 21, 271. Whereas in 1869, Fiske described himself as "neither a Christian nor a theist," in 1873 he informed his mother that he regarded his view as an espousal of Christianity. Even allowing for a certain impulse to pull his punches, his later works suggest that he was moving in the direction of a greater sympathy for religion. Berman, *John Fiske*, pp. 75, 103–104; John Fiske to his mother, March 31, 1872, in John Spencer Clarke, *The Life and Letters of John Fiske* (Boston, 1917), 1:394.

23. John Tyndall, "The 'Prayer for the Sick': Hints towards a Serious Attempt to Estimate Its Value," *Contemporary Review*, 20 (1872), 205–210. The most complete treatment of the life and thought of Tyndall is A. S. Eve and C. H. Creasy, *Life and Work of John Tyndall* (London, 1945). See also the essays in W. H. Brock, N. D. McMillan, and R. C. Mollan, eds., *John Tyndall: Essays on a Natural Philosopher* (Dublin, 1981).

24. John Tyndall, "On Prayer," *Contemporary Review*, 20 (1872), 764–766.

25. For Tyndall's comments on the "stir" his discussion of prayer raised in America, see Eve and Creasy, *Life and Work of Tyndall*, p. 169.

26. James McCosh, "On Prayer," in Professor Tyndall et al., *The Prayer-Gauge Debate* (Boston, 1876), pp. 142–144, 137–139, 143. See also William M. Taylor, "Conditions of Successful Prayer," *Princeton Review*, 4th ser. (1878), pp. 180–181; C. A. Stork, "Professor Tyndall's Test of Prayer," *Quarterly Review of the Evangelical Lutheran Church*, n.s. 3 (1873), 82–86; Noah K. Davis, "The Prayer Test," *Baptist Quarterly*, 7 (1873), 63–65; Willis J. Beecher, "Faith as an Ambiguous Middle Term," *Presbyterian Quarterly and Princeton Review*, n.s. 2 (1873), 467; James McCosh, *Ideas in Nature Overlooked by Dr. Tyndall, Being an Examination of Dr. Tyndall's Belfast Address* (New York, 1875), p. 14n; Hugh Miller Thompson, "The Christian Doctrine of Prayer," in C. S. Henry et al., *Christian Truth and Modern Opinion* (New York, 1874), pp. 61–62.

27. McCosh, "On Prayer," p. 144. See also McCosh, *Ideas in Nature*, p. iv; Eve and Creasy, *Life and Work of Tyndall*, p. 168.

28. [John Tyndall], *Advancement of Science: The Inaugural Address of Professor John Tyndall . . . and Articles of Prof. Tyndall and Sir Henry Thompson on Prayer* (New York, 1874), pp. 19, 21–37.

29. Ibid., pp. 64–65, 75–79, 54–63; John Tyndall, *Fragments of Science for Unscientific People: A Series of Detached Essays, Lectures, and Reviews* (New York, 1871), p. 159.

30. John W. Mears, "Theistic Reactions in Modern Speculation," *Presbyterian Quarterly and Princeton Review*, n.s. 4 (1875), 331–332, 337. See also John Laing, "An Open Letter to Professor Tyndall," ibid., pp. 235, 237–238, 247–249; McCosh, *Ideas in Nature*, pp. 16, 43–44; Anon., "Professor Tyndall," *Southern Review*, 15 (1874), 452. In 1875 Professor John Trowbridge of Harvard observed that Tyndall's address had been "criticized from a hundred pulpits." John Trowbridge, "Science from the Pulpit," *Popular Science Monthly*, 6 (1875), 735.

31. O. B. Frothingham, *The Religion of Humanity* (New York, 1873), p. 30. See also Anon., "Man in Darwinism and Christianity," *American Quarterly Church Review*, 24 (1872), 288. Statements affirming the popularity of the productions of scientific naturalists in the United States include T. H. Huxley, *On the Physical Basis of Life*, 2d ed. (New Haven, 1870), publisher's note; Alexander Winchell, "Huxley and Evolution," *Methodist Quarterly Review*, 4th ser., 29 (1877), 290; Spencer, *Autobiography*, 2:113n, 476–479.

32. Henry M. Harmon, "Natural Theology," *Methodist Review*, 4th ser., 15 (1863), 183; Thompson, "Does Science Tend," p. 87; Francis L. Patton, Inaugural Address, *Addresses at the Induction of Francis L. Patton into the "Cyrus H. McCormick Professor of Didactic and Polemic Theology" in the Presbyterian Theological Seminary of the North West* (Chicago, 1873), p. 28; Burr, *Pater Mundi*, p. 19. Historians who have analyzed scientific naturalism in the nineteenth century have called attention to essentially the same salient characteristics as did religious thinkers. Perceptive discussions include Donald Fleming, *John William Draper and the Religion of Science* (Philadelphia, 1950), passim; Frank Miller Turner, *Between Science and Religion: The Reaction to Scientific Naturalism in Late Victorian England* (New Haven, 1974), pp. 8–30; Susan Budd, *Varieties of Unbelief: Atheists and Agnostics in English Society, 1850–1960* (London, 1977), pp. 124–149; and John C. Greene, "Darwinism as a World View," *Science, Ideology, and World View: Essays in the History of Evolutionary Ideas* (Berkeley, 1981), pp. 128–157.

33. Burr, *Pater Mundi*, p. 14. See also B[enjamin] W. B[acon], "Burr, Enoch Fitch," *Dictionary of American Biography*, 3:321–322 (hereafter cited as *DAB*).

34. Thomas Henry Huxley, "On the Advisableness of Improving Natural Knowledge [1868]," *Lay Sermons, Addresses and Reviews* (New York, 1871), p. 16; Anon., Review of *Illustrations of Progress*, by Herbert Spencer, *Atlantic Monthly*, 13 (1864), 776; J. E. Barnes, "Herbert Spencer on Ultimate Religious Ideas," *New Englander*, 22 (1863), 728, 724–725, 703, 723. When the essay was reprinted in *Huxley's Essays*, the phrase "and Unknowable" was dropped, possibly because of Huxley's growing hostility to Spencer. *Huxley's Essays*, 1:38. See also [Charles Hodge], "Can God Be Known?" *Biblical Repertory and Princeton Review*, 36 (1864), 149–150; Abbot, "Positivism in Theology," p. 255; Anon., "The Idea of God," *Southern Review*, 15 (1874), 253–254; [Lyman Atwater], "Herbert Spencer's Philosophy: Atheism, Pantheism, and Materialism," *Biblical Repertory and Princeton Review*, 37 (1865), 264–265.

I cannot agree with the claim that Protestant thinkers sought to show that their theology could be reconciled with Spencerianism. See, for example, Moore, *Post-Darwinian Controversies*, pp. 167–168; Richard Hofstadter, *Social Darwinism in American Thought*, rev. ed. (New York, 1955), pp. 37–38. Whether or not such reconciliation was theoretically possible, I see little evidence beyond the work of John Fiske, Minot Savage, and, at least arguably, Henry Ward Beecher to suggest that Protestant intellectuals were willing to countenance Spencer's view of religion.

35. M. Stuart Phelps, "Cosmism," *New Englander*, 34 (1875), 530; Fiske, *Outlines*, 4:232; Anon., Review of *Outlines of Cosmic Philosophy*, by John Fiske, *Atlantic Monthly*,

34 (1875), 619. See also John Bascom, "The Synthetic or Cosmic Philosophy," *Bibliotheca Sacra*, 33 (1876), 636; Joseph Le Conte, *Religion and Science. A Series of Sunday Lectures on the Relation of Natural and Revealed Religion, or the Truths Revealed in Nature and Scripture* (1873; New York, 1874), pp. 13–14.

36. Anon., "Man in Darwinism," pp. 291–292; Thompson, "Does Science Tend," p. 87. See also Ort, "Controversy between the Theist," pp. 211–212; Richards, "Sources of Divine Knowledge," p. 488; Gast, "Modern Skepticism," pp. 320–323.

37. Anon., "How to Treat Modern Skepticism," *American Church Review*, 25 (1873), 101. See also Thomas Nichols, "Modern Skepticism," *Presbyterian Quarterly and Princeton Review*, n.s. 3 (1874), 239; Gast, "Modern Skepticism," p. 318.

38. Ort, "Controversy between the Theist," p. 218. See also E. A. Washburn, "Moral Responsibility and Physical Law," in Henry et al., *Christianity and Modern Opinion*, pp. 69–70.

39. Bixby, "Science and Religion," p. 330; W. Streissguth, "Modern Materialism Viewed from a Scientific-Religious Standpoint," trans. J. G. Morris, *Quarterly Review of the Evangelical Lutheran Church*, n.s. 5 (1875), 408, 404.

40. Anon., Review of *Christianity and Positivism*, by James McCosh, *Southern Review*, 13 (1873), 493; Lewis, "Nature and Prayer," pp. 208–209; Eli Fay, "Religion For the Heart Rather than the Head," *Religious Magazine and Monthly Review*, 44 (1870), 272–273. See also Haven, "Place and Value of Miracles," p. 349n; William W. Patton, "The Tendency of Scientific Men to Skepticism," *Methodist Quarterly Review*, 4th ser., 14 (1862), 541–542, 548–550; Anon., "Man in Darwinism," p. 288; Joseph H. Wythe, *The Agreement of Science and Religion* (Philadelphia, 1872), p. 15; Crawford H. Toy, "The Place of Theological Science in the Sciences Comprised in a Liberal Education," *Proceedings of the National Baptist Educational Convention, 28–30 May 1872* (New York, 1872), pp. 155–156; Stearns, "Recent Questions," p. 461; Thompson, "Does Science Tend," pp. 84, 94–95; Anon., "Darwinianism," *American Quarterly Church Review*, 21 (1870), 525, 527; Dabney, "Caution against Anti-Christian Science," *Discussions*, 3:146–148. It would be a mistake, of course, to suggest that apprehensions about the hazards of scientific investigation were entirely new. From the outset of the Reformation, as I suggested in Chapter 1, some Protestants had warned that such investigation would divert attention from the supernatural. What altered was the volume of expression of such concern, which increased during the third quarter of the nineteenth century.

41. Anon., "Philosophy versus Darwinism," *Southern Review*, 13 (1873), 269, 267. See also William Rupp, "The Bible and Science," *Mercersburg Review*, n.s. 8 (1874), 56–57; Welch, "Admissions," p. 638; Gast, "Modern Skepticism," p. 327; Brumby, "Relations of Science," pp. 2–3, 25–27; Lewis E. Hicks, "Scientists and Theologians: How They Disagree and Why," *Baptist Quarterly*, 8 (1874), 267; Patton, "Tendency of Scientific Men," p. 541; Gardiner, "Darwinism," p. 248; Thomas Hill, "The Struggles of Science," *Unitarian Review and Religious Magazine*, 3 (1875), 349–350; Noah Porter, "Professor Tyndall's Last Deliverance," *New Englander*, 37 (1878), 35–36.

42. Anon., "Darwinism," *Southern Review*, n.s. 12 (1873), 407. See also Samuel M. Shute, "Professor Tyndall's Belfast Address," *Baptist Quarterly*, 9 (1875), 27; Streissguth, "Modern Materialism," p. 404; Anon., Review of *History of the Conflict between Religion and Science*, by John William Draper, *Methodist Quarterly Review*, 4th ser., 27 (1875), 162–163.

43. John William Draper, *History of the Conflict between Religion and Science* (New

York, 1874), p. vi. The best discussion of Draper's life and thought is Fleming, *John William Draper*.

44. Anon., Review of *History of the Conflict between Religion and Science*, by John Draper, *Quarterly Review of the Evangelical Lutheran Church*, n.s. 5 (1875), 150. See also Laing, "Open Letter," pp. 231–232; Anon., "Draper's Religion and Science," *Presbyterian Quarterly and Princeton Review*, n.s. 4 (1875), 158, 165; Koller, "Should Clergymen Study," p. 597.

45. Winchell, "Voices from Nature," p. 386; Brumby, "Relations of Science," pp. 2–3. See also Edward A. Walker, "The Present Attitude of the Church toward Critical and Scientific Inquiry," *New Englander*, 19 (1861), 345–346; Anon., "Agassiz on Provinces of Creation and the Unity of the Race," *Biblical Repertory and Princeton Review*, 41 (1869), 5–6; Julius H. Seelye, *A Criticism of the Development Hypothesis, as Held by Charles Darwin, Thomas Huxley, Alfred Russel Wallace, Herbert Spencer, and the New School of Naturalists* (New York, 1871), p. 8; Ort, "Controversy between the Theist," pp. 212–213; James B. Tyler, "Evolutionism in Natural History as Related to Christianity," *New Englander*, 3 (1871), 465; Anon., "Darwinism," pp. 409, 422; [L. J. Livermore], "The Origin of Man," *Christian Examiner*, n.s. 1 (1866), 62; Anon., "Origin of Species," pp. 721–722; Anon., "Philosophy versus Darwinism," pp. 254–255; Howard Crosby, Introduction to the American Edition, in John T. Leifchild, *The Great Problem: The Higher Ministry of Nature Viewed in the Light of Modern Science, as an Aid to an Advanced Christian Philosophy* (New York, 1872), n.p.

46. Darwin to Asa Gray, July 23 [1862], *More Letters of Charles Darwin*, ed. Francis Darwin and A. C. Seward (London, 1903), 1:202 (hereafter cited as *MLD*). See also Chadbourne, *Lectures on Natural Theology*, p. 175. Darwin was often more explicit in discussing his religious beliefs in his private correspondence. See, for example, Darwin to Charles Lyell, October 11 [1859], *LLD*, 2:210–211; Darwin to Sir John Herschel, 23 May [1861], reprinted in "Some Unpublished Letters of Charles Darwin," ed. Gavin de Beer, Royal Society of London, *Notes and Records*, 14 (1959), 35; Darwin to Gray, November 26, 1860, *LLD*, 2:353; Darwin to Gray, June 5 [1861], ibid., p. 373; Darwin to Lyell, June 17 [1860], *MLD*, 1:154; Darwin to Lyell [August 2, 13, 21, 1861], ibid., pp. 191–194; Darwin to Lyell, October 20 [1859], *LLD*, 2:174; Darwin to Joseph Hooker [March 29, 1863], ibid., 3:18; Darwin to W. Graham, July 3, 1881, ibid., 1:315–316.

Valuable studies of the controverted question of Darwin's changing views of God's role in nature include John Hedley Brooke, "The Relations between Darwin's Science and His Religion," in John Durant, ed., *Darwinism and Divinity: Essays on Evolution and Religious Belief* (New York, 1985), pp. 40–75; Dov Ospovat, "God and Natural Selection: The Darwinian Idea of Design," *Journal of the History of Biology*, 13 (1980), 169–194; Neal C. Gillespie, *Charles Darwin and the Problem of Creation* (Chicago, 1979); Howard E. Gruber and Paul H. Barrett, *Darwin on Man: A Psychological Study of Scientific Creativity* (New York, 1974), esp. pp. 209–217; Maurice Mandelbaum, "Darwin's Religious Views," *Journal of the History of Ideas*, 19 (1958), 363–378. Alvar Ellegård has speculated that Darwin may have wished his views concerning the role of God in his theory to be misunderstood in the *Origin of Species* in order to deflect criticism and to encourage readers to give his theory a fair hearing. Alvar Ellegård, "The Darwinian Theory and the Argument from Design," *Lynchnos* (1956), p. 185.

47. Charles Darwin, *The Variation of Animals and Plants under Domestication* (London, 1868), 2:431–432; Anon., "The Reign of Law," *Biblical Repertory and Princeton Review*, 42 (1870), 59–60; McCosh, *Ideas in Nature*, pp. 2–3; Anon., "The Origin and Antiquity of Man: Darwin, Huxley, and Lyell," *American Quarterly Church Review and*

Ecclesiastical Register, 17 (1865), 195, 189–190. See also Stearns, "Recent Questions," p. 481; Andrew P. Peabody, "Religion and Chemistry," *Bibliotheca Sacra*, 22 (1865), 450; Anon., "Modern Atheism," *Southern Review*, 10 (1872), 125; Anon., "Idea of God," pp. 253–254; [Atwater], "Herbert Spencer's Philosophy," p. 269; Augustus Hopkins Strong, "Materialistic Skepticism [1873]," *Philosophy and Religion: A Series of Addresses, Essays and Sermons Designed to Set Forth Great Truths in Popular Form* (New York, 1888), p. 31.

48. Not all religious thinkers were unmindful of the increasing popularity of the transmutation hypothesis within the scientific community. For example, one observer told readers of the *Independent* in 1871 that "Darwinism is spreading among all the younger scientists—and we might add among the older too—like the measles in a school." Anon., "Periodicals," *Independent*, March 16, 1871, p. 6. Such statements, however, were relatively rare in the early 1870s.

49. Asa Gray, "Species as to Variation, Geographical Distribution, and Succession [1863]," *Darwiniana: Essays and Reviews Pertaining to Darwinism*, ed. A. Hunter Dupree (1876; Cambridge, Mass., 1963), p. 164. See also Martin J. S. Rudwick, *The Meaning of Fossils: Episodes in the History of Palaeontology*, 2d ed. (New York, 1976), pp. 222, 226; David L. Hull, *Darwin and His Critics: The Reception of Darwin's Theory of Evolution by the Scientific Community* (Cambridge, Mass., 1973), pp. 15, 52, 74–75; Gillespie, *Charles Darwin*, pp. 19–36. Gillespie has suggested that American scientists, possibly because of the influence of Agassiz, were more willing than their English counterparts to consider special creations as miraculous (p. 162 n. 15).

50. James Dwight Dana, "Science and the Bible," *Bibliotheca Sacra*, 13 (1856), 124; Rice, "Darwinian Theory," pp. 608–609, 618; Huxley, "Mr. Darwin's Critics," p. 165. See also Rudwick, *Meaning of Fossils*, pp. 153–154; Gillespie, *Charles Darwin*, pp. 34–36. A valuable case study of changing views among one segment of the scientific community is Neal C. Gillespie, "Preparing for Darwin: Conchology and Natural Theology in Anglo-American Natural History," *Studies in History of Biology*, 7 (1984), 93–145, esp. pp. 114–135.

51. Charles Darwin, *The Expression of the Emotions in Man and Animals* (1872; New York, 1873), p. 12; Simon Newcomb, "Evolution and Theology. A Rejoinder," *North American Review*, 128 (1879), 660; John Tyndall, "Reply to the Critics of the Belfast Address," *Popular Science Monthly*, 6 (1875), 429; George F. Wright, "Recent Works Bearing on the Relation of Science to Religion. No. 2: The Divine Method of Producing Living Species," *Bibliotheca Sacra*, 38 (1876), 479–480; [Asa Gray], "Darwin on the Origin of Species," *Atlantic Monthly*, 6 (1860), 112–113; Thomas Huxley, "The Rise and Progress of Paleontology [1881]," *Huxley's Essays*, 4:44–45; [Thomas Huxley], "Professor Huxley's Lectures," *Popular Science Monthly*, 10 (1877), 296; [E. L. Youmans], "Evolution and the Copernican Theory," *Popular Science Monthly*, 10 (1876), 240; Hull, *Darwin and His Critics*, p. 51; Alvar Ellegård, "The Darwinian Theory and Nineteenth-Century Philosophies of Science," *Journal of the History of Ideas*, 18 (1957), 392; Darwin, *Descent of Man*, 1:31–32; Charles Darwin, *On the Origin of Species by Means of Natural Selection, or the Preservation of Favoured Races in the Struggle for Life* (1859; facsimile ed., Cambridge, Mass., 1964), pp. 413, 420, 453, 485–486; Darwin to Lyell, August 21 [1861], *MLD*, 1:194.

Frank M. Turner has linked demands for scientific explanation to the growing maturity and specialization of the scientific community. Frank M. Turner, "The Victorian Conflict between Science and Religion: A Professional Dimension," *Isis*, 69 (1978), 356–376, especially p. 364.

52. O. C. Marsh, "Notice of New Equine Mammals from the Tertiary Formation,"

American Journal of Science and Arts, 3d ser., 7 (1874), 247–258 (quotation is from p. 258); Huxley, "Rise and Progress of Paleontology," pp. 44, 39–42. See also [B. D. Walsh], quoted in "Gradation from 'Individual Peculiarities' to Species in Insects," *American Journal of Science and Arts*, 2d ser., 40 (1865), 282–283; [E. S. Morse], "Address by Professor E. S. Morse," American Association for the Advancement of Science, *Proceedings*, 25 (1877), 145–163; Rudwick, *Meaning of Fossils*, pp. 219–220, 246–252; O. C. Marsh, "Introduction and Succession of Vertebrate Life in North America," *Nature*, 16 (1877), 448–450, 470–472, 489–491.

53. Charles Kingsley to F. D. Maurice [1863], in *Charles Kingsley: His Letters and Memories of His Life*, ed. [Mrs. Fanny E. Kingsley] (London, 1877), 2:171; William North Rice, "Twenty-Five Years of Scientific Progress [1893]," *Twenty-Five Years of Scientific Progress and Other Essays* (New York, 1894), pp. 4, 52. See also Rudwick, *Meaning of Fossils*, pp. 237–238, 245, 255–258, 261; Peter J. Bowler, *Fossils and Progress: Paleontology and the Idea of Progressive Evolution in the Nineteenth Century* (New York, 1976), pp. 129–130.

Joseph Le Conte's conversion can be seen by comparing Joseph Le Conte, "Lectures on Coal," *Annual Report of the Board of Regents of the Smithsonian Institution* (Washington, D.C., 1858), p. 168, with Le Conte, *Religion and Science*, p. 23. Alexander Winchell's conversion can be seen by comparing Alexander Winchell, *Sketches of Creation: A Popular View of Some of the Grand Conclusions of the Sciences in Reference to the History of Matter and of Life* (New York, 1970), p. 321, with Winchell, "Huxley and Evolution," p. 295. For discussion of the conversion of a number of other American scientists to the evolutionary hypothesis, see Edward Justin Pfeifer, "The Reception of Darwinism in the United States, 1859–1880," Ph.D. diss., Brown University, 1957, pp. 87–89.

54. James D. Dana, *A Textbook of Geology*, 2d ed. (New York, 1874), pp. 260–263. For a more extensive discussion of Dana's conversion to evolution, see William F. Sanford, Jr., "Dana and Darwinism," *Journal of the History of Ideas*, 26 (1965), 531–546.

55. Theodore Gill, "On the Relations of the Order of Mammals," American Association for the Advancement of Science, *Proceedings*, 19 (1871), 267–270; David Starr Jordan, *The Days of a Man* (Yonkers, N.Y., 1922), 1:113–114; [Morse], "Address," p. 140; [Nathaniel Southgate Shaler], *The Autobiography of Nathaniel Southgate Shaler with a Supplementary Memoir by His Wife* (Boston, 1909), pp. 110–111, 181; Edward J. Pfeiffer, "United States," in Thomas F. Glick, ed., *The Comparative Reception of Darwinism* (Austin, 1974), p. 195. Detailed research on the pattern of conversion of British scientists to the transmutation hypothesis has shown that it is easy to overestimate the role of youth in accounting for receptivity to the hypothesis. David L. Hull, Peter O. Tessner, and Arthur M. Diamond, "Planck's Principle," *Science*, 202 (November 17, 1978), 722.

56. Louis Agassiz to Sir Philip De Grey Egerton, March 26, 1867, in *Louis Agassiz: His Life and Correspondence*, ed. Elizabeth Cary Agassiz (Boston, 1885), 2:647; Louis Agassiz, "Evolution and the Permanence of Type," *Atlantic Monthly*, 33 (1874), 94, 99–101.

57. J. W. Dawson, *The Story of the Earth and Man* (New York, 1873), pp. 317, 322–330, 339; J. W. Dawson, *Nature and the Bible* (New York, 1875), pp. 137, 142–145, 240; J. W. Dawson, *The Origin of the World, According to Revelation and Science* (New York, 1877), pp. 226–228. A valuable discussion of Dawson's life and thought is Charles F. O'Brien, *Sir William Dawson: A Life in Science and Religion* (Philadelphia, 1971), especially pp. 17–18, 99–144.

58. [J. Lawrence Smith], "Address," American Association for the Advancement of Science, *Proceedings*, 22 (1874), 12, 16. See also Robert Stebbins, "France," in Glick, ed., *Comparative Reception of Darwinism*, pp. 117–163; Yvette Conry, *L'introduction du Darwinisme en France au XIXe siècle* (Paris, 1974).

59. Gray's speech appears in Asa Gray, "Sequoia and Its History [1872]," *Darwiniana*, pp. 169–194, with minor changes (quotation on p. 193); Marsh, "Introduction and Succession of Vertebrate Life," p. 448. Equally indicative of the conversion of scientists to the transmutation hypothesis was the fact that Princeton was unable to find in America a biologist who was not an evolutionist and had to go elsewhere. William Hayes Ward, "Princeton College," *Independent*, 28 (June 29, 1876), 5.

60. Jordan, *Days of a Man*, 1:114; Thomas H. Huxley, "The Coming of Age of 'The Origin of Species' [1880]," *Huxley's Essays*, 2:229.

61. G. J. Romanes, "Conscience in Animals," *Popular Science Monthly*, 9 (1876), 80; Anon., "Science," *Atlantic Monthly*, 30 (1872), 508; Theodore Gill, "The Doctrine of Darwin," *Proceedings of the Biological Society of Washington, with the Address Read on the Occasion of the Darwin Memorial Meeting, May 12, 1882* (Washington, 1882), 1:69; Joseph Le Conte, "Man's Place in Nature," *Princeton Review*, 4th ser. (1878), pp. 787–788; [Henry Ware Holland], "Gray's *Darwiniana*," *Nation*, 23 (December 14, 1876), 358; H. W. Conn, *Evolution of To-Day* (New York, 1886), pp. 1–2, 240–241; Joseph Le Conte, "Evolution in Relation to Materialism," *Princeton Review*, n.s. 7 (1881), 150.

A list of Darwin's honors, including his numerous elections to scientific societies in America and elsewhere, can be found in *LLD*, App. 4, 3:373–376. Darwin himself believed that he had been instrumental in converting scientists to belief in the theory of evolution. Darwin to J. D. Hooker, July 28 [1868], *MLD*, 1:304.

62. Darwin realized that the critics of his work had convinced many scientists that his explanation of the evolutionary process was inadequate. In 1871 he expressed concern to T. H. Huxley that "the pendulum is now swinging against our side." Darwin to Huxley, September 21 [1871], *LLD*, 3:148. Though he had often declared that he was more interested in replacing the "dogma of special creation" with transmutation than in establishing his own particular explanation of how the latter had occurred, he was hardly willing to acquiesce in assaults on his position. Darwin, *Descent of Man*, 1:153. Accordingly, in the last two editions of the *Origin of Species*, published in 1869 and 1872, Darwin responded to the major objections advanced against his theory. A number of secondary accounts deal with these responses and the revisions that Darwin himself made in his theory. These include Peter J. Vorzimmer, *Charles Darwin: The Years of Controversy: The Origin of Species and Its Critics, 1859–1882* (Philadelphia, 1970); Moore, *Post-Darwinian Controversies*, pp. 125–152; Joe D. Burchfield, "Darwin and the Dilemma of Geological Time," *Isis*, 65 (1974), 301–321; Hull, *Darwin and His Critics*.

63. A. S. Packard, Jr., "Rapid as Well as Slow Evolution," *Independent*, 29 (August 23, 1877), 6. Useful discussions of American neo-Lamarckianism include Edward J. Pfeiffer, "The Genesis of American Neo-Lamarckianism," *Isis*, 56 (1965), 156–167; Alpheus S. Packard, *Lamarck the Founder of Evolution: His Life and Work* (New York, 1901), pp. 382–424; Peter J. Bowler, *The Eclipse of Darwinism: Anti-Darwinian Evolution Theories in the Decades around 1900* (Baltimore, 1983), pp. 118–140.

64. Ernst Mayr, "The Nature of the Darwinian Revolution," *Science*, 176 (June 2, 1972), 988; Rudwick, *Meaning of Fossils*, pp. 255, 260–261; Bowler, *Eclipse of Darwinism*.

65. Anon., Review of Schmid's "The Theories of Darwin," *New Englander*, n.s. 6

(1883), 275. See also Peabody, "Bearing of Modern Scientific Theories," p. 715; Burrit A. Smith, "Evolutionism versus Theism," New Englander, 33 (1874), 92; Anon., "Some Thoughts on Evolution," *Independent*, 28 (September 21, 1876), 16; Frederic Gardiner, "The Bearing of Recent Scientific Thought upon Theology," *Bibliotheca Sacra*, 35 (1878), 66; Anon., Review of *Reconciliation of Science and Religion*, by Alexander Winchell, *Methodist Quarterly Review*, 4th ser., 29 (1877), 751; George Frederick Wright, "Recent Works Bearing on the Relation of Science to Religion. No. 5: Some Analogies between Calvinism and Darwinism," *Bibliotheca Sacra*, 37 (1880), 50; William Hayes Ward, "Whether It Is Right to Study the Bible," *Independent*, 32 (February 26, 1880), 4; J. A. Clutz, "Goldwin Smith on the Decay of Faith," *Lutheran Quarterly*, n.s. 9 (1880), 262.

Chapter 4. "Put on the Whole Armor of God"

1. E. Nisbet, *The Science of the Day and Genesis* (Rochester, N.Y., 1886), pp. 67–73. See also Benjamin Tefft, *Evolution and Christianity* (Boston, 1885), pp. 239–240; Luther Tracy Townsend, *Evolution or Creation: A Critical Review of the Scientific and Scriptural Theories of Creation and Certain Related Subjects* (New York, 1896), p. 75; Robert Patterson, *The Errors of Evolution: An Examination of the Nebular Theory, Geological Evolution, the Origin of Life, and Darwinism*, ed. H. L. Hastings (Boston, 1885), pp. 213–215.

2. John Moore, "Science against Darwinism," *Universalist Quarterly and General Review*, n.s. 15 (1878), 187–188; Thomas Hill, "Geometry and Biology," *Unitarian Review and Religious Magazine*, 9 (1878), 149; W. D. Wilson, "The Recent and Supernatural Origin of Man, Considered from a Purely Scientific Point of View," *American Church Review*, 42 (1883), 543–544. See also S. E. Shepard, "Animal Life," *Christian Quarterly*, 8 (1876), 469–470, 473, 477; Clark Braden, *The Problem of Problems, and Its Various Solutions; or, Atheism, Darwinism, and Theism* (Cincinnati, 1876), pp. 146, 163–169.

3. R. L. Dabney, *The Sensualistic Philosophy of the Nineteenth Century* (New York, 1876), pp. 195–197; Anon., Review of *The Origin of the World According to Revelation and Science*, by J. W. Dawson, *Methodist Quarterly Review*, 4th ser., 30 (1878), 370.

4. L. Curtis, "Relation of Evolution to Christianity and Rational Truth," *New Englander*, 39 (1880), 670, 667–668; Dabney, *Sensualistic Philosophy*, p. 183.

5. Curtis, "Relation of Evolution," pp. 670, 667–668; Ransom B. Welch, *Faith and Modern Thought* (New York, 1876), p. 96; Samuel Porter, "Is Thought Possible without Language? Case of a Deaf-Mute," *Princeton Review*, n.s. 7 (1881), 127; Samuel Z. Beam, "Evolution a Failure," *Reformed Quarterly Review*, 35 (1888), 506. See also Moore, "Science against Darwinism," pp. 195–196.

6. Moore, "Science against Darwinism," pp. 195–196; J. H. McIlvaine, "Evolution in Relation to Species," *Presbyterian Review*, 1 (1880), 627.

7. L. T. Townsend, *Bible Theology and Modern Thought* (1882: Boston, 1883), p. 271. See also Patterson, *Errors of Evolution*, p. 266; Townsend, *Evolution or Creation*, p. 44; W. J. Wright, "A Generation of Darwinism," *Presbyterian Quarterly*, 7 (1883), 236–237.

8. Enoch Fitch Burr, *Ecce Terra; or, The Hand of God in the Earth* (Philadelphia, 1883), pp. 166–167. See also Braden, *Problem of Problems*, pp. 164–165, 311.

9. Shepard, "Animal Life," pp. 468–469; Thomas Hill, "Creation Is Revelation," *Unitarian Review*, 30 (1888), 3; Thomas Hill, "Organic Forms," *Bibliotheca Sacra*, 36

(1879), 21–22; Hill, "Geometry and Biology," pp. 149, 157; Curtis, "Relation of Evolution," p. 665. See also Braden, *Problem of Problems*, pp. 185–186, 188.

10. William G. T. Shedd, *Dogmatic Theology* (New York, 1888), 1:503; W. E. Hamilton, "Recent Ethical Theory," *Presbyterian Review*, 3 (1882), 465; D. S. Gregory, "Is Evolution Science?" *Independent*, 32 (May 27, 1880), 2–3; John A. Earnest, "Evolution and the Scriptures," *Lutheran Quarterly*, n.s. 12 (1882), 101.

11. Moore, "Science against Darwinism," p. 186; McIlvaine, "Evolution in Relation," p. 613. See also Charles F. Deems, "Is There Any Theory of Evolution Proven?" *Homiletic Monthly*, 8 (1884), 709; Townsend, *Evolution or Creation*, pp. 88–94.

12. George Ticknor Curtis, *Creation or Evolution? A Philosophical Inquiry* (New York, 1887), pp. 22–23, ix. See also C[arl] B. F[ish], "Curtis, George Ticknor," *Dictionary of American Biography*, 4:613–614.

13. McIlvaine, "Evolution in Relation," pp. 621–622. See also J. B. Drury, "Darwinism," *Scribner's Monthly*, 10 (1875), 351.

14. Curtis, *Creation or Evolution?* pp. 127–128; Drury, "Darwinism," pp. 351, 359; Curtis, "Relation of Evolution," pp. 664–665; John P. Gulliver, "A Symposium on Evolution: Is the Darwinian Theory of Evolution Reconcilable with the Bible? If So, with What Limitations?" *Homiletic Monthly*, 8 (1884), 595–596. See also Burr, *Ecce Terra*, pp. 40–41.

15. Gregory, "Is Evolution Science?" p. 2; Gulliver, "Symposium on Evolution," pp. 595–596; Thomas Hill, "Charles Darwin," *Unitarian Review*, 29 (1888), 391–392.

16. F. A. P. Barnard, "The Law of Disease," *College Courant*, 14 (January 17, 1874), 27.

17. Deems, "Is There Any Theory," p. 715; S. A. Gardner, "Theology and Science," *Universalist Quarterly and General Review*, n.s. 20 (1883), 188. See also Braden, *Problem of Problems*, p. 214.

18. Noah Porter, "The Collapse of Faith," *Princeton Review*, n.s. 9 (1882), 164–165; Francis Patton, "Evolution and Apologetics," *Presbyterian Review*, 6 (1885), 140. See also M. E. Dwight, "The Contest As It Is To-Day," *New Englander*, n.s. 7 (1884), 584. Henry King Carroll, who served as director of the Division of Churches for the 1890 census, estimated that "one out of every twelve persons is either an active or passive opponent of religion." H. K. Carroll, *The Religious Forces of the United States, Enumerated, Classified, and Described on the Basis of the Government Census of 1890*, rev. ed. (New York, 1896), p. xxvi. For a perceptive discussion of faith and doubt in late-nineteenth-century America, see D. H. Meyer, "American Intellectuals and the Victorian Crisis of Faith," in Daniel Walker Howe, ed., *Victorian America* (Philadelphia, 1976), pp. 59–77.

19. Archibald A. Hodge, Introduction, in Joseph S. Van Dyke, *Theism and Evolution: An Examination of Modern Speculative Theories as Related to Theistic Conceptions of the Universe*, 2d ed. (New York, 1886), pp. xvii–xviii; Francis Bowen, "Malthusianism, Darwinism, and Pessimism," *North American Review*, 129 (1879), 463; Tefft, *Evolution and Christianity*, pp. 6, 9; L. J. Livermore, "What Is Darwinism?" *Unitarian Review and Religious Magazine*, 3 (1875), 240–241. See also Wright, "Generation of Darwinism," pp. 224, 231, 233, 236; Gardner, "Theology and Science," p. 185; George B. Cheever, "The Philosophy of Evolution," *Presbyterian Quarterly and Princeton Review*, n.s. 4 (1875), 130; Earnest, "Evolution and the Scriptures," pp. 94–95. Those who cited Darwin's own disavowals of design include ibid., p. 105; Wright, "Generation of Darwinism," p. 234.

20. Benjamin B. Warfield, "Charles Darwin's Religious Life: A Sketch in Spiritual Biography," *Presbyterian Review*, 9 (1888), 578, 575. See also B. B. Warfield, "Darwin's Arguments against Christianity and against Religion," *Homiletic Review*, 17 (1889), 15–16; G. Macloskie, Review of *Life and Letters of Charles Darwin*, by Francis Darwin, *Presbyterian Review*, 9 (1888), 521; J. William Dawson, *Modern Ideas of Evolution as Related to Revelation and Science*, 2d ed. (New York, 1890), p. 12. A useful discussion of Warfield's theological position is Samuel G. Craig, "Benjamin B. Warfield," in Benjamin Breckinridge Warfield, *Biblical and Theological Studies*, ed. Samuel G. Craig (Philadelphia, 1952), pp. xi–xlviii. In the period after 1900, Warfield was more insistent in claiming that the transmutation hypothesis could be reconciled with theism, though he continued to believe that it was inconsistent with several features of the biblical narrative concerning human creation. Deryl Freeman Johnson, "The Attitudes of the Princeton Theologians toward Darwinism and Evolution from 1859–1929," Ph.D. diss., University of Iowa, 1968, pp. 235–242.

21. Anon., Review of *What Is Darwinism?* by Charles Hodge, *Methodist Quarterly Review*, 4th ser., 34 (1882), 591; Wright, "Generation of Darwinism," pp. 223, 234–236.

22. John T. Duffield, "Evolutionism, Respecting Man and the Bible," *Princeton Review*, 4th ser. (1878), pp. 173–174; Earnest, "Evolution and the Scriptures," pp. 101–105 (quotations on pp. 105 and 102–103).

23. Jacob Todd, "A Common Basis of Knowledge for Science and Religion," *Methodist Quarterly Review*, 4th ser., 37 (1875), 27; J. MacBride Sterrett, "Apologetics—Its Proper Attitude at the Present Time," *American Church Review*, 43 (1884), 143, 141. See also Drury, "Darwinism," p. 359; Dwight, "Contest," p. 588; T. De Witt Talmage, *Sermons: 2nd Series* (New York, 1875), pp. 60–61.

24. George W. Samson, "Modern Evolution Theories," *Baptist Quarterly*, 11 (1877), 148. See also Dwight, "Contest," p. 588.

25. Joseph Haven, "Place and Value of Miracles in the Christian System," *Bibliotheca Sacra*, 19 (1862), 339; Leonard Woods, "Divine Agency and Government, Together with Human Agency and Freedom," *American Biblical Repository*, 2d ser., 12 (1844), 411–413; Charles Hodge, *Systematic Theology* (New York, 1872–73), 1:600, 575, 579–580, 595–597, 621, 690. See also Henry Ware, *An Inquiry into the Foundations, Evidences, and Truths of Religion* (Cambridge, 1842), pp. 157–158, 169–170, 250; S. W. Culver, "The Natural and the Supernatural—How Distinguished and How Related," *Baptist Quarterly*, 7 (1873), 362–369; George H. Daniels, *American Science in the Age of Jackson* (New York, 1968), pp. 145, 194; [Robert L. Dabney], "Geology and the Bible," *Southern Presbyterian Review*, 14 (1861), 271–272; C. H. Hitchcock, "The Relations of Geology to Theology," *Bibliotheca Sacra*, 24 (1867), 475; John Harris, *The Pre-Adamite Earth: Contributions to Theological Science* (Boston, 1849), pp. 100–101; [Samuel John Baird], "The Providential Government of God," *Biblical Repertory and Princeton Review*, 42 (1870), 76; E. Nisbet, "Darwinism," *Baptist Quarterly*, 7 (1873), 218–223; James McCosh, *The Method of the Divine Government, Physical and Moral* (New York, 1851), pp. 191–193, 204, 222–225; Curtis, *Creation or Evolution?* p. 128; Anon., "The Nebular Hypothesis," *Southern Quarterly Review*, 28 (1856), 115–116; [Albert Baldwin Dod], "Vestiges of the Natural History of Creation," *Biblical Repertory and Princeton Review*, 17 (1845), 553; [Lyman Atwater], "The Positive Philosophy of Auguste Comte," *Biblical Repertory and Princeton Review*, 28 (1856), 61, 87; Jaroslav Pelikan, "Creation and Causality in the History of Christian Thought," in Sol Tax and Charles Callender, eds., *Evolution after Darwin* (Chicago, 1960), 3:38–39; William W.

Patton, "The Tendency of Scientific Men to Skepticism," *Methodist Quarterly Review*, 4th ser., 14 (1862), 552–553.

For scientists' view of the immanence of power in matter, see P. M. Heimann and J. E. McGuire, "Newtonian Forces and Lockean Powers: Concepts of Matter in Eighteenth-Century Thought," *Historical Studies in the Physical Sciences*, 3 (1971), 233–306, esp. 235–236, 305; P. M. Heimann, "Voluntarism and Immanence: Conceptions of Nature in Eighteenth-Century Thought," *Journal of the History of Ideas*, 39 (1978), 271–283; Richard Westfall, *Science and Religion in Seventeenth-Century England* (New Haven, 1958), pp. 75–105; Alexandre Koyré, *Newtonian Studies* (Chicago, 1965), pp. 144, 155–163; J. E. McGuire, "Boyle's Conception of Nature," *Journal of the History of Ideas*, 33 (1972), 530–531; Ernan McMullen, *Newton on Matter and Activity* (Notre Dame, 1978), pp. 119–121; Dov Ospovat, *The Development of Darwin's Theory: Natural History, Natural Theology, and Natural Selection* (Cambridge, 1981), pp. 20–21; Charles Darwin, *On the Origin of Species by Means of Natural Selection, or the Preservation of Favoured Races in the Struggle for Life* (1859; facsimile ed., Cambridge, Mass., 1964), p. 488.

26. John Bascom, "The Natural Theology of Social Science," *Bibliotheca Sacra*, 25 (1868), 270; John E. Todd, "New Theology," *Bibliotheca Sacra*, 43 (1886), 353. See also D. E. Frierson, "Professor Drummond's Apology to Scientists," *Presbyterian Quarterly*, 2 (1888), 479.

27. Duffield, "Evolutionism," pp. 171–173; Anon., Review of *What Is Darwinism?* by Charles Hodge [1882], p. 592; Wright, "Generation of Darwinism," p. 241.

28. Drury, "Darwinism," pp. 359–360; F. D. Hoskins, "Evolution and the Christian Doctrine of the Fall," *American Church Review* (1881), p. 33; Tefft, *Evolution and Christianity*, p. 9; Braden, *Problem of Problems*, pp. 106, 108; Cheever, "Philosophy of Evolution," p. 130; Wright, "Generation of Darwinism," pp. 233–234, 238; Miner Raymond, *Systematic Theology* (Cincinnati, 1877), 1:296–297; John Pindar Bland, "Some Implications of the Philosophy of Evolution," *Unitarian Review and Religious Magazine*, 3 (1875), 585–586.

29. Jesse B. Thomas, "Symposium on Evolution," p. 533. See also Curtis, "Relation of Evolution," p. 654; Joseph T. Duryea, "Symposium on Evolution," p. 284; Dawson, *Modern Ideas of Evolution*, pp. 28–29; Braden, *Problem of Problems*, p. 110; E. James, "Pantheism," *New Englander*, 42 (1883), 639; A. A. H[odge], Review of *Natural Science and Religion*, by Asa Gray, *Presbyterian Review*, 1 (1880), 588; Robert Young, "The Historiographic and Ideological Contexts of the Nineteenth-Century Debate on Man's Place in Nature," in Mikuláš Teich and Robert Young, eds., *Changing Perspectives in the History of Science: Essays in Honor of Joseph Needham* (London, 1973), p. 367.

30. J. M. Buckley, "Symposium on Evolution," pp. 645–646; Duffield, "Evolutionism," pp. 156, 159–160, 173–175; Anon., "Agassiz on Provinces of Creation and the Unity of the Race," *Biblical Repertory and Princeton Review*, 41 (1869), 6. See also Lyman Atwater, "Evolution and Supernaturalism," *Independent*, 32 (March 11, 1880), 4; A. A. Hodge, *Outlines of Theology* (New York, 1878), p. 296; T. De Witt Talmage, *Live Coals; or, Truths That Burn*, collated by Lydia D. White (Chicago, 1886), p. 255; Francis L. Patton, "Symposium on Evolution," p. 410; Duryea, "Symposium on Evolution," p. 287; George D. Armstrong, "The Word of God versus the Bible of Modern Scientific Theology," *Presbyterian Quarterly*, 2 (1888), 46–48; Hodge, *Systematic Theology*, 2:2.

31. Mark Hopkins, *The Scriptural Idea of Man: Six Lectures Given before the Theological Students at Princeton* (New York, 1883), p. 98; [Charles Hodge], "Can God Be

Known?" *Biblical Repertory and Princeton Review*, 36 (1864), 145. See also Charles Hodge, *What Is Darwinism?* (New York, 1874), p. 5.

32. D. D. Wheedon, "Prayer and Science," *Methodist Quarterly Review*, 4th ser., 36 (1884), p. 9; E. P. Barrows, "Revelation and Inspiration," *Bibliotheca Sacra*, 25 (1868), 334–335. See also Hopkins, *Scriptural Idea of Man*, p. 1.

33. Duffield, "Evolutionism," pp. 166, 175; Noah Porter, "Force, Law, and Design," *Princeton Review*, 4th ser. (1879), p. 485; Porter, "Is Thought Possible?" p. 128; Bland, "Some Implications," p. 578. See also Dabney, *Sensualistic Philosophy*, pp. 180–181, 202; W. Streissguth, "Modern Materialism Viewed from a Scientific-Religious Standpoint," *Quarterly Review of the Evangelical Lutheran Church*, n.s. 5 (1875), 397; Hopkins, *Scriptural Idea of Man*, pp. 1, 98, 103, 125; Edward Thomson, "The Image of God," *Methodist Review*, 5th ser., 4 (1888), 723–724.

34. Bland, "Some Implications," p. 578; Anon., "The Religion of Today," *North American Review*, 129 (1879), 564; Darwin to W. Graham, July 3, 1881, in *The Life and Letters of Charles Darwin, Including an Autobiographical Chapter*, ed. Francis Darwin (London, 1887), 1:316; Warfield, "Darwin's Religious Life," p. 591; Dawson, *Modern Ideas of Evolution*, pp. 13–14. See also Dwight, "Contest," p. 584; Macloskie, Review of *Life and Letters of Charles Darwin*, p. 521.

35. Noah Porter, "Seek First the Kingdom of God [1881]," *Fifteen Years in the Chapel of Yale College* (New York, 1888), p. 280; Noah Porter, "Darwin's Theory of Knowledge vs. His Theory of Evolution," *New Englander and Yale Review*, n.s. 12 (1888), 205.

36. Noah Porter, *Evolution: A Lecture before the Nineteenth Century Club, May 25, 1886* (New York, 1886), pp. 6, 20–21; Porter, "Darwin's Theory of Knowledge," p. 208; Porter, "Force, Law, and Design," pp. 485–486.

37. George S. Morris, "The Immortality of the Human Soul," *Bibliotheca Sacra*, 33 (1876), 711; H[odge], Review of *Natural Science*, p. 588; Bland, "Some Implications," pp. 584–586; Hamilton, "Recent Ethical Theory," pp. 471–472. See also John Bascom, "The Synthetic or Cosmic Philosophy," *Bibliotheca Sacra*, 33 (1876), 622–623, 627–628; Curtis, *Creation or Evolution?* pp. 14, 61–64, 78–80; Braden, *Problem of Problems*, pp. 175–176, 183; W. H. Wynn, "The Religion of Evolution as against the Religion of Jesus," *Lutheran Quarterly*, n.s. 12 (1882), 11–12. A perceptive brief discussion of the tendency of the "revivalist tradition" to think in terms of dichotomies can be found in George M. Marsden, *Fundamentalism and American Culture: The Shaping of Twentieth-Century Evangelicalism, 1870–1925* (New York, 1980), pp. 224–225. The dualism embraced by Unitarians has been noted in Daniel Walker Howe, *The Unitarian Conscience: Harvard Moral Philosophy, 1805–1861* (Cambridge, Mass., 1970), pp. 40–44.

38. Patton, "Evolution and Apologetics," pp. 143–144; Drury, "Darwinism," p. 360; Raymond, *Systematic Theology*, 2:15–16; Cyrus Cort, "The Evolution Heresy in Modern Theology," *Reformed Quarterly Review*, 36 (1889), 487–490; Anon., "God and Moral Obligation," *Southern Presbyterian Review*, 29 (1878), 330. For a valuable discussion of the various positions American Protestant thinkers took with regard to the Fall, see H. Shelton Smith, *Changing Conceptions of Original Sin: A Study in American Theology since 1750* (New York, 1955).

39. Charles Darwin, *The Descent of Man, and Selection in Relation to Sex* (London, 1871), 1:177, 181, 134–135, 184; George A. Armstrong, quoted in John B. Adger, *My Life and Times, 1810–99* (Richmond, 1899), p. 546. See also Earnest, "Evolution and the Scriptures," pp. 103–104; Duryea, "Symposium on Evolution," p. 288; Hamilton, "Recent Ethical Theory," pp. 470–471.

40. Duffield, "Evolutionism," p. 152. For a brief discussion of Duffield's career, see Thomas Jefferson Wertenbaker, *Princeton, 1746–1896* (Princeton, 1946), p. 261, and Anon., "Duffield, John Thomas," *Appleton's Cyclopedia of American Biography*, 2:249.

41. Duffield, "Evolutionism," pp. 164–167, 172–173.

42. Hoskins, "Evolution and the Christian Doctrine," pp. 27, 33–35.

43. Ibid., pp. 35–36; J. W. Dawson, *The Story of the Earth and Man* (New York, 1973), p. 372; Mark Hopkins, "Personality and Law—the Duke of Argyll," *Princeton Review*, n.s. 10 (1882), 194–195. See also Henry Colman, "Pre-Adamites," *Methodist Review*, 5th ser., 7 (1891), 894–896, 902; Maurice Mandelbaum, *History, Man, and Reason: A Study in Nineteenth-Century Thought* (Baltimore, 1971), pp. 96–100. As a number of historians have noted, it would be an error to ascribe belief in social evolution solely to commitment to the theory of organic evolution. Anthropology provided a number of independent insights into the early history of mankind. See, for example, ibid., pp. 93–94; J. W. Burrow, *Evolution and Society: A Study in Victorian Social Theory* (Cambridge, 1966).

For an insightful discussion of "degenerationism" in nineteenth-century Great Britain, see Neal C. Gillespie, "The Duke of Argyll, Evolutionary Anthropology, and the Art of Scientific Controversy," *Isis*, 68 (1977), 40–54. The popularity of this position in the United States requires much more investigation than historians have thus far given it.

44. J. W. Dawson, *The Origin of the World, According to Revelation and Science* (New York, 1877), pp. 238–239; Hoskins,"Evolution and the Christian Doctrine," p. 35. See also John W. Dawson, "Points of Contact between Science and Revelation," *Princeton Review*, 4th ser. (1879), 584.

45. John Bascom, "Atheism in Colleges," *North American Review*, 132 (1881), 37; [Dabney], "Geology and the Bible," p. 274. See also Merle Curti and Vernon Carstensen, *The University of Wisconsin: A History, 1848–1925* (Madison, 1949), pp. 246–295; D. H. Meyer, *The Instructed Conscience: The Shaping of the American National Ethic* (Philadelphia, 1972), pp. 3–11; E. Brooks Holifield, *The Gentlemen Theologians: American Theology in Southern Culture, 1795–1860* (Durham, N.C., 1978), pp. 127, 138; Conrad Cherry, *Nature and Religious Imagination: From Edwards to Bushnell* (Philadelphia, 1980), pp. 119–125 and passim.

46. Meyer, *Instructed Conscience*, esp. pp. 19–20, 47, 49–50, 90–95, 140; Howe, *Unitarian Conscience*, pp. 49–56, 135–136; William G. McLoughlin, ed., *The American Evangelicals, 1800–1860* (New York, 1968), pp. 2–4; Wilson Smith, *Professors and Public Ethics: Studies of Northern Philosophers before the Civil War* (Ithaca, N.Y., 1956), pp. 28–43. A work that puts discussions of morality at the center of nineteenth-century American Protestant thought is James Turner, *Without God, Without Creed: The Origins of Unbelief in America* (Baltimore, 1985).

47. Darwin, *Descent of Man*, 1:106, 97–98, 73, 162.

48. Herbert Spencer, "Morals and Moral Sentiments," *Fortnightly Review*, 15 (1871), 419–432. The most comprehensive survey of various systems of "evolutionary ethics" with which I am familiar is still William F. Quillian, Jr., *The Moral Theory of Evolutionary Naturalism* (New Haven, 1945), esp. pp. 1–72. My discussion of Spencer's ethical philosophy is indebted to this work.

49. Herbert Spencer, *The Data of Ethics* (London, 1879), pp. 55, 123, iv, 30, 32, 38–40.

50. Ibid., pp. 25, 27, 281, 13–15, 261.

51. Ibid., pp. 40, 13–20 (quotation on p. 20), 114, 25. See also J. D. Y. Peel, *Herbert Spencer: The Evolution of a Sociologist* (London, 1971), pp. 149–152.

52. Spencer, *Data of Ethics*, pp. 120–129; Herbert Spencer, *An Autobiography* (New York, 1904), 2:545–547.

53. McIlvaine, "Evolution in Relation," p. 627; Van Dyke, *Theism and Evolution*, pp. 87–88; Drury, "Darwinism," p. 360. See also F. L. Patton, Review of *The Science of Ethics*, by Leslie Stephen, *Presbyterian Review*, 4 (1883), 216; Smith, *Professors and Public Ethics*, pp. 63–64, 204.

54. Bascom, "Synthetic or Cosmic Philosophy," pp. 648–649; V. D. Davis, "Herbert Spencer's Theory of Morals," *Unitarian Review and Religious Magazine*, 20 (1883), 51–56 (quotation on p. 56); [Francis Patton], *Addresses at the Induction of Rev. Francis L. Patton into "The Cyrus H. McCormick Professorship of Didactic and Polemic Theology," in the Presbyterian Theological Seminary of the North-west* (Chicago, 1873), pp. 28–29; George B. Stevens, "The Authority of Faith," *New Englander*, n.s. 4 (1881), 436; Henry T. Steele, "Scientific Ethics," *New Englander*, n.s. 7 (1884), 174; Moore, "Science against Darwinism," p. 196; Hamilton, "Recent Ethical Theory," p. 470.

55. C. A. Stork, "Notes on Some Postulates of the New Ethics," *Lutheran Quarterly*, n.s. 11 (1881), 51–52, 45–46; T. B. Stork, "The Ethics of Herbert Spencer," *Lutheran Quarterly*, 30 (1900), 4; Porter, "Christianity an Ethical Force [1875]," *Fifteen Years*, p. 148. See also D. M. Hodge, "Ethics and Evolution," *Universalist Quarterly and General Review*, n.s. 17 (1880), 186.

56. Steele, "Scientific Ethics," pp. 171–174 (quotation on p. 171); Stork, "Notes on Some Postulates," pp. 45–46, 51. See also Braden, *Problem of Problems*, pp. 184, 186, 398–400.

57. Drury, "Darwinism," p. 360; Porter, "The Light of the World [1878]," *Fifteen Years*, p. 214; Stork, "Ethics of Herbert Spencer," pp. 17–18; Duryea, "Symposium on Evolution," p. 288. See also Anon., "The Data of Ethics," *New Englander*, n.s. 6 (1883), 838; Talmage, *Live Coals*, p. 273; Tefft, *Evolution and Christianity*, pp. 471, 477–478; Bland, "Some Implications," p. 586.

Chapter 5. "Canst Thou by Searching Find Out God?"

1. John B. Drury, *Truths and Untruths of Evolution* (New York, 1876), pp. 3, 13, 20–21, 30. Cf. J. B. Drury, "Darwinism," *Scribner's Monthly*, 10 (1875), 348–360. Even before 1875, a number of American Protestants had argued that Christianity and the theory of organic evolution were not in principle irreconcilable. See, for example, E. P. Barrows, "Revelation and Inspiration," *Bibliotheca Sacra*, 25 (1868), 323; Anon., "Synopsis of the Quarterlies and Others of the Higher Periodicals," *Methodist Quarterly Review*, 4th ser., 20 (1868), 124; Samuel Adams, "Darwinism," *Congregational Review*, 11 (1871), 359–360; Charles E. Hamlin, "The Attitude of the Christian Teacher in Respect of Science," *Baptist Quarterly*, 6 (1872), 23.

2. Alexander Winchell, *The Doctrine of Evolution: Its Data, Its Principles, Its Speculations, and Its Theistic Bearings* (New York, 1874), pp. 111–112. See also Anon., "Some Thoughts on Evolution," *Independent*, 28 (September 21, 1866), 16; David N. Beach, "The Reconstruction of Theology," *Bibliotheca Sacra*, 54 (1897), 121; William Newton Clarke, *An Outline of Christian Theology* (New York, 1898), pp. 51–52; S. R. Calthrop, "Religion and Science," *Unitarian Review and Religious Magazine*, 3 (1874), 313; W. S. Bean, "The Outlook of Modern Science," *Southern Presbyterian Review*, 25 (1874), 335;

[Daniel Curry], "About Evolution," *Methodist Review*, 5th ser., 1 (1885), 285; T. T. Munger, "Evolution and the Faith," *Century Magazine*, n.s. 10 (1886), 109; J. H. Rylance, "Theological Re-Adjustments," *North American Review*, 138 (1884), 47; Lyman Abbott, *The Theology of an Evolutionist* (Boston, 1897), pp. 7–8.

The literature on the growing deference of Americans to scientific expertise is enormous but unsystematic. See, for example, George H. Daniels, *American Science in the Age of Jackson* (New York, 1968), pp. 34–36; Sally Gregory Kohlstedt, *The Formation of the American Scientific Community: The American Association for the Advancement of Science, 1848–1860* (Urbana, 1976), pp. 17–21 and passim; both the Introduction and the essays in Thomas L. Haskell, ed., *The Authority of Experts: Studies in History and Theory* (Bloomington, Ind., 1985); Alexandra Oleson and John Voss, eds., *The Organization of Knowledge in Modern America* (Baltimore, 1979); and James Turner, *Without God, Without Creed: The Origins of Unbelief in America* (Baltimore, 1985), esp. pp. 121–124, 133–140, 189–192, 201–202, 213–214, 240–241.

George M. Marsden has suggested that one of the important factors enabling many Protestants to accept the tenets of modern thought was a commitment to a philosophical tradition that viewed "perception as an interpretive process." This perspective enabled them, Marsden argues, to remain "more open to speculative theories" such as the theory of evolution. George M. Marsden, *Fundamentalism and American Culture: The Shaping of Twentieth-Century Evangelicalism, 1870–1925* (New York, 1980), p. 215. Though I would not discount altogether the importance of this factor in prompting many Protestants to countenance the theory of organic evolution, my reading of the sources has convinced me that the most important consideration underlying the more favorable view of the theory within the American Protestant intellectual community was the conviction that the problem of speciation was preeminently a scientific issue that was to be determined by the scientific community. I should hasten to add, however, that Protestants typically continued jealously to assert the right to draw the appropriate philosophical and religious inferences from the transmutation hypothesis and other scientific theories.

3. C. W. Ernst, "St. George Mivart's 'Contemporary Evolution,' " *Unitarian Review and Religious Magazine*, 7 (1877), 15; George F. Moore, "The Modern Historical Movement and Christian Faith," *Andover Review*, 10 (1888), 333; F[rancis] A[lbert] C[hristie], "Bixby, James Thompson," *Dictionary of American Biography*, 2: 306–307 (hereafter cited as *DAB*).

4. James T. Bixby, *Similarities of Physical and Religious Knowledge* (New York, 1876), pp. 10–11, 73; James T. Bixby, "Cook's Biology," *Unitarian Review and Religious Magazine*, 9 (1878), 72.

5. George P. Fisher, "The Alleged Conflict of Natural Science and Religion," *Princeton Review*, n.s. 12 (1883), 34; Anon., "Do Our Colleges Teach Evolution?" *Independent*, 31 (December 18, 1879), 15; Alexander Winchell, "Huxley and Evolution," *Methodist Quarterly Review*, 4th ser., 29 (1877), 295. See also James McCosh, "A Symposium on Evolution: Is the Darwinian Theory of Evolution Reconcilable with the Bible? If So, with What Limitations?" *Homiletic Monthly*, 8 (1884), 230; Myron Adams, *The Continuous Creation: An Application of the Evolutionary Philosophy to the Christian Religion* (Boston, 1889), pp. 40–41; Gideon J. Burton, "What Should Be the Attitude of the Church towards Evolution as a Working Theory of the Universe?" *Christian Literature*, 13 (1895), 125; Munger, "Evolution and the Faith," p. 108.

6. Newman Smyth, *Old Faiths in New Light*, 2d ed. (New York, 1879), pp. 24, 28. See also Munger, "Evolution and the Faith," pp. 108–109.

7. S. R. Calthrop, "Religion and Evolution," *Religious Magazine and Monthly Review*, 50 (1873), 206; Anon., Review of *Life and Letters of Charles Darwin*, ed. Francis Darwin, *Bibliotheca Sacra*, 45 (1888), 370; McCosh, "Symposium on Evolution," p. 232. See also Borden P. Bowne, *Studies in Theism* (New York, 1879), p. 147; F. A. Mansfield, "Teleology, Old and New," *New Englander*, n.s. 7 (1884), 213; J. M. Whiton, "Darwin and Darwinism," *New Englander*, n.s. 6 (1883), 54; Anon., "Do Our Colleges Teach Evolution?" pp. 14–15; Joseph Le Conte, "Evolution in Relation to Materialism," *Princeton Review*, n.s. 7 (1881), 153–154, 159–160; Ernst, "St. George Mivart's 'Contemporary Evolution,' " p. 18; George T. Ladd, "The Concept of God as the Ground of Progress," *Bibliotheca Sacra*, 36 (1878), 643–646; Lewis French Stearns, *The Evidence of Christian Experience* (New York, 1890), p. 74.

8. George Frederick Wright, "Recent Works Bearing on the Relation of Science to Religion. No. 4: Concerning the True Doctrine of Final Cause or Design in Nature," *Bibliotheca Sacra*, 34 (1877), 357, 359, 363; George P. Fisher, *Faith and Rationalism with Short Supplementary Essays on Related Topics* (New York, 1879), pp. 107–112; James McCosh, *The Religious Aspect of Evolution*, 2d ed. (New York, 1890), p. 38; Anon., "Some Thoughts on Evolution," p. 16; George W. Samson, "Modern Evolution Theories," *Baptist Quarterly*, 11 (1877), 163; Anon., Review of *Evolution and Christianity*, by Benjamin F. Tefft, *Methodist Review*, 5th ser., 1 (1885), 481. Historians who have suggested that liberal Protestants, who tended to endorse the evolutionary hypothesis, substantially abandoned natural theology in the late nineteenth century include Cynthia Eagle Russett, *Darwin in America: The Intellectual Response, 1865–1912* (San Francisco, 1976), p. 43; Herbert Hovenkamp, *Science and Religion in America, 1800–1860* (Philadelphia, 1978), p. 44; and Turner, *Without God*, pp. 184–187 (but cf. p. 183). Actually, the decline of interest in natural theology occurred after 1900, and even then natural theology retained a place in liberal apologetics.

9. H. W. Conn, *Evolution of To-day* (New York, 1886), p. 16. See also George T. Ladd, "The Origin of the Concept of God," *Bibliotheca Sacra*, 34 (1877), 34; Joseph Le Conte, *Evolution and Its Relation to Religious Thought* (New York, 1888), pp. 324–325; F. H. Johnson, "Mechanical Evolution," *Andover Review*, 1 (1884), 631; James T. Bixby, "The Know-Nothing Position in Religion," *Bibliotheca Sacra*, 38 (1881), 437; Henry Ward Beecher, *Evolution and Religion* (New York, 1885), p. 153; William James, "Rationality, Activity and Faith," *Princeton Review*, n.s. 10 (1882), 63–64; W. R. Benedict, "Theism and Evolution," *Andover Review*, 6 (1886), 338–339.

10. Borden P. Bowne, *Philosophy of Theism* (New York, 1887), p. 82; James T. Bixby, "The Argument from Design in the Light of Modern Science," *Unitarian Review and Religious Magazine*, 8 (1877), 18, 13, 20. See also Clarke, *An Outline*, pp. 115–117; George T. Ladd, "History and the Concept of God," *Bibliotheca Sacra*, 37 (1880), 633; George P. Fisher, *The Grounds of Theistic and Christian Belief* (New York, 1883), pp. 46, 54.

11. Bixby, "Argument from Design," pp. 21–23. See also Francis Howe Johnson, *What Is Reality? An Inquiry as to the Reasonableness of Natural Religion, and the Naturalness of Revealed Religion* (Boston, 1891), pp. 264–276; Conn, *Evolution of To-day*, p. 213; Whiton, "Darwin and Darwinism," p. 53; Anon., "The Scientific Basis of Faith," *Methodist Review*, 5th ser., 8 (1892), 953.

12. Morse Peckham, ed., *The Origin of Species by Charles Darwin: A Variorum Text* (Philadelphia, 1959), p. 179 (95.14f); George F. Wright, "Recent Works Bearing on the Relation of Science to Religion. No. 3: Objections to Darwinism, and the Rejoinders of Its Advocates," *Bibliotheca Sacra*, 33 (1876), 672–681 (quotation on p. 674). See also

Burton, "What Should Be the Attitude," pp. 127–128; Conn, *Evolution of To-day*, pp. 212, 245, and passim; John Bascom, *Natural Theology* (New York, 1880), pp.136–137; Anon., "Christian Evolution," *Independent*, 32 (January 8, 1880), 16; Frederic Gardiner, "The Bearing of Recent Scientific Thought upon Theology," *Bibliotheca Sacra*, 35 (1878), 66; Abbott, *Theology of an Evolutionist*, pp. 6–7.

13. The most articulate statement of the view I am attempting to refute can be found in James R. Moore, *The Post-Darwinian Controversies: A Study of the Protestant Struggle to Come to Terms with Darwin in Great Britian and America, 1870–1900* (Cambridge, 1979), pp. 343, 300–303. For the scientific community's reception of "orthodox" Darwinism, see Ernst Mayr, *The Growth of Biological Thought: Diversity, Evolution, and Inheritance* (Cambridge, Mass., 1982), pp. 510–536; Peter J. Bowler, *The Eclipse of Darwinism: Anti-Darwinian Evolution Theories in the Decades around 1900* (Baltimore, 1983); Martin J. S. Rudwick, *The Meaning of Fossils: Episodes in the History of Palaeontology*, 2d ed. (New York, 1976), pp. 225, 260; and my discussion in the concluding section of Chapter 3.

14. Asa Gray, *Natural Science and Religion: Two Lectures Delivered to the Theological School of Yale College* (New York, 1880), p. 47; Mansfield, "Teleology," p. 220; Andrew P. Peabody, "Science and Revelation," *Princeton Review*, 4th ser. (1878), p. 766. See also James McCosh, "On Causation and Development," *Princeton Review*, n.s. 7 (1881), 383–386; James McCosh, "Is the Development Hypothesis Sufficient?" *Popular Science Monthly*, 10 (1876), 97; Wright, "Recent Works [1877]," pp. 365–366; James Freeman Clarke in Simon Newcomb et al., "Law and Design in Nature," *North American Review*, 128 (1879), 556; W. E. Parson, "Evolution—Shall It Be Atheistic?" *Lutheran Quarterly*, n.s. 9 (1879), 190; McCosh, *Religious Aspect*, pp. 7, 70. The popularity of the practice of attributing the factors making up natural selection to design belies the claim that after Charles Hodge, "no one undertook seriously to reconcile natural selection with design." Stow Persons, "Evolution and Theology," in Persons, ed., *Evolutionary Thought in America* (New Haven, 1950), p. 426. Peter J. Bowler may be correct in claiming that "any mechanism for producing adaptation naturally will undermine the argument from design." Peter J. Bowler, "Edward Drinker Cope and the Changing Structure of Evolutionary Theory," *Isis*, 68 (1977), 265. The evidence indicates, however, that many American Protestant evolutionists in the last quarter of the nineteenth century did not believe this to be the case.

15. J. Lewis Diman, *The Theistic Argument as Affected by Recent Theories* (Boston, 1881), pp. 165, 178–179. See also H[arris] E[llwood] S[tarr], "Diman, Jeremiah Lewis," *DAB*, 3: 312–313.

16. Darwin to A. Hyatt, December 4, 1872, *More Letters of Charles Darwin*, ed. Francis Darwin and A. C. Seward (London, 1903), 1: 344 (hereafter cited as *MLD*); Charles Darwin, *On the Origin of Species by Means of Natural Selection, or the Preservation of Favoured Races in the Struggle for Life* (1859; facsimile ed., Cambridge, Mass., 1964), pp. 489–490, 84, 314–315, 336–337, 345. See also Darwin to J. D. Hooker [1854], *MLD*, 1: 76; Darwin to J. D. Hooker, December 30 [1858], ibid., pp. 114–115.

17. Joseph Le Conte, "Scientific Relation of Sociology to Biology," *Popular Science Monthly*, 14 (1879), 331; George Harris, *Moral Evolution* (Boston, 1896), pp. 187, 164–165; Alexander Winchell, "Speculative Consequences of Evolution," University of Michigan, *Philosophical Papers*, 2d ser., 1 (1888), 21. See also McCosh, "On Causation," pp. 384–386; James McCosh, "Herbert Spencer's 'Data of Ethics,' " *Princeton Review*, 4th ser. (1879), 623; Ladd, "Concept of God," pp. 636–640.

18. Diman, *Theistic Argument*, pp. 166–167; M. Valentine, *Natural Theology; or, Ra-*

tional Theism (Chicago, 1885), p. 132; Ladd, "Concept of God," pp. 621–622, 624, 640. See also A. S. Packard, "The Law of Evolution," *Independent*, 32 (February 5, 1880), 10; Bixby, "Argument from Design," pp. 21–22; Smyth, *Old Faiths*, pp. 306–307.

19. Winchell, "Speculative Consequences of Evolution," pp. 20–21; Bixby, "Argument from Design," p. 24; Wright, "Recent Works [1877]," pp. 357–359, 364–365; D. B. Purinton, *Christian Theism: Its Claims and Sanctions* (New York, 1889), pp. 31, 46; Harris, *Moral Evolution*, pp. 185–188; R. S. MacArthur, "Christianity and the Secular Spirit," *New Princeton Review*, n.s. 5 (1888), 180. See also Clarke, *An Outline*, pp. 105–109, 131; Stearns, *Evidence*, pp. 63–65; George P. Fisher, "Materialism and the Pulpit," *Princeton Review*, 4th ser. (1878), 207–209; Bixby, "Cook's Biology," p. 72.

20. J. W. Chadwick, "The Basis of Religion," *Unitarian Review and Religious Magazine*, 26 (1886), 255–256; Gardiner, "Bearing of Recent Scientific Thought," pp. 66–67. See also Munger, "Evolution and the Faith," pp. 110–111; [G. F.] W[right], Review of *The Human Species*, by A. de Quatrefages, *Bibliotheca Sacra*, 36 (1879), 784; William Rupp, "The Theory of Evolution and the Christian Faith," *Reformed Quarterly Review*, 35 (1888), 161–162; L. E. Hicks, *A Critique of Design-Arguments: A Historical Review and Free Examination of the Methods of Reasoning in Natural Theology* (New York, 1883), p. 334; Parson, "Evolution—Shall It Be Atheistic?" pp. 189–190. Not surprisingly, scientists were among the most enthusiastic proponents of this position. See, for example, Packard, "Law of Evolution," p. 10; Josiah Parsons Cooke, *The Credentials of Science the Warrant of Faith* (New York, 1888), pp. 245–247; William North Rice, "Evolution [1890]," *Twenty-five Years of Scientific Progress and Other Essays* (New York, 1894), p.86.

21. James McCosh, *Realistic Philosophy Defended in a Philosophic Series* (New York, 1887), 1: 217. See also Samuel Harris, *The Philosophical Basis of Theism* (New York, 1883), p. 455; J. H. Hyslop, "Limitations of Evolution in Ethical Problems," *New Englander and Yale Review*, n.s. 12 (1888), 263. For representative statements of the virtually unanimous opposition of Protestant evolutionists during the last quarter of the nineteenth century to the Spencerian view of God and his approach to the reconciliation of science and religion, see Benedict, "Theism and Evolution," pp. 338–339; Ladd, "Origin of the Concept of God," p. 625; W.S. Lilly, "The Present Outlook for Christianity," *Forum*, 2 (1886), 325–326; Stearns, *Evidence*, pp. 16–17. Even Henry Ward Beecher, often cited as an enthusiastic disciple of Spencer, declared in 1885 that it was "preposterous" to assume that "a God that is inconceivable, unthinkable, unknowable" warranted humanity's religious devotion. Beecher, *Evolution and Religion*, pp.152–153. To suggest, as some historians have done, that the theology embodied in the work of Protestant evolutionists was more indebted to Spencer than to Darwin is to assume mistakenly that acceptance of cosmic evolution implied an acceptance of the Spencerian world view. See, for example, Russett, *Darwin in America*, pp. 29–30; Moore, *Post-Darwinian Controversies*, pp. 236–237. In view of their prior acceptance of the nebular hypothesis and geological uniformitarianism, Protestants did not require the imprimatur of Spencer to believe that a universal system of evolution was the direction in which science was moving. See Munger, "Evolution and the Faith," p. 109. I do not wish to deny that Spencer may well have helped to publicize the concept of cosmic evolution, but Protestant intellectuals chose to turn that concept to their own purposes. I do think, however, that Jim Moore has succeeded in showing resonance between the social views of Spencer and those of certain American Protestant thinkers of the late nineteenth century. Jim Moore,

"Herbert Spencer's Henchmen: The Evolution of Protestant Liberals in Late Nineteenth Century America," in John Durant, ed., *Darwinism and Divinity: Essays in Evolution and Religious Belief* (New York, 1985), pp. 76–100.

22. The most reliable study of Le Conte's life is Lester D. Stephens, *Joseph Le Conte: Gentle Prophet of Evolution* (Baton Rouge, 1982). Le Conte was one of numerous Protestant evolutionists who claimed to be "the pioneer" in opposition to "the materialistic and irreligious implication of the doctrine of evolution." [Joseph Le Conte], *The Autobiography of Joseph Le Conte*, ed. William Dallam Armes (New York, 1903), pp. 335–337.

23. Le Conte, "Evolution in Relation to Materialism," p. 165. See also Le Conte, *Evolution and Its Relation*, pp. 3–4, 65, 277, 325. Expressions of similar views include Bixby, "Know-Nothing Position," pp. 456–457; Stearns, *Evidence*, pp. 64–65; Alexander Winchell, *Walks and Talks in the Geological Field* (New York, 1886), p. 311.

24. Lewis F. Stearns, "Reconstruction in Theology," *New Englander*, n.s. 5 (1882), 86; Winchell, "Huxley and Evolution," p. 302; Mansfield, "Teleology," p. 222. See also Fisher, "Alleged Conflict," p. 34; Hicks, *Critique of Design-Arguments*, p. 331; Anon., Review of *Faith and Rationalism*, by George P. Fisher, *Bibliotheca Sacra*, 37 (1880), 199; M. Stuart Phelps, "Anthropomorphism," *Princeton Review*, n.s. 8 (1881), 132–133; Washington Gladden, "The New Evolution," *McClure's Magazine*, 3 (1894), 237.

25. Bowne, *Studies in Theism*, p. 148; McCosh, *Religious Aspect*, p. 70; Stearns, "Reconstruction," p. 86; Chadwick, "Basis of Religion," pp. 256–257. See also H. M. Goodwin, "The Bible as a Book of Education," *New Englander*, n.s. 6 (1883), 262; Newman Smyth, "Professor Harris's Contributions to Theism," *Andover Review*, 1 (1884), 134, 138; Fisher, *Faith and Rationalism*, pp. 48–49. A few Protestants were harsher in their critique of natural theology. They insisted that arguments that made the existence of God "a deduction from experience" had "always failed under the ultimate tests both of philosophy and theology." George Harris, Review of *The Idea of God as Affected by Modern Knowledge*, by John Fiske, *Andover Review*, 5 (1886), 100. For the use of intuitional modes of theology prior to 1875, see Turner, *Without God*, pp. 104–113. D. H. Meyer has appropriately termed the "inward" emphasis of apologetics during the late nineteenth century "a natural theology of the mind." D. H. Meyer, "American Intellectuals and the Victorian Crisis of Faith," Daniel Walker Howe, ed., *Victorian America* (Philadelphia, 1976), p. 69.

26. George P. Fisher, "The Personality of God and Man," *Princeton Review*, n.s. 10 (1882), 30. A useful discussion of the role of the German theological tradition in American theology during the nineteenth century is Jurgen Herbst, *The German Historical School in American Scholarship: A Study in the Transfer of Culture* (Ithaca, 1965), pp. 73–97. For a contemporary assessment, see James McCosh, "The Scottish Philosophy as Contrasted with the German," *Princeton Review*, n.s. 10 (1882), 337. John Herman Randall, Jr., has credited the theory of organic evolution with impelling liberal Protestants in America and England to come to terms with German theology in the last quarter of the nineteenth century by forcing them to search for a new foundation of religion. John Herman Randall, Jr., "The Changing Impact of Darwin on Philosophy," *Journal of the History of Ideas*, 22 (1961), 443, 446. See also Turner, *Without God*, pp. 187–199, 267.

27. Newman Smyth, *The Religious Feeling: A Study for Faith* (New York, 1877), p. vi. See also H[arris] E[llwood] S[tarr], "Smyth, Newman," *DAB*, 17: 376–377; Claude Welch, *Protestant Thought in the Nineteenth Century*, Vol. 1: 1799–1870 (New Haven,

1972), pp. 59–85. A number of late-nineteenth-century thinkers commented on the popularity of Schleiermacher's thought in America. See, for example, Alexander V. G. Allen, *The Continuity of Christian Thought: A Study of Modern Theology in the Light of Its History* (Boston, 1884), p. 397; F. G. Peabody, "The New Theology," *Unitarian Review and Religious Magazine*, 11 (1879), 354. Other European theologians who influenced American Protestants who sought to adjust Christian theology to developments in science and biblical scholarship during the last quarter of the nineteenth century include Frederick Denison Maurice, Frederick Robertson, and Isaac A. Dorner. In the 1890s Protestants began to devote some attention to the work of Albrecht Ritschl and his followers. William R. Hutchison, *The Modernist Impulse in American Protestantism* (Cambridge, Mass., 1976), pp. 80–87, 122–132.

28. Smyth, *Religious Feeling*, pp. 148, 157–158, 35. See also Newman Smyth, "Orthodox Rationalism," *Princeton Review*, n.s. 9 (1882), 299–300; Smyth, "Professor Harris's Contributions," pp. 138–139. Smyth viewed "physical evolution" as only a "half-truth" that "finds its complement only in a higher truth." Smyth, *Old Faiths*, pp. 383–384.

29. Smyth, *Religious Feeling*, pp. 33–34, 106–108, 35–41, 114, 118–126, 159–160. Favorable reviews of Smyth's work include Anon., Review of *The Religious Feeling*, by Newman Smyth, *Quarterly Review of the Evangelical Lutheran Church*, n.s. 7 (1877), 627; Anon., Review of *The Religious Feeling: A Study for Faith*, by Newman Smyth, *Presbyterian Quarterly and Princeton Review*, n.s. 6 (1877), 759–760; Anon., Review of *The Religious Feeling*, by Newman Smyth, *Methodist Quarterly Review*, 4th ser., 30 (1878), 365–366.

30. Benedict, "Theism and Evolution," p. 347; James C. Parsons, "Religious Experience," *Unitarian Review and Religious Magazine*, 26 (1886), 460–461. See also Harris, *Philosophical Basis of Theism*, pp. 15–16; Fisher, "Personality of God and Man," p. 31; Henry Graham, "God in Human Consciousness," *Methodist Review*, 5th ser., 3 (1887), 582; James C. Parsons, "The Three Fundamental Truths of Religion," *Unitarian Review and Religious Magazine*, 26 (1881), 130–133; William B. Clarke, "The Nature and Working of the Christian Consciousness," *Andover Review*, 7 (1887), 381; George P. Fisher, "The Folly of Atheism," *New Englander*, 36 (1877), 84–85; James G. Roberts, "The Inductive Method in Theology," *New Englander*, n.s. 4 (1881), 748; Stearns, "Reconstruction," pp. 86–87; Valentine, *Natural Theology*, pp. 26–31, 206–213, 221. I discuss the position of Protestant evolutionists regarding the moral experience of humanity at greater length in Chapter 7.

31. George B. Stevens, "The Authority of Faith," *New Englander*, n.s. 4 (1881), 437. See also Roberts, "Inductive Method," p. 748; Borden P. Bowne, "Some Difficulties of Modern Materialism," *Princeton Review*, n.s. 8 (1881), 360–362; Parsons, "Three Fundamental Truths," pp. 130–131; Winchell, *Walks and Talks*, p. 317.

32. Graham, "God in Human Consciousness," p. 586; Smyth, "Orthodox Rationalism," pp. 300–301; James S. Candlish, "The Personality of God," *Princeton Review*, n.s. 14 (1884), 135. See also Fisher, "Personality of God and Man," p. 38.

33. Fisher, *Grounds of Theistic and Christian Belief*, p. 59; MacArthur, "Christianity and the Secular Spirit," p. 181; Theodore T. Munger, *The Freedom of Faith* (Boston, 1883), p. 359; McCosh, *Religious Aspect*, pp. 61–62. See also Lewis G. Janes, "Religion in the Light of Modern Science," *Unitarian Review*, 32 (1889), 319.

34. Washington Gladden, *Recollections* (Boston, 1909), pp. 223–224; Elizabeth Stuart Phelps, "Is God Good?" *Atlantic Monthly*, 48 (1881), 533. See also Valentine, *Natural Theology*, pp. 231–232; Munger, *Freedom of Faith*, pp. 359–360; Turner, *Without*

God, pp. 71–72, 88–95, 142–143, 204–207, 221–222; James Turner, *Reckoning with the Beast: Animals, Pain, and Humanity in the Victorian Mind* (Baltimore, 1980), pp. 1–14, 34–37, 79–82, and passim. The increasing compassion and sensibility in the nineteenth century represented the culmination of a much longer development. See Keith Thomas, *Man and the Natural World: A History of the Modern Sensibility* (New York, 1983).

35. Hyslop, "Limitations of Evolution," p. 267; Le Conte, *Evolution and Its Relation*, p. 328. See also George Frederick Wright, "Recent Works Bearing on the Relation of Science to Religion. No. 5: Some Analogies between Calvinism and Darwinism," *Bibliotheca Sacra*, 37 (1880), 55; Cooke, *Credentials of Science*, p. 318; F. H. Johnson, "Coöperative Creation," *Andover Review*, 3 (1885), 437–438; George F. Genung, "The Trustworthiness of Spiritual Apprehension," *Andover Review*, 7 (1887), 144. Other accounts of the difficulties that the theory of organic evolution raised with regard to the doctrine of God's benevolence include David Hull, *Darwin and His Critics: The Reception of Darwin's Theory of Evolution by the Scientific Community* (Cambridge, Mass., 1973), p. 56; Alvar Ellegård, "The Darwinian Theory and the Argument from Design," *Lynchnos* (1956), 182–183.

36. Darwin to J. D. Hooker, July 13, 1856, *MLD*, 1: 94; Darwin, *Origin of Species*, p. 79; [Charles Darwin], *The Autobiography of Charles Darwin, 1809–1882, With original omissions restored*, ed. Nora Barlow (New York, 1958), p. 90. See also Darwin to Asa Gray, May 22 [1860] in *The Life and Letters of Charles Darwin, Including an Autobiographical Chapter*, ed. Francis Darwin (London, 1887) 2: 311–312; Charles Darwin, *The Variation of Plants and Animals under Domestication* (London, 1878), 2: 431–432; Donald Fleming, "Charles Darwin, the Anaesthetic Man," *Victorian Studies*, 4 (1961), 219–236. For a somewhat different interpretation of Darwin's reflections on God's benevolence, see Neal C. Gillespie, *Charles Darwin and the Problem of Creation* (Chicago, 1979), pp. 125–133.

37. B. F. Cocker, *The Theistic Conception of the World: An Essay in Opposition to Certain Tendencies of Modern Thought* (New York, 1875), p. 131; [Asa Gray], "Darwin and His Reviewers," *Atlantic Monthly*, 6 (1860), 410–413 (quotation on p. 411), 417. Arthur Lovejoy has suggested that the combination of special creationism and progressionism "had not even the poor merit of being anthropomorphic. For no man outside of a madhouse ever behaved in such a manner as that in which, by this hypothesis, the Creator of the universe was supposed to have behaved." Arthur Lovejoy, "The Argument for Organic Evolution before the Origin of Species, 1830–1858," in Bentley Glass, Owsei Temkin, and William L. Strauss, Jr., eds., *Forerunners of Darwin, 1745–1859* (Baltimore, 1968), pp. 412–413.

38. McCosh, *Religious Aspect*, p. 68. See also Gray, *Natural Science and Religion*, p. 64; Johnson, "Coöperative Creation," p. 330; Calthrop, "Religion and Science," p. 314.

39. For useful discussions of Wright's life and thought, see William James Morison, "George Frederick Wright: In Defense of Darwinism and Fundamentalism, 1838–1921" Ph.D. diss., Vanderbilt, 1971; and Moore, *Post-Darwinian Controversies*, pp. 280–298. In my judgment, Moore's claim that "Wright's work served to show liberal Christians that the best science of the age was on the side of orthodoxy" rests on an anachronistic view of science and an exaggerated vision of Wright's influence. Ibid., p. 295.

40. Wright, "Recent Works [1877]," pp. 368–383 (quotations on pp. 368, 375–376).

41. Wright, "Recent Works [1880]," pp. 53–54, 76, 61–69 (quotations on pp. 64, 68).

William James Morison has maintained that Wright's attempt to reconcile Calvinism and Darwinism was his only really original contribution to the evolutionary controversy. Morison, "George Frederick Wright," p. 14.

42. James McCosh, "Religious Aspects of the Doctrine of Development," in Philip Schaff and S. Irenaeus Prime, eds., *History, Essays, Orations, and Other Documents of the Sixth General Conference of the Evangelical Alliance, Held in New York, October 2–12, 1873* (New York, 1874), p. 269; James McCosh, *Christianity and Positivism: A Series of Lectures to the Times on Natural History and Apologetics* (New York, 1871), pp. 86, 71–72, 339. Others who noted a certain similarity between the Darwinian vision of natural history and the Calvinist conception of the scheme of redemption include Gray, *Natural Science and Religion*, p. 102; John Fiske, *Through Nature to God* [1899], *The Miscellaneous Writings of John Fiske* (Boston, 1902), 9: 276; A. W. Jackson, "The Old Faith and the New," *Unitarian Review*, 28 (1887), 42–43; W. E. C. Wright, Review of *Social Evolution*, by Benjamin Kidd, *Bibliotheca Sacra*, 52 (1895), 201; Daniel Coit Gilman, "Johns Hopkins University Celebration of the Twenty-fifth Anniversary . . . [1902]," in Richard Hofstadter and Wilson Smith, eds., *American Higher Education* (Chicago, 1961), 2: 644. Not all of these thinkers, however, were themselves proponents of orthodox Darwinism or orthodox Calvinism. Asa Gray, for example, not only rejected Darwin's view of the randomness of variation, but also rejected the doctrine of election and endorsed a liberal version of evangelicalism. A. Hunter Dupree, *Asa Gray: 1810–1888* (Cambridge, Mass., 1959), pp. 44–45, 365–366. Some thinkers used the analogy between Calvinism and Darwinism as a kind of heuristic device to convince readers that the conclusions modern science was reaching about natural history were not altogether different from familiar modes of thinking.

43. Stearns, "Reconstruction," p. 90. See also Newman Smyth, *The Orthodox Theology of To-day* (New York, 1881), pp. 56–57. Trenchant contemporary criticisms of Calvinism include A Presbyterian Minister, "Scripture or Logic—Which?" *Bibliotheca Sacra*, 47 (1890), 676–681; Roberts, "Inductive Method," p. 744; Beecher, *Evolution and Religion*, p. 18; George A. Gordon, *The Christ of To-day* (Boston, 1896), pp. 184–185. For the decline of belief in Calvinism's theodicy, see E. Brooks Holifield, *The Gentlemen Theologians: American Theology in Southern Culture, 1795–1860* (Durham, N.C., 1978), pp. 187, 190–191. For the decline of Calvinism, see Joseph Haroutunian, *Piety versus Moralism: The Passing of the New England Theology* (New York, 1932); Paul Carter, *The Spiritual Crisis of the Gilded Age* (De Kalb, Ill., 1971), pp. 45–49, 58–60, 80, 95; Daniel Walker Howe, "The Decline of Calvinism: An Approach to Its Study," *Comparative Studies in Society and History*, 14 (1972), 306–327.

44. Packard, "Law of Evolution," p. 10. See also Samuel Harris, *The Self-Revelation of God* (1886; New York, 1887), pp. 314–315.

45. Le Conte, *Evolution and Its Relation*, pp. 336, 329; Asa Gray, "Evolutionary Teleology," *Darwiniana: Essays and Reviews Pertaining to Darwinism*, ed. A. Hunter Dupree (1876; Cambridge, Mass., 1963), pp. 308–311; John Fiske, *Outlines of Cosmic Philosophy* [1874], *Miscellaneous Writings*, 4: 221–226; John Fiske, *The Idea of God as Affected by Modern Knowledge* [1885], *Miscellaneous Writings*, 9: 177–178, 210, 204–206; Joseph Le Conte, "Scientific Relation," p. 336. See also Nathaniel Southgate Shaler, "Darwinism," in Mrs. John T. Sargent, ed., *Sketches and Reminiscences of the Radical Club* (Boston, 1880), p. 263; Cooke, *Credentials of Science*, p. 251; W. H. Furness, "Natural Selection in Relation to Man," *Unitarian Review and Religious Magazine*, 5 (1876), 293; Beecher, *Evolution and Religion*, p. 115.

46. Le Conte, *Evolution and Its Relation*, p. 329; Joseph S. Van Dyke, *Theism and Ev-*

olution: An Examination of Modern Speculative Theories as Related to Theistic Conceptions of the Universe, 2d ed. (New York, 1886), p. 47. See also Smyth, *Religious Feeling*, pp. 163–164; Munger, "Evolution and the Faith," p. 111; Genung, "Trustworthiness of Spiritual Apprehension," pp. 145–146.

47. Smyth, *Orthodox Theology*, pp. 56–57; Bowne, *Philosophy of Theism*, pp. 227–228, 222–223, 233–235; Beecher, *Evolution and Religion*, pp. 339, 87–88, 247; Joseph Le Conte, *Religion and Science: A Series of Sunday Lectures on the Relation of Natural and Revealed Religion, or the Truths Revealed in Nature and Scripture* (1873; New York, 1874), pp. 243–246 (quotation on p. 243), 145–146; Le Conte, "Evolution in Relation to Materialism," pp. 163–164. See also Cocker, *Theistic Conception*, p. 130; Valentine, *Natural Theology*, pp. 250–251, 270; McCosh, *Realistic Philosophy*, 1: 248; Wright, "Recent Works [1877]," p. 368.

48. Cocker, *Theistic Conception*, pp. 173–174.

49. Le Conte, *Evolution and Its Relation*, pp. 277, iv. See also Le Conte, "Evolution in Relation to Materialism," pp. 173–174; F. H. Johnson, "Revelation as a Factor in Evolution," *Andover Review*, 5 (1886), 21; Lewis E. Hicks, "Scientists and Theologians: How They Disagree and Why," *Baptist Quarterly*, 9 (1875), 65.

50. Chadwick, "Basis of Religion," p. 253; M. H. Valentine, "The Influence of the Theory of Evolution on the Theory of Ethics," *Lutheran Quarterly*, 28 (1898), 218; MacArthur, "Christianity and the Secular Spirit," p. 180; Mansfield, "Teleology," pp. 219–220. See also McCosh, *Realistic Philosophy*, 1: 156–157, 223–224, 2: 272–274; McCosh, *Religious Aspect*, pp. 54–55; James McCosh in Newcomb et al., "Law and Design," pp. 558–560; Purinton, *Christian Theism*, pp. 274–277; Lewis French Stearns, *Present Day Theology: A Popular Discussion of Leading Doctrines of the Christian Faith* (New York, 1893), pp. 266–270; W. Douglas MacKenzie, "Evolution Theories and Christian Doctrine," *Bibliotheca Sacra*, 54 (1897), 551–553; McCosh, "On Causation," p. 387; Rylance, "Theological Re-Adjustments," p. 48; Clarke, in Newcomb et al., "Law and Design," pp. 556–557; Wright, "Recent Works [1876]," pp. 687–688.

51. Parsons, "Religious Experience," p. 456; Edwin Stuteley Carr, "Spencer's Philosophy of Religion," *Bibliotheca Sacra*, 54 (1897), 240; Henry Churchill King, "Reconstruction in Theology," *American Journal of Theology*, 3 (1899), 308. See also Le Conte, *Evolution and Its Relation*, pp. 280–281; Gardiner, "Bearing of Recent Scientific Thought," p. 48; Jackson, "Old Faith," pp. 47–48; Johnson, "Revelation as a Factor," p. 20; Hyslop, "Limitations of Evolution," p. 263; George A. Thayer, "Christianity in the Process of Evolution," *Unitarian Review*, 34 (1890), 7; James DeKoven, *Sermons Preached on Various Occasions* (New York, 1880), p. 158; James T. Bixby, "Science and Religion," *Religious Magazine and Monthly Review*, 45 (1871), 695; Bowne, *Studies in Theism*, pp. 287–289; Gladden, "New Evolution," pp. 237–238. Significantly, some Protestants held that there was every reason to assume that science would eventually discover the causes of variation. See, for example, F. H. Johnson, "Theistic Evolution," *Andover Review*, 1 (1884), 371; H. S. Stanley, "Evolution as Bearing on Method in Teleology," *New Englander*, n.s. 6 (1883), 590–591; Gray, *Natural Science and Religion*, p. 75.

52. Joseph Le Conte, "Man's Place in Nature," *Princeton Review*, 4th ser. (1878), 794; George T. Ladd, "History and the Concept of God," *Bibliotheca Sacra*, 37 (1880), 597. See also Editors of the *Andover Review, Progressive Orthodoxy: A Contribution to the Christian Interpretation of Christian Doctrines* (Boston, 1885), p. 16; John Tunis, "The Doctrine of the Divine Immanence," *Andover Review*, 14 (1890), 401; Allen, *Continuity of Christian Thought*, p. 1. Protestants who credited the theory of evolution with rein-

forcing belief in God's immanent presence in the world include Beecher, *Evolution and Religion*, p. 78; Adams, *Continuous Creation*, pp. 16, 95–96; Rupp, "Theory of Evolution," p. 156; Tunis, "Doctrine of the Divine Immanence," pp. 399–401; Thayer, "Christianity in the Process of Evolution," pp. 15–16; Joseph May, "The Twofold Symbol of Godhead," *Unitarian Review and Religious Magazine*, 26 (1886), 101–102; Diman, *Theistic Argument*, p. 179; Le Conte, *Evolution and Its Relation*, pp. 262, 279, 281–282; Frank Hugh Foster, "Evolution and the Evangelical System of Doctrine," *Bibliotheca Sacra*, 50 (1893), 414; Henry Davies, "Social Evolution and the Churches," *Bibliotheca Sacra*, 54 (1897), 720; King, "Reconstruction in Philosophy," p. 307.

Although the doctrine of God's immanent presence in the world was fundamental to many Protestant intellectuals' understanding of God's relationship to His creation, the doctrine has received surprisingly little sustained attention from historians of religious thought. The most sustained treatment of nineteenth-century Protestant views of the doctrine of divine immanence is Arthur Cushman McGiffert, *The Rise of Modern Religious Ideas* (New York, 1922), pp. 187–221. Briefer treatments of the importance of immanentism in late-nineteenth-century Protestant theology in the United States include Persons, "Evolution and Theology," pp. 450–451; H. Shelton Smith, Robert T. Handy, and Lefferts A. Loetscher, *American Christianity: An Historical Interpretation with Representative Documents* (New York, 1963), 2: 258–259; Russett, *Darwin in America*, p. 30; Moore, *Post-Darwinian Controversies*, pp. 224–231 and passim. Hutchison, *Modernist Impulse*, deals at length with the role of "cultural immanentism" in American liberal theology but devotes little space to a consideration of the immanentist perception of the natural world.

53. James Douglas, "The Divine Immanency," *Bibliotheca Sacra*, 45 (1888), 504, 331 (the original phrase is in italics); Johnson, "Theistic Evolution," p. 372; Smyth, *Old Faiths*, p. 269; Alexander Winchell, "Symposium on Evolution," p. 347. See also David Nelson Beach, *The Newer Religious Thinking* (Boston, 1893), p. 58; Peabody, "Science and Revelation," pp. 767–768; Gardiner, "Bearing of Recent Scientific Thought," pp. 71–73; David Hume, *A Treatise of Human Nature* (1739; London, 1960), pp. 74–94; Jacob Gould Schurman, *Belief in God: Its Origin, Nature, and Basis* (1890; New York, 1902), pp. 162–165.

54. Johnson, "Theistic Evolution," p. 365. See also Fisher, *Faith and Rationalism*, p. 106. A. J. DuBois, "Science and the Supernatural," *New Englander and Yale Review*, n.s. 17 (1890), 466; King, "Reconstruction in Theology," p. 308; Frederic Gardiner, "The Persistence of Force: A Point in the Argument of Natural Theology," *Bibliotheca Sacra*, 50 (1881), 24; Bixby, *Similarities*, pp. 62, 226; Beecher, *Evolution and Religion*, p. 45; Harris, *Moral Evolution*, p. 189.

55. Le Conte, *Religion and Science*, pp. 20, 278; Le Conte, "Evolution in Relation to Materialism," p. 166. See also Le Conte, *Evolution and Its Relation*, pp. 282–283. Even in *Religion and Science*, however, there were indications that Le Conte's ideas were undergoing transition. Le Conte, *Religion and Science*, pp. 88, 152–153, 278–279.

56. Winchell, "Huxley and Evolution," p. 291; Rice, "Evolution [1890]," p. 86; Conn, *Evolution of To-day*, p. 17; Gray, *Natural Science and Religion*, p. 77; Asa Gray [1860], in American Academy of Arts and Sciences, *Proceedings*, 4 (May 1857–May 1860), 426. See also Asa Gray, "Darwin's Life and Letters," *Nation*, 27 (November 17, 1887), 402; [Gray], "Darwin and His Reviewers," pp. 417–419.

57. Douglas, "Divine Immanency," p. 498; Cocker, *Theistic Conception*, pp. 175, 236–243, 342; A. H. Strong, "The Fall and the Redemption of Man in the Light of Evolution," *Sixteenth Annual Session of the Baptist Congress for Discussion of Current Questions, November 15-17, 1898* (New York, 1898), pp. 6–10 (quotations on pp. 7, 9);

Calthrop, "Religion and Evolution," p. 199. See also Fiske, *Idea of God*, pp. 166–167, 209–210; Fiske, *Through Nature*, pp. 338–339; Minot J. Savage, *The Religion of Evolution* (Boston, 1876), pp. 144–145, 188; Abbott, *Theology of an Evolutionist*, pp. 5–15, 76–77; J. Max Hark, *The Unity of the Truth in Christianity and Evolution* (New York, 1888), pp. 139–140; L. Bell, "Unbelief, Half-Belief, and a Remedy," *New Englander*, n.s. 7 (1884), 73; Gardiner, "Bearing of Recent Scientific Thought," pp. 57, 74; T. S. Lathrop, "Evolution and Conscience," *Universalist Quarterly*, n.s. 16 (1879), 305; Rupp, "Theory of Evolution," p. 158; Anson P. Atterbury, "Five Points in an Evolutionary Confession of Faith," *Christian Thought*, 7 (1889), 44; Schurman, *Belief in God*, pp. 161–173.

58. Douglas, "Divine Immanency," p. 332; Bowne, *Studies in Theism*, p. 286. See also Winchell, "Speculative Consequences of Evolution," pp. 19–20; Cocker, *Theistic Conception*, pp. 236–238; Le Conte, *Evolution and Its Relation*, pp. 283–284, 317, 326. For the role of idealism in American philosophy, see Herbert W. Schneider, *A History of American Philosophy*, 2d ed. (New York, 1963), pp. 375–424; Sydney E. Ahlstrom, "Theology in America: A Historical Survey," in James Ward Smith and A. Leland Jamison, eds., *The Shaping of American Religion* (Princeton, 1961), pp. 288–290; G. Watts Cunningham, *The Idealistic Argument in Recent British and American Philosophy* (1933; New York, 1969); Bruce Kuklick, *The Rise of American Philosophy: Cambridge, Massachusetts, 1860–1930* (New Haven, 1977), pp. 46, 157–158, and passim.

59. Charles Hodge, *Systematic Theology* (New York, 1872–73), 1: 618; John Milton Williams, "Divine Limitation," *Bibliotheca Sacra*, 47 (1890), 262–263. See also Lyman Abbott, *The Evolution of Christianity* (Boston, 1892), pp. 112–113; Douglas, "Divine Immanency," pp. 503–504; Winchell, "Huxley and Evolution," pp. 302–303; Bowne, *Studies in Theism*, pp. 314–315; A. A. Berle, "The Passing of Agnosticism," *Bibliotheca Sacra*, 52 (1895), 530; James Douglas, "Miracles and the Divine Immanency," *Bibliotheca Sacra*, 45 (1888), 573, 582; Augustus Jay DuBois, "Science and Miracle," *New Englander and Yale Review*, n.s. 15 (1889), 20; Bell, "Unbelief, Half-Belief," pp. 79–80; Gardiner, "Bearing of Recent Scientific Thought," p. 67; Cocker, *Theistic Conception*, pp. 134, 342. George Harris held that the very term "supernatural" was an unhappy phrase coined in the "modern" era. Both the idea and the word were absent from the Bible. Harris, *Moral Evolution*, pp. 432–433; Joseph Le Conte, *Evolution: Its Nature, Its Evidences, and Its Relation to Religious Thought*, 2d rev. ed. (New York, 1891), pp. 355–356 (2d ed. hereafter cited as *Evolution*).

60. G. Frederick Wright, "The Debt of the Church to Asa Gray," *Bibliotheca Sacra*, 45 (1888), 527; G. F. W[right], "Bad Philosophy Going to Seed," *Bibliotheca Sacra*, 52 (1895), 559–561. See also G. Frederick Wright, *Story of My Life and Work* (Oberlin, 1916), p. 399.

61. May, "Twofold Symbol," p. 110; Tunis, "Doctrine of the Divine Immanence," p. 402. See also Stearns, *Present Day Theology*, pp. 269–270; John J. Elmendorf, "The Continuity of Christian Thought," *American Church Review*, 46 (1885), 345; M. Valentine, "Symposium on the 'New Theology': What Are Its Essential Features? Is It Better Than the Old?" *Homiletic Review*, 12 (1886), 283.

62. Douglas, "Divine Immanency," pp. 330, 339–342; Ladd, "History and the Concept of God," p. 597; Le Conte, "Man's Place," p. 794; Le Conte, *Evolution and Its Relation*, pp. 282–284. See also Atterbury, "Five Points," p. 44; Cocker, *Theistic Conception*, pp. 174–175, 241–242; Rupp, "Theory of Evolution," p. 158; Abbott, *Theology of an Evolutionist*, pp. 14–15; Clarke, *An Outline*, pp. 129–130; Beach, *Newer Religious Thinking*, p. 59; Schurman, *Belief in God*, pp. 173–174; Johnson, *What Is Reality?* p. 252.

63. Winchell, "Speculative Consequences of Evolution," p. 23; Bowne, *Philosophy*

of Theism, p. 8; Fisher, "Personality of God and Man," p. 16; Fisher, *Grounds of Theistic and Christian Belief*, pp. 107–108; Le Conte, *Evolution and Its Relation*, pp. 284, 314–329. See also Le Conte, "Evolution in Relation to Materialism," p. 162; Gardiner, "Bearing of Recent Scientific Thought," pp. 70–71; Phelps, "Anthropomorphism," pp. 142–144; Candlish, "Personality of God," pp. 135, 137; Alexander T. Ormund, "The Agnostic Dilemma," *New Princeton Review*, n.s. 2 (1886), 172–173; Gardiner, "Persistence of Force," pp. 22–23.

64. Johnson, "Revelation as a Factor," p. 21.

65. Fisher, *Grounds of Theistic and Christian Belief*, p. 108. See also Peabody, "Science and Revelation," pp. 768–769; Strong, "Fall and the Redemption," pp. 7–8; Gardiner, "Bearing of Recent Scientific Thought," pp. 57–58; William W. Kinsley, *Views on Vexed Questions* (Philadelphia, 1881), p. 75; Stearns, *Present Day Theology*, pp. 272–273; Gray, *Natural Science and Religion*, p. 108, Le Conte, *Evolution*, pp. 355–357.

66. Munger, "Evolution and the Faith," p. 110. See also Douglas, "Divine Immanency," p. 337; Foster, "Evolution and the Evangelical System of Doctrine," pp. 413–414; J. H. Allen, "Present Aspects of the Liberal Movement," *Unitarian Review and Religious Magazine*, 26 (1886), 242; Jackson, "Old Faith," p. 51.

67. Wright, "Debt of the Church," pp. 527–528; Wright, "Recent Works [1880]," pp. 75–76. See also George F. Wright, "Recent Works Bearing on the Relation of Science to Religion. No. 2: The Divine Method of Producing Living Species," *Bibliotheca Sacra*, 33 (1876), 489; Stearns, *Present Day Theology*, pp. 275–281. Many immanentists also maintained that special providence most frequently occurred in the transaction between God and human consciousness. See, for example, Cocker, *Theistic Conception*, pp. 253, 310; Le Conte, "Evolution in Relation to Materialism," p. 173.

68. McCosh, *Realistic Philosophy*, 1: 221–224, 145, 156–157, 221–222, 229. See also Gardiner, "Bearing of Recent Scientific Thought," pp. 54, 56; C. A. Row, "God's Threefold Revelation of Himself," *Princeton Review*, 4th ser. (1878), p. 714; Rupp, "Theory of Evolution," p. 156; Wright, "Recent Works [1880]," p. 54; Winchell, "Huxley and Evolution," p. 303; Wright, "Recent Works [1877]," pp. 375–376, 379–383; Bell, "Unbelief, Half-Belief," p. 75; Louis Paine, "God's Beneficence in Nature," *Methodist Review*, 5th ser., 5 (1889), 760–761; Bascom, *Natural Theology*, p. 270; Savage, *Religion of Evolution*, p. 147; Peabody, "Science and Revelation," p. 768; Beecher, *Evolution and Religion*, p. 172.

69. Fisher, *Grounds of Theistic and Christian Belief*, p. 108; Joseph Le Conte, "Science and Mental Improvement," *Popular Science Monthly*, 13 (1878), 98. See also William W. Kinsley, "Science and Prayer," *Bibliotheca Sacra*, 49 (1892), 90; McCosh, *Realistic Philosophy*, 1: 220; [Henry Ware Holland], "Gray's Darwiniana," *Nation*, 23 (December 14, 1876), 358.

70. Smyth, *Old Faiths*, pp. 16, 18, 33; Abbott, *Theology of an Evolutionist*, pp. 76–77, 9–10, 40–41. See also Gladden, "New Evolution," p. 237; H. W. Conn, "The Three Great Epochs of World Evolution," *Methodist Review*, 5th ser., 12 (1896), 885; William Jewett Tucker, *My Generation: An Autobiographical Interpretation* (Boston, 1919), pp. 2–3; MacArthur, "Christianity and the Secular Spirit," p. 179; Foster, "Evolution and the Evangelical System of Doctrine," pp. 409–410; Rupp, "Theory of Evolution," pp. 145–146.

71. Clarke, *An Outline*, p. 225. See also Munger, "Evolution and the Faith," p. 109; Le Conte, "Science and Mental Improvement," p. 101; Abbott, *Evolution of Christianity*, p. 14.

Chapter 6. "Where Is the Place of Understanding?"

1. J. A. Clutz, "Goldwin Smith on the Decay of Faith," *Lutheran Quarterly*, n.s. 9 (1880), 262–263; Lewis E. Hicks, "Scientists and Theologians: How They Disagree and Why," *Baptist Quarterly*, 9 (1875), 71; Alexander Winchell, *Preadamites; or, A Demonstration of the Existence of Men before Adam; together with a Study of Their Condition, Antiquity, Racial Affinities, and Progressive Dispersion over the Earth* (Chicago, 1880), p. 6. See also Frederic Gardiner, "The Bearing of Recent Scientific Thought upon Theology," *Bibliotheca Sacra*, 35 (1878), 68–69; J. Max Hark, *The Unity of the Truth in Christianity and Evolution* (New York, 1888), pp. 28–29; R. T. Brumby, "Gradualness Characteristic of All God's Operations," *Southern Presbyterian Review*, 25 (1874), 540–541; George Frederick Wright, "Recent Works Bearing on the Relation of Science to Religion. No. 5: Some Analogies between Calvinism and Darwinism," *Bibliotheca Sacra* 37, (1880), 73; S. H. Kellogg, "The Creative Laws and the Scripture Revelation,"*Bibliotheca Sacra*, 46 (1889), 393. Winchell argued that the insistence of conservatives that the Bible should be interpreted literally was actually an implicit denial that the authors had been inspired to speak truth that transcended the scope of their understanding. Winchell, *Preadamites*, pp. 456–457.

2. G[eorge] F. W[right], "Adjustments between the Bible and Science," *Bibliotheca Sacra*, 49 (1892), 154; Frederic Gardiner, " 'Errors' of the Scriptures," *Bibliotheca Sacra*, 36 (1879), 507–508, 533. See also R. S. MacArthur, "Christianity and the Secular Spirit," *New Princeton Review*, n.s. 5 (1888), 176; John W. Chadwick, "The Revelation of God," *Unitarian Review*, 27 (1887), 498–499.

3. Arnold Guyot, *Creation; or, The Biblical Cosmogony in the Light of Modern Science* (New York, 1884), pp. vi–xi, 127–128, 4–5, 135. For a useful brief discussion of Guyot's life and thought, see Ronald L. Numbers, *Creation by Natural Law: Laplace's Nebular Hypothesis in American Thought* (Seattle, 1977), pp. 91–94.

4. G. Frederick Wright, *Story of My Life and Work* (Oberlin, 1916), p. 427. See also W[right], "Adjustments," p. 154; Augustus Hopkins Strong, *Systematic Theology: A Compendium and Commonplace-Book Designed to Set Forth Great Truths in Popular Form* (New York, 1888), pp. 193–194; Alexander Winchell, *Reconciliation of Science and Religion* (New York, 1877), pp. 356–363, 381–382; James McCosh, "A Symposium on Evolution: Is the Darwinian Theory of Evolution Reconcilable with the Bible? If So, with What Limitations?" *Homiletic Monthly*, 8 (1884), 234; Anon., "The Cosmogony of Genesis: Professor Driver's Critique of Professor Dana," *Bibliotheca Sacra*, 45 (1888), 356–365.

5. G. Frederick Wright, *Studies in Science and Religion* (Andover, 1882), pp. 368–369; W[right], "Adjustments," pp. 156, 154; George F. Wright, "Recent Works Bearing on the Relation of Science to Religion. No. 2: The Divine Method of Producing Living Species," *Bibliothea Sacra*, 33 (1876), 457–458. For Wright's belief in plenary inspiration, see, for example, [George Frederick Wright], "Dr. Ladd on Alleged Discrepancies and Errors of the Bible," *Bibliotheca Sacra*, 41 (1884), 389.

For views similar to those of Wright, see James D. Dana, "Creation; or, The Biblical Cosmogony in the Light of Modern Science," *Bibliotheca Ṣacra*, 42 (1885), 217–218; Alexander Winchell, "Symposium on Evolution," pp. 345–346.

6. George P. Fisher, "The Alleged Conflict of Natural Science and Religion," *Princeton Review*, n.s. 12 (1883), 37–38. See also F. H. Johnson, "Theistic Evolution," *Andover Review*, 1 (1884), 377; James T. Bixby, *Similarities of Physical and Religious Knowledge* (New York, 1876), p. 14; J. S. Candlish, "Reformation Theology in the Light of Modern Knowledge," *Presbyterian Review*, 8 (1887), 231.

7. Minot J. Savage, *The Irrepressible Conflict between Two World Theories* (Boston, 1892), p. 20; William North Rice, "Genesis and Geology [1892]," in *Twenty-five Years of Scientific Progress and Other Essays* (New York, 1894), pp. 160–173 (quotation on p. 160). See also William North Rice, "Evolution [1890]," ibid., pp. 84–85; Charles Augustus Briggs, *Whither? A Theological Question for the Times* (New York, 1889), p. 106; Henry Morton, "The Cosmogony of Genesis and Its Reconcilers," *Bibliotheca Sacra*, 54 (1897), 267, 272–292, 436–461.

8. S. R. Calthrop, "The Great Synthesis; or, The Foundation on Which All Things Rest," *Unitarian Review and Religious Magazine*, 16 (1881), 1. See also Morton, "Cosmogony of Genesis," p. 266.

9. William R. Hutchison, *The Modernist Impulse in American Protestantism* (Cambridge, Mass., 1976), p. 95.

10. Theodore T. Munger, *The Freedom of Faith* (Boston, 1883), pp. 16–21.

11. Newman Smyth, *Old Faiths in New Light*, 2d ed. (New York, 1879), pp. 171–172, 151, 180–181, 175, 138, 166, 183; Newman Smyth, *Recollections and Reflections* (New York, 1926), p. 208. A somewhat different interpretation of Smyth's views concerning science and Genesis can be found in Hutchison, *Modernist Impulse*, pp. 89–90. For an expression of ambivalence about the relationship between science and religion similar to that of Smyth, see Asa Gray, *Natural Science and Religion: Two Lectures Delivered to the Theological School of Yale College* (New York, 1880), pp. 8–9.

12. William Rupp, "The Bible and Science," *Mercersburg Review*, n.s. 8 (1874), 58–60; William Rupp, "The Theory of Evolution and the Christian Faith," *Reformed Quarterly Review*, 35 (1888), 162–165, 146, 149.

13. Henry A. Stimson, "The Bible in the Conditions Created by Modern Scholarship," *Bibliotheca Sacra*, 57 (1900), 375; B. F. Cocker, *The Theistic Conception of the World: An Essay in Opposition to Certain Tendencies of Modern Thought* (New York, 1875), pp. 136–138; Henry Ward Beecher, *Evolution and Religion* (New York, 1885), p. 32; Frank Hugh Foster, "The Authority and Inspiration of the Scriptures," *Bibliotheca Sacra*, 52 (1895), 254; E. S. Breidenbaugh, "Concerning Certain Misconceptions in Inquiries into the Relation between Science and Religion," *Lutheran Quarterly*, n.s. 9 (1880), 280; Morton, "Cosmogony of Genesis," pp. 267–268; [Thomas] Howard MacQueary, *The Evolution of Man and Christianity* (New York, 1890), pp. 81–82; Lyman Abbott, *The Evolution of Christianity* (Boston, 1892), pp. 45–46.

14. J. M. Whiton, "The Alleged Infallibility of the Scriptures Practically Considered," *New Englander*, n.s. 5 (1882), 66–67; Smyth, *Old Faiths*, pp. 36, 34; Beecher, *Evolution and Religion*, pp. 61, 56; Henry Ward Beecher, "Symposium on Evolution," p. 471. See also Myron Adams, *The Continuous Creation: An Application of the Evolutionary Philosophy to the Christian Religion* (Boston, 1889), pp. 46–47; George B. Stevens, "Professor Shedd's Dogmatic Theology," *New Englander and Yale Review*, n.s. 14 (1889), 94–95; Washington Gladden, *Who Wrote the Bible? A Book for the People* (Boston, 1891), pp. 354–355.

A perceptive discussion of the conflicts among American Protestant intellectuals regarding the authority and inspiration of the Bible is Grant Wacker, "The Demise of Biblical Civilization," in Nathan O. Hatch and Mark A. Noll, eds., *The Bible in America: Essays in Cultural History* (New York, 1982), pp. 121–138.

15. Beecher, *Evolution and Religion*, pp. 35–37, 68; David J. Hill, "Antecedent Probabilities of a Revelation," *Princeton Review*, n.s. 12 (1883), 176–177. See also Smyth, *Old Faiths*, pp. 38, 62–127; Adams, *Continuous Creation*, p. 47; Minot J. Savage, *The*

Religion of Evolution (Boston, 1876), pp. 54–55; W. M. Lisle, "The Evolution of Christianity," *Bibliotheca Sacra*, 49 (1892), 436–445; W. Douglas MacKenzie, "Evolution Theories and Christian Doctrine," *Bibliotheca Sacra*, 54 (1897), 555; Abbott, *Evolution of Christianity*, pp. 40–41, 53–57, 66. Jerry Wayne Brown has noted that in the period prior to 1875 Moses Stuart adopted a similar view of the Scriptures but did not recognize its consistency with the notion that they conveyed one system of truth. Jerry Wayne Brown, *The Rise of Biblical Criticism in America, 1800–1870: The New England Scholars* (Middletown, Conn., 1969), p. 58.

16. W[illiam] H. A[llison], "Clarke, William Newton," *Dictionary of American Biography*, 4: 164 (hereafter cited as *DAB*).

17. William Newton Clarke, *Sixty Years with the Bible* (New York, 1912), pp. 40, 42, 56–57, 159–160, 144, 178, 104–105. See also William Newton Clarke, *An Outline of Christian Theology* (New York, 1898), pp. 22, 27, 32–33.

18. Robert Collyer in Elizabeth Stuart Phelps et al., "The Combat for the Faith: The Field-Ingersoll-Gladstone Controversy," *North American Review*, 147 (1888), 19–20. See also Savage, *Religion of Evolution*, p. 189; Clarke, *An Outline*, pp. 40, 45–47; Beecher, *Evolution and Religion*, pp. 37–39; Henry B. Smith, *Apologetics: A Course of Lectures*, ed. William S. Karr (New York, 1881), pp. 208–209; R. Heber Newton, *The Right and Wrong Uses of the Bible* (New York, 1883), p. 2; Lyman Abbott, *The Theology of an Evolutionist* (Boston, 1897), p. 57; Gladden, *Who Wrote*, p. 356; Briggs, *Whither?* pp. 69, 76–77; Alan Richardson, *The Bible in the Age of Science* (Philadelphia, 1961), p. 68.

19. Foster, "Authority and Inspiration," p. 254. A useful brief biographical treatment of Stearns is George L. Prentiss, "Biographical Sketch," in Lewis French Stearns, *Present Day Theology: A Popular Discussion of Leading Doctrines of the Christian Faith* (New York, 1893), pp. v–xxiv.

20. Lewis F. Stearns, "Reconstruction in Theology," *New Englander*, n.s. 5 (1882), 91; Lewis French Stearns, "The Present Direction of Theological Thought in the Congregational Churches of the United States [1891]," *Present Day Theology*, pp. 538–539.

21. Foster, "Authority and Inspiration," pp. 255, 235–237. See also Strong, *Systematic Theology*, p. 103; Egbert C. Smyth, "Dogma in Religion," *Andover Review*, 14 (1890), 507; James H. Fairchild, "Authenticity and Inspiration of the Scriptures," *Bibliotheca Sacra*, 49 (1892), 23; Morton, "Cosmogony of Genesis," p. 462; Charles A. Briggs, *Biblical Study*, 2d ed. (New York, 1885), pp. 241–242; Asher H. Wilcox, "The Ultimate Criteria of Christian Doctrine," *Andover Review*, 8 (1887), 337.

22. Foster, "Authority and Inspiration," p. 251.

23. Rice, "Genesis and Geology," pp. 134–135; Whiton, "Alleged Infallibility," p. 68. See also James Morris Whiton, *The Evolution of Revelation: A Critique of Conflicting Opinions Concerning the Old Testament* (New York, 1885), pp. 8–10; Rice, "Evolution [1890]," p. 85; F. H. Hedge in F. H. Hedge et al., "What Is Inspiration?" *North American Review*, 127 (1878), 307; William Hayes Ward, "Whether It Is Right to Study the Bible," *Independent*, 32 (February 26, 1880), 4; Beecher, *Evolution and Religion*, p. 60.

24. Joseph Le Conte, *Evolution and Its Relation to Religious Thought* (New York, 1888), p. 311. See also Munger, *Freedom of Faith*, p. 19.

25. Smyth, *Old Faiths*, pp. 76, 43. See also Munger, *Freedom of Faith*, pp. 16–17; Morton, "Cosmogony of Genesis," p. 267; Stevens, "Shedd's Dogmatic Theology," p. 94; Jacob Gould Schurman, *Belief in God: Its Origin, Nature, and Basis* (1890; New York, 1902), p. 261.

For my discussion of the reception of "higher criticism" in the United States, I have drawn on Ira V. Brown, "The Higher Criticism Comes to America, 1880–1900," *Journal of the Presbyterian Historical Society*, 38 (1960), 193–212; Norman H. Maring, "Baptists and Changing Views of the Bible, 1865–1918," *Foundations*, 1 (July 1958), 52–75, and (October 1958), 30–61; Jurgen Herbst, *The German Historical School in American Scholarship: A Study in the Transfer of Culture* (Ithaca, 1965), pp. 73–97; Wacker, "Demise," pp. 124–125, and passim; and Richardson, *Bible in the Age of Science*, pp. 68–69. I should also take note of an excellent essay that appeared after I had written the section on higher criticism: James R. Moore, "Geologists and Interpreters of Genesis in the Nineteenth Century," in David C. Lindberg and Ronald L. Numbers, eds., *God and Nature: Historical Essays on the Encounter between Christianity and Science* (Berkeley, 1986), pp. 322–350.

26. Stimson, "Bible in the Conditions," p. 371; Josiah Royce, "Is There a Philosophy of Evolution?" *Unitarian Review*, 32 (1889), 14; MacKenzie, "Evolution Theories," p. 555. For the relationship of the theory of organic evolution to biblical criticism in the work of the Baptist biblical theologian Crawford H. Toy, see David G. Lyon, "Crawford Howell Toy," *Harvard Theological Review*, 13 (1920), 8. A useful discussion of historicism is Maurice Mandelbaum, *History, Man, and Reason: A Study in Nineteenth-Century Thought* (Baltimore, 1971), pp. 41–49, and passim; for the connection between Darwinism and historicism, see pp. 47, 77. For a discerning discussion of the importance of historicism in late-nineteenth-century America and its impact on ideas concerning the Bible, see Wacker, "Demise," pp. 126–133. See also Sydney E. Ahlstrom, *A Religious History of the American People* (New Haven, 1972), pp. 771–774; and James Turner, *Without God, Without Creed: The Origins of Unbelief in America* (Baltimore, 1985), pp. 135–136, 150–153.

Some contemporaries testified that historical criticism of the Bible provoked even more controversy than the theory of evolution among American Protestants. See, for example, William Jewett Tucker, *My Generation: An Autobiographical Interpretation* (Boston, 1919), p. 6. As John C. Greene has suggested, however, Darwin's work acted as a "catalyst" for the controversy over biblical criticism. John C. Greene, "Darwin and Religion," *Proceedings of the American Philosophical Society*, 103 (1959), 716–717.

27. Chadwick, "Revelation of God," pp. 494–495; Samuel Harris, "Have We a Theology?" *New Englander and Yale Review*, n.s. 9 (1886), 23. See also Henry Ward Beecher, "Progress of Thought in the Church," *North American Review*, 135 (1882), 106–107; Briggs, *Whither?* pp. 9–10; Clarke, *An Outline*, p. 23; George T. Ladd, *The Doctrine of Sacred Scripture* (New York, 1883), 2: 459; T. T. Munger, "Evolution and the Faith," *Century Magazine*, n.s. 10 (1886), 114; John C. Greene, *Darwin and the Modern World View* (Baton Rouge, 1961), pp. 46–48.

28. Alexander V. G. Allen, "The Theological Renaissance of the Nineteenth Century," *Princeton Review*, n.s. 10 (1882), 280–281; Clarke, *Sixty Years*, pp. 147–149, 220–221; Adams, *Continuous Creation*, p. 51. See also Beecher, "Progress of Thought," p. 107; George T. Ladd, "History and the Concept of God," *Bibliotheca Sacra*, 37 (1880), 597–599, 624–625.

29. Bixby, *Similarities*, p. 221; Beecher, *Evolution and Religion*, pp. 46, 24. See also Philip S. Moxom, "Symposium on the 'New Theology': What Are Its Essential Features? Is It Better Than the Old?" *Homiletic Review*, 11 (1886), 207; Newman Smyth, *The Religious Feeling: A Study for Faith* (New York, 1877), p. 147; Clarke, *An Outline*, pp. 50–51; Gardiner, "Bearing of Recent Scientific Thought," p. 63; David N. Beach,

"The Reconstruction of Theology," *Bibliotheca Sacra*, 54 (1897), 121; Greene, *Darwin and the Modern World View*, p. 48.

30. Allen, "Theological Renaissance," p. 281; MacQueary, *Evolution of Man*, p. 251. See also Smyth, *Old Faiths*, pp. 35, 36–37, 184–185, 253; Smyth, "Dogma in Religion," p. 497; Clarke, *An Outline*, p. 16; George Harris, *Moral Evolution* (Boston, 1896), p. 195; Ladd, "History and the Concept of God," pp. 609–610; Whiton, *Evolution of Revelation*, p. 22. For a fuller discussion of the centrality of "cultural immanentism" in Protestant liberalism, see Hutchison, *Modernist Impulse*, pp. 2, 79, and passim.

31. Frank Hugh Foster, "Evolution and the Evangelical System of Doctrine," *Bibliotheca Sacra*, 50 (1893), 419; Foster, "Authority and Inspiration," pp. 72–73. See also George F. Genung, "The Trustworthiness of Spiritual Apprehension," *Andover Review*, 7 (1887), 139–140; Abbott, *Evolution of Christianity*, pp. 118–120. Discussions of the Christian consciousness include George Harris, "The Function of the Christian Consciousness," *Andover Review*, 2 (1884), 338–352; Smyth, *Religious Feeling*; Frank Hugh Foster, "Christian Experience as a Source of Systematic Theology," *Bibliotheca Sacra*, 48 (1897), 586–604; Asher H. Wilcox, "The Ultimate Criteria of Christian Doctrine," *Andover Review*, 8 (1887), 343; William B. Clarke, "The Nature and Working of the Christian Consciousness," *Andover Review*, 7 (1887), 376–390; Savage, *Religion of Evolution*, pp. 186–187; Lewis F. Stearns, *Evidence of Christian Experience* (New York, 1890), pp. 295–296 and passim. Useful secondary accounts include Daniel Day Williams, *The Andover Liberals: A Study in American Theology* (1941; New York, 1970), esp. pp. 92–93; Richardson, *Bible in the Age of Science*, pp. 82–84; Herbst, *German Historical School*, pp. 86–92. A perceptive discussion of the varied means that have been attached to the concept of religious experience during the course of American religious history is Daniel D. Williams, "Tradition and Experience in American Theology," in James Ward Smith and A. Leland Jamison, eds., *The Shaping of American Religion* (Princeton, 1961), pp. 443–495. Although the idea that religious experience was a source of divine revelation had appeared in the thought of some American Protestants prior to 1875, it was not prominent among a significant segment of the Protestant intellectual community until the last quarter of the nineteenth century. The sources, content, and function of the concept of religious experience and the Christian consciousness merit a good deal more study than they have received from historians. As Frank M. Turner has demonstrated, the appeal of subjective experience was not limited to liberal Protestants. Frank Miller Turner, *Between Science and Religion: The Reaction to Scientific Naturalism in Late Victorian England* (New Haven, 1974), p. 23 and passim. I suspect that a clearer understanding of the popularity of such experience would reveal a good deal about the nature of American culture in the late nineteenth century.

32. Allen, "Theological Renaissance," pp. 280–281; Harris, "Function of the Christian Consciousness," pp. 351, 339–340; Smyth, *Religious Feeling*, pp. 169–170, 106. See also G[eorge] H[arris], "The Christian Consciousness—Criticism and Comment," *Andover Review*, 2 (1884), 594; Clarke, "Nature and Working," pp. 376–378, 387; James T. Bixby, "From What Faculties Does Religion Spring?—The Psychology of Religion," *New Englander and Yale Review*, n.s. 9 (1886), 1022–1023; W. R. Benedict, "Theism and Evolution," *Andover Review*, 6 (1886), 347; Chadwick, "Revelation of God," p. 497; Foster, "Authority and Inspiration," p. 72; Samuel Harris, *The Philosophical Basis of Theism* (New York, 1883), pp. 15–16; Wilcox, "Ultimate Criteria," pp. 339–340.

33. Henry Graham, "God in Human Consciousness," *Methodist Review*, 5th ser.,

3 (1887), 579; Allen, "Theological Renaissance," pp. 280–281; Clarke, *Sixty Years*, p. 221. See also Smyth, *Old Faiths*, p. 253; Washington Gladden, *Recollections* (Boston, 1909), p. 426; John Coleman Adams, "The Christ and the Creation," *Andover Review*, 17 (1892), 227; Abbott, *Theology of an Evolutionist*, p. 73; Moxom, "Symposium on the 'New Theology,' " p. 205; James Douglas, "The Divine Immanency," *Bibliotheca Sacra*, 45 (1888), 341; Alexander Mair, "Contributions of Christianity to Science," *Presbyterian Review*, 9 (1888), 48–49; Whiton, *Evolution of Revelation*, p. 23.

34. F. H. Johnson, "Coöperative Creation," *Andover Review*, 3 (1885), 438; G. B. Willcox, "Is Theology a Progressive Science?" *New Englander and Yale Review*, n.s. 15 (1889), 306. See also Stearns, "Reconstruction," p. 101; Munger, *Freedom of Faith*, pp. 58–59; Abbott, *Evolution of Christianity*, pp. 21–25; George F. Moore, "The Modern Historical Movement and Christian Faith," *Andover Review*, 10 (1888), 340; Foster, "Evolution and the Evangelical System of Doctrine," p. 424.

35. Smyth, *Old Faiths*, pp. 38, 76. See also Clarke, *An Outline*, pp. 31–34; Abbott, *Theology of an Evolutionist*, pp. 60–67; MacQueary, *Evolution of Man*, pp. 250–251; Foster, "Evolution and the Evangelical System of Doctrine," p. 423. In itself, of course, this view of the Bible was not notably different from that adopted by proponents of plenary inspiration. The difference lay elsewhere. In the first place, Smyth and others did not assume that all ideas in the Bible had been inspired by God. Hence, they did not feel compelled to hold that the language God had "condescended" to use was compatible with truth. Especially important, they did not limit their concern with God's gradual revelation and inspiration to the scriptural narrative.

36. E[dward] M. W[eyer], "Ladd, George Trumbull," *DAB*, 10: 525–526; Edwin G. Boring, *A History of Experimental Psychology*, 2d ed. (New York, 1950), pp. 524–526.

37. Ladd, "History and the Concept of God," pp. 612, 599–600, 624; George T. Ladd, "The Difficulties of the Concept of God," *Bibliotheca Sacra*, 34 (1877), 597.

38. Ladd, "Difficulties of the Concept of God," p. 597; Johnson, "Coöperative Creation," p. 438. See also Graham, "God in Human Consciousness," p. 579; Adams, *Continuous Creation*, p. 178; Smyth, *Old Faiths*, pp. 71–118; MacKenzie, "Evolution Theories," pp. 555, 558–559; Moxom, "Symposium on the 'New Theology,' " pp. 205–206.

39. Ladd, *Doctrine of Sacred Scripture*, 2: 453–454, 465, 459, 488; Smyth, *Religious Feeling*, pp. 169–170. See also Gladden, *Recollections*, p. 426; Douglas, "Divine Immanency," p. 341; MacQueary, *Evolution of Man*, p. 242; Beach, "Reconstruction," p. 131.

40. Elizabeth Stuart Phelps, "What Does Revelation Reveal?" *North American Review*, 134 (1882), 470. See also Beecher, *Evolution and Religion*, pp. 40–41.

41. Stimson, "Bible in the Conditions," p. 370; Hill, "Antecedent Probabilities," p. 177. See also Adams, *Continuous Creation*, pp. 54–55, 124; Lisle, "Evolution of Christianity," p. 433; Foster, "Evolution and the Evangelical System of Doctrine," pp. 413–414; Moxom, "Symposium on the 'New Theology,' " p. 206; Abbott, *Theology of an Evolutionist*, pp. 9–10; J. Lewis Diman, *Orations and Essays: With Selected Parish Sermons* (Boston, 1882), p. 406; Adams, "Christ," p. 227.

42. Moore, "Modern Historical Movement," pp. 333–335, 340–341; Harris, *Philosophical Basis of Theism*, pp. 455-456; Stearns, *Present Day Theology*, p. 30; John Fiske, "What Is Inspiration?" *The Miscellaneous Writings of John Fiske* (Boston, 1902), 8: 111; Mair, "Contributions of Christianity," pp. 48–49. See also Beecher, *Evolution and Religion*, p. 54; Smyth, *Religious Feeling*, p. 155; Abbott, *Theology of an Evolutionist*, p. 52;

Lyman Abbott, *Reminiscences* (Boston, 1915), pp. 456–460; George A. Thayer, "Christianity in the Process of Evolution," *Unitarian Review*, 34 (1890), 17; H. G. Wood, *Belief and Unbelief since 1850* (Cambridge, 1955), p. 55.

43. Smyth, *Old Faiths*, p. 119; Gladden, *Recollections*, p. 426.

44. Stearns, *Present Day Theology*, pp. 100, 97, 93; Stearns, "Reconstruction," p. 101. See also Stearns, *Evidence*, p. 314; Stearns, "Present Direction," p. 539; Lisle, "Evolution of Christianity," p. 445; Harris, "Function of the Christian Consciousness," p. 344.

45. Stearns, *Evidence*, pp. 239, 24–25; Stearns, "Reconstruction," pp. 95, 101; Wilcox, "Ultimate Criteria," pp. 343, 348. See also Stearns, *Present Day Theology*, p. 97; Harris, "Function of the Christian Consciousness," pp. 343–345, 349; The Editors of the *Andover Review*, *Progressive Orthodoxy: A Contribution to the Christian Interpretation of Christian Doctrines* (1885; Boston, 1886), p. 10; Lisle, "Evolution of Christianity," p. 445. For a summary of the views of the Andover theologians on this subject, see Williams, *Andover Liberals*, p. 171.

46. Clarke, *Sixty Years*, p. 149; Abbott, *Theology of an Evolutionist*, pp. 65, 62. See also Briggs, *Whither?* pp. 11, 15, 17; Savage, *Religion of Evolution*, p. 189.

47. Harris, "Function of the Christian Consciousness," p. 350. See also Moore, "Modern Historical Movement," p. 340; Briggs, *Whither?* pp. 281–282; Clarke, *An Outline*, pp. 18, 21; Abbott, *Evolution of Christianity*, p. 27; Augustus Jay DuBois, "What Has Science to Do with Religion?" *Century Magazine*, 49 (1894), 233; Frank H. Foster, "The Argument from Christian Experience for the Inspiration of the Bible," *Bibliotheca Sacra*, 40 (1883), 98.

48. Harris, *Moral Evolution*, p. 426; Clarke, "Nature and Working," p. 385; Willcox, "Is Theology," p. 303. See also Stearns, "Reconstruction," p. 101.

49. Hill, "Antecedent Probabilities," p. 177; Harris, "Christian Consciousness," pp. 597–598; James H. Fairchild, "Progress of Religious Thought," *Bibliotheca Sacra*, 49 (1892), 414; Beach, "Reconstruction," p. 135. See also Harris, "Function of the Christian Consciousness," p. 349; Smyth, *Old Faiths*, pp. 116–118, 253; Editors of the *Andover Review*, *Progessive Orthodoxy*, p. 10; Abbott, *Reminiscences*, pp. 461–462; Beecher, *Evolution and Religion*, p. 41.

50. Adams, *Continuous Creation*, p. 258. See also Smyth, *Recollections*, p. 93; Harris, "Function of the Christian Consciousness," p. 348.

51. Foster, "Evolution and the Evangelical System of Doctrine," pp. 410–411.

52. Smyth, *Old Faiths*, pp. 253, 244–245; Briggs, *Biblical Study*, pp. 186, 364. See also Savage, *Religion of Evolution*, p. 190; Abbott, *Theology of an Evolutionist*, pp. 70–73; Whiton, *Evolution of Revelation*, pp. 27–28; Egbert C. Smyth, Review of *The Continuity of Christian Thought*, by Alexander V. G. Allen, *Andover Review*, 3 (1885), 291; Stearns, "Present Direction," pp. 540–541; Wilcox, "Ultimate Criteria," pp. 350–351; Foster, "Authority and Inspiration," p. 234; Moore, "Modern Historical Movement," pp. 338–340; Editors of the *Andover Review*, *Progressive Orthodoxy*, pp. 16, 205, 231; Williams, *Andover Liberals*, pp. 94–95, 104–113, 171.

53. Charles W. Eliot, "On the Education of Ministers," *Princeton Review*, n.s. 11 (1883), 346; Benjamin W. Bacon, "Is Theology Scientific?" *New Englander and Yale Review*, n.s. 10 (1887), 57–58; James G. Roberts, "The Inductive Method in Theology," *New Englander*, n.s. 4 (1881), 745; Beach, "Reconstruction," pp. 135, 130–131. See also Smyth, "Dogma in Religion," p. 495; Harris, *Philosophical Basis of Theism*, pp. 15–16; James De Koven, *Sermons Preached on Various Occasions* (New York, 1880), p. 202;

Beecher, "Progress of Thought," p. 104; Theodore T. Munger, *The Appeal to Life* (Boston, 1887), pp. v–vi; J. H. Allen, "Present Aspects of the Liberal Movement," *Unitarian Review and Religious Magazine*, 26 (1886), 242–243; Edward A. Lawrence, "Natural Law in the Spiritual World," *Andover Review*, 6 (1886), 22; Foster, "Evolution and the Evangelical System of Doctrine," p. 410; DuBois, "What Has Science," p. 228; Williams, *Andover Liberals*, p. 89.

54. Le Conte, *Evolution and Its Relation*, pp. 310–311; Beecher, "Progress of Thought," p. 107. See also Wilcox, "Ultimate Criteria," p. 342.

55. James Thompson Bixby, "Science and Religion as Allies," *Popular Science Monthly*, 9 (1876), 692; Harris, "Function of the Christian Consciousness," pp. 349, 340, 346. See also Thayer, "Christianity and the Process of Evolution," p. 5; Wilcox, "Ultimate Criteria," pp. 339, 344; Benedict, "Theism and Evolution," pp. 346–348; Moore, "Modern Historical Movement," p. 339; Clarke, "Nature and Working," p. 379; Alexander V. G. Allen, *The Continuity of Christian Thought: A Study of Modern Theology in the Light of Its History* (Boston, 1884), pp. 17–18; Stearns, *Evidence*, pp. 265–266, 289–290.

56. Benedict, "Theism and Evolution," p. 346; Bixby, *Similarities*, p. 225. See also Harris, "Function of the Christian Consciousness," p. 341; Harris, *Philosophical Basis of Theism*, pp. 15–16; Stearns, *Evidence*, p. 258.

57. E[dward] C. M[oore], "Harris, George," *DAB*, 8: 308–309.

58. Harris, "Function of the Christian Consciousness," pp. 338–352 (quotations on pp. 345 and 338). See also Stearns, *Evidence*, pp. 29–31, 265–266, 317–318, and passim; Foster, "Argument from Christian Experience," pp. 104–105, 136; Foster, "Authority and Inspiration," pp. 72–73.

59. Francis A. Henry, "Reconstruction in Religious Thought," *Princeton Review*, n.s. 14 (1884), 24; Stearns, *Evidence*, pp. 320–321; Lyman Abbott, "Evolution and Theology," *Andover Review*, 4 (1885), 567. See also Smyth, *Recollections*, p. 145; Anon., "Tradition, Criticism, and Science," *Andover Review*, 3 (1885), 53.

60. Harris, "Function of the Christian Consciousness," p. 340.

61. Wilcox, "Ultimate Criteria," pp. 345, 341, 347; Abbott, *Reminiscences*, pp. 450–452; Harris, "Function of the Christian Consciousness," p. 339. See also Foster, "Evolution and the Evangelical System of Doctrine," pp. 418–419, 422–423; Foster, "Argument from Christian Experience," pp. 132, 137; F. H. Johnson, "Revelation as a Factor in Evolution," *Andover Review*, 5 (1886), 30; R. Jackson Wilson, *In Quest of Community: Social Philosophy in the United States, 1860–1920* (New York, 1968), pp. 44–48. John Chadwick observed that whereas scientific investigation was open only to a finite number of individuals, religious experience, in principle at least, was available to everyone. J. W. Chadwick, "The Basis of Religion," *Unitarian Review and Religious Magazine*, 26 (1886), 257–258.

62. Wilcox, "Ultimate Criteria," pp. 345, 349–350. See also Harris, "Function of the Christian Consciousness," p. 345; Clarke, "Nature and Working," p. 390, and passim; Beecher, *Evolution and Religion*, pp. 40–41; Editors of the *Andover Review, Progressive Orthodoxy*, p. 5. Daniel Day Williams has made this point with specific regard to the Andover liberals. Williams, *Andover Liberals*, pp. 88–91. My discussion of this issue is indebted to Williams' treatment of it.

63. Harris, "Function of the Christian Consciousness," p. 341; Stearns, *Evidence*, pp. 322, 298–299, 313–318, 323–338. See also Wilcox, "Ultimate Criteria," pp. 342, 350; Harris, "Christian Consciousness," p. 597; Stearns, "Present Direction," p.

535. For a perceptive discussion of the "vague and shifting" nature of the epistemology embraced by the Andover theologians, see Williams, *Andover Liberals*, pp. 113, 171–176.

64. Stearns, *Evidence*, p. 25; Foster, "Evolution and the Evangelical System of Doctrine," pp. 410–411, 422–423. See also Wilcox, "Ultimate Criteria," p. 350; Willcox, "Is Theology," p. 303; Anon., "Religious Authority," *Andover Review*, 17 (1892), 305–306; Moore, "Modern Historical Movement," p. 339; Smyth, *Religious Feeling*, p. 166; Briggs, *Whither?* pp. 21–22.

65. Harris, *Moral Evolution*, p. 424; Foster, "Evolution and the Evangelical System of Doctrine," pp. 419–420; Edward J. Young, "The Sufficiency of Christianity," *Unitarian Review and Religious Magazine*, 25 (1886), 342; Smyth, *Religious Feeling*, p. 149. See also Anon., "How Religions Grow," *Unitarian Review*, 33 (1890), 247. Bruce Kuklick has noted that the American pragmatists employed a similar line of reasoning. Bruce Kuklick, *The Rise of American Philosophy: Cambridge, Massachusetts, 1860–1930* (New Haven, 1977), p. xix.

66. Willcox, "Is Theology," p. 303. See also Smyth, *Religious Feeling*, pp. 115–117. The idea of scriptural development proved particularly popular in accounting for the Old Testament conception of a vengeful God. See, for example, Alexander Winchell, "Anthropomorphism," *Methodist Review*, 5th ser., 1 (1885), 525.

67. Stearns, "Reconstruction," p. 101; Roberts, "Inductive Method," p. 745; Newman Smyth in Newman Smyth, Lyman Abbott, and Henry Ward Beecher (Symposium), "The Revision of Creeds," *North American Review*, 136 (1883), 3; Fairchild, "Progress," p. 414. See also Willcox, "Is Theology," pp. 302–303; Thomas Hitchcock, "The Functions of Unbelief," *North American Review*, 125 (1877), 470; Munger, *Appeal to Life*, p. vii; Smyth, *Old Faiths*, p. 16; Clarke, "Nature and Working," pp. 386–387; Clarke, *An Outline*, p. 19.

68. Smyth in Smyth et al., "Revision of Creeds," p. 2; Harris, "Function of the Christian Consciousness," p. 348; Newman Smyth, *The Orthodox Theology of To-day* (New York, 1881), p. 39. See also Foster, "Evolution and the Evangelical System of Doctrine," p. 418; Joseph Le Conte, "Illustrations of a Law of Evolution of Thought," *Princeton Review*, n.s. 8 (1881), 390; Stearns, "Reconstruction," pp. 82, 101; Whiton, *Evolution of Revelation*, p. 12; Briggs, *Biblical Study*, pp. 36–37.

69. Henry, "Reconstruction," pp. 33, 19, 24; Daniel Curry, "Present Necessity for a Restatement of Christian Beliefs," *Methodist Review*, 5th ser., 2 (1886), 750. See also Stearns, "Reconstruction"; Briggs, *Whither?* pp. 21–22, and passim; S. W. Culver, "Progress in Theology," *Baptist Quarterly*, 10 (1876), 244; Beach, "Reconstruction"; Anon., "The Accountability of the Ultra-Conservatives," *Andover Review*, 1 (1884), 654; Smyth, *Old Faiths*, pp. 31–32; J. M. Whiton, "Darwin and Darwinism," *New Englander*, n.s. 6 (1883), 57. A valuable discussion of demands for reconstruction of theology among Protestants in the late nineteenth century is Hutchison, *Modernist Impulse*, pp. 48–144. I have chosen not to use "New Theology" as an organizing principle for my discussion because proponents of that position responded to and employed the theory of organic evolution in a variety of different ways.

70. Moxom, "Symposium on the 'New Theology,' " pp. 205–206; Harris, *Moral Evolution*, p. 426; Smyth, *Religious Feeling*, p. 166; DuBois, "What Has Science," p. 234. See also Willcox, "Is Theology," p. 303; Allen, *Continuity of Christian Thought*, p. viii.

71. M. Stuart Phelps, "Anthropomorphism," *Princeton Review*, n.s. 8 (1881), 127; Beecher, *Evolution and Religion*, p. 41. See also Harris, "Function of the Christian Consciousness," pp. 352, 344; Adams, *Continuous Creation*, p. 9; Moore, "Modern

Historical Movement," p. 339; Clarke, *Sixty Years*, p. 251; J. G. Schurman, Review of *A History of the Warfare of Science with Theology in Christendom*, by Andrew Dickson White, *Science*, 4 (December 11, 1896), 880.

72. Moore, "Modern Historical Movement," p. 337. See also Briggs, *Whither?* pp. 21–22; Willcox, "Is Theology," p. 303; Savage, *Religion of Evolution*, p. 230; F. B. Hornbrooke, "Religion and Morality," *Unitarian Review and Religious Magazine*, 24 (1885), 310; Phelps, "Anthropomorphism," pp. 127–128. For the role of the evolutionary hypothesis in encouraging uncertainty and relativism, see also Arthur Cushman McGiffert, *The Rise of Modern Religious Ideas* (New York, 1915), pp. 184–185.

Chapter 7. "What Is Man, That Thou Art Mindful of Him?"

1. Henry Ward Beecher, "Progress of Thought in the Church," *North American Review*, 135 (1882), 110. See also Myron Adams, *The Continuous Creation: An Application of the Evolutionary Philosophy to the Christian Religion* (Boston, 1889), p. 257; J. M. Whiton, "Darwin and Darwinism," *New Englander*, n.s. 6 (1883), 57.

2. G[eorge] F. W[right], "Adjustments between the Bible and Science," *Bibliotheca Sacra*, 49 (1892), 154–155. See also J. Max Hark, *The Unity of the Truth in Christianity and Evolution* (New York, 1888), p. 138; B. F. Cocker, *The Theistic Conception of the World* (New York, 1875), pp. 165–166; A. H. Strong, "The Fall and the Redemption of Man in the Light of Evolution," *Sixteenth Annual Session of the Baptist Congress for the Discussion of Current Questions, Nov. 15–17, 1898* (New York, 1898), p. 14; Henry W. Parker, *The Spirit of Beauty: Essays Scientific and Aesthetic* (New York, 1888), p. 128n; Alexander Winchell, *Preadamites; or, A Demonstration of the Existence of Men before Adam; together with a Study of Their Condition, Antiquity, Racial Affinities, and Progressive Dispersion over the Earth* (Chicago, 1880), pp. 293–294.

3. Lyman Abbott, "Evolution and Theology," *Andover Review*, 4 (1885), 564–565; Anon., "Some Thoughts on Evolution," *Independent*, 28 (September 21, 1876), 16; William Hayes Ward, "Whether It Is Right to Study the Bible," *Independent*, 32 (February 26, 1880), 4.

4. Beecher, "Progress of Thought," p. 108; Samuel Harris, *The Philosophical Basis of Theism* (New York, 1883), pp. 527–528. See also F. G. Peabody, "The New Theology," *Unitarian Review and Religious Magazine*, 11 (1879), 366, 368; Henry Ward Beecher, *Evolution and Religion* (New York, 1885), p. 152; Lewis French Stearns, *The Evidence of Christian Experience* (New York, 1890), pp. 65–66, 71; Joseph Le Conte, *Evolution and Its Relation to Religious Thought* (New York, 1888), p. 284; C. C. Everett, "The Theistic Argument as Affected by Recent Theories," *Unitarian Review and Religious Magazine*, 16 (1881), 457.

5. Stearns, *Evidence*, p. 72; George Harris, *Moral Evolution* (Boston, 1896), pp. 233–234. See also Joseph Le Conte, "Man's Place in Nature," *Princeton Review*, 4th ser. (1878), 788–789.

6. Lewis French Stearns, *Present Day Theology: A Popular Discussion of Leading Doctrines of the Christian Faith* (New York, 1893), p. 298; Anon., "Do Our Colleges Teach Evolution?" *Independent*, 31 (December 18, 1879), 14; Anon., "Christian Evolution," *Independent*, 32 (January 8, 1880), 16; Alexander Winchell, "Man and Evolution," *Homiletic Review*, 14 (1887), 538; H. W. Conn, *Evolution of To-day* (New York, 1886), p. 328.

A minority of Christians who accepted the general theory of organic evolution reasoned that if God had created the human mind immediately, He had also created the human body immediately. See for example, Joseph S. Van Dyke, *Theism and Evolution: An Examination of Modern Speculative Theories as Related to Theistic Conceptions of the Universe*, 2d ed. (New York, 1886), pp. 77–78. Augustus H. Strong revised his opinion with regard to the evolution of the human body in response to his altered estimate of the status of scientific opinion on this subject. Cf. Augustus Hopkins Strong, *Systematic Theology: A Compendium and Commonplace-Book Designed for the Use of Theological Students* (Rochester, 1886), pp. 234–236, with Strong, "The Fall," p. 10.

7. F. H. Johnson, "Coöperative Creation," *Andover Review*, 3 (1885), 345; Le Conte, "Man's Place," pp. 788–789; William Rupp, "The Theory of Evolution and the Christian Faith," *Reformed Quarterly Review*, 35 (1888), 165–166. See also George S. Morris, "The Immortality of the Human Soul," *Bibliotheca Sacra*, 33 (1876), 712–713; Cocker, *Theistic Conception*, pp. 165, 360; Edward Thompson, "The Image of God," *Methodist Review*, 5th ser., 4 (1888), 723; Stearns, *Evidence*, p. 72; Newman Smyth, *Old Faiths in New Light*, 2d ed. (New York, 1879), p. 282. The increased emphasis on the doctrine of immanence in the nineteenth century seemed to some Protestants to reinforce humanity's sense of kinship with God. See, for example, Egbert C. Smyth, Review of *The Continuity of Christian Thought*, by Alexander V. G. Allen, *Andover Review*, 3 (1885), 286; Joseph May, "The Twofold Symbol of Godhead," *Unitarian Review and Religious Magazine*, 26 (1886), 105–106.

8. Stearns, *Evidence*, pp. 89–90, 73–75; G. Frederick Wright, *Story of My Life and Work* (Oberlin, 1916), p. 422. See also Van Dyke, *Theism and Evolution*, pp. 71–115; S. H. Kellogg, "The Creative Laws and Scripture Revelation," *Bibliotheca Sacra*, 46 (1889), 407–409; M. H. Valentine, "The Influence of the Theory of Evolution on the Theory of Ethics," *Lutheran Quarterly*, 28 (1898), 226; Stearns, *Present Day Theology*, pp. 296–297; James McCosh, *The Religious Aspect of Evolution*, 2d ed. (New York, 1890), p. 103; George F. Wright, "Recent Works Bearing on the Relation of Science to Religion. No. 2: The Divine Method of Producing Living Species," *Bibliotheca Sacra*, 33 (1876), 455n; James D. Dana, "Creation; or, The Biblical Cosmogony in the Light of Modern Science," *Bibliotheca Sacra*, 42 (1885), 220.

9. F. H. Johnson, "Theistic Evolution," *Andover Review*, 1 (1884), 377; Federic Gardiner, "The Bearing of Recent Scientific Thought upon Theology," *Bibliotheca Sacra*, 35 (1878), 68; Strong, "The Fall," pp. 9–10; T. T. Munger, "Evolution and the Faith," *Century Magazine*, n.s. 10 (1886), 112–113. See also William Newton Clarke, *An Outline of Christian Theology* (New York, 1898), pp. 223–225; Beecher, *Evolution and Religion*, pp. 48–49; Hark, *Unity of the Truth*, pp. 144–149, 152; Lyman Abbott, *The Theology of an Evolutionist* (Boston, 1897), pp. 38–41.

10. Lyman Abbott, *Reminiscences* (Boston, 1915), p. 459; Alexander Winchell, *The Doctrine of Evolution: Its Data, Its Principles, Its Speculations, and Its Theistic Bearings* (New York, 1874), p. 115; Morris, "Immortality," p. 711. See also J. Lewis Diman, *The Theistic Argument as Affected by Recent Theories* (Boston, 1881), p. 181; Frank Hugh Foster, "Evolution and the Evangelical System of Doctrine," *Bibliotheca Sacra*, 50 (1893), 412; Gardiner, "Bearing of Recent Scientific Thought," p. 68; Whiton, "Darwin and Darwinism," pp. 58, 60–61; Beecher, *Evolution and Religion*, p. 49; Gideon J. Burton, "What Should Be the Attitude of the Church toward Evolution as a Working Theory of the Universe?" *Christian Literature*, 13 (1895), 129–130; Clarke, *An Outline*, p. 223; Minot J. Savage, *The Religion of Evolution* (Boston, 1876), p. 82; Rupp, "Theory of Evolution," pp. 151–152.

11. Rupp, "Theory of Evolution," p. 154; Le Conte, "Man's Place," pp. 776–777, 800; Joseph Le Conte, "The Psychical Relation of Man to Animals," *Princeton Review*,

n.s. 13 (1884), 239–261; James T. Bixby, "Immortality and Science," *Bibliotheca Sacra*, 41 (1884), 57; Munger, "Evolution and the Faith," pp. 117–118; Abbott, *Theology of an Evolutionist*, pp. 37–38; Beecher, *Evolution and Religion*, p. 28.

12. F. H. Johnson, "The Evolution of Conscience," *Andover Review*, 2 (1884), 537–543. See also Johnson, "Theistic Evolution," pp. 366–367; Thomas S. Lathrop, "Evolution, Morals, Religion," *Universalist Quarterly and General Review*, n.s. 23 (1886), 459; Harris, *Moral Evolution*, p. 181. Similar enunciations of this position from Protestant evolutionists who affirmed that the human species was the product of a special act of supernatural intervention include Stearns, *Evidence*, pp. 66, 90–91; Valentine, "Influence of the Theory," pp. 212–213.

13. Munger, "Evolution and the Faith," pp. 112–113. See also Lathrop, "Evolution, Morals, Religion," p. 459; Newman Smyth, *The Religious Feeling: A Study for Faith* (New York, 1877), pp. 104–105.

14. Le Conte, "Man's Place," pp. 790–791; Orlando O. A. Rounds, "Evolution and Materialism," *Universalist Quarterly and General Review*, n.s. 17 (1880), 411–414; Morris, "Immortality," pp. 703–704, 708; Burrit A. Smith, "Evolutionism versus Theism," *New Englander*, 33 (1874), 92; George T. Ladd, "The Origin of the Concept of God," *Bibliotheca Sacra*, 34 (1877), 20; J. P. Gordy, "Science and Phenomenalism," *New Englander*, n.s. 5 (1882), 209–210.

15. Johnson, "Theistic Evolution," pp. 373–374; Anson P. Atterbury, "Five Points in an Evolutionary Confession of Faith," *Christian Thought*, 7 (1889), 54, 50–51; G. Frederick Wright, "The Evolutionary Fad," *Bibliotheca Sacra*, 57 (1900), 309–310. See also Le Conte, "Man's Place," p. 788; Joseph Le Conte, "Science and Mental Improvement," *Popular Science Monthly*, 13 (1878), 97; Clarence King, "Catastrophism and Evolution," *American Naturalist*, 11 (1877), 468–470; Winchell, "Man and Evolution," pp. 537–538; Abbott, *Reminiscences*, pp. 459–460.

16. Le Conte, *Evolution and Its Relation*, p. 309; Dana, "Creation," p. 220. See also Morris, "Immortality," pp. 709–710; Thomson, "Image of God," pp. 725–726.

17. W. E. Parson, "The Materialistic Heresy," *Lutheran Quarterly*, 18 (1888), 470, 462–463; Beecher, *Evolution and Religion*, p. 46. See also Peter J. Bowler, *Fossils and Progress: Paleontology and the Idea of Progressive Evolution in the Nineteenth Century* (New York, 1976), p. 117; Munger, "Evolution and the Faith," pp. 111, 118; Clarke, *An Outline*, pp. 116, 224; Harris, *Moral Evolution*, p. 184; Anon., Review of *A Critique of Design-Arguments*, by L. E. Hicks, *Methodist Quarterly Review*, 4th ser., 35 (1883), 571; Adams, *Continuous Creation*, pp. 83–84; M. Valentine, *Natural Theology; or, Rational Theism* (Chicago, 1885), p. 267; Cocker, *Theistic Conception*, pp. 131–132, 169, 254; Paul Carter, *The Spiritual Crisis of the Gilded Age* (De Kalb, Ill., 1971), pp. 27–28.

18. Rupp, "Theory of Evolution," p. 151.

19. John Fiske, *The Destiny of Man Viewed in the Light of His Origin* [1884], *The Miscellaneous Writings of John Fiske* (Boston, 1902), 9: 48, 4, 14, 19–20, 75, 80, 101–102; John Fiske, *The Idea of God as Affected by Modern Knowledge* [1885], ibid., p. 100.

20. Fiske, *Destiny of Man*, pp. 16–19 (quotation on pp. 18–19), 51–52; Fiske, *Idea of God*, p. 101.

21. Fiske, *Destiny of Man*, p. 18. See also Charles Darwin, *The Descent of Man, and Selection in Relation to Sex* (London, 1871), 1: 158; Conn, *Evolution of To-day*, pp. 330–331; Atterbury, "Five Points," p. 55; Adams, *Continuous Creation*, p. 50; Theodore T. Munger, *The Appeal to Life* (Boston, 1887), pp. 297–299; Vida D. Scudder, "Immortality and Evolution," *New Englander*, n.s. 7 (1884), 715–716; Parson, "Materialistic

Heresy," pp. 462–463; Howard N. Brown, "The Divine Humanity," *Unitarian Review and Religious Magazine*, 24 (1885), 27–30.

22. Atterbury, "Five Points," p. 56. See also Smyth, *Religious Feeling*, pp. 68–69; George T. Ladd, "History and the Concept of God," *Bibliotheca Sacra*, 37 (1880), 621–624; Clarke, *An Outline*, p. 242; John Brooks Leavitt, "Has the Time Come to Revise the Thirty-nine Articles?" *American Church Review*, 42 (1883), 129. Useful discussions of the prominent role that the idea of progress played in nineteenth-century thought in the United States and Europe include Arthur Alphonse Ekirch, *The Idea of Progress in America, 1815–1860* (New York, 1944); David W. Marcell, *Progress and Pragmatism: James, Dewey, Beard, and the American Idea of Progress* (Westport, Conn., 1974); Maurice Mandelbaum, *History, Man, and Reason: A Study in Nineteenth-Century Thought* (Baltimore, 1971); and W. Warren Wagar, *Good Tidings: The Belief in Progress from Darwin to Marcuse* (Bloomington, Ind., 1972). For a brief discussion of the importance of the concept of progress held by one group of American liberal Protestants, see Daniel Day Williams, *The Andover Liberals: A Study in American Theology* (1941; New York, 1970), pp. 48–49.

Not all Protestant evolutionists participated in the celebration of progress. Borden Parker Bowne, for example, maintained that "the actual man is a poor affair at best; and it is doubtful if he will ever amount to much. We know more and appear better than past generations, but it is not clear that character is much superior." Borden Parker Bowne, *Philosophy of Theism* (New York, 1887), pp. 259–260.

23. Adams, *Continuous Creation*, pp. 64–65, 187–188; Atterbury, "Five Points," p. 56. See also Mandelbaum, *History, Man, and Reason*, pp. 93–111, esp. 95; J. W. Burrow, *Evolution and Society: A Study in Victorian Social Theory* (Cambridge, 1968).

24. Valentine, "Influence of the Theory," p. 224. See also Anon., "Christianity and Its Modern Competitors," *Andover Review*, 6 (1886), 512, 656; Stearns, *Evidence*, pp. 365–367; Harris, *Moral Evolution*, pp. 5–7, 189–191, 418–419; John Coleman Adams, "The Christ and the Creation," *Andover Review*, 17 (1892), 232; Christopher Stuart Patterson, "Christianity the Conservator of American Civilization," *Century Magazine*, 36 (1888), 855; W. S. Lilly, "The Present Outlook for Christianity," *Forum*, 2 (1886), 317–318; Anon., "The Contributors' Club," *Atlantic Monthly*, 45 (1880), 423; James T. Bixby, "Morality on a Scientific Basis," *Andover Review*, 19 (1893), 220.

25. Harris, *Moral Evolution*, p. 158; Smyth, *Old Faiths*, p. 69; Cocker, *Theistic Conception*, pp. 253–254. See also Adams, *Continuous Creation*, p. 209; George T. Ladd, "The Concept of God as the Ground of Progress," *Bibliotheca Sacra*, 36 (1878), 621–622, 624, 649; Anon., "Christianity and Its Modern Competitors," p. 648.

26. Philip S. Moxom, "Symposium on the 'New Theology': What Are Its Essential Features? Is It Better Than the Old?" *Homiletic Review*, 11 (1886), 206; Charles Loring Brace, quoted in *The Life of Charles Loring Brace*, ed. Emma Brace (New York, 1894), p. 302; Adams, *Continuous Creation*, pp. 192–193. See also James McCosh, *Christianity and Positivism: A Series of Lectures to the Times on Natural Theology and Apologetics* (New York, 1871), p. 70; T. S. Lathrop, "Evolution and Conscience," *Universalist Quarterly*, n.s. 16 (1879), 306; Lewis O. Brastow, "Christian Anthropology and Christian Philanthropy," *New Englander and Yale Review*, n.s. 9 (1886), 130; Johnson, "Coöperative Creation," pp. 451–452.

27. [Thomas] Howard MacQueary, *The Evolution of Man and Christianity* (New York, 1890), pp. 361–362. See also John H. Bellows, "The Moral Element in Science, Literature, and Religion," *Unitarian Review and Religious Magazine*, 22 (1884), 296;

Beecher, *Evolution and Religion*, p. 79; James Freeman Clarke, "Have Animals Souls?" *Atlantic Monthly*, 34 (1874), 421.

28. E. D. Cope, "On the Hypothesis of Evolution, Physical and Metaphysical [1870]," *The Origin of the Fittest: Essays on Evolution* (1886; New York, 1887), p. 168; Adams, *Continuous Creation*, pp. 188, 193, 197–198. See also Thomas Nixon Carver, "The Economic Interpretation of the Fall of Man," *Bibliotheca Sacra*, 57 (1900), 493.

29. Cope, "On the Hypothesis," pp. 168, 172. See also Lyman Abbott, *The Evolution of Christianity* (Boston, 1892), p. 8; A. Jay DuBois, "Science and the Spiritual," *New Englander and Yale Review*, n.s. 10 (1887), 432; Valentine, "Influence of the Theory," p. 224; Munger, *Appeal to Life*, pp. 231, 301–302.

30. DuBois, "Science and the Spiritual," pp. 431–432; Clarke, *An Outline*, p. 245. See also Bellows, "Moral Element," p. 295.

31. Beecher, *Evolution and Religion*, pp. 15, 53; John Dewey, "Ethics and Physical Science," *Andover Review*, 7 (1887), 576. See also Harris, *Moral Evolution*, pp. 189, 215; Stearns, *Evidence*, p. 88; George M. Marsden, *Fundamentalism and American Culture: The Shaping of Twentieth-Century Evangelicalism, 1870–1925* (New York, 1980), p. 24; Sydney E. Ahlstrom, *A Religious History of the American People* (New Haven, 1972), p. 779.

32. Lathrop, "Evolution and Conscience," pp. 318–319. See also Harris, *Moral Evolution*, pp. 82, 85, 95–96, 200, 224–226, 229, 246, 284; Valentine, "Influence of the Theory," pp. 223–224; Augustus Jay DuBois, "Science and Miracles," *New Englander*, n.s. 15 (1889), 28–29; George P. Fisher, *The Grounds of Theistic and Christian Belief* (New York, 1883), p. 67; George A. Gordon, *Immortality and the New Theodicy* (Boston, 1897), p. 85; James McCosh, "Herbert Spencer's 'Data of Ethics,' " *Princeton Review*, 4th ser. (1879), 627.

33. C. C. Everett, "The Ultimate Facts of Ethics," *Unitarian Review*, 28 (1887), 479; Johnson, "Evolution of Conscience," pp. 544–545, 541. See also J. H. Hyslop, "Limitations of Evolution in Ethical Problems," *New Englander and Yale Review*, n.s. 12 (1888), 262; Jacob Gould Schurman, *The Ethical Import of Darwinism* (New York, 1887), pp. 255–256; F. H. Johnson, "Revelation as a Factor in Evolution," *Andover Review*, 5 (1886), 271; Valentine, *Natural Theology*, pp. 210–211; M. J. Savage, "Natural Ethics," *North American Review*, 133 (1881), 233; Charles F. Dole, "The Problem of Duty: A Study in the Philosophy of Ethics," *Andover Review*, 12 (1889), 634–635; Savage, *Religion of Evolution*, pp. 113–119.

34. Harris, *Moral Evolution*, pp. 218–219, 9; Lathrop, "Evolution, Morals, Religion," p. 459; Lathrop, "Evolution and Conscience," pp. 313–315. See also James Thompson Bixby, "Transmutational Ethics," *Unitarian Review and Religious Magazine*, 18 (1882), 307.

35. Schurman, *Ethical Import*, pp. 122–123, 37; George Frederick Wright, "Recent Works Bearing on the Relation of Science to Religion. No. 4: Concerning the True Doctrine of Final Cause or Design in Nature," *Bibliotheca Sacra*, 34 (1877), 384; Borden P. Bowne, "The Ethics of Evolution," *Methodist Quarterly Review*, 4th ser., 32 (1880), 450, 453–454; Johnson, "Evolution of Conscience," p. 539; Bowne, *Philosophy of Theism*, pp. 249, 219–220; Stearns, *Evidence*, pp. 89–91; Valentine, *Natural Theology*, p. 210; Hyslop, "Limitations of Evolution," pp. 275–277; Lathrop, "Evolution and Conscience," pp. 317–319. Taking an exception to this position was Minot Savage, who endorsed the Spencerian notion that the proper "object of all free, sentient activity" was a happy, abundant life. Savage, "Natural Ethics," pp. 237–238.

36. Stearns, *Evidence*, p. 91; Harris, *Moral Evolution*, pp. 9, 131–132. See also James

McCosh, "Development and Growth of Conscience," *Princeton Review*, 4th ser. (1880), 140; Andrew P. Peabody, "Is Pantheism the Legitimate Outcome of Modern Science?" *Journal of Speculative Philosophy*, 19 (1885), 351; Schurman, *Ethical Import*, p. 160; Bixby, "Transmutational Ethics," pp. 306–307; Anon., Review of *The Science of Ethics*, by Leslie Stephen, *New Englander*, n.s. 5 (1882), 706; Valentine, "Influence of the Theory," pp. 209, 222.

37. McCosh, "Herbert Spencer's 'Data,' " pp. 623–624, 627; Bixby, "Transmutational Ethics," p. 307. See also Valentine, "Influence of the Theory," pp. 220–221.

38. Hyslop, "Limitations of Evolution," pp. 266, 269. Biographical details of Hyslop's early career are discussed in R. Laurence Moore, *In Search of White Crows: Spiritualism, Parapsychology, and American Culture* (New York, 1977), pp. 156–159. Moore has maintained that by the time Hyslop published his articles on the relationship between evolution and ethics he had broken with Christianity. The articles themselves provide little help in determining whether this was the case, but the fact that he chose to publish his articles in Protestant journals surely served to disguise this fact.

39. Hyslop, "Limitations of Evolution," pp. 270–280 (quotation on p. 270); J. H. Hyslop, "Evolution and Ethical Problems," *Andover Review*, 9 (1888), 351–353 (quotation on p. 351). See also Bowne, *Philosophy of Theism*, p. 215; Dewey, "Ethics and Physical Science," p. 587.

40. Valentine, "Influence of the Theory," p. 223. See also Bowne, *Philosophy of Theism*, p. 252; Anon., "Christianity and Its Modern Competitors," p. 649. For a perceptive discussion of Huxley's view of the relationship between evolution and ethics, see James G. Paradis, *T. H. Huxley: Man's Place in Nature* (Lincoln, Nebr., 1978), pp. 141–163. Huxley's position is noted in J. H. Hyslop, "The Ethics of Evolution," *New Englander and Yale Review*, n.s. 17 (1890), 270, 273; Valentine, "Influence of the Theory," pp. 216–217; and Burton, "What Should Be the Attitude," p. 127.

41. Dewey, "Ethics and Physical Science," pp. 576, 584–585, 580, 578, 588. On Dewey's realignment with ethical naturalism, see Elizabeth Flower and Murray G. Murphey, *A History of Philosophy in America* (New York, 1977), 2: 818.

42. Dewey, "Ethics and Physical Science," pp. 580–584, 587–591 (quotations on pp. 581, 583, 580).

43. Lathrop, "Evolution and Conscience," p. 319; Hyslop, "Limitations of Evolution," pp. 266–267. See also McCosh, "Herbert Spencer's 'Data,' " p. 622; Anon., Review of *The Science of Ethics*, p. 707.

44. Theodore T. Munger, *The Freedom of Faith* (Boston, 1883), p. 218; McCosh, *Christianity and Positivism*, pp. 64–67. See also Bowne, *Philosophy of Theism*, p. 249; Lathrop, "Evolution and Conscience," p. 319.

45. Hyslop, "Limitations of Evolution," pp. 271, 266–269; Anon., "Christianity and Its Modern Competitors," p. 649; McCosh, *Christianity and Positivism*, p. 62. See also Mattoon M. Curtis, "Sympathy with the Lower Animals," *Bibliotheca Sacra*, 54 (1897), 46; Augustus Hopkins Strong, "The Philosophy of Evolution [1878]," *Philosophy and Religion: A Series of Addresses, Essays and Sermons Designed to Set Forth Great Truths in Popular Form* (New York, 1888), p. 56.

46. Hyslop, "Ethics of Evolution," p. 270. See also Stearns, *Evidence*, p. 91; Harris, *Philosophical Basis*, p. 467; McCosh, *Christianity and Positivism*, p. 64; Lathrop, "Evolution and Conscience," pp. 318–319; Barry Gale, "Darwin and the Concept of a Struggle for Existence: A Study in the Extrascientific Origins of Scientific Ideas," *Isis*,

63 (1972), 322–344; John Greene, "Darwin as a Social Evolutionist," *Science, Ideology, and World View: Essays in the History of Evolutionary Ideas* (Berkeley, 1981), pp. 121–123.

47. Anon., Review of *Immortality and the New Theodicy*, by George A. Gordon, *Bibliotheca Sacra*, 54 (1897), 399; Bixby, "Morality on a Scientific Basis," pp. 210, 217, 219–220; Washington Gladden, "The New Evolution," *McClure's Magazine*, 3 (1894), 242; Clarke, *An Outline*, p. 245. See also Anon., "Current Skepticism—The Scientific Basis of Faith," *Methodist Review*, 5th ser., 8 (1892), 954; W. H. Furness, "Natural Selection in Relation to Man," *Unitarian Review and Religious Magazine*, 5 (1876), 295–296.

48. Johnson, "Evolution of Conscience," pp. 532–534; H. W. Conn, "The Three Great Epochs of World Evolution," *Methodist Review*, 5th ser., 12 (1896), 892; Joseph Le Conte, "Relation of Sociology to Biology," *Popular Science Monthly*, 14 (1879), 336. See also Everett, "Ultimate Facts," p. 498; Harris, *Moral Evolution*, p. 132. A good short sketch of Drummond can be found in James R. Moore, *The Post-Darwinian Controversies: A Study of the Protestant Struggle to Come to Terms with Darwin in Great Britain and America, 1870–1900* (Cambridge, 1979), p. 224. Moore has also written a perceptive longer piece on Drummond, "Evangelicals and Evolution: Henry Drummond, Herbert Spencer, and the Naturalisation of the Spiritual World," *Scottish Journal of Theology*, 38 (1985), 383–417. American Protestant evolutionists who cited Drummond and Spencer in support of the reality of altruistic impulses include Francis D. Kelsey, "Drummond's 'Ascent of Man,' " *Bibliotheca Sacra*, 52 (1895), 351–357, esp. p. 357; Abbott, *Theology of an Evolutionist*, pp. 98–99; and Gladden, "New Evolution," pp. 238–239.

49. Johnson, "Evolution of Conscience," p. 533; Harris, *Moral Evolution*, pp. 29, 418, 10, 26, 130–154; Furness, "Natural Selection," p. 294. See also Everett, "Ultimate Facts," p. 484; Washington Gladden, *Applied Christianity* (1886; New York, 1976), pp. 234–235; Conn, "Three Great Epochs," pp. 892, 899; Gordon, *Immortality*, pp.83–85; Abbott, *Theology of an Evolutionist*, pp. 112–113.

50. Conn, "Three Great Epochs," pp. 900–901, 895–898; Savage, "Natural Ethics," p. 240; Bixby, "Morality on a Scientific Basis," p. 212; Gladden, "New Evolution," p. 242. See also Harris, *Moral Evolution*, pp. 420–422; Newman Smyth, *Christian Ethics* (New York, 1892), pp. 247–249; Francis Howe Johnson, *What Is Reality? An Inquiry as to the Reasonableness of Natural Religion, and the Naturalness of Revealed Religion* (Boston, 1891), p. 247.

51. S. R. Calthrop, "Religion and Evolution," *Religious Magazine and Monthly Review*, 50 (1873), 226.

52. Johnson, "Evolution of Conscience," p. 534. See also Munger, *Appeal to Life*, pp. 300–302; Abbott, *Theology of an Evolutionist*, pp. 41–42, 112; McCosh, *Christianity and Positivism*, pp. 76–77; James Douglas, "The Divine Immanancy," *Bibliotheca Sacra*, 46 (1889), 65; Harris, *Moral Evolution*, pp. 203–204; Lathrop, "Evolution, Morals, Religion," p. 459; Kelsey, "Drummond's 'Ascent,' " p. 357; Gladden, *Applied Christianity*, pp. 235–236; Williams, *Andover Liberals*, pp. 57, 83.

53. John Cotton Smith, "Evolution and a Personal Creator," in C. S. Henry et al., *Christian Truth and Modern Opinion* (New York, 1874), pp. 216–217; George Frederick Wright, "Recent Works Bearing on the Relation of Science to Religion. No. 5: Some Analogies between Calvinism and Darwinism," *Bibliotheca Sacra*, 37 (1880), 54–57.

54. John Thomas Gulick, "Evolution and the Fall of Man," *Bibliotheca Sacra*, 49 (1892), 516–519. See also A. J. Baker, "The Fall of Man a Scientific Fact," *Methodist*

Review, 5th ser., 10 (1894), 872–874, and passim; D. W. Simon, "Evolution and the Fall of Man," *Bibliotheca Sacra*, 54 (1897), 12–20.

55. Clarke, *An Outline*, p. 241; Ward, "Whether It Is Right," p. 4. See also Anon., "A Darwinian Theologian," *Independent*, 29 (March 8, 1877), 23; Anon., "The Religion of To-day," *North American Review*, 129 (1879), 557–558; O. B. Frothingham, in O. B. Frothingham and T. W. Chambers, "Is Man a Depraved Creature?" *North American Review*, 126 (1878), 468–469; J. A. Biddle, "The New Theology," *Bibliotheca Sacra*, 54 (1897), 98; Lyman Abbott, in Newman Smyth et al., "The Revision of Creeds," *North American Review*, 136 (1883), 12; Oliver Wendell Holmes, *The Poet at the Breakfast Table* [1872], *The Works of Oliver Wendell Holmes* (Boston, 1892), 3: 304–305.

56. C[harles] H. L[yttle], "Savage, Minot Jackson," *Dictionary of American Biography*, 16: 389–390.

57. Minot J. Savage, *The Irrepressible Conflict between Two World-Theories* (Boston, 1892), pp. 8–9, 11.

58. Ibid., pp. 25, 77, 170.

59. Ibid., pp. 192, 193, 195; Savage, *Religion of Evolution*, p. 205.

60. Useful discussions of Beecher's life and thought include Clifford E. Clark, Jr., *Henry Ward Beecher: Spokesman for Middle-Class America* (Urbana, 1978); William G. McLoughlin, *The Meaning of Henry Ward Beecher: An Essay on the Shifting Values of Mid-Victorian America, 1840–1870* (New York, 1970); Ernest Trice Thompson, *Changing Emphases in American Preaching* (Philadelphia, 1943), pp. 53–98.

61. Henry Ward Beecher, quoted in Paxton Hibben, *Henry Ward Beecher: An American Portrait* (1927; New York, 1942), pp. 300–301.

62. Beecher, "Progress of Thought," pp. 112–114; Beecher, *Evolution and Religion*, p. 90.

63. Beecher, *Evolution and Religion*, p. 92.

64. Ibid., pp. 92, 248, 139; Henry Ward Beecher, "A Symposium on Evolution: Is the Darwinian Theory of Evolution Reconcilable with the Bible? If So, with What Limitations?" *Homiletic Monthly*, 8 (1884), 471. For views akin to those of Beecher and Savage, see George A. Thayer, "Christianity in the Process of Evolution," *Unitarian Review*, 34 (1890), 14; Adams, *Continuous Creation*, pp. 60–65.

65. William North Rice, "Evolution [1890]," *Twenty-five Years of Scientific Progress and Other Essays* (New York, 1894), pp. 87–88; Abbott, "Evolution and Theology," p. 565. See also Abbott, *Theology of an Evolutionist*, pp. 88, 44–45; Abbott, *Evolution of Christianity*, pp. 209–211, 226–227. The best biographical treatment of Abbott is Ira V. Brown, *Lyman Abbott, Christian Evolutionist: A Study in Religious Liberalism* (Cambridge, Mass., 1953).

66. Harris, *Moral Evolution*, p. 29.

67. F. H. Johnson, "Creation and Salvation," *Andover Review*, 7 (1887), 278–280, 284. See also Johnson, *What Is Reality?* pp. 448–450.

68. Johnson, "Theistic Evolution," p. 379; Abbott, *Evolution of Christianity*, p. 226; Stearns, *Evidence*, p. 100; Clarke, *An Outline*, p. 232. See also Munger, *Appeal to Life*, p. 231; H. H. Peabody, "Man's Fall and Redemption in the Light of Evolution," *Sixteenth Annual Session of the Baptist Congress for the Discussion of Current Questions, Nov. 15–17, 1898* (New York, 1898), p. 30; Savage, *Irrepressible Conflict*, pp. 26–27; Stearns, *Present Day Theology*, pp. 307–308; Abbott, *Theology of an Evolutionist*, p. 45.

69. Lewis F. Stearns, "Reconstruction in Theology," *New Englander*, n.s. 5 (1882), 94–95; Clarke, *An Outline*, pp. 242–244; Rupp, "Theory of Evolution," pp. 167–168.

See also Strong, "The Fall," pp. 11–12; W. M. Barbour, "Fit Truths for Fit Times," *New Englander*, n.s. 5 (1882), 78–79; Stearns, *Present Day Theology*, pp. 334–335, 337, 341; Adams, *Continuous Creation*, p. 64; Washington Gladden, *How Much Is Left of the Old Doctrines? A Book for the People* (Boston, 1899), pp. 121–124, 130; DuBois, "Science and the Spiritual," p. 431; Daniel S. Martin, "Christian Evolutionism and Its Influence on Religious Thought," *Christian Thought*, 5 (1887), 120. This was not a new idea. Prior to the publication of *Origin of Species*, Horace Bushnell, for example, had asserted that sinful tendencies had been biologically inherited. H. Shelton Smith, *Changing Conceptions of Original Sin: A Study in American Theology since 1750* (New York, 1955), pp. 155–156. The role that the evolutionary hypothesis played in fostering this idea stemmed largely from its effect in encouraging thinking about problems of heredity and descent.

70. Beecher, *Evolution and Religion*, pp. 141, 84–85, 353; Abbott, "Evolution and Theology," p. 565; L. C. Barnes, "Man's Fall and Redemption in the Light of Evolution," *Sixteenth Annual Session of the Baptist Congress for the Discussion of Current Questions, Nov. 15–17, 1898* (New York, 1898), p. 35. See also Martin, "Christian Evolutionism," pp. 119; Adams, *Continuous Creation*, pp. 70–71, 114; W. M. Lisle, "The Evolution of Christianity," *Bibliotheca Sacra*, 49 (1892), 434–435; Johnson, "Creation and Salvation," p. 283; Abbott, *Evolution of Christianity*, pp. 226–227; Abbott, *Theology of an Evolutionist*, pp. 48–49; Munger, *Appeal to Life*, pp. 301–302; Fiske, *Destiny of Man*, p. 72.

71. Fiske, *Destiny of Man*, p. 72; Clarke, *An Outline*, pp. 240, 232; Le Conte, *Evolution and Its Relation*, pp. 337–338. See also Cope, "On the Hypothesis," p. 167; Savage, *Irrepressible Conflict*, pp. 29–30; William W. McLane, "Evolution as Involving the Doctrine of Sin," *New Englander and Yale Review*, 18 (1891), 187; Strong, "The Fall," pp. 10–11; Daniel Walker Howe, *The Unitarian Conscience: Harvard Moral Philosophy, 1805–1861* (Cambridge, Mass., 1970), pp. 57–61; E. Brooks Holifield, *The Gentlemen Theologians: American Theology in Southern Culture, 1795–1860* (Durham, N.C., 1978), pp. 122–145. Cf. Carter, *Spiritual Crisis*, pp. 50–55. In my judgment, Carter has exaggerated the degree to which most Protestant evolutionists equated humanity's animality with sinfulness. This has led him wrongly to assume that Le Conte's was a minority view.

72. Harris, *Moral Evolution*, pp. 279–281; Clarke, *An Outline*, p. 232. See also Stearns, *Present Day Theology*, p. 307; Carter, *Spiritual Crisis*, p. 51. It is worth noting that the idea that the vestiges of bestial tendencies remaining in the human species were responsible for individuals committing heinous acts of sex and violence was a prominent theme in the writing of American literary naturalists. Malcolm Cowley, "Naturalism in American Literature," in Stow Persons, ed., *Evolutionary Thought in America* (New Haven, 1950), pp. 300–333.

73. Beecher, *Evolution and Religion*, pp. 351, 82; Adams, *Continuous Creation*, pp. 59–61, 114; Munger, *Appeal to Life*, p. 301; Le Conte, "Man's Place," p. 800.

74. Harris, *Moral Evolution*, pp. 274–275, 283–284; Savage, *Religion of Evolution*, pp. 87, 100–101, 108; Clarke, *An Outline*, pp. 237, 241, 247. See also Wright, "Recent Works [1880]," pp. 55–56; McLane, "Evolution as Involving," pp. 186–188; James H. Fairchild, "The Religious Life: Its Nature and Claims," *Bibliotheca Sacra*, 54 (1897), 29–30. Useful treatments of the increasingly anthropocentric thrust of American theology in the nineteenth century include Joseph Haroutunian, *Piety versus Moralism: The Passing of the New England Theology* (1932; New York, 1970), pp. 87–96, and passim; and Ann Douglas, *The Feminization of American Culture* (New York, 1977), pp. 121–130.

75. Savage, *Religion of Evolution*, pp. 108–109.

76. Beecher, *Evolution and Religion*, pp. 84–85, 353; Abbott, "Evolution and Theology," p. 566. See also Le Conte, *Evolution and Its Relation*, pp. 335–336.

77. Adams, *Continuous Creation*, p. 114. See also Cocker, *Theistic Conception*, pp. 131–132; Stearns, *Present Day Theology*, pp. 26–27, 30–31; Wright, "Evolutionary Fad," pp. 315–316; Abbott, *Theology of an Evolutionist*, pp. 75–76; Johnson, "Creation and Salvation," pp. 283–284; Peabody, "Man's Fall," pp. 33–34.

78. Francis A. Henry, "Reconstruction in Religious Thought," *Princeton Review*, n.s. 14 (1884), 25; Savage, *Religion of Evolution*, p. 190; Abbott, *Evolution of Christianity*, p. 242; H. Shelton Smith, Robert T. Handy, and Lefferts A. Loetscher, *American Christianity: An Historical Interpretation with Representative Documents* (New York, 1963), 2: 261–262. Stow Persons has offered the perceptive suggestion that one of the sources of the great veneration for Jesus in the late nineteenth century was that he supplied an "element of personal leadership and inspiration" that seemed to be so difficult to perceive in God. Stow Persons, "Evolution and Theology," in Persons, ed., *Evolutionary Thought in America*, p. 450.

Useful discussions of the orthodox view of the Atonement include Holifield, *Gentlemen Theologians*, pp. 193–196; and Frank Hugh Foster, *A Genetic History of the New England Theology* (1927; New York, 1963), pp. 113–117, 189–223, 510–524.

It would be a mistake to infer from my discussion of the significant role that moral issues played in the analysis of Protestants who emphasized the life and teachings of Jesus that this was the only focus of attention. Protestants also laid great stress, to cite one example, on the role of Jesus in teaching men and women that God was a loving Father. See, for example, The Editors of the *Andover Review, Progressive Orthodoxy: A Contribution to the Christian Interpretation of Christian Doctrines* (1885; Boston, 1886), pp. 57–58; Beecher, *Evolution and Religion*, pp. 248–249.

79. Gordon, *Immortality*, p. 91. See also Savage, *Religion of Evolution*, p. 222; Abbott, *Theology of an Evolutionist*, pp. 120–128; Clarke, *An Outline*, pp. 260–362, esp. pp. 276–278, 308–309, 339–340; George Harris, "Ethical Christianity and Biblical Criticism," *Andover Review*, 15 (1891), 465–467; Johnson, "Creation and Salvation," pp. 284, 286–287. Some thinkers maintained that the content of Jesus' moral message was a stronger proof of his divinity than the plenary inspiration of the Scriptures or the miracles he performed. See, for example, Harris, "Ethical Christianity," pp. 469–470. This position, which was based on the prior assumption that the teachings of Jesus embodied the divine moral law, was a different argument from that which predicated the normative quality of Jesus' teachings on belief in his divinity.

80. Peabody, "Man's Fall," p. 34; Johnson, "Creation and Salvation," p. 277; Harris, *Moral Evolution*, pp. 419, 428. See also Joseph Le Conte, *Evolution: Its Nature, Its Evidences, and Its Relation to Religious Thought*, 2d rev. ed. (New York, 1891), p. 363.

81. Smyth, *Old Faiths*, p. 265; Abbott, *Theology of an Evolutionist*, pp. 72–74; Le Conte, *Evolution*, pp. 360, 362; Lisle, "Evolution of Christianity," p. 436; Henry, "Reconstruction," p. 26; Clarke, *An Outline*, pp. 290–294, 298.

82. Smyth, *Religious Feeling*, p. 170; Adams, "Christ," pp. 233, 227–230; Smith, "Evolution and a Personal Creator," pp. 226–227. See also Strong, "The Fall," pp. 14–15; MacQueary, *Evolution of Man*, p. 220; Harris, *Moral Evolution*, pp. 428–431.

83. Adams, "Christ," pp. 232–233; MacQueary, *Evolution of Man*, p. 220; Cocker, *Theistic Conception*, p. 132; Abbott, *Evolution of Christianity*, pp. 250–251; Abbott, *Theology of an Evolutionist*, pp. 75–76. See also Harris, *Moral Evolution*, pp. 419–420; Lisle, "Evolution of Christianity," p. 436; Le Conte, *Evolution*, pp. 360–361; Smyth, *Old Faiths*, p. 287.

84. Smyth, *Christian Ethics*, p. 241; Editors of the *Andover Review, Progressive Orthodoxy*, pp. 53–55.

85. Abbott, "Evolution and Theology," p. 566; Anon., "Christianity and Its Modern Competitors," p. 648; Martin, "Christian Evolutionism," p. 120; Johnson, "Coöperative Creation," p. 451; McCosh, *Religious Aspect*, p. 113; Valentine, "Influence of the Theory," p. 227; Abbott, *Theology of an Evolutionist*, pp. 84–85.

86. Abbott, *Theology of an Evolutionist*, p. 112; Abbott, *Evolution of Christianity*, pp. 8–9, 233. See also Smyth, *Christian Ethics*, pp. 242–243; Clarke, *An Outline*, pp. 402–403; Le Conte, *Evolution*, p. 363; Stearns, *Present Day Theology*, pp. 336–338; Adams, *Continuous Creation*, p. 71.

87. Beecher, *Evolution and Religion*, pp. 248–249, 81, 94–95, 99; Harris, *Moral Evolution*, p. 298. See also Le Conte, *Evolution and Its Relation*, p. 335; Johnson, "Creation and Salvation," pp. 288–289; Johnson, *What Is Reality?* pp. 468–469; Clarke, *An Outline*, pp. 386–389, 397, 418; Williams, *Andover Liberals*, pp. 60–63.

88. Abbott, *Reminiscences*, p. 466. See also Abbott, *Theology of an Evolutionist*, pp. 127–128; Clarke, *An Outline*, pp. 422–423; Beecher, *Evolution and Religion*, pp. 81, 94–99; Abbott, *Evolution of Christianity*, p. 222.

89. Bixby, "Immortality and Science," p. 57; Scudder, "Immortality and Evolution," pp. 715–717, 712. See also Adams, *Continuous Creation*, pp. 75, 85; Hark, *Unity of Truth*, pp. 153–154, 158; Fiske, *Destiny of Man*, p. 83; Gordon, *Immortality*, pp. 82–83, 85–86; Whiton, "Darwin and Darwinism," pp. 63–64.

90. Adams, *Continuous Creation*, p. 87; Savage, *Religion of Evolution*, p. 250; Le Conte, *Evolution and Its Relation*, p. 306. See also Johnson, "Coöperative Creation," p. 451; William W. McLane, "The Scientific and Scriptural Basis of Immortality," *New Englander and Yale Review*, n.s. 17 (1890), 55; Johnson, "Creation and Salvation," pp. 276–277; Bixby, "Immortality and Science," pp. 63–64; Scudder, "Immortality and Evolution," pp. 712, 716–717; Augustus Jay DuBois, "Science and Immortality," *Century Magazine*, 43 (1891), 257–258. For other arguments for immortality that invoked the concept of evolution, see, for example, Bixby, "Immortality and Science," p. 56; Whiton, "Darwin and Darwinism," p. 63; Hark, *Unity of the Truth*, pp. 158–159.

Chapter 8. "Get Thee Hence, Satan"

1. W. J. Wright, "A Generation of Darwinism," *Presbyterian Quarterly*, 7 (1893), 223. See also A A. H[odge], Review of *Natural Science and Religion*, by Asa Gray, *Presbyterian Review*, 1 (1880), 588–589; Archibald Alexander Hodge, *Popular Lectures on Theological Themes* (Philadelphia, 1887), p. 176; A. A. Hodge, Introduction, in Joseph S. Van Dyke, *Theism and Evolution: An Examination of Modern Speculative Theories as Related to Theistic Conceptions of the Universe*, 2d ed. (New York, 1886), pp. xviii–xxi. Several students of the Princeton theology have placed Archibald Hodge in the camp of cautious evolutionists. See, for example, Gary Scott Smith, *The Seeds of Secularization: Calvinism, Culture, and Pluralism in America, 1870–1915* (Grand Rapids, Mich., 1985), pp. 98, 110; David N. Livingstone, "The Idea of Design: The Vicissitudes of a Key Concept in the Princeton Response to Darwin," *Scottish Journal of Theology*, 37 (1984), 342–344. My reading of the sources has convinced me that Hodge remained essentially hostile to the theory of organic evolution. I should be quick to concede that it is possible to find statements from him to the effect that the theory, rightly constructed, was not inherently irreconcilable with theism. When one examines what

he meant by a "right" construction, however, I think it is very difficult to differentiate his view from that of the special creationists.

2. Livingstone, "Idea of Design," pp. 329–357; Cynthia Eagle Russett, *Darwin in America: The Intellectual Response, 1865–1912* (San Francisco, 1976), pp. 26, 32; Alvar Ellegård, "The Darwinian Theory and the Argument from Design," *Lynchnos* (1956), 173–174; Milton Berman, *John Fiske: The Evolution of a Popularizer* (Cambridge, Mass., 1961), pp. 109–110; R. J. Wilson, *Darwinism and the American Intellectual* (Homewood, Ill., 1967), pp. 39–40; Thomas Hill, "Charles Darwin," *Unitarian Review*, 29 (1888), 391–392; H[odge], Review of *Natural Science*, p. 587; Charles Hodge, *What Is Darwinism?* (New York, 1874), p. 141; George D. Armstrong, "The Word of God versus 'The Bible of Modern Scientific Theology,' " *Presbyterian Quarterly*, 2 (1888), 46; John T. Duffield, "Evolutionism, Respecting Man and the Bible," *Princeton Review*, 4th ser. (1878), 150; J. H. McIlvaine, "Evolution in Relation to Species," *Presbyterian Review*, 1 (1880), 611–612; Francis L. Patton, "A Symposium on Evolution: Is the Darwinian Theory of Evolution Reconcilable with the Bible? If So, with What Limitations?" *Homiletic Monthly*, 8 (1884), 405; L. T. Townsend, *Bible Theology and Modern Thought* (1882; Boston, 1883), pp. 269–270; R. L. Dabney, *The Sensualistic Philosophy of the Nineteenth Century* (New York, 1876), pp. 198–199.

3. James R. Moore, *The Post-Darwinian Controversies: A Study of the Protestant Struggle to Come to Terms with Darwin in Great Britain and America, 1870–1900* (Cambridge, 1979), pp. 213–215, 194–196, 205–206; Sydney E. Ahlstrom, *A Religious History of the American People* (New Haven, 1972), p. 771. George Marsden has similarly contended that opponents of the transmutation hypothesis "were judging the later [Darwinian] scientific revolution by the standards of the first—the revolution of Bacon and Newton." George M. Marsden, *Fundamentalism and American Culture: The Shaping of Twentieth-Century Evangelicalism, 1870–1925* (New York, 1980), p. 214. In my judgment, the philosophy of science embraced by critics of the evolutionary hypothesis was largely an *effect* of prior biblical commitments rather than a primary causal agent. Still, I can agree with Marsden's view that insofar as these issues did play a role, they did so primarily because of their concern with the "fixed character of supernaturally guaranteed truth." Ibid., pp. 215–216. For the views of Curtis and Hill on fixity, see my discussion in Chapter 4.

4. Charles Hodge, *Systematic Theology* (New York, 1872–73), 2: 12–19; Hodge, *What Is Darwinism?* p. 141.

5. A. A. Hodge, *Outlines of Theology* (New York, 1878), p. 69; Wright, "Generation of Darwinism," p. 239.

6. T. De Witt Talmage, *Sermons: 2d Series* (New York, 1875), pp. 58–60. See also Wright, "Generation of Darwinism," p. 234; Robert Patterson, *The Errors of Evolution: An Examination of the Nebular Theory, Geological Evolution, the Origin of Life, and Darwinism*, ed. H. L. Hastings (Boston, 1885), pp. 211–212; George D. Armstrong, *The Two Books of Nature and Revelation Collated* (New York, 1886), pp. 96–97; T. M. Griffin, "Evolution on Trial," *Methodist Review*, 5th ser., 10 (1894), 122.

7. D. E. Frierson, "Professor Drummond's Apology to Scientists," *Presbyterian Quarterly*, 2 (1888), 479. See also John E. Todd, "New Theology," *Bibliotheca Sacra*, 43 (1886), 353; Samuel M. Smith, "The Andover Renaissance in Theology," *Presbyterian Quarterly*, 1 (1887), 38n; Anon., "Prayer Answerable without Any Violation of Nature," *Southern Presbyterian Review*, 29 (1878), 278.

8. Samuel Buel, "The Christian Revelation, Christian Theology, and Philosophy: Their Mutual Connections and Their Relative Authority," *American Church Review*

(1882), pp. 125–126; M. E. Dwight, "The Contest As It Is To-day," *New Englander,* n.s. 7 (1884), 586; Miner Raymond, *Systematic Theology* (Cincinnati, 1877), 2: 13–16 (quotation on p. 16). See also S. E. Shepard, "Animal Life," *Christian Quarterly,* 8 (1876), 468; Wright, "Generation of Darwinism," p. 239; William G. T. Shedd, *Dogmatic Theology* (New York, 1888), 1: 484–500; R. D. Malone, "The Instability of Science and the Incomparable Stability of the Bible," *Christian Quarterly,* 8 (1876), 231; John L. Girardeau, quoted in John B. Adger, *My Life and Times, 1810–99* (Richmond, Va., 1899), pp. 484–486; Duffield, "Evolutionism," pp. 150–177; T. W. Chambers in O. B. Frothingham and T. W. Chambers, "Is Man a Depraved Creature?" *North American Review,* 126 (1878), 471; Lyman Atwater, "Evolution and Supernaturalism," *Independent,* 32 (March 11, 1880), 4; Henry Darling, "Preaching and Modern Skepticism," *Presbyterian Review,* 2 (1881), 762; General Assembly of the Presbyterian Church in the United States, *Minutes* [1886], p. 18. For a useful discussion of the Biblicism of the Seventh-Day Adventists, a group I have not studied, see Ronald L. Numbers, "Science Falsely So-Called: Evolution and Adventists in the Nineteenth Century," *Journal of the American Scientific Affiliation,* 27 (1975), pp. 18–23.

It is worth noting that many Protestant evolutionists perceived that what precluded some of their brethren within the religious community from endorsing the transmutation hypothesis was the conviction that it conflicted with essential elements of the biblical message. See, for example, E. D. Cope, "On the Hypothesis of Evolution, Physical and Metaphysical [1870]," *The Origin of the Fittest: Essays on Evolution* (1886; New York, 1887), p. 128; Charles Loring Brace to Asa Gray [1879], in *The Life of Charles Loring Brace,* ed. Emma Brace (New York, 1894), pp. 367–368.

9. Historians who have been inclined to reject the idea that biblical questions were crucial in the evolutionary controversy within the American intellectual community include Moore, *Post-Darwinian Controversies,* pp. 205, 218–219; Russett, *Darwin in America,* pp. 31–32; Alvar Ellegård, *Darwin and the General Reader: The Reception of Darwin's Theory of Evolution in the British Periodical Press, 1859–1872* (Göteborg, 1958), pp. 172, 203; Wilson, *Darwinism and the American Intellectual,* pp. 4, 39; and Berman, *John Fiske,* p. 110. Other historians who have found that biblical considerations were crucial include John C. Greene, *Darwin and the Modern World View* (Baton Rouge, 1961), pp. 10, 14–15; and Mark A. Noll, " 'My Anchor Holds'—A Great Divide (1870–1930)," in John D. Woodbridge, Mark Noll, and Nathan O. Hatch, eds., *The Gospel in America: Themes in the Story of America's Evangelicals* (Grand Rapids, Mich., 1979), pp. 49–50.

10. John L. Girardeau, "The Glorious Gospel of the Blessed God [1860]," *Sermons,* ed. George A. Blackburn (Columbia, S.C., 1907), p. 200; Girardeau, "The Discretionary Power of the Church [1875]," ibid., pp. 370–371, 384, 391. See also Girardeau, "The Signs of the Times—In the Church [n.d.]," ibid., p. 117; George B. Cheever, "The Philosophy of Evolution," *Presbyterian Quarterly and Princeton Review,* n.s. 4 (1875), 155; Thomas O. Summers, *Systematic Theology: A Complete Body of Wesleyan Arminian Divinity Consisting of Lectures on the Twenty-five Articles of Religion* (Nashville, Tenn., 1888), 1: 42–43, 497–498; Edward D. Morris, "The Religious Consciousness Viewed as a Help and Test in Belief," *Presbyterian and Reformed Review,* 1 (1890), 606; Jacob Todd, "A Common Basis of Knowledge for Science and Religion," *Methodist Quarterly Review,* 4th ser., 27 (1875), 49; H. M. Goodwin, "The Bible as a Book of Education," *New Englander,* n.s. 6 (1883), 270; [Francis L. Patton], *Addresses at the Induction of Rev. Francis L. Patton into "The Cyrus H. McCormick Professorship of Didactic and Polemic Theology" in the Presbyterian Theological Seminary of the North-west*

(Chicago, 1873), p. 52. For a valuable discussion of the life and thought of John L. Girardeau, see Morton H. Smith, *Studies in Southern Presbyterian Theology* (Jackson, Miss., 1962), pp. 234–248.

11. Morris, "Religious Consciousness," pp. 604–609 (quotation on p. 607); Girardeau, "Discretionary Power," pp. 380, 373–375. See also Girardeau, "Signs of the Times," pp. 116–117; Frederick Alvord, "The Bible: Shall We Take It As We Find It, or As We Like It?" *New Englander and Yale Review*, n.s. 10 (1887), 517–518; George N. Boardman, "Inspiration,—with Remarks on the Theory Presented in Ladd's Doctrine of Sacred Scripture,"*Bibliotheca Sacra*, 41 (1884), 517–521, 548–549; W. Andrew Hoffecker, *Piety and the Princeton Theologians: Archibald Alexander, Charles Hodge, and Benjamin Warfield* (Phillipsberg, N.J., 1981).

12. S. L. Bowman, "Inspiration and Infallibility," *Methodist Review*, 5th ser., 5 (1889), 180–182, 174, 169–170. See also Talmage, *Sermons*, pp. 61–62; Armstrong, *Two Books*, p. 168; Archibald A. Hodge and Benjamin B. Warfield, "Inspiration," *Presbyterian Review*, 2 (1881), 225–260, esp. 226, 236–237, 243; Francis L. Patton, "The Dogmatic Aspect of Pentateuchal Criticism," *Presbyterian Review*, 4 (1883), 362–363; Girardeau, "Discretionary Power," pp. 370–372; J. S. Beekman, "The Development Theory," *Presbyterian Quarterly and Princeton Review*, n.s. 6 (1877), 606. John Woodbridge has noted that in the nineteenth century, Protestants commonly equated the terms "infallibility" and "inerrancy." John Woodbridge, *Biblical Authority: A Critique of the Rogers/McKim Proposal* (Grand Rapids, 1982), pp. 134, 217, n. 77.

13. Boardman, "Inspiration," p. 521; E. F. Burr, "Infallible Scripture," *Bibliotheca Sacra*, 44 (1887), 136, 122; Hodge, *Systematic Theology*, 1: 14. See also Armstrong, *Two Books*, pp. 168–169; John L. Girardeau, Review of *Supernatural Revelation: An Essay Concerning the Basis of the Christian Faith*, by C. M. Mead, *Presbyterian Quarterly*, 4 (1890), 308; Girardeau, "Discretionary Power," p. 389; Enoch Fitch Burr, *Ecce Terra; or, The Hand of God in the Earth* (Philadelphia, 1883), pp. 201–202, 214; Hodge and Warfield, "Inspiration," pp. 233–234; Anon., "God and Moral Obligation," *Southern Presbyterian Review*, 29 (1878), 330; Grant Wacker, "The Demise of Biblical Civilization," in Nathan O. Hatch and Mark A. Noll, eds., *The Bible in America: Essays in Cultural History* (New York, 1982), pp. 127–128; Marsden, *Fundamentalism*, p. 56; Bowman, "Inspiration and Infallibility," p. 173; Darling, "Preaching," p. 763; George B. Cheever, *God's Timepiece for Man's Eternity* (1883; New York, 1888), pp. xlv, xlix–1; H. Liebhardt, "Present State of Protestant Theology," *Methodist Quarterly Review*, 4th ser., 35 (1883), 126.

14. Bowman, "Inspiration and Infallibility," ip. 171. See also Patton, "Dogmatic Aspect," p. 363; Hodge and Warfield, "Inspiration," pp. 226, 237, 245; Burr, "Infallible Scripture," pp. 122, 127; Hodge, *Outlines of Theology*, pp. 66–67, 75; Woodbridge, *Biblical Authority*, pp. 127–128; Randall Balmer, "The Princetonians and Scripture: A Reconsideration," *Westminster Theological Journal*, 44 (1982), 358–365.

15. Townsend, *Bible Theology*, p. 3; L. T. Townsend, *The Bible and Other Ancient Literature in the Nineteenth Century* (1884; New York, 1888), pp. 5–9 (quotation on p. 8); G. T. Bedell, "The Decline of Religion," *American Church Review*, 41 (1883), 14. See also Clark Braden, *The Problem of Problems, and Its Various Solutions; or, Atheism, Darwinism, and Theism* (Cincinnati, 1876), pp. 213–214; Hodge and Warfield, "Inspiration," pp. 237–238, 245; Shedd, *Dogmatic Theology*, 1: 104–105; Malone, "Instability of Science," pp. 236–239; Patterson, *Errors of Evolution*, pp. 154–155; Samuel Z. Beam, "Science Vindicating Revelation," *Reformed Quarterly Review*, 30 (1888), 227; J. P. Newman in F. H. Hodge et al., "What Is Inspiration?" *North American Review*, 127

(1878), 324; Benjamin B. Warfield, "Charles Darwin's Religious Life: A Sketch in Spiritual Biography," *Presbyterian Review*, 9 (1888), 575; Bowman, "Inspiration and Infallibility," p. 173; Armstrong, "Word of God," pp. 46–47.

16. Smith, "Andover Renaissance," p. 39; E. R. Craven, "The Inductive Sciences of Nature and the Bible," *Presbyterian Quarterly and Princeton Review*, n.s. 6 (1877), 678; Stuart Robinson, "The Pulpit and Skeptical Culture," *Princeton Review*, 4th ser. (1879), 148. See also Morris, "Religious Consciousness," p. 606; Anon., Review of *Creation*, by Arnold Guyot, *New Englander*, n.s. 7 (1884), 593; [Patton], *Addresses*, p. 60; E[rnest] T[rice] T[hompson], "Robinson, Stuart," *Dictionary of American Biography*, 16: 53 (hereafter cited as *DAB*).

17. Townsend, *The Bible*, p. 192; J. M. Cromer, "The Lutheran Conception of Divine Truth," *Lutheran Quarterly*, n.s. 15 (1885), 73; George M. Marsden, "Everyone One's Own Interpreter? The Bible, Science, and Authority in Mid-Nineteenth-Century America," in Hatch and Noll, eds., *Bible in America*, pp. 80, 90, 92–93; Marsden, *Fundamentalism*, pp. 110–111; Ferenc Morton Szasz, *The Divided Mind of Protestant America, 1880–1930* (University, Ala., 1982), pp. 16–17; Samuel Tyler, "Connection between Philosophy and Revelation," *Biblical Repertory and Princeton Review*, 17 (1845), 405–406; Malone, "Instability of Science," pp. 238–240; Wacker, "Demise," p. 127; Robinson, "The Pulpit," pp. 136–137, 143, 146; Duffield, "Evolutionism," p. 175. There were exceptions. Some Biblicists continued to concede that the results of scientific and historical inquiry had sometimes helped to shed light on difficult passages. See, for example, Burr, *Ecce Terra*, p. 21.

18. Alvord, "The Bible," p. 527.

19. Charles B. Warring, *The Mosaic Account of Creation, the Miracle of To-day; or, New Witnesses to the Oneness of Genesis and Science* (New York, 1875), p. 22; Darling, "Preaching," pp. 763–764. See also Robinson, "The Pulpit," p. 147; Hodge, Introduction, in Van Dyke, *Theism and Evolution*, p. xix; Anon., Review of *Creation*, pp. 593–594; Cromer, "Lutheran Conception," pp. 73–74; Samuel Z. Beam, "Evolution a Failure," *Reformed Quarterly Review*, 35 (1888), 496. The hostility to periodic compromise in response to developments from the secular realm was not altogether new. See, for example, Robert Lewis Dabney, quoted in James Woodrow, *An Examination of Certain Recent Assaults on Physical Science* (Columbia, S.C., 1873), pp. 51–52.

20. Thomas H. Huxley, "Science and Pseudo Science [1887]," *Collected Essays by T. H. Huxley* (1897; New York, 1968), 5: 115–116 (hereafter cited as *Huxley's Essays*); [Thomas Huxley], "Professor Huxley's Lectures," *Popular Science Monthly*, 10 (1876–77), 51–52. See also Thomas H. Huxley, *Science and Hebrew Tradition, Huxley's Essays*, 4: vii–viii; Darling, "Preaching," p. 762; J. H. McIlvaine, "Revelation and Science," *Bibliotheca Sacra*, 34 (1877), 261; Duffield, "Evolutionism," pp. 174–175; Timothy P. Weber, "The Two-Edged Sword: The Fundamentalist Use of the Bible," in Hatch and Noll, eds., *Bible in America*, p. 111. For a discussion of the dispensationalists' view of the importance of the "literal sense" of the Scriptures, see Marsden, *Fundamentalism*, p. 60.

21. Robinson, "The Pulpit," p. 147; Morris, "Religious Consciousness," p. 606; Luther Tracy Townsend, *Evolution or Creation: A Critical Review of the Scientific and Scriptural Theories of Creation and Certain Related Subjects* (New York, 1896), pp. 29–33. See also Warring, *Mosaic Account*, pp. 11–18; George W. Samson, "Modern Evolution Theories," *Baptist Quarterly*, 11 (1877), 150. The roots of Americans' faith in the "plain sense" meaning of the Bible could be found in their allegiance to Scottish

common-sense philosophy as well as to the Reformed tradition. George Marsden, "From Fundamentalism to Evangelicalism: A Historical Analysis," in David F. Wells and John D. Woodbridge, eds., *The Evangelicals: What They Believe, Who They Are, Where They Are Changing* (Nashville, 1975), p. 137.

The commitment to the plain sense of the Bible accounts for many American religious thinkers' distaste for allegory. See E. Brooks Holifield, *The Gentlemen Theologians: American Theology in Southern Culture, 1795–1860* (Durham, N.C., 1978), pp. 97–98; and Ernest R. Sandeen, *The Roots of Fundamentalism: British and American Millenarianism, 1800–1930* (Chicago, 1970), pp. 110–111.

22. Morris, "Religious Consciousness," p. 606; James W. Richard, "How Shall We Train the Ministry for the Times?" *Lutheran Quarterly*, n.s. 8 (1878), 484. See also Samuel Smith, "Frederick W. Robertson," *Southern Presbyterian Review*, 33 (1882), 91–92; Warring, *Mosaic Account*, p. 21; Burr, *Ecce Terra*, p. 20; Braden, *Problem of Problems*, pp. 92, 213.

23. George Armstrong, quoted in Adger, *My Life*, p. 546; Armstrong, "Word of God," p. 58. See also H[arris] E[lwood] S[tarr], "Armstrong, George Dod," *DAB*, 1: 352–353.

24. Malone, "Instability of Science," pp. 232–234. See also McIlvaine, "Evolution in Relation," p. 613; Buel, "Christian Revelation," pp. 125–126; Robinson, "The Pulpit," p. 147; Anon., "Relation of Theology to Other Sciences," *Bibliotheca Sacra*, 33 (1876), 289–290; Jacob Cooper, "What Is Truth?" *Presbyterian Quarterly and Princeton Review*, n.s. 6 (1877), 514; Laurens P. Hickok, "Evolution from Mechanical Force," *Princeton Review*, 4th ser. (1878), 605; Darling, "Preaching," p. 763; Henry Coleman, "Pre-Adamites," *Methodist Review*, 5th ser., 7 (1891), 894–896; Alfred G. Mortimer, in Mortimer and R. Heber Newton, "Recent Criticisms of the Bible," *North American Review*, 138 (1884), 397–398; Byron Sunderland, "The Impotence of Science," *Preacher and Homiletic Monthly*, 3 (1879), 517–519; Howard Osgood, "President Harper's Lectures," *Bibliotheca Sacra*, 52 (1895), 334; Braden, *Problem of Problems*, pp. 215–216; F. H. Kerfoot, *The Demand of the Scientific Spirit upon Theology* (Louisville, Ky., 1889), pp. 18–19; Patterson, *Errors of Evolution*, p. 156.

25. Duffield, "Evolutionism," pp. 150–177 (quotations on pp. 157, 175, 160). See also J. P. Newman in Hodge et al., "What Is Inspiration?" p. 324; Hodge and Warfield, "Inspiration," p. 239; Townsend, *The Bible*, pp. 5–8; Armstrong, "Word of God," pp. 47–48; Atwater, "Evolution and Supernaturalism," p. 4.

26. S. A. Gardner, "Theology and Science," *Universalist Quarterly and General Review*, n.s. 20 (1883), 188; Wright, "Generation of Darwinism," p. 239. See also Malone, "Instability of Science," p. 234; Duffield, "Evolutionism," pp. 175–176.

27. [Patton], *Addresses*, p. 30; Lionel S. Beale, "The Materialist Revival and the Miracle of the Raising of the Dead," *Princeton Review*, 4th ser. (1878), 113; John Moore, "Science against Darwinism," *Universalist Quarterly and General Review*, n.s. 15 (1878), 198; Robinson, "The Pulpit," p. 138; Jesse B. Thomas, "A Symposium on Evolution: Is the Darwinian Theory of Evolution Reconcilable with the Bible? If So, with What Limitations?" *Homiletic Monthly*, 8 (1884), 534. See also J. M. Buckley, ibid., p. 647; Wright, "Generation of Darwinism," p. 229; Talmage, *Sermons*, pp. 58–59; Braden, *Problem of Problems*, pp. 93–94, 147, 216–217; Alfred G. Mortimer, in Mortimer and Newton, "Recent Criticisms," pp. 397–398; H. H. Moore in James Strong et al., "Theology: A Symposium," *Methodist Review*, 5th ser., 5 (1889), 535.

28. Girardeau, "Discretionary Power," pp. 385–391 (quotation on p. 387); [Patton], *Addresses*, pp. 58, 52. George Marsden has suggested that the thrust of the re-

vivalist tradition, which disposed individuals to think in terms of a "fixed antithesis between truth and error[,] allowed little room for historical and developmental views." Marsden, "From Fundamentalism," pp. 137–138.

29. Girardeau, "Discretionary Power," pp. 385–387; Townsend, *The Bible*, pp. 192–193; T. De Witt Talmage, *Live Coals; or, Truths That Burn*, collated by Lydia D. White (Chicago, 1886), p. 291; Darling, "Preaching," p. 763; Charles Hodge, quoted in Alexander A. Hodge, *The Life of Charles Hodge*, (London, 1881), pp. 593–595, 521 (quotation on p. 594). See also Robinson, "The Pulpit," p. 147.

30. Washington Gladden, *Who Wrote the Bible? A Book for the People* (Boston, 1891), pp. 356–357; Minot J. Savage, *The Religion of Evolution* (Boston, 1876), pp. 185–187; J. H. Rylance, "Inspiration and Infallibility," *North American Review*, 139 (1884), 228–229; Weber, "Two-Edged Sword," pp. 105–106; Noll, " 'My Anchor Holds,' " p. 56. For a perceptive treatment of the role that isolation from the centers of cultural and political authority played in breeding dissent from the conventional wisdom during the late nineteenth century, see James Turner, "Understanding the Populists," *Journal of American History*, 67 (1980), 368–373.

31. Warring, *Mosaic Account*, p. 21; Girardeau, "Signs of the Times," p. 116. See also Samson, "Modern Evolution Theories," p. 148; Burr, *Ecce Terra*, pp. 201–202; Anon., "God and Moral Obligation," p. 331; James M. Ludlow, "Symposium on the 'New Theology': What Are Its Essential Features? Is It Better Than the Old?" *Homiletic Review*, 11 (1886), 14. As George Marsden has noted, the doctrine of biblical inerrancy carried the "scientific" connotations of precision and reliability. Marsden, *Fundamentalism*, pp. 56–57.

32. Anon., "Relation of Theology," p. 288; Gardner, "Theology and Science," p. 186; Kerfoot, *Demand of the Scientific Spirit*, p. 5. See also Townsend, *Evolution or Creation*, pp. 16–17, 35–45; Braden, *Problem of Problems*, pp. 90–91, 376–378; Weber, "Two-Edged Sword," pp. 108–113; Marsden, *Fundamentalism*, p. 20; Todd, "Common Basis," p. 27; Cheever, *God's Timepiece*, p. xlix; Richard, "How Shall We Train," pp. 479–481; W. H. Wynn, "The Religion of Evolution as against the Religion of Jesus," *Lutheran Quarterly*, n.s. 12 (1882), 1–2, 25; B. B. Warfield, "Darwin's Arguments against Christianity and against Religion," *Homiletic Review*, 17 (1889), 9; E. R. L. Gould, "Modern Materialism," *New Englander*, n.s. 5 (1882), 440; Anon., "Synopsis of the Quarterlies," *Methodist Quarterly Review*, 4th ser., 34 (1882), 534; Armstrong, *Two Books*, p. 8.

33. Patterson, *Errors of Evolution*, pp. 156–157; Cheever, "Philosophy of Evolution," pp. 152–155 (quotation on p. 152). See also McIlvaine, "Evolution in Relation," pp. 629–630; Patton, "Symposium on Evolution," pp. 410–411; L. J. Livermore, "What Is Darwinism?" *Unitarian Review and Religious Magazine*, 3 (1875), 249; Armstrong, *Two Books*, p. 87; J. H. Potts, "Relation of the Pulpit to Skeptical Scientific Theories," *Methodist Quarterly Review*, 4th ser., 34 (1882), 41; Beam, "Evolution a Failure," p. 496; Heman Lincoln, "Science Not Supreme, but Subordinate," *Bibliotheca Sacra*, 42 (1885), 227. As D. H. Meyer has noted, with the theory of organic evolution "the wider cultural implications of the scientific revolution became clear to the entire intellectual community." D. H. Meyer, "American Intellectuals and the Victorian Crisis of Faith," in Daniel Walker Howe, ed., *Victorian America* (Philadelphia, 1976), p. 62.

34. Patterson, *Errors of Evolution*, p. 156. See also C. W. Ernst, "St. George Mivart's 'Contemporary Evolution,' " *Unitarian Review and Religious Magazine*, 7 (1877), 18;

Gail Hamilton, "A Bible Lesson for Mr. Herbert Spencer," *North American Review*, 156 (1893), 87.

35. J. William Dawson, *Modern Ideas of Evolution as Related to Revelation and Science*, 2d ed. (New York, 1890), p. 21; [Patton], *Addresses*, p. 25. See also Mortimer, in Mortimer and Newton, "Recent Criticisms," pp. 397–398; Armstrong, *Two Books*, p. 181; Talmage, *Sermons*, p. 61; Kerfoot, *Demand of the Scientific Spirit*, p. 5. Ira V. Brown has also concluded that "Higher criticism and the theory of evolution went hand in hand." Ira V. Brown, "The Higher Criticism Comes to America," *Journal of Presbyterian History*, 38 (1960), 195.

36. Townsend, *Evolution or Creation*, pp. 33–34; Darling, "Preaching," pp. 763–764; Cromer, "Lutheran Conception," pp. 73–74; Gardner, "Theology and Science," pp. 182, 188. See also Braden, *Problem of Problems*, p. 83; Buel, "Christian Revelation," pp. 125–126; Wright, "Generation of Darwinism," pp. 239–240; Dwight, "The Contest," p. 585.

37. Beale, "Materialist Revival," pp. 98–99. For factual details concerning Woodrow's career, see J[ohn] E. P[omfret], "Woodrow, James," *DAB*, 20: 495–496. My discussion of the Woodrow case has been informed by the following works: T. Watson Street, "The Evolution Controversy in the Southern Presbyterian Church with Attention to the Theological and Ecclesiastical Issues Raised," *Journal of the Presbyterian Historical Society*, 37 (1959), 232–250; Clement Eaton, "Professor James Woodrow and the Freedom of Teaching in the South," *Journal of Southern History*, 28 (1962), 3–17; Ernest Trice Thompson, *Presbyterians in the South* (Richmond, Va., 1973), 2: 457–490.

38. Woodrow, *An Examination*, pp. 46, 29, 5, 10–11, and passim. See also James Woodrow, "Inaugural Address," *Southern Presbyterian Review*, 14 (1862), 528–529. An account of the Woodrow-Dabney controversy, seen largely from Dabney's perspective, can be found in Thomas Cary Johnson, *The Life and Letters of Robert Lewis Dabney* (Richmond, Va., 1903), pp. 340–348.

39. Woodrow, *An Examination*, pp. 17–20; Thompson, *Presbyterians*, pp. 457–461; Johnson, *Life and Letters of Dabney*, pp. 343–344.

40. James Woodrow, *Evolution: An Address Delivered May 7, 1884, before the Alumni Association of the Columbia Theological Seminary, Columbia, S.C.*, republished in Joseph Blau, ed., *American Philosophic Addresses, 1700–1900* (New York, 1946), pp. 489–490, 493–494, 491, 512–513.

41. Ibid., pp. 499–502.

42. General Assembly of the Presbyterian Church in the United States, *Minutes*, pp. 18, 41, 44. See also Thompson, *Presbyterians*, pp. 463–465, 482; Armstrong, *Two Books*, pp. 93–96. Woodrow remained as a professor and later became president of South Carolina College, and ironically, although his teaching had been condemned, he remained, institutionally at least, a clergyman in good standing with his denomination.

43. Alexander Winchell, *Adamites and Preadamites; or, A Popular Discussion Concerning the Remote Representatives of the Human Species and Their Relation to the Biblical Adam* (Syracuse, 1878), pp. 21, 17; Alexander Winchell, quoted in Walter P. Metzger, "Academic Freedom in the Age of the University," in Richard Hofstadter and Walter P. Metzger, *The Development of Academic Freedom in the United States* (New York, 1955), p. 331. See also Alexander Winchell, *Preadamites; or, A Demonstration of the Existence of Men before Adam; together with a Study of Their Condition, Antiquity, Racial Affinities, and Progressive Dispersion over the Earth* (Chicago, 1880), pp. 293–294, 285–286. Edward

Justin Pfeifer has wrongly inferred from the fact that Winchell denied that all races had descended from Adam that he was espousing polygenism. Edward Justin Pfeifer, "The Reception of Darwinism in the United States, 1859–1880," Ph.D. diss., Brown University, 1957, pp. 149–150. Actually, it was central to Winchell's argument that all races had descended from a common stock. Winchell merely considered Adam a subsequent arrival to the first organic being that could be legitimately called a man. See Winchell, *Adamites and Preadamites*, pp. 19–21; Winchell, *Preadamites*, p. 297.

In my treatment of the Winchell case I have drawn heavily on two secondary accounts: Edwin Mims, *History of Vanderbilt University* (Nashville, 1946), pp. 100–103; and Dickson Hunter Farish, *The Circuit Rider Dismounts: A Social History of Southern Methodism, 1865–1900* (Richmond, Va., 1938), pp. 293–297.

44. Winchell, *Adamites and Preadamites*, pp. 43, 46.

45. Tennessee Conference, quoted in [E. L. or W. J. Youmans], "Vanderbilt University Again," *Popular Science Monthly*, 14 (1878), 237–238. See also E. L. or W. J. Youmans, "Religion and Science at Vanderbilt University," *Popular Science Monthly*, 13 (1878), 492–495. Vanderbilt invoked financial considerations as justification of its actions. Mims, *History of Vanderbilt*, pp. 101–102. Winchell himself believed that both his preadamitism and his endorsement of the transmutation hypothesis contributed to his downfall at Vanderbilt. See Alexander Winchell to A. D. White, August 31, 1878, quoted in Walter P. Rogers, *Andrew D. White and the Modern University* (Ithaca, 1942), pp. 229–230 n. 30.

46. The Woodrow and Winchell episodes were not the only instances of the conservative counteroffensive against modern thought. For a perceptive account of the trial of David Swing, see William R. Hutchison, *The Modernist Impulse in American Protestantism* (Cambridge, Mass., 1976), pp. 48–75. For useful discussions of other heresy cases, see George H. Shriver, ed., *American Religious Heretics: Formal and Informal Trials* (Nashville, 1966), and Marsden, *Fundamentalism*, pp. 102–108.

47. Robinson, "The Pulpit," pp. 139, 147; Duffield, "Evolutionism," p. 174; Darling, "Preaching," p. 763; Archibald Hodge, Introduction, in Van Dyke, *Theism and Evolution*, p. xix. See also Patterson, *Errors of Evolution*, pp. iv, xi; Cromer, "Lutheran Conception," p. 73; Dawson, *Modern Ideas of Evolution*, pp. 227–228; Beale, "Materialist Revival," pp. 99, 108–109, 113.

48. Smith, "Andover Renaissance," pp. 37–38; Thomas, "Symposium on Evolution," p. 531. See also Todd, "New Theology," p. 352; J. A. Biddle, "The New Theology," *Bibliotheca Sacra*, 54 (1897), 97–98; Braden, *Problem of Problems*, p. 111.

49. Anon., "Synopsis of the Quarterlies and Others of the Higher Periodicals," *Methodist Quarterly Review*, 4th ser., 34 (1882), 750–751; Malone, "Instability of Science," pp. 229–231. See also Talmage, *Live Coals*, pp. 293–295, 299.

Conclusion

1. Henry Adams, *The Education of Henry Adams*, ed. Ernest Samuels (1918; Boston, 1973), p. 53. (a slightly different version of Adams' work was published privately in 1907). In addition to my concluding remarks in Chapter 5, see M. H. Valentine, "The Influence of the Theory of Organic Evolution on the Theory of Ethics," *Lutheran Quarterly*, 28 (1898), 208–209; Henry Davies, "Social Evolution and the Churches," *Bibliotheca Sacra*, 54 (1897), 716–717; W. S. Rainsford, *The Story of a Varied Life: An Autobiography* (Garden City, N. Y., 1922), p. 179.

2. J. M. Cromer, "The Lutheran Conception of Divine Truth," *Lutheran Quarterly*, n.s. 15 (1885), 73.

3. Philip S. Moxom, "Symposium on the 'New Theology': What Are Its Essential Features? Is It Better Than the Old?" *Homiletic Review*, 11 (1886), 206; George Harris, "The Function of the Christian Consciousness," *Andover Review*, 2 (1884), 352. See also Octavius Brooks Frothingham, *Recollections and Impressions, 1822–1890* (New York, 1891), p. 142; Anon., "Religious Authority," *Andover Review*, 17 (1892), 306.

4. Michael E. Ruse, "Two Biological Revolutions," *Dialectica*, 25 (1971), 20.

5. R. Lawrence Moore has maintained that groups who have resided outside the mainstream of culture have often consciously attempted to maintain sharp boundary lines to ensure the retention of their group status as "outsiders." R. Lawrence Moore, "Insiders and Outsiders in American Historical Narrative and American History," *American Historical Review*, 87 (1982), 400–401. In my judgment, a strong case could be made for suggesting that American Protestant intellectuals who rejected the transmutation hypothesis exemplified this phenomenon.

6. Borden P. Bowne, *Philosophy of Theism* (New York, 1887), p. vii. See also Daniel Dorchester, *Christianity in the United States from the First Settlement Down to the Present Time* (New York, 1888), p. 654; Lewis F. Stearns, "The Present Direction of Theological Thought in the Congregational Churches of the United States [1891]," *Present Day Theology: A Popular Discussion of Leading Doctrines of the Christian Faith* (New York, 1893), pp. 534–535; James McCosh, *The Religious Aspect of Evolution*, 2d ed. (New York, 1890), pp. ix–x.

7. Lyman Abbott, *Reminiscences* (Boston, 1915), p. 464; Bowne, *Philosophy of Theism*, p. vii. See also Anon., "The Religion of To-day," *North American Review*, 129 (1879), 554; Theodore T. Munger, *The Freedom of Faith* (Boston, 1883), p. 51; J. B. Harrison, *Certain Dangerous Tendencies in American Life* (Boston, 1880), pp. 7–10, 28.

8. William Paley, *Natural Theology; or, Evidences of the Existence and Attributes of the Deity, Collected from the Appearances of Nature* (London, 1802), p. 3; Myron Adams, *The Continuous Creation: An Application of the Evolutionary Philosophy to the Christian Religion* (Boston, 1889), p. 31. See also A. W. Jackson, "The Old Faith and the New," *Unitarian Review*, 28 (1887), 49; Davies, "Social Evolution," pp. 720–721.

9. James DeKoven, *Sermons Preached on Various Occasions* (New York, 1880), pp. 156–157; Charles E. Rosenberg, *No Other Gods: On Science and American Social Thought* (Baltimore, 1976), pp. 138–139; Donald Fleming, *John William Draper and the Religion of Science* (Philadelphia, 1950), pp. 129–134.

10. James Turner has advanced the argument that the effort of antebellum American religious thinkers to exploit the results of science for theological ends was one of the crucial factors that "gave birth to unbelief." James Turner, *Without God, Without Creed: The Origins of Unbelief in America* (Baltimore, 1985), esp. pp. 261, xiii. Though I am not unsympathetic to the thrust of Turner's argument, my concern is less with the role of religion in fostering unbelief than with the failure of the American Protestant intellectual community during the late nineteenth century to stem the growing tide of indifference to theology among educated Americans.

11. Fleming, *John William Draper*, pp. 131–134; Turner, *Without God*, pp. 124, 250–251.

Index

DESIGNED BY JIM MENNICK
COMPOSED BY BRUCE GRAPHICS, INC., BIRMINGHAM, ALABAMA
MANUFACTURED BY CUSHING-MALLOY, INC. ANN ARBOR, MICHIGAN
TEXT AND DISPLAY LINES ARE SET IN PALATINO

Library of Congress Cataloging-in-Publication Data
Roberts, Jon H.
Darwinism and the divine in America.
(History of American thought and culture)
Includes index.
1. Evolution—Religious aspects—Christianity—
History of doctrines—19th century. 2. Theology,
Doctrinal—United States—History—19th century.
I. Title.   II. Series.
BT712.R63   1987   231.7'65   87-40374
ISBN 0-299-11590-9